A HOUSE

Presented to Alan Barnes
15.8.04
from the Congregation and Friends of
St. John the Baptist Church, Mayfield,
with grateful thanks for 12 years faithful
service as Organist.

A HOUSE OF PRAISE

Collected Hymns 1961–2001

by
TIMOTHY
DUDLEY-SMITH

Oxford University Press

Hope Publishing Company

For Europe and Africa:
Oxford University Press
Great Clarendon Street, Oxford OX2 6DP, England
198 Madison Avenue, New York, NY10016, USA

Oxford University Press is a department of the University of Oxford.
It furthers the University's aim of excellence in research, scholarship,
and education by publishing worldwide

Oxford is a registered trade mark of Oxford University Press
in the UK and in certain other countries

For the rest of the world including the USA and Canada:
Hope Publishing Company, 380 South Main Place, Carol Stream, IL 60188
Toll Free: 800-323-1049; Fax 630-665-2552; Email: hope@hopepublishing.com
www.hopepublishing.com

Code No. 8203

First published 2003

1 3 5 7 9 10 8 6 4 2

Oxford University Press ISBN 0-19-100159-7
Hope Publishing Company ISBN 0-916642-74-7
Library of Congress Control Number 2003108657

Printed in the USA

With love and thankfulness to my wife Arlette
for more than forty years of marriage
and to those who shared
our Seacroft summers

O magnify the Lord with me,
and let us exalt his Name together

PSALM 34.3

Here may faith and love increase,
flowing forth in joy and peace
from the Father, Spirit, Son,
undivided, Three-in-One:
his the glory all our days
in this house of prayer and praise!

from hymn 103
written for Norwich Cathedral,
January 1978 at Bramerton

Contents

Preface

'It is the best of all trades to make songs,' Hilaire Belloc declared in one of his innumerable essays, 'and the second-best to sing them.' Hyperbole apart, it still comes as a happy surprise to me, even after the forty years spanned by this collection, to find myself a hymn writer. In the 1940s and 50s, a young Christian with a love of verse, I longed to write hymns; but having no music whatsoever, it seemed that door was closed. As for my attempts at singing, I could only hope for the same toleration accorded by John Wesley, as described in a published lecture of 1862:

> 'One good man sang out of tune, to the offence of Mr Wesley's delicate ear. "John," said he, "you do not sing in tune." The man stopped, but soon began again. The rebuke was repeated. "Please, sir, I sing with my heart," was the sufficient reply. "Then sing on," said Mr W.'

This is therefore a book of hymn texts, words only without music, and in addition to more recent writing it subsumes four earlier collections: *Lift Every Heart*, 1984; *Songs of Deliverance*, 1988; *A Voice of Singing*, 1993; and *Great is the Glory*, 1997. Its relationship to *Lift Every Heart* is such that it can be regarded as a new, updated and enlarged edition. Much of what was written in the Foreword there, as well as the substance of the dedication and the main pattern of the book, remains unchanged; though this edition now contains more than twice the number of hymns. Besides those published in the three smaller and later books named above, the last five or six years have added a further fifty or so new texts, here collected for the first time; and I have also taken the opportunity to make and list some corrections and revisions of earlier work, minor changes for the most part. The Notes have been entirely revised or rewritten, and the ten indexes cover the whole collection of 285 hymns. They are designed to make the book as user-friendly as possible to editors, composers, and leaders of worship, as well as those who simply have an interest in hymnody. It is the purpose of this Preface to explain and comment briefly on the different sections of the book.

The Hymns

The dates in the subtitle, 1961-2001, show that these were written over the course of forty years, an average therefore of seven or eight a year. For me, this seems about right and I hope to continue it, if I can, for a few years more. Those with an observant eye may spot in the Notes to 22 'Had he not loved us', and to 55 'Upon a tree the sin of man', a reference to the 1940s. In part or whole, these two texts draw on the Christian verse which I was then writing and beginning to see published, but never regarded as hymnody. Indeed, a number of the texts in this collection, including 212 'Tell out, my soul', were written simply as verse, with no thought that they might be sung. For this and other reasons, some of the texts that follow have been found more suitable as the words of anthems or choral settings, than for congregational use.

In the four earlier collections, the hymns appeared simply in alphabetical order, supported by indexes of Biblical references and of themes and subjects. This seemed sense with the 36 or so texts in each of the smaller collections, and even with the 124 hymns in *Lift Every Heart*. But with nearly 300 texts, some system of arrangement into manageable divisions seemed essential as an aid to the browser and general reader: or, as I dare to hope, the use of the book in preparing for public worship, or in personal devotion.

The nine divisions chosen simply reflect the nature of my hymn writing; and I have added on the introductory page to each section a repeated warning that many texts might have appeared in more than one section. 'Sing a new song to the Lord' (161), for example, could be classified as a metrical psalm, or as a liturgical canticle (it forms the Cantate Domino in the *Book of Common Prayer*) or under one of a number of themes. The divisions, therefore, are bound to be somewhat arbitrary; and those wanting something more comprehensive should look in the appropriate Index at the back of the book.

The Notes: dates, places and tunes

Since my MS book gives the place as well as the date of writing, I have included these for each text. It may be helpful to explain that for much of my earliest hymn writing we were living in Sevenoaks, Kent; that we moved to Bramerton, near Norwich, in the early 1970s; and that we retired to Ford, on the edge of Salisbury, in 1992. But during my years of active ministry most of my writing was done in August, at 'Seacroft', our very ordinary but much-loved holiday home in Cornwall, in the village of Ruan Minor on the Lizard. Here, for some twenty years, I wrote six or eight hymns each summer. This explains the inclusion of Seacroft in the dedication of this book, and the many nostalgic references to Ruan Minor and South Cornwall.

Hymns, I have learned, only truly exist when they are sung in the heart, if not by a congregation. I am therefore specially grateful to those who have written some of the music here listed, and to those who have advised me on the choice of existing tunes. Derek Kidner was the first to help me in this way, and I have recorded my measureless debt to him in earlier books. More recently two retired physicians, Dr Peter Tucker and Dr Jonathan West, friends of long standing, have given much painstaking and informed advice; while various editors have made their own choices which are here listed for the benefit of others. A special feature of this collection is the work of Dr Donald Hustad, himself a Professor of Church Music, who has patiently and expertly listed tunes likely to be known to North American congregations; and for this I owe him a particular debt of gratitude. It is therefore on the work of others that the Index of Tunes is based and I gratefully acknowledge this; while affirming that all errors, whether of judgment, taste or substance are entirely mine. Perhaps I should add that the composers or sources given for the tunes in this book are meant primarily as an aid to identification. They do not claim to address debatable questions of authorship or origin, and seldom acknowledge the often substantial contributions of arrangers, harmonizers or subsequent editors. To my pleasure, contemporary composers sometimes send me tunes written to these hymn texts. As I indicated in *Lift Every Heart*, I maintain a file of these (by now a few hundred) which editors consult from time to time, and I am always happy to add to it.

Each of the Notes, with a few exceptions, lists one or more 'suggested tunes' for that text; and the Index of Tunes offers some help in locating many of these tunes in a selected range of published hymnals from the United Kingdom and North America. These 'suggested tunes' are not necessarily to be preferred over those chosen by editors, which are also listed: the needs of congregations vary considerably. They are offered, for the most part, simply as tunes to which the text can be sung; especially where there are no published tunes, or where such as there are seem inappropriate or unavailable.

The Notes: hymnals, recordings and translations

The hymnals and other publications listed under many texts, and in

Index 1, are mainly of books intended for congregational use. There are a number of anthems (these are listed by date of publication in Index 2) and a few 'words only' collections. Anthologies of verse, books of prayers, devotional readings and the like are only included if they seem of special significance; if, for example, they contain the only publication of a text to date. No reference is made to electronic databases or to the various CD-Roms on which the texts are included. The CD-Rom 'HymnQuest' published by Stainer and Bell, London, is an excellent resource for those who want these texts in digital form; while the most popular also appear on 'Songselect', a CD-Rom from Christian Copyright Licensing (Europe) Ltd., of Eastbourne, Sussex: there is a growing range of North American counterparts. I have also omitted many hymnals privately published for individual local churches, colleges and schools, which contain one or more texts from this collection.

Recordings, again, are generally limited to commercial recordings—cassettes and CDs, with some LPs in the early days—catalogued and offered for sale. Even so, I am aware that there are bound to be a number of omissions. Again, 'domestic' recordings such as now can be produced with relative ease and economy for a local choir or school, are generally omitted.

Translations present problems not only in oriental but even in the main European languages. Those listed are therefore the responsibility of the foreign publisher. A note about copyright appears at the start of Index 5.

The Notes: commentary

Apart from the tabulated information already discussed, I see the purpose of the Notes as to give, where applicable, some brief comment or information about the origin and nature of the text; for example, if it was a commission, or written to meet a particular need. Sometimes I go further and highlight background sources of images, phrases, or even single words. When Professor J.R. Watson published his definitive study *The English Hymn* (Oxford 1997) I was encouraged to read a pertinent quotation from T.S. Eliot, there applied to Charles Wesley, about how 'immature poets imitate: mature poets steal...' making their borrowings into something different. I hope this may be true of the many borrowings here listed.

In particular, the Notes are concerned to show biblical correspondences, or biblical sources for statements or expressions; or, more simply, the verse or passage which often lies behind a stanza or a line. It is, I believe, a particular duty of teachers of the faith (and this certainly includes hymn writers) to be guided firmly by the revealed truths of Scripture, and not be led into such speculative realms as the 'wistful agnosticism' satirized by T.R. Glover (the Cambridge classical scholar and historian) in his mischievous pastiche of modernist theology. It is quoted by T.E.B. Howarth in *Cambridge Between Two Wars* (London 1978):

> *'We know Thee not, not guess Thee,*
> *O vague beyond our dreams:*
> *We praise Thee not nor bless Thee,*
> *Dim source of all that seems;*
> *Unconscious of our witness,*
> *The music of our heart,*
> *O It beyond all Itness*
> *If aught indeed Thou art.'*

Since the publication of my earlier collection, the Church of England has moved in its liturgy, not indeed from the *Book of Common Prayer* which remains normative, but from the *Alternative Service Book, 1980* to *Common Worship, 2000*. While retaining references to the ASB where this was, and therefore remains, a source or starting point, the rest of the contemporary liturgical references now look mainly to *Common Worship*.

The Indexes

Most of these need no explanation. On Index 4, 'Biblical and other Sources', I repeat what I have explained in earlier collections, that this includes mainly those verses or passages which form the substantial basis of a hymn or stanza, and does not set out to be a comprehensive list of biblical allusions or brief quotations. In the same way, the description 'based on' in the Notes is meant to indicate no more than that. I use it where I have had a passage of Scripture before me, and have been aiming at some kind of 'metrical version'. The end result has often been a good deal freer than even 'metrical version' properly implies.

When deciding to include Index 6, 'Discontinued or Altered Texts', I had expected to consign more texts to the 'discontinued' category. However, while some that I regarded as borderline remain in use in current hymnals or continue in demand, it seemed best to give them the benefit of the doubt. Many of the changes listed in Index 6 simply incorporate the 'permitted variations' listed in *Lift Every Heart,* Appendix 5. Not all of these have been adopted, since a few now seem to me an attempt to secure 'inclusive language' at too great a cost to the integrity of an early text. Inevitably some hymns from the 1960s and 70s have proved resistant to 'invisible mending' in the interests of gender-free language of persons; but no editor or worship leader is obliged to use them, and they form only a small proportion of the book. Inclusive language of Deity, as the most casual reading of these texts will show, is another matter altogether. It seems to me that the surest way to address Almighty God, and think and write about him, is in the language of revelation. This is not to suggest that God has gender as we know it, but simply to remember that Jesus taught his followers unambiguously to call God 'Father'. While the Bible includes female imagery, it consistently uses words such as 'Lord' and 'King' and pronouns such as 'he', 'him' and 'his'. I take this as clear guidance for us to do the same.

It has become plain to me, reading the proofs of my work in hymnals over the years, that some editors have greatly improved on my original punctuation. I have tried to learn from this; and also to reduce, if not eliminate, the use of a dash in place of a comma or perhaps a colon. Until experience demonstrated it, I would not have believed how hard it is to maintain a definitive version of a text. Not all editors send proofs to contributors; proof-reading is in any event a fallible art; and once a variant of a text has appeared in any hymnal, it is impossible to ensure that it is not used as a source for further publications. I hope therefore (obvious misprints apart) that future editors will use the versions printed here, rather than copy from even my own earlier collections, or from other hymnals. The changes listed in Index 6 do not take account of the many other texts where there has been a change in punctuation, and this is an added reason for regarding this collection as now definitive, even where no entry against a particular text appears in Index 6.

This Index of Alterations would be far longer than it is if I had not resolved to resist, except for compelling necessity, the urge to tinker which besets many writers whose work is later reprinted. W.H. Auden is a notorious example, while the young C.S. Lewis in a letter to his friend Arthur Greeves (Walter Hooper, ed., *Collected Letters, Vol. 1,* London 2000) asserted that 'corrections made afterwards are usually for the worse...'. Again, A.E. Housman wrote to Grant Richards, his publisher, on 24 July 1898 (Archie Burnett, ed., *The Poems of A.E. Housman,* Oxford 1997) to say:

> 'I think it best not to make any alterations, even the slightest,
> after one has once printed a thing. It was Shelley's plan, and
> is much wiser than Wordsworth's perpetual tinkering...'

Admittedly, he concluded his sentence with the words '...as it makes the public fancy one is inspired', but however firmly his tongue was in his cheek, it remained his policy not to change what was once in print. The humblest hymn writer, more even than the most distinguished poet, has an obligation not to alter in later books, save for cogent reasons, words which may already have become familiar to a congregation. I believe the same to be generally true of the hymnal editor—but that is another story!

Before leaving the question of alterations (which sometimes means corrections) I ought to remedy a lapse of memory in the Foreword to *Lift Every Heart* (page 8). The 'snowy day at the Albert Hall' was in fact 29 November 1969 and marked the launch of *Youth Praise 2*. *Psalm Praise* was published four years later in 1973, and enthusiastic launchings were held that September in eight British cities.

Finally, on the subject of the Indexes, I repeat my recommendation that anyone in search of a hymn for a special service or occasion, or on a particular theme, should turn first to Index 9, 'Themes and Subjects', which I have sought by cross-referencing to make as comprehensive as I can within the limits of what I have to offer.

* * *

For myself, my overwhelming feeling as this book goes to press is one of thankfulness: to my family, who have borne with this preoccupation for so long; to the many friends, in Great Britain and Ireland, in North America and beyond, whom I have gained through a shared love of hymns, not least as fellow-members of their respective Hymn Societies; to those who offered me early encouragement: and to the musical friends named above who have advised me with patience and long-suffering. I include with pride and affection the name of George Shorney, who has done so much to encourage hymn writers and to introduce the names of British writers and composers to North American congregations.

I thank too Mrs Susanna Tovey of Salisbury who has put the whole of this book on a word-processor from a much-corrected MS; and the new generation of Shorneys at the Hope Publishing Company who like George, their former Chairman, are not only my publishers but my friends. In Europe the book is co-published by the Oxford University Press with its distinguished tradition in the service of hymnody. It is our joint intention that OUP will become the administrator of my hymn copyrights, in the territories not served by Hope Publishing Company, whenever I do not wish, or become unable, to go on doing this myself. I therefore thank Julian Elloway and Joyce Horn from longstanding previous links with the Press and Simon Wright, Nigel Lynn and David Blackwell for their help towards this present publication.

Hymn writing has been for me a most enriching and entirely unexpected gift: indeed, with other aspects of Christian ministry, 'the best of all trades'. So the title chosen for this collection, and the verse printed as epigraph by way of explanation, express chiefly my thankfulness to the Giver of all good gifts, to whose praise these hymns were written, and to whose praise may they be sung!

T. D. S.

Ford, July 2002

THE HYMNS

Throughout this section, the number of the hymn is the same as the number of the page.

1. The Christian Year

Certain texts which might have been listed here are classified under other headings, for example as metrical psalms or other Scriptures, metrical canticles and so on.

The Index of Themes and Subjects on page 544 contains entries under all the headings listed above, generally with a wider selection of suitable texts.

Some other regular occasions in the life of a local congregation (New Year, Harvest and so on) will be found in Section 3, 'Occasional Services'; but these too, with other headings such as 'The Transfiguration', will be found listed more fully in the Index of Biblical and other Sources and the Index of Themes and Subjects on pages 499 and 544.

1 AWAKE, AS IN THE SKIES ABOVE

Awake, as in the skies above
the darkness yields to dawn;
so came God's gift of light and love,
our Saviour Christ was born.

Awake and watch! The hour draws on
of his return to reign;
our night of sin and sorrow gone
when Christ shall come again.

Awake from sleep, from time and place
to God's eternal now,
when every eye shall see his face
and every knee shall bow.

Behold the Sun of Righteousness
whose glories blaze abroad,
till every tongue on earth confess
that Jesus Christ is Lord!

2 FROM THE FATHER'S THRONE ON HIGH

based on Mark 13.24–27

From the Father's throne on high
Christ returns to rule and reign:
child of earth, he came to die;
    judge of all he comes again.

Darkened be the day at noon
    when the stars of heaven fall:
earth and sky and sun and moon,
    cloudy darkness covers all.

Ancient powers of sin and death
    shake to hear the trumpet blown;
from the winds' remotest breath
    God will gather in his own.

So behold the promised sign,
    sky and sea by tumult riven,
and the King of kings divine
    coming in the clouds of heaven.

Come then, Lord, in light and power,
    at whose word the worlds began;
in the unexpected hour
    come in glory, Son of Man!

3 HERE ON THE THRESHOLD OF A NEW BEGINNING

Here on the threshold of a new beginning,
  by grace forgiven, now we leave behind
our long-repented selfishness and sinning,
    and all our blessings call again to mind:
Christ to redeem us, ransom and restore us,
    the love that holds us in a Saviour's care,
faith strong to welcome all that lies before us,
    our unknown future, knowing God is there.

May we, your children, feel with Christ's compassion
    an earth disordered, hungry and in pain;
then, at your calling, find the will to fashion
    new ways where freedom, truth and justice reign;
where wars are ended, ancient wrongs are righted,
    and nations value human life and worth;
where in the darkness lamps of hope are lighted
    and Christ is honoured over all the earth.

So may your wisdom shine from Scripture's pages
    to mould and make us stones with which to build
God's holy temple, through eternal ages,
    one church united, strong and Spirit-filled;
heirs to the fullness of your new creation,
    in faith we follow, pledged to be your own;
yours is the future, ours the celebration,
    for Christ is risen! God is on the throne!

4 HIGH PEAKS AND SUNLIT PRAIRIES

High peaks and sunlit prairies,
　　earth's silent places, hark!
lost caves where nothing varies
　　the dank and secret dark:
to oceans depths unseeing,
　　to circling planets dumb,
the source of all your being,
　　your absent Lord, is come!

Earth's countless living creatures,
　　all nature's legions, hark!
the myriad forms and features
　　that peopled Noah's ark.
In creaturehood, and sharing
　　the narrow gate of birth,
the news goes forth declaring
　　your King has come to earth!

And nature's child and master,
　　have we no news to mark?
no cheer against disaster,
　　no comfort through the dark?
A lost world's new beginning,
　　a dark night's blaze of morn!
to hearts grown old in sinning,
　　to us, a child is born.

5 WHEN HE COMES

When he comes,
  when he comes,
we shall see the Lord in glory when he comes!
As I read the gospel story
we shall see the Lord in glory,
we shall see the Lord in glory when he comes!
> With the Alleluias ringing to the sky,
> with the Alleluias ringing to the sky!
> As I read the gospel story
> we shall see the Lord in glory
> with the Alleluias ringing to the sky!

When he comes,
when he comes,
we shall hear the trumpet sounded when he comes!
We shall hear the trumpet sounded,
see the Lord by saints surrounded,
we shall hear the trumpet sounded when he comes!
> With the Alleluias ringing to the sky,
> with the Alleluias ringing to the sky!
> We shall hear the trumpet sounded,
> see the Lord by saints surrounded,
> with the Alleluias ringing to the sky!

When he comes,
when he comes,
we shall all rise up to meet him when he comes!
When he calls his own to greet him
we shall all rise up to meet him,
we shall all rise up to meet him when he comes!
> With the Alleluias ringing to the sky,
> with the Alleluias ringing to the sky!
> When he calls his own to greet him
> we shall all rise up to meet him
> with the Alleluias ringing to the sky!

6 WHEN THE LORD IN GLORY COMES

When the Lord in glory comes,
not the trumpets, not the drums,
not the anthem, not the psalm,
not the thunder, not the calm,
not the shout the heavens raise,
not the chorus, not the praise,
not the silences sublime,
not the sounds of space and time,
but his voice when he appears
shall be music to my ears;
> but his voice when he appears
> shall be music to my ears.

When the Lord is seen again,
not the glories of his reign,
not the lightnings through the storm,
not the radiance of his form,
not his pomp and power alone,
not the splendours of his throne,
not his robe and diadems,
not the gold and not the gems,
but his face upon my sight
shall be darkness into light;
> but his face upon my sight
> shall be darkness into light.

When the Lord to human eyes
shall bestride our narrow skies,
not the child of humble birth,
not the carpenter of earth,
not the man by all denied,
not the victim crucified,
but the God who died to save,
but the victor of the grave,
he it is to whom I fall,
Jesus Christ, my all in all;
> he it is to whom I fall,
> Jesus Christ, my all in all.

7 A NEW SONG GOD HAS GIVEN

A new song God has given,
a new thing God has done,
when from the courts of heaven
he sent to us his Son.
Rejoice in song and story
to tell of Jesus' birth,
who laid aside his glory
and came, a child, to earth.

A new-born baby sleeping,
a mother's tender care,
while ox and ass are keeping
their night-long vigil there;
to greet the infant stranger
the shepherds make their way,
to find, within a manger,
the child of Christmas Day.

A new-found star is shining
upon the eastern skies,
that kings may come, divining
the way of all the wise.
O child of our salvation,
receive the gifts we bring,
the songs of adoration
that love alone can sing.

A new world now is waking,
the old must pass away;
a new-made morning breaking
on God's eternal day.
A new song God has given
to tell his praise abroad,
who came, a child, from heaven,
a Saviour, Christ the Lord.

8 A SONG WAS HEARD AT CHRISTMAS

A song was heard at Christmas
　　to wake the midnight sky:
a Saviour's birth, and peace on earth,
　　and praise to God on high.
The angels sang at Christmas
　　with all the hosts above,
and still we sing the new-born King,
　　his glory and his love.

A star was seen at Christmas,
　　a herald and a sign,
that all might know the way to go
　　to find the child divine.
The wise men watched at Christmas
　　in some far eastern land,
and still the wise in starry skies
　　discern their Maker's hand.

A tree was grown at Christmas,
　　a sapling green and young;
no tinsel bright with candlelight
　　upon its branches hung.
But he who came at Christmas
　　our sins and sorrows bore,
and still we name his tree of shame
　　our life for evermore.

A child was born at Christmas
　　when Christmas first began;
the Lord of all a baby small,
　　the Son of God made man.
For love is ours at Christmas,
　　and life and light restored,
and so we praise through endless days
　　the Saviour, Christ the Lord.

9 A STONE TO BE THE LINTEL

a carol for a carpenter

A stone to be the lintel
 above the open door,
a bed of straw for stable
 and trampled earth a floor;
but wood is for the manger,
 so patterned, smooth and worn,
O, wood is for the cradle
 where Jesus Christ is born.

As seed is for the sower
 and bread is for the home,
so bronze is for the breastplate
 and all the might of Rome.
But wood is for the Craftsman
 by whom the world was made,
O, wood is for the workshop
 where Jesus learned his trade.

A colt to be his charger
 and palms for glory now,
a reed shall be for sceptre
 and thorn upon his brow;
but wood is for the crosses
 against a darkened sky,
O, wood and nails together
 when Jesus came to die.

With wood to work our ransom
 he mastered death and grave;
the gates of heaven opened
 on all he came to save:
a tree of life unfading
 beyond our mortal pains,
whose leaves are for our healing
 where Jesus lives and reigns.

10 CAROLS TO CHRIST BE SUNG

C arols to Christ be sung,
   joy be on every tongue,
    welcome his birth!
where in the starry sky
legions of angels cry
'Glory to God on high,
    peace upon earth'.

Shepherds behold the sight,
keeping their flocks by night,
    safe till the morn:
down through the dark they tread,
finding the cattle-shed,
where in a manger bed
    Jesus is born.

Kings from the East arise,
worshippers strange and wise,
    journeying far;
incense and gold they bring,
gifts for a God and King,
myrrh for his suffering,
    led by a star.

Though, like the star that shone,
shepherds and kings are gone
    long past recall,
he who by faith is known,
Saviour and Son alone,
reigns from his Father's throne,
    Christ over all!

11 CHILD OF MARY, NEWLY BORN

Child of Mary, newly born,
    softly in a manger laid,
wake to wonder on this morn,
    view the world your fingers made.
Starlight shone above your bed,
    lantern-light about your birth:
morning sunlight crown your head,
    light and life of all the earth!

Child of Mary, grown and strong,
    traveller, teacher, young and free,
see him stride the hills along,
    Christ the Man of Galilee.
Wisdom from a world above
    now by waiting hearts is heard:
hear him speak the words of love,
    Christ the true eternal Word.

Child of Mary, grief and loss,
    all the sum of human woe,
crown of thorn and cruel cross,
    mark the path you choose to go.
Man of sorrows, born to save,
    bearing all our sins and pains:
from his cross and empty grave
    Christ the Lord of glory reigns.

Child of Mary, gift of grace,
    by whose birth shall all be well,
one with us in form and face,
    God with us, Emmanuel!
Night is past and shadows fled,
    wake to joy on Christmas morn:
sunlight crown the Saviour's head,
    Christ the Prince of peace is born.

12 CHILD OF THE STABLE'S SECRET BIRTH

Child of the stable's secret birth,
the Lord by right of the lords of earth,
let angels sing of a King new born,
the world is weaving a crown of thorn:
    a crown of thorn for that infant head
    cradled soft in the manger bed.

Eyes that shine in the lantern's ray;
a face so small in its nest of hay,
face of a child who is born to scan
the world he made through the eyes of man:
    and from that face in the final day
    earth and heaven shall flee away.

Voice that rang through the courts on high
contracted now to a wordless cry,
a voice to master the wind and wave,
the human heart and the hungry grave:
    the voice of God through the cedar trees
    rolling forth as the sound of seas.

Infant hands in a mother's hand,
for none but Mary may understand
whose are the hands and the fingers curled
but his who fashioned and made our world;
    and through these hands in the hour of death
    nails shall strike to the wood beneath.

Child of the stable's secret birth,
the Father's gift to a wayward earth,
to drain the cup in a few short years
of all our sorrows, our sins and tears;
    ours the prize for the road he trod:
    risen with Christ; at peace with God.

13 CHILL OF THE NIGHTFALL

C hill of the nightfall,
    lamps in the windows,
letting their light fall
clear on the snow;
    bitter December
    bids us remember
Christ in the stable
long, long ago.

Silence of midnight,
voices of angels,
singing to bid night
yield to the dawn;
    darkness is ended,
    sinners befriended,
where in the stable
Jesus is born.

Splendour of starlight
high on the hillside,
faint is the far light
burning below;
    kneeling before him
    shepherds adore him,
Christ in the stable
long, long ago.

Glory of daybreak!
Sorrows and shadows,
suddenly they break
forth into morn;
    sing out and tell now
    all shall be well now,
for in the stable
Jesus is born!

14 CHOIRS OF ANGELS, TELL ABROAD

C hoirs of angels, tell abroad
  all the glories of the Lord;
sound on high what God has done,
sending us his only Son.
    Christ is come on Christmas morn,
      Christ for us in flesh arrayed,
    Christ our God incarnate born
      and within a manger laid.

Shepherds, leave your flock and fold,
he of whom the prophets told,
born to bring salvation down,
comes at last to David's town.
    Christ the Lord of David's line,
      Christ the Shepherd of the sheep,
    Christ the Lamb of God divine
      in a stable lies asleep.

Watchers of the midnight skies,
follow wisdom and be wise;
take your treasures, journey far,
ride beneath the shining star.
    Christ your King has come to birth,
      Christ the Wisdom from on high;
    Christ the Light of all the earth
      sleeps to Mary's lullaby.

Christ is come, the child adored,
Christ the Saviour, Christ the Lord;
Christ who calls his servants friends,
Christ whose kingdom never ends;
    Christ the true and living Way,
      Christ in whom shall all be well,
    Christ the dawn of heaven's day,
      Christ with us, Emmanuel!

15 CHRIST FROM HEAVEN'S GLORY COME

Christ from heaven's glory come,
in a stable make your home.
Helpless new-born babe-in-arms,
dream of terror's night-alarms.
Lullaby, my little love,
Herod's troops are on the move.

Cradled on a mother's knee,
immigrant and refugee,
talking, walking hand in hand,
homeless in a foreign land,
child of Mary, full of grace,
exile of an alien race.

Christ whose hand the hungry fed,
stones were yours in place of bread;
Christ whose love our ransom paid,
by a kiss at last betrayed;
friendless now, and nothing worth,
join the outcasts of the earth.

Soon the soldiers' jest is done,
'They will reverence my Son.'
On the gallows hang him high,
'By our law he ought to die.'
Perished, all the flower of youth:
wash your hands, for what is truth?

*   *   *

Christ who once at Christmas came,
move our hearts who name your Name.
By your body, bring to birth
truth and justice, peace on earth,
sinners pardoned, love restored:
reign among us, risen Lord!

16 CHRIST IS COME! LET EARTH ADORE HIM

C hrist is come! Let earth adore him;
      God appears in mortal frame.
Saints and angels bow before him,
      praise his high and holy Name.
Word of our salvation's story,
      helpless babe of human birth,
Christ has laid aside his glory,
      born for us a child of earth.

Christ is come and calls us to him;
      here by faith behold your King;
with the shepherds kneel to view him,
      with the wise your treasures bring.
Child today and man tomorrow,
      by his cross and crown of thorn
he shall vanquish sin and sorrow,
      sing we then that Christ is born.

Christ is come! Let all enthrone him,
      every tongue declare his praise;
every heart rejoice to own him
      King of everlasting days.
Christ is come, our sure salvation,
      Christ the ransomed sinner's friend,
so with all his new creation
      sing the song that knows no end.

17 COME NOW WITH AWE, EARTH'S ANCIENT VIGIL KEEPING

Come now with awe, earth's ancient vigil keeping;
cold under starlight lies the stony way.
Down from the hillside see the shepherds creeping,
hear in our hearts the whispered news they say:
'Laid in a manger lies an infant sleeping,
Christ our Redeemer, born for us today.'

Come now with joy to worship and adore him;
hushed in the stillness, wonder and behold,
Christ in the stable where his mother bore him,
Christ whom the prophets faithfully foretold:
High King of Ages, low we kneel before him,
starlight for silver, lantern-light for gold.

Come now with faith, the age-long secret guessing,
hearts rapt in wonder, soul and spirit stirred;
see in our likeness love beyond expressing,
all God has spoken, all the prophets heard;
born for us sinners, bearer of all blessing,
flesh of our flesh, behold the eternal Word!

Come now with love; beyond our comprehending
love in its fullness lies in mortal span!
How should we love, whom Love is so befriending?
Love rich in mercy since our race began
now stoops to save us, sighs and sorrows ending,
Jesus our Saviour, Son of God made man.

18 COME, WATCH WITH US THIS CHRISTMAS NIGHT

C ome, watch with us this Christmas night;
  our hearts must travel far
to darkened hills and heavens bright
with star on shining star;
to where in shadowy silence sleep
    the fields of Bethlehem,
as shepherds wake their watch to keep
and we will watch with them.

Who would not join the angel songs
that tell the Saviour's birth?
The Lord for whom creation longs
has come at last to earth;
the fullness of the Father's love
    is ours at Bethlehem,
while angels throng the skies above
and we will sing with them.

Who would not journey far to share
the wisdom of the wise,
and gaze with them in wonder where
the world's Redeemer lies?
The Lord of all the lords that are
    is born at Bethlehem,
and kings shall kneel beneath his star
and we will bow with them.

Lift every heart the hymn of praise
that all creation sings;
the angel host its homage pays,
the shepherds and the kings.
For earth and sky with one accord,
    O child of Bethlehem,
are come to worship Christ the Lord
and we will come with them.

19 DONKEY PLOD AND MARY RIDE

Donkey plod and Mary ride,
weary Joseph walk beside,
theirs the way that all men come,
dark the night and far from home:
    down the years remember them,
    come away to Bethlehem.

Mary's child, on Christmas Eve,
none but ox and ass receive;
theirs the manger and the stall
where is laid the Lord of all:
    down the years remember them,
    come away to Bethlehem.

Angels throng the midnight sky:
'Glory be to God on high!'
Theirs the song that sounds abroad,
'Born a Saviour, Christ the Lord':
    down the years remember them,
    come away to Bethlehem.

Shepherds haste the watch to keep
where their Maker lies asleep;
theirs the angels' promised sign,
'Born for us a child divine':
    down the years remember them,
    come away to Bethlehem.

Ancient kings from eastern skies
trace the way of all the wise,
theirs the shining star, to find
light to lighten all mankind:
    down the years remember them,
    come away to Bethlehem.

Shepherds, kings and angel throngs,
teach us where our joy belongs;
souls restored and sins forgiven,
Christ on earth the hope of heaven:
    down the years rejoice in them,
    come away to Bethlehem.

20 EXULT, O MORNING STARS AFLAME

Exult, O morning stars aflame!
with all the works of God proclaim
the Child of Bethlehem who came
for love and love alone.

Come earth and air and sky and sea,
bear witness to his deity
who lived, the Man of Galilee,
for love and love alone.

By faith behold the Crucified,
his arms of mercy open wide,
the Lamb of Calvary, who died
for love and love alone.

Let every eye his glories see,
who was, and is, and is to be;
who reigns as Christ in Majesty
for love and love alone.

*   *   *

O world, by strife and sorrow torn,
new hope is yours on Christmas morn,
the Prince of Peace a child is born,
for love and love alone.

21 GOLD FOR A MANGER BED

G old for a manger bed,
  Jesus enshrining;
straw where he lays his head,
    softly reclining;
        so small and still he lies
        as on his infant eyes
        high in the darkened skies
    the stars are shining.

King and Creator see,
    whose hands have wrought us;
Saviour and Shepherd he,
    who loved and sought us;
        our God in human frame
        who to a lost world came
        and on the cross of shame
    so dearly bought us.

Gold for a monarch's state,
    all things sustaining;
High Prince and Potentate,
    death's dread disdaining;
        to him the ransomed raise
        unceasing songs of praise,
        through everlasting days
    in glory reigning.

22 HAD HE NOT LOVED US

Had he not loved us
    he had never come,
yet is he love
    and love is all his way;
low to the mystery
    of the virgin's womb
Christ bows his glory,
    born on Christmas Day.

Had he not loved us
    he had never come;
had he not come
    he need have never died,
nor won the victory
    of the vacant tomb,
the awful triumph
    of the Crucified.

Had he not loved us
    he had never come;
still were we lost
    in sorrow, sin and shame,
the doors fast shut
    on our eternal home
which now stand open,
    for he loved and came.

23 HE COMES, THE WAY THAT ALL MAY TREAD

He comes, the Way that all may tread,
the Shepherd King of David's line,
the radiance from his manger bed
through all the earth shall shine:
Alleluia, Alleluia,
our promised Light divine.

He comes, the Truth the prophets heard,
who was and is and is to be,
God's timeless, true, eternal Word
whom wise men longed to see:
Alleluia, Alleluia,
the Truth that makes us free.

He comes, the Life who for us gave
a ransom none but he could pay,
the child who conquered death and grave,
our Life, our Truth, our Way:
Alleluia, Alleluia,
the Christ of Christmas Day.

24 HEAR HOW THE BELLS OF CHRISTMAS PLAY

H ear how the bells of Christmas play!
Well may they ring for joy and say,
 O praise him! Alleluia!
God has fulfilled his promised word,
born is our Saviour and our Lord,
 O praise him! Alleluia!

Let all the waiting earth rejoice,
lift every heart and every voice,
 O praise him! Alleluia!
Sing now the song to angels given,
Glory to God in highest heaven!
 O praise him! Alleluia!

As through the silence of the skies
shepherds in wonder heard arise,
 O praise him! Alleluia!
So may we hear again with them
songs in the night at Bethlehem,
 O praise him! Alleluia!

All nature sang at Jesus' birth,
Hail the Creator come to earth!
 O praise him! Alleluia!
Sun, moon and shining stars above,
tell out the story of his love,
 O praise him! Alleluia!

Hear how the bells of Christmas play!
Well may they ring for joy and say,
 O praise him! Alleluia!
Come now to worship and adore,
Christ is our peace for evermore,
 O praise him! Alleluia!

For Europe and Africa: © Timothy Dudley-Smith
For the rest of the world including the USA and Canada: © 1987 Hope Publishing Company

25 HERE IS THE CENTRE: STAR ON DISTANT STAR

H ere is the centre: star on distant star
  shining unheeded in the depths of space,
worlds without number, all the worlds there are,
turn in their travelling to this holy place.
> Here in a stable and an ox's stall
> laid in a manger lies the Lord of all.

Now is the moment: God in flesh appears,
down from the splendours of his throne sublime,
High King of Ages, Lord of all the years,
God everlasting stoops to space and time.
> All that was promised now is brought to birth,
> Jesus our Saviour come at last to earth.

Son of the Father, God's eternal Word,
emptied of glory, born to cross and grave;
ours is the secret ancient prophets heard,
God in our likeness come to seek and save:
> Christ in his passion, bearer of our sins;
> and, from his rising, risen life begins.

Come then rejoicing! Praise be all our songs!
Love lies among us in the stable bare,
light in our darkness, righting of all wrongs,
hope for the future, joy enough to share.
> Peace to our hearts for God is on the throne!
> Christ our Redeemer comes to claim his own.

26 HOLY CHILD, HOW STILL YOU LIE

Holy child, how still you lie!
safe the manger, soft the hay;
faint upon the eastern sky
breaks the dawn of Christmas Day.

Holy child, whose birthday brings
shepherds from their field and fold,
angel choirs and eastern kings,
myrrh and frankincense and gold:

Holy child, what gift of grace
from the Father freely willed!
In your infant form we trace
all God's promises fulfilled.

Holy child, whose human years
span like ours delight and pain;
one in human joys and tears,
one in all but sin and stain:

Holy child, so far from home,
all the lost to seek and save,
to what dreadful death you come,
to what dark and silent grave!

Holy child, before whose Name
powers of darkness faint and fall;
conquered, death and sin and shame,
Jesus Christ is Lord of all!

Holy child, how still you lie!
safe the manger, soft the hay;
clear upon the eastern sky
breaks the dawn of Christmas Day.

27 HOW FAINT THE STABLE-LANTERN'S LIGHT

How faint the stable-lantern's light
    but in the east afar
upon the darkness burning bright
    there shines a single star.

A homeless child is brought to birth,
    yet love and faith shall find
a candle lit for all the earth,
    the hope of humankind;

A flame to warm the barren hearth,
    a lamp for all who roam,
to shine upon the heavenward path
    and light our journey home.

28 HOW SILENT WAITS THE LISTENING EARTH

How silent waits the listening earth
        beneath a cloud-dark sky,
no star to mark the midnight birth,
        the new-born baby's cry;
till angel voices lift their songs
        and glory shines abroad,
for him to whom all praise belongs,
        a Saviour, Christ the Lord.

On trembling feet, from flock and fold,
        the shepherds hasten down;
the child of whom the angel told
        is born in David's town.
They gaze in wide-eyed wonder there
        on Mary's child asleep,
the Lamb of God, our sins to bear,
        the Shepherd of his sheep.

By mountain ways and deserts wide,
        from kingly courts afar,
the wise men in their wisdom ride
        beneath a travelling star.
Beyond the treasures wealth can buy,
        the truths by sages heard,
there shines the wisdom from on high
        in God's incarnate Word.

To him whom now by faith we know
        with angel choirs we sing;
and like the wise, so long ago,
        our treasures too we bring.
O child, to whom the shepherds came
        and knelt to you alone,
we name your everlasting Name,
        the Lamb upon his throne!

29 HUSH YOU, MY BABY

Hush you, my baby,
the night wind is cold,
the lambs from the hillside
are safe in the fold.
Sleep with the starlight
and wake with the morn,
    the Lord of all glory
a baby is born.

Hush you, my baby,
so soon to be grown,
watching by moonlight
on mountains alone,
toiling and travelling
so sleep while you can,
    till the Lord of all glory
is seen as a man.

Hush you, my baby,
the years will not stay;
the cross on the hilltop
the end of the way.
Dim through the darkness,
in grief and in gloom,
    the Lord of all glory
lies cold in the tomb.

Hush you, my baby,
the Father on high
in power and dominion
the darkness puts by;
bright from the shadows,
the seal and the stone,
    the Lord of all glory
returns to his own.

Hush you, my baby,
the sky turns to gold;
the lambs on the hillside
are loose from the fold;
fast fades the midnight
and new springs the morn,
    for the Lord of all glory
a Saviour is born.

30 IN OUR DARKNESS LIGHT HAS SHONE

based on John 1.1–14

I n our darkness light has shone,
    Alleluia,
still today the light shines on,
    Alleluia;
Word made flesh in human birth,
    Alleluia,
Light and Life of all the earth,
    Alleluia!

Christ the Son incarnate see,
    Alleluia,
by whom all things came to be,
    Alleluia;
through the world his splendours shine,
    Alleluia,
full of grace and truth divine,
    Alleluia!

All who now in him believe,
    Alleluia,
everlasting life receive,
    Alleluia;
born of God and in his care,
    Alleluia,
we his Name and nature share,
    Alleluia!

Christ a child on earth appears,
    Alleluia,
crown of all creation's years,
    Alleluia;
God's eternal Word has come,
    Alleluia,
he shall lead his people home,
    Alleluia!

31 NOT IN LORDLY STATE AND SPLENDOUR

Not in lordly state and splendour,
 lofty pomp and high renown;
infant-form his robe most royal,
 lantern-light his only crown;
see the new-born King of glory,
 Lord of all to earth come down!

His no rich and storied mansion,
 kingly rule and sceptred sway;
from his seat in highest heaven
 throned among the beasts he lay;
see the new-born King of glory
 cradled in his couch of hay!

Yet the eye of faith beholds him,
 King above all earthly kings;
Lord of uncreated ages,
 he whose praise eternal rings;
see the new-born King of glory
 panoplied by angels' wings!

Not in lordly state and splendour,
 lofty pomp and high renown;
infant-form his robe most royal,
 lantern-light his only crown;
Christ the new-born King of glory,
 Lord of all to earth come down!

32 O CHILD OF MARY, HARK TO HER

O child of Mary, hark to her
    and to the song she sings,
of gold and frankincense and myrrh,
    the shepherds and the kings.
The light of love is in her eyes
    and music on her breath,
that tells of Galilean skies,
    and home, and Nazareth.

She sings of sunlight through the door,
    the olive and the vine,
and shavings on the workshop floor
    of resin-scented pine;
of winter stars, and fires alight,
    and bed and hearth and board,
and only sometimes, in the night,
    the shadow of a sword.

O sinless child, for sinners born
    to suffering and loss,
the bitter nails, the cruel thorn,
    the darkness and the cross;
no song, since ever time began,
    can tell the path you trod,
O Son of Mary, Son of Man,
    redeeming Son of God.

Yet have we songs: no death and grave,
    no cross with all its pains,
can master him who died to save
    and now in glory reigns.
To him, our ever-living Lord,
    new songs are ours to sing:
the crown, the triumph and the sword
    are yours, O Christ our King.

33 O PRINCE OF PEACE WHOSE PROMISED BIRTH

O Prince of peace whose promised birth
　the angels sang with 'Peace on earth',
peace be to us and all beside,
　　peace to us all,
peace to the world this Christmastide.

O child who found to lay your head
no place but in a manger bed,
come where our doors stand open wide,
　　peace to us all,
　　peace to the world,
peace in our homes this Christmastide.

O Christ whom shepherds came to find,
their joy be ours in heart and mind;
let grief and care be laid aside,
　　peace to us all,
　　peace to the world,
　　peace in our homes,
peace in our hearts this Christmastide.

O Saviour Christ, ascended Lord,
our risen Prince of life restored,
our Love who once for sinners died,
　　peace to us all,
　　peace to the world,
　　peace in our homes,
　　peace in our hearts,
peace with our God this Christmastide.

34 PEACE BE YOURS AND DREAMLESS SLUMBER

Peace be yours and dreamless slumber,
　　heaven's King
　　come to bring
blessings without number.

Helpless now in love's surrender,
　　by your birth,
　　child of earth,
emptied of all splendour.

Dearest Jesus! So we name you,
　　born to save;
　　cross and grave
soon will come to claim you.

Then to heaven's throne ascended!
　　All our tears,
　　wasted years,
sins and sorrows ended.

Sing we then, O Saviour sleeping,
　　our Noel,
　　all is well,
in the Father's keeping.

35 SEE, TO US A CHILD IS BORN

Choir (or solo)   See, to us a child is born:
All   glory breaks on Christmas morn!

Choir   Now to us a Son is given:
All   praise to God in highest heaven!

Choir   On his shoulder rule shall rest:
All   in him all the earth be blest!

Choir   Wise and wonderful his Name:
All   heaven's Lord in human frame!

Choir   Mighty God, who mercy brings:
All   Lord of lords and King of kings!

Choir   Father of eternal days:
All   every creature sing his praise!

Choir   Everlasting Prince of peace:
All   truth and righteousness increase!

Choir   He shall reign from shore to shore:
All   Christ is King for evermore!

36 SOFT THE EVENING SHADOWS FALL

a carol for Christmas pilgrims

Soft the evening shadows fall,
    still journey on;
darkness soon be over all,
    still journey on.
Weary now, and travel-worn,
night must come before the morn:
where will Mary's son be born?
    still journey on.

Shepherds, hasten from the fold;
    this God has done.
Here in human form behold
    this God has done.
Christ the Lord of David's line,
born a Saviour and a sign,
King immortal, child divine,
    this God has done.

Kings who from the east afar
    still journey on,
seeking Christ beneath a star,
    still journey on.
For his worship incense bring,
gold to crown an infant King,
myrrh to mark his suffering,
    still journey on.

Lord of all, enthroned above,
    God sent his Son.
Gift of everlasting love,
    God sent his Son.
He himself a ransom gave,
bowed himself to cross and grave,
came himself to seek and save,
    God sent his Son.

So the Christmas story tell;
    still journey on.
At the last shall all be well;
    still journey on.
Love be ours, and joy and praise,
one with Christ to walk his ways,
in his service all our days
    still journey on.

37 STARS OF HEAVEN, CLEAR AND BRIGHT

Stars of heaven, clear and bright,
shine upon this Christmas night.
Vaster far than midnight skies
are its timeless mysteries.
Trampled earth and stable floor
lift the heart to heaven's door:
God has sent to us his Son,
earth and heaven meet as one.

Sleepy sounds of beast and byre
mingle with the angel choir.
Highest heaven bends in awe
where he lies amid the straw,
who from light eternal came
aureoled in candle-flame:
God has sent to us his Son,
earth and heaven meet as one.

Wide-eyed shepherds mutely gaze
at the child whom angels praise.
Threefold gifts the wise men bring
to the infant Priest and King;
to the Lord immortal, myrrh
for an earthly sepulchre:
God has sent to us his Son,
earth and heaven meet as one.

Heaven of heavens hails his birth,
King of glory, child of earth,
born in flesh to reign on high,
Prince of life to bleed and die.
Throned on Mary's lap he lies,
Lord of all eternities:
God has sent to us his Son,
earth and heaven meet as one.

'Glory be to God on high,
peace on earth,' the angels cry.
Ancient enmities at rest,
ransomed, reconciled and blest,
in the peace of Christ we come,
come we joyful, come we home:
God has sent to us his Son,
earth and heaven meet as one.

38 THE DARKNESS TURNS TO DAWN

The darkness turns to dawn,
the dayspring shines from heaven,
for unto us a child is born,
to us a son is given.

The Son of God most high,
before all else began,
a virgin's son behold him lie,
the new-born Son of Man.

God's Word of truth and grace
made flesh with us to dwell;
the brightness of the Father's face,
the child Emmanuel.

How rich his heavenly home!
How poor his human birth!
As mortal man he stoops to come,
the light and life of earth.

A servant's form, a slave,
the Lord consents to share;
our sin and shame, our cross and grave,
he bows himself to bear;

Obedient and alone
upon that cross to die,
and then to share the Father's throne
in majesty on high.

And still God sheds abroad
that love so strong to send
a Saviour, who is Christ the Lord,
whose reign shall never end.

39 THE HUSH OF MIDNIGHT HERE BELOW

The hush of midnight here below,
the shining stars above,
a night of wonder long ago
when in the stable lantern's glow
is born God's gift of love.

To all the waiting world belongs
the child now brought to birth,
who comes to right our human wrongs,
his praises told in angel songs,
proclaiming peace on earth.

Judean shepherds stand in awe,
in wide-eyed wonder dumb,
to see amid the stable's straw,
fulfilling all the ancient law,
the Lamb of God is come.

The kings of earth in homage ride
to where the child is born;
a King to whom a star shall guide,
whose throne is at the Father's side,
his crown a crown of thorn.

This child, whose birth the angels tell,
whose death our life restored,
by whom at last shall all be well,
is God with us, Immanuel,
our Saviour, Christ the Lord.

40 THE KING OF GLORY COMES TO EARTH

The King of glory comes to earth
from God the Father given,
the heralds of his royal birth
the angel host of heaven;
> his kingly robe the swathing bands,
> his homage Mary's gaze,
> beyond the stars his kingdom stands
> to everlasting days.

The King of glory comes unknown,
the infant Lord of all;
a mother's lap his only throne,
his state a cattle stall.
> Before their naked new-born King
> the ox and ass are dumb,
> while countless choirs of angels sing
> to see his kingdom come.

The King of glory comes to die
in poverty and scorn,
upon a donkey riding by
to claim a crown of thorn.
> Creation's Lord of time and space
> is come to meet his hour,
> his triumph-song the word of grace,
> and love his only power.

The King of glory comes in peace,
and hope is ours again,
as life and love and joy increase
and faith and freedom reign.
> The child of all our Christmas songs,
> his cross and passion past,
> will right the sum of human wrongs
> and bring us home at last.

41 THE LIGHT OF GLORY BREAKS

The light of glory breaks,
  angelic splendours shine;
our God our nature takes,
    a human child divine:
        to cattle-shed as earthly home
        the long-awaited Christ has come.

He lies in slumber deep,
    his manger-bed of hay,
while shepherds leave their sheep,
    his only courtiers, they:
        on trembling feet in haste they trod
        to find the new-born Lamb of God.

The treasures Wisdom gave
    those infant eyes behold,
the myrrh to mark his grave,
    the frankincense and gold:
        prophetic gifts for God Most High,
        our King and Priest who comes to die.

Come, join the angel throngs,
    the shepherds and the kings,
to lift on high the songs
    renewed creation sings:
        for peace with God, for hope restored,
        all glory be to Christ the Lord!

42 THE SHINING STARS UNNUMBERED

T he shining stars unnumbered
on Bethlehem looked down;
unnumbered, too, the travellers
    who thronged to David's town;
no place to rest, no room to spare,
but what the ox and ass may share
    for Mary's son so tender;
she laid him in a manger there,
    the crown of heaven's splendour!

While earth lies hushed and sleeping
    nor dreams of Jesus' birth,
hushed deep in new-born slumbers
    lies he who made the earth;
and from that stable through the night
there shines a lantern burning bright,
    a sign for mortals' seeing,
that Christ is come, the Light of light,
    the Lord of all our being!

A sound of angels singing
    the watching shepherds heard;
our songs of praise are bringing
    anew the promised word;
so let all hearts be joyful when
we hear what angels carolled then
    and tell the Christmas story,
of peace on earth, goodwill to men,
    through Christ the King of glory!

43 THROUGH CENTURIES LONG
THE PROPHETS OF OLD

Through centuries long the prophets of old
in story and song this promise foretold:
a Saviour anointed, a Sovereign supreme,
divinely appointed to rule and redeem.

In judgment and peace his power shall be shown,
his kingdom increase, his justice be known;
from nation to nation his reign shall extend
the hope of salvation and life without end.

He comes not in state with sceptre and crown,
with panoply great of rank or renown,
but choosing in weakness, his glory put by,
majestic in meekness, to serve and to die.

In mercy he came our burden to bear,
our sorrow and shame, our guilt and despair;
an outcast and stranger, he carried our loss
from Bethlehem's manger to Calvary's cross.

He rose from the grave, exalted again,
almighty to save, immortal to reign;
let sorrows be ended and joy be restored
for Christ is ascended, for Jesus is Lord!

Then honour his Name, rejoice at his birth,
his wonders proclaim through all the wide earth!
the child of our story in Bethlehem's stall
is reigning in glory, our God over all.

44 TO THIS OUR WORLD OF TIME AND SPACE

To this our world of time and space,
a destined hour, a chosen place,
    our Saviour Christ has come:
let earth and sky alike bow down
before his everlasting crown,
    the Lord himself has come!

To this our world his hands had made,
in human form and flesh arrayed,
    our Saviour Christ has come:
the light of God's eternal light
to end our fallen nature's night,
    the Lord himself has come!

To this our world, to seek and save,
to crib and crown, to cross and grave,
    our Saviour Christ has come:
the promised gift of God above,
amazing grace, immortal love,
    the Lord himself has come!

To this our world of joy and pain,
to die for us and rise again,
    our Saviour Christ has come:
to die for us and rise again,
and over all the earth to reign,
    the Lord himself has come!

45 WHERE DO CHRISTMAS SONGS BEGIN?

Where do Christmas songs begin?
By the stable of an inn
where the song of hosts on high
mingled with a baby's cry.
There, for joy and wonder, smiled
man and maid and holy child.
Christmas songs begin with them:
Sing the songs of Bethlehem!

Who is this, whose human birth
here proclaims him child of earth?
He it is who formed the skies,
saw the new-made stars arise:
life immortal, light divine,
blinking in the candle-shine;
born our darkness to dispel,
God with us, Emmanuel!

Only love can answer why
he should come to grieve and die,
share on earth our pain and loss,
bear for us the bitter cross.
Love is come to seek and save,
life to master death and grave,
so in Christ is all restored,
risen and redeeming Lord!

Praise we then, in Christmas songs,
him to whom all praise belongs.
Hear the angel host reply,
'Glory be to God on high,
joy and peace to mortals given,
peace on earth and peace with heaven!'
Join we now, as one with them:
sing the songs of Bethlehem!

46 WITHIN A CRIB MY SAVIOUR LAY

Within a crib my Saviour lay,
a wooden manger filled with hay,
come down for love on Christmas Day:
all glory be to Jesus!

Upon a cross my Saviour died,
to ransom sinners crucified,
his loving arms still open wide:
all glory be to Jesus!

A victor's crown my Saviour won,
his work of love and mercy done,
the Father's high-ascended Son:
all glory be to Jesus!

47 CHRIST OUR REDEEMER KNEW TEMPTATION'S HOUR

Christ our Redeemer knew temptation's hour
in desert places, silent and apart;
and three times over met the tempter's power
    with God's word written, hidden in his heart.

He makes not bread what God has made a stone,
    he at whose bidding water turns to wine:
we are not meant to live by bread alone
    but as God speaks the word of life divine.

He will not ask the fickle crowd's acclaim,
    nor flaunt the Sonship which is his by right,
nor seem distrustful of the Father's Name
    who bids us walk by faith and not by sight.

He seeks no kingdom but by cross and grave,
    for love of sinners spurning Satan's throne:
his triumph seen in those he died to save
    who, to his glory, worship God alone.

48 O CHRIST, WHO FACED IN DESERTS BARE

O Christ, who faced in deserts bare
    the fiercest test temptation brings,
to win for us a pasture fair
    and water from eternal springs:
        now, lest our feet be led astray,
        Good Shepherd, walk with us today.

We know the voice that calls our name,
    the patient, low, insistent word;
a voice, for evermore the same,
    that James and John and Peter heard:
        to follow where their steps have gone,
        Good Shepherd, lead your people on.

For all your scattered flock we pray,
    whose eyes the Lamb of God behold;
come as their true and living Way
    to other sheep of every fold:
        from powers of sin and death and grave,
        Good Shepherd, stoop to seek and save.

Good Shepherd of the life laid down,
    Great Shepherd of the ransom paid,
that life, and glory, and a crown,
    be ours, in righteousness arrayed:
        our ways direct, our wants provide,
        Good Shepherd, still be guard and guide.

Teach us to journey here below
    as those who seek their rest above,
and daily by your grace to grow
    in truth and holiness and love:
        and when our pilgrim days are past,
        Good Shepherd, bring us home at last.

49 NO TRAMP OF SOLDIERS' MARCHING FEET

No tramp of soldiers' marching feet
　　with banners and with drums,
no sound of music's martial beat:
　　　'The King of glory comes!'
To greet what pomp of kingly pride
no bells in triumph ring,
no city gates swing open wide:
　　　'Behold, behold your King!'

And yet he comes. The children cheer;
with palms his path is strown.
With every step the cross draws near:
　　　the King of glory's throne.
Astride a colt he passes by
as loud hosannas ring,
or else the very stones would cry
　　　'Behold, behold your King!'

What fading flowers his road adorn;
the palms, how soon laid down!
No bloom or leaf but only thorn
　　　the King of glory's crown.
The soldiers mock, the rabble cries,
the streets with tumult ring,
as Pilate to the mob replies,
　　　'Behold, behold your King!'

Now he who bore for mortals' sake
the cross and all its pains
and chose a servant's form to take,
　　　the King of glory reigns.
Hosanna to the Saviour's Name
till heaven's rafters ring,
and all the ransomed host proclaim
　　　'Behold, behold your King!'

50 IN THE SAME NIGHT
IN WHICH HE WAS BETRAYED

In the same night in which he was betrayed,
the supper ended, and the dark come down,
there in that lonely garden Jesus prayed,
beyond the lamplight of the sleeping town:
above the trees the Paschal moon is high,
the olive branches black against the sky.

What agony of spirit bowed his head
lies far beyond our human heart to frame;
yet 'Not my will but yours' at last he said,
as lights and torches through the garden came:
so Judas ends what love of self began,
and with a kiss betrays the Son of Man.

The hour is come: the power of darkness reigns.
See, like a lamb, the Lord is led away.
Of twelve disciples only one remains
to wait the dawning of the final day:
alone before his captors Jesus stands,
while in the courtyard Peter warms his hands.

*   *   *

Turn, Lord, and look: for many a cock has crowed;
we too betray, forsake you, or deny.
For us, like Peter, bitter tears have flowed,
lost in the dark, no language but a cry;
a cry of weakness, failure and despair:
Lord, in your mercy, stoop to hear our prayer.

51 A PURPLE ROBE, A CROWN OF THORN

A purple robe, a crown of thorn,
    a reed in his right hand;
before the soldiers' spite and scorn
    I see my Saviour stand.

He bears between the Roman guard
    the weight of all our woe;
a stumbling figure bowed and scarred
    I see my Saviour go.

Fast to the cross's spreading span,
    high in the sunlit air,
all the unnumbered sins of man
    I see my Saviour bear.

He hangs, by whom the world was made,
    beneath the darkened sky;
the everlasting ransom paid,
    I see my Saviour die.

He shares on high his Father's throne,
    who once in mercy came;
for all his love to sinners shown
    I sing my Saviour's Name.

52 APPROACH WITH AWE THIS HOLIEST PLACE

Approach with awe this holiest place,
the last of death's domain;
the shuttered heavens hide their face,
the powers of darkness reign;
for there beneath those sombre skies
the Prince of life, forsaken, dies.

The Prince of life! For us he came
from that high throne above,
his cross the measure of our shame,
his death the price of love;
and at his cross, my soul, begin
to feel the weight of love and sin.

Can this poor broken form be he
who taught the words of truth,
who strode the hills of Galilee
in all the flower of youth?
Can this be he, this lifeless head,
with grace and strength and beauty fled?

By wood and nails the work is done
that answers all our need,
the prize of full salvation won,
the ransomed sinner freed.
Draw near with faith, my soul, and see
the Prince of life who died for me.

The Prince of life! While time shall last
his cross and grave remain
sure signs of sin and sorrow past,
bright morning come again:
an empty cross, an empty grave,
a risen Christ to seek and save!

53 BEHOLD, AS LOVE MADE MANIFEST

Behold, as love made manifest,
  the Lamb of God divine:
redeeming love perceived, possessed,
    in sacrifice and sign;

A sign of saving grace displayed,
    a sign of sinners' worth;
by wood and nails a ransom paid
    for all the sins of earth.

A sign of love beyond belief,
    where every failing breath
affirms through agony and grief
    a love that conquers death;

A sign of mercy's wide extent
    and universal sway;
the evil powers of darkness spent
    for Christ has won the day.

A sign of triumph over sin
    and dread devouring grave,
a sign of all he died to win
    for all he longs to save;

Herein is love beyond all price,
    the Lamb of God divine:
his all-sufficient sacrifice,
    his all-prevailing sign.

54 DEAR LORD, WHO BORE OUR WEIGHT OF WOE

Dear Lord, who bore our weight of woe
and for our pardon died,
incline our hearts to feel and know
those arms yet open wide.

Those loving arms enfold us still
nor turn one soul away;
to him who welcomes all who will
we come anew today.

In penitence and faith we come
on Jesus' promise stayed:
of all our sin, the final sum
for love alone he paid.

He paid what none may comprehend;
what all have lost, restored;
the sinner's advocate and friend,
our gracious loving Lord.

Our loving Lord! We rest within
that Name all names above,
for vaster far than all our sin
is Christ our Saviour's love.

55 UPON A TREE THE SIN OF MAN

Upon a tree the sin of man
    found its primeval root,
where thick upon each burdened branch
    there hung forbidden fruit.

The tree of knowledge rudely robbed,
    the tree of life decayed,
another tree was grown and hewn,
    the tree of death was made.

And there the sin of Adam's race
    shall end as it began:
for high between the barren boughs
    there hangs the Son of Man.

56 WE TURN IN FAITH TO CHRIST THE LAMB OF GOD

We turn in faith to Christ the Lamb of God
  and in him rest;
he who the path of pain and sorrow trod,
  by sin oppressed.
Sinless himself, he died to bear our shame
when to the loveless and the lost he came.

Lord Jesus, bearer of our grief and loss
  and all our sins,
we come to kneel anew beneath that cross
  where life begins:
that cross of shame become the healing tree
where we and all your children may be free.

Christ our Redeemer, bringing life to birth
  from death's dark grave,
Saviour and Sovereign over all the earth
  you died to save,
take now our love, that comes from sins forgiven;
teach us on earth to live the life of heaven.

57 ALL SHALL BE WELL

All shall be well!
for on our Easter skies
see Christ the Sun
of Righteousness arise.

All shall be well!
the sacrifice is made;
the sinner freed,
the price of pardon paid.

All shall be well!
the cross and passion past;
dark night is done,
bright morning come at last.

All shall be well!
within our Father's plan
death has no more
dominion over man.

Jesus alive!
Rejoice and sing again,
'All shall be well
for evermore, Amen!'

58 AND SLEEPS MY LORD IN SILENCE YET

And sleeps my Lord in silence yet,
  within the darkness laid away;
where none remember nor forget,
    where breaks no more the sunlit day?
and sleeps my Lord in silence yet,
    where cold his lifeless body lay?

And does the sting of death remain
    to work unchanged its bitter will?
were cross and passion all in vain,
    no battle won on Calvary's hill?
and does the sting of death remain,
    and gapes the grave in triumph still?

Have faith in Christ, the risen Son,
    who reigns eternal, glorified!
who death destroyed, who triumph won,
    who flung the gates of heaven wide!
Have faith in Christ, the risen Son,
    the living Lord of Eastertide!

59 BY LOVING HANDS THE LORD IS LAID

By loving hands the Lord is laid,
　　no voice or pulse or breath;
as close within the shuttered gloom,
the sealed and silent garden tomb,
　　he sleeps the sleep of death.

There through the dark of Easter dawn
　　before the break of day,
before the dew was off the grass
with none to see their footsteps pass,
　　the women make their way.

No seal, no stone, secures the tomb,
　　as low within the cave
they stoop to find, beyond belief,
where late the Lord was laid with grief,
　　there stands an empty grave.

An empty grave! A risen Lord!
　　A ransomed world reborn,
to see upon the shining skies
the Sun of Righteousness arise
　　on that first Easter morn!

60 CHRIST IS RISEN AS HE SAID

Choir (or solo) Christ is risen as he said,
All   Christ the firstborn from the dead:

Choir   See, the stone is rolled away,
All   see the place where Jesus lay.

Choir   Lord of life, he lives again;
All   Lord of lords, to rule and reign:

Choir   Every tongue confess him now,
All   every knee before him bow.

Choir   Christ who died our life to win,
All   Christ has conquered death and sin:

Choir   Now is all his warfare done,
All   now is every triumph won.

Choir   Son of God, his life he gave,
All   Son of Man, to seek and save:

Choir   Risen now, the Son who died,
All   risen, ascended, glorified.

61 COME AND SEE WHERE JESUS LAY

C ome and see where Jesus lay,
　　cold within the silent cave;
see, the stone is rolled away,
　　　void and tenantless the grave:
clothes to shroud his form and head
　　　still their absent Lord display;
Christ is risen from the dead!
　　　Come and see where Jesus lay.

Go and tell that Jesus reigns,
　　　sin and death are overthrown;
dead to sin and all its pains,
　　　live to make his glories known.
Raised in triumph, as he said,
　　　he who all the world sustains:
Christ is risen from the dead!
　　　Go and tell that Jesus reigns!

62 FROM AFAR A COCK IS CROWING

From afar a cock is crowing,
every star is paler showing,
    night is on the wane;
dark is done, the dawn is breaking,
with the sun the world is waking,
    life is come again!

Gone is gloom and grief despairing!
See the tomb the truth declaring
    as the Saviour said:
Christ at last, his work completed,
passion past and death defeated,
    risen from the dead!

All the powers of darkness broken,
life is ours, from death awoken,
    born to joy again.
Open lies our ancient prison:
come, arise, with Jesus risen,
    and with Jesus reign!

63 JESUS, PRINCE AND SAVIOUR

Jesus, Prince and Saviour,
 Lord of life who died,
Christ, the friend of sinners,
mocked and crucified;
for a world's salvation
he his body gave,
lay at last death's victim
lifeless in the grave.
> *Lord of life triumphant,*
> *risen now to reign!*
> *King of endless ages,*
> *Jesus lives again!*

In his power and Godhead
every victory won,
pain and passion ended,
all his purpose done:
Christ the Lord is risen!
sighs and sorrows past,
death's dark night is over,
morning comes at last!
> *Chorus*

Resurrection morning,
sinners' bondage freed!
Christ the Lord is risen,
he is risen indeed!
Jesus, Prince and Saviour,
Lord of life who died,
Christ the King of glory
now is glorified!
> *Chorus*

64 LONG BEFORE THE WORLD IS WAKING

based on John 21

Long before the world is waking,
  morning mist on Galilee,
from the shore, as dawn is breaking,
Jesus calls across the sea;
    hails the boat of weary men,
    bids them cast their net again.

So they cast, and all their heaving
cannot haul their catch aboard;
John in wonder turns, perceiving,
cries aloud, 'It is the Lord!'
    Peter waits for nothing more,
    plunges in to swim ashore.

Charcoal embers brightly burning,
bread and fish upon them laid:
Jesus stands at day's returning
in his risen life arrayed;
    as of old his friends to greet,
    'Here is breakfast; come and eat.'

Christ is risen! Grief and sighing,
sins and sorrows, fall behind;
fear and failure, doubt, denying,
full and free forgiveness find.
    All the soul's dark night is past,
    morning breaks in joy at last.

Morning breaks, and Jesus meets us,
feeds and comforts, pardons still;
as his faithful friends he greets us,
partners of his work and will.
    All our days, on every shore,
    Christ is ours for evermore!

65 NOW IS CHRIST RISEN FROM THE DEAD

Now is Christ risen from the dead,
now are the powers of darkness fled,
Alleluia...
Gone is the night of sin and gloom,
Jesus is risen from the tomb.
Alleluia...

Now is Christ risen from the dead,
empty there lies his narrow bed,
Alleluia...
Christ and his cross have won the day,
come, see the grave in which he lay.
Alleluia...

Now is Christ risen from the dead,
he who his blood for sinners shed,
Alleluia...
In him who died to bear our sins
our resurrection-life begins.
Alleluia...

Now is Christ risen from the dead,
risen and reigning as he said,
Alleluia...
Praise him who light and life restored,
praise him, our ever-living Lord!
Alleluia...

66 OUR RISEN LORD, OUR KING OF KINGS

Our risen Lord, our King of kings,
earth with your Easter triumph rings;
hear how the whole creation sings,
Alleluia...

O holy child, whose saving Name
the angels sang when first you came,
let every tongue your love proclaim,
Alleluia...

O Son of Man, your life you gave,
and chose for us the cross and grave;
we sing with all you came to save,
Alleluia...

O Lamb of God, ordained to die,
and lifeless in that tomb to lie,
immortal praise be yours on high,
Alleluia...

O Prince of life who lives again,
risen indeed from death's domain,
come to our hearts, and rule and reign,
Alleluia...

67 WHO IS THERE ON THIS EASTER MORNING

Who is there on this Easter morning
runs not with John to find the grave?
Nor sees how, death's dominion scorning,
Jesus is risen, strong to save?
    Who is there on this Easter morning
    runs not with John to find the grave?

Who has not stood where Mary grieving
to that first Easter garden came;
for very joy but half believing
whose is the voice that calls her name?
    Who has not stood where Mary grieving
    to that first Easter garden came?

Who is there doubts that night is ended?
Hear from on high the trumpets call!
Christ is in triumph now ascended,
risen and reigning, Lord of all!
    Who is there doubts that night is ended?
    Hear from on high the trumpets call!

68 CHRIST HIGH-ASCENDED, NOW IN GLORY SEATED

Christ high-ascended, now in glory seated,
  throned and exalted, victory completed,
death's dread dominion finally defeated,
    we are his witnesses.

Christ from the Father every power possessing,
who on his chosen lifted hands in blessing,
sends forth his servants, still in faith confessing,
    we are his witnesses.

Christ, who in dying won for us salvation,
lives now the first-born of the new creation;
to win disciples out of every nation,
    we are his witnesses.

Christ in his splendour, all dominion gaining,
Christ with his people evermore remaining,
Christ to all ages gloriously reigning,
    we are his witnesses.

As at his parting, joy shall banish grieving,
faith in his presence strengthen our believing;
filled with his Spirit, love and power receiving,
    we are his witnesses.

69 HEAVEN'S THRONE ASCENDING

H eaven's throne ascending,
death's dominion ending,
  Christ the strong to save!
now in glory seated,
work on earth completed,
  risen from the grave!
join to praise through all our days
Christ the Lord of love who sought us,
  and in dying bought us.

Powers of darkness broken,
earth from sleep awoken,
  and to life re-born!
from our nature's prison
we with Christ are risen
  by that Easter morn.
Join to sing our glorious King,
risen, reigning, high ascending,
  Lord of life unending!

70 RISEN LORD IN SPLENDOUR SEATED

Risen Lord in splendour seated,
throned at God the Father's side,
Prince of life who death defeated,
Lamb who once for sinners died,
　　Christ for ever Son and Saviour
reigns in triumph glorified.

He who came our nature bearing,
child of earth from heaven's throne,
human trials and troubles sharing,
God himself in flesh made known,
　　Christ for ever with his people
sends his Spirit on his own.

Love of God, unwearied, reaching
furthest bounds of time and space,
still by foolishness of preaching
holding forth the word of grace,
　　Christ for ever interceding
builds his church in every place.

Earth awaits her new creation
when from sin and death restored,
in the strength of full salvation
Christ is honoured and adored,
　　Christ for ever high ascended,
sovereign, universal Lord!

71 BE PRESENT, SPIRIT OF THE LORD

Be present, Spirit of the Lord,
let sounds of earth be dumb;
the Father's love be shed abroad,
the dew of blessing on us poured:
    O silent Spirit, come!

In power unseen upon us rest,
    your gracious gifts impart:
a mind renewed, a spirit blessed,
a life where Christ is manifest,
    an understanding heart.

Love's sovereign work of grace fulfil,
    our souls to Christ incline,
intent to do the Father's will
and stand by faith before him still
    in righteousness divine.

O Spirit come, and with us stay;
    make every heart your home.
So work in us that we who pray
may walk with Christ in wisdom's way:
    O Holy Spirit, come!

72 SPIRIT OF FAITH, BY FAITH BE MINE

Spirit of faith, by faith be mine;
Spirit of truth, in wisdom shine;
Spirit of holiness divine,
    Spirit of Jesus, come!

Come to our hearts and there remain;
Spirit of life, our life sustain;
Spirit of grace and glory, reign!
    Spirit of Jesus, come!

73 SPIRIT OF GOD WITHIN ME

Spirit of God within me,
    possess my human frame;
fan the dull embers of my heart,
    stir up the living flame.
Strive till that image Adam lost,
    new minted and restored,
in shining splendour brightly bears
    the likeness of the Lord.

Spirit of truth within me,
    possess my thought and mind;
lighten anew the inward eye
    by Satan rendered blind;
shine on the words that wisdom speaks
    and grant me power to see
the truth made known to all in Christ,
    and in that truth be free.

Spirit of love within me,
    possess my hands and heart;
break through the bonds of self-concern
    that seeks to stand apart:
grant me the love that suffers long,
    that hopes, believes and bears,
the love fulfilled in sacrifice,
    that cares as Jesus cares.

Spirit of life within me,
    possess this life of mine;
come as the wind of heaven's breath,
    come as the fire divine!
Spirit of Christ, the living Lord,
    reign in this house of clay,
till from its dust with Christ I rise
    to everlasting day.

74 WHEN GOD THE SPIRIT CAME

When God the Spirit came
upon his church outpoured
in sound of wind and sign of flame
they spread his truth abroad,
    and filled with the Spirit
proclaimed that Christ is Lord.

What courage, power and grace
that youthful church displayed!
to those of every tribe and race
they witnessed unafraid,
    and filled with the Spirit
they broke their bread and prayed.

They saw God's word prevail,
his kingdom still increase,
no part of all his purpose fail,
no promised blessing cease,
    and filled with the Spirit
knew love and joy and peace.

Their theme was Christ alone,
the Lord who lived and died,
who rose to his eternal throne
at God the Father's side;
    and filled with the Spirit
the church was multiplied.

So to this present hour
our task is still the same,
in pentecostal love and power
his gospel to proclaim,
    and filled with the Spirit,
rejoice in Jesus' Name.

75 GOD AND FATHER, EVER GIVING

God and Father, ever giving
from the fruitful dust of earth
form and flesh to all things living,
life and being, breath and birth,
    living Lord, whose life we share,
    lift our hearts in love and prayer.

Son of God who came and sought us,
shared our pleasure and our pain,
who in dying loved and bought us
and triumphant rose again,
    living Lord, whose life we share,
    lift our hearts in love and prayer.

Holy Spirit, life bestowing,
breath of God on all our ways,
wind of heaven, freely blowing,
fire to set the soul ablaze,
    living Lord, whose life we share,
    lift our hearts in love and prayer.

God eternal, all sustaining,
King immortal, throned above,
Father, Son and Spirit reigning,
One in everlasting love,
    living Lord, whose life we share,
    lift our hearts in love and prayer.

76 GOD IS NOT FAR,
WHOSE THREEFOLD MERCIES SHINE

God is not far, whose threefold mercies shine
about our ways as wisdom judges best:
in grace and love and fellowship divine
    he comes as Father, Son and Spirit blest.

God is but One, who ever reigns above.
    Deep in the Godhead is his love expressed.
Before he formed us, children of his love,
    he loved as Father, Son and Spirit blest.

For God is love, unquenchable and strong;
    see in our Saviour love made manifest!
Praises unending to our God belong
    who lives as Father, Son and Spirit blest.

77 GOD LIES BEYOND US, THRONED IN LIGHT RESPLENDENT

God lies beyond us, throned in light resplendent,
Father eternal, source of all creation.
To him in glory, timeless and transcendent,
    High King of Ages, come with adoration.

God walks beside us, born to be our neighbour,
    died to redeem us, risen and ascended;
love to the loveless, friend of all who labour,
    Christ our Companion, till our days are ended.

God lives within us, breath and life instilling,
    daily transforming ways of thought and seeing.
Spirit all-holy, all our spirits filling,
    blow, Wind, about us! burn within our being.

God in three Persons, Trinity of splendour!
    To God the Father, all in all sustaining,
and God the Saviour, adoration render,
    with God the Spirit, One in glory reigning.

78 THE EVERLASTING FATHER REIGNS

The everlasting Father reigns
from his eternal throne;
his will created and sustains
    our world and worlds unknown:
to him we lift our voices high,
    who was, and is to be,
and 'Holy, holy, holy,' cry
    to God, the One-in-Three.

To Christ the Son, incarnate Lord,
    we bring unending praise;
his Name be honoured and adored
    through everlasting days:
who loved, and loosed us from our sins,
    who died to make us free,
in whom abundant life begins
    with God, the One-in-Three.

O Spirit blest, who life imparts,
    by whom all gifts are given,
who makes his home in human hearts,
    the harbinger of heaven:
that life of love we long to share,
    that holiness to see,
who helps us breathe our wordless prayer
    to God, the One-in-Three.

Lift every heart to God above,
    beyond all time and space,
who loves us with a Father's love,
    a Son's redeeming grace:
who by his Spirit makes us one,
    to him all glory be,
eternal Father, Spirit, Son,
    our God, the One-in-Three.

2. Regular Daily and Weekly Church Services

Certain texts which might have been listed here are classified under other headings, for example as metrical psalms or other Scriptures, metrical canticles and so on.

The Index of Themes and Subjects on page 544 contains entries under all the headings listed above, generally with a wider selection of suitable texts. There is also a heading for 'Evening'; and a very much larger list of suggestions for 'Praise and worship'.

79 IN ENDLESS EXULTATION

In endless exultation
all earth unites to raise
her chorus of creation,
    her ancient hymn of praise.
To tell abroad his wonders
    the very stones give tongue;
by ocean's mighty thunders
    the praise of God is sung.

Unnumbered creatures share it,
    they make their homage heard;
the wind and storm declare it
    fulfilling all his word.
Earth's varied voices blending
    give praise to God on high,
one anthem never-ending
    from earth and sea and sky.

In solemn high thanksgiving
    his Name be now adored,
and bless with all things living
    our Saviour and our Lord!
Sing out with all creation
    the song of saints above,
to God our great salvation
    whose very Name is love.

80 LET US SING THE GOD OF GLORY
WHO HAS SET THE STARS IN PLACE

Let us sing the God of glory who has set the stars in place,
with the planets in their courses as they cross the heaven's face,
and the constellations shining to the boundaries of space,
    our God whose Name is love!
Glory, glory, Alleluia . . . our God whose Name is love!

Let us sing the God of beauty in the mountains and the seas,
all the colours of the rainbow and the tracery of trees,
in the thunder of the breakers and the whisper of the breeze,
    our God whose Name is love!
Glory, glory, Alleluia . . . our God whose Name is love!

Let us sing the God of bounty for a fruitful earth and fair,
who provides for us in plenty so that all may have a share,
and who loves his human family and has us in his care,
    our God whose Name is love!
Glory, glory, Alleluia . . . our God whose Name is love!

Let us sing the God of mercy for the wonders he has done,
how he loved us in our sinfulness and sent to us his Son,
who has died for us, and lives for us, and life and freedom won,
    our God whose Name is love!
Glory, glory, Alleluia . . . our God whose Name is love!

Let us sing the Saviour Jesus as he makes the Father known,
let us hear his Spirit's call to us to come and be his own,
and to worship him in glory on his everlasting throne,
    our God whose Name is love!
Glory, glory, Alleluia . . . our God whose Name is love!

81 REJOICE IN GOD! LET TRUMPETS SOUND

Rejoice in God! let trumpets sound
in witness to the world around,
   his faithfulness proclaim;
who led his people by the hand
and brought them to their promised land
that all the earth should understand
   the greatness of his Name.

Rejoice in God, the God of grace,
and come with thanks before his face
   for all his tender care;
whose mercy meets us in our need,
whose word of life is life indeed,
on whom, in Christ, our spirits feed,
   who loves to answer prayer.

Rejoice in God whose only Son
a fallen world's salvation won
   and broke the sinner's chain.
He came in love to seek and save
when for us all his life he gave,
and then from cross and death and grave
   triumphant rose again.

Rejoice in God and for him build
a living temple, Spirit-filled,
   of everlasting worth;
a church united, true and strong,
where all who love the Lord belong,
and find in him their strength and song,
   the joy of all the earth.

Rejoice in God! your voices raise
in honour, blessing, love and praise
   to his eternal throne;
that every heart, with one accord,
and every tongue may tell abroad
the loving-kindness of the Lord,
   and make his glory known.

82 YOUR VOICES RAISE TO THE FATHER'S PRAISE

Your voices raise to the Father's praise,
  our God of eternal grace;
he formed our earth and he gave us birth
    as children of time and space.
The moon to rise in the starry skies,
    the seas and the sunlit land,
we see displayed in the world he made
    the touch of its Maker's hand.

In wonder sing of the Lord our King,
    the Saviour who loved and came
to seek and save, when his life he gave
    and died on a cross of shame.
Our flesh he wore and our sins he bore
    till, back from the grave again,
he came at dawn on that Easter morn
    in triumph to rise and reign.

To God above, and the Saviour's love,
    whose Spirit his life imparts,
all glory be as the One-in-Three,
    the homage of all our hearts.
Our love be shown not in word alone:
    we come with no empty praise,
as faithful friends till our journey ends,
    to follow him all our days.

83 LORD, AS THE DAY BEGINS

L ord, as the day begins
lift up our hearts in praise;
take from us all our sins,
guard us in all our ways:
 our every step direct and guide
 that Christ in all be glorified!

Christ be in work and skill,
serving each other's need;
Christ be in thought and will,
Christ be in word and deed:
 our minds be set on things above
 in joy and peace, in faith and love.

Grant us the Spirit's strength,
teach us to walk his way;
so bring us all at length
safe to the close of day:
 from hour to hour sustain and bless,
 and let our song be thankfulness.

Now as the day begins
make it the best of days;
take from us all our sins,
guard us in all our ways:
 our every step direct and guide
 that Christ in all be glorified!

84 LORD, FOR THE GIFT OF THIS NEW DAY

Lord, for the gift of this new day
receive alike our praise and prayer,
that all we think and do and say
be in your care.

Our minds be set on things of worth,
things excellent and good and true;
so may we love not only earth
but heaven too.

Our actions match the faith we claim,
integrity attend our ways;
let all be done in Jesus' Name
and to his praise.

Our speech express a heart renewed
and lightened by the Spirit's love,
with words of grace and truth endued
from God above.

So may your benediction rest
on us and all we meet this day,
who walk with Jesus, doubly blest,
the pilgrim way.

85 THIS DAY ABOVE ALL DAYS

This day above all days
　　glad hymns of triumph bring;
lift every heart to love and praise
and every voice to sing:
　　　for Jesus is risen,
our glorious Lord and King!

Christ keeps his Eastertide!
The Father's power descends;
the shuttered tomb he opens wide,
the rock-hewn grave he rends:
　　　for Jesus is risen,
and death's dominion ends!

What sovereign grace is found
in Christ for all our need!
The powers of sin and death are bound,
the ransomed captives freed:
　　　for Jesus is risen,
the Prince of life indeed!

So lift your joyful songs
with all the hosts on high,
where angel and archangel throngs
his ceaseless praises cry:
　　　for Jesus is risen,
and lives no more to die!

86 AN UPPER ROOM WITH EVENING LAMPS ASHINE

An upper room with evening lamps ashine,
the twelve disciples, and the table spread;
now in our turn Christ bids us pour the wine,
    and in remembrance bless and break the bread.

We see by faith upon the cross displayed
    his body broken and his blood outpoured;
in that dread robe of majesty arrayed
    we gaze in worship on the dying Lord.

Dead for our sins, yet reigning now above,
    still to our hearts we find his presence given;
take for ourselves the pledges of his love,
    foretaste and token of that feast in heaven.

So send us out to love and serve and praise,
    filled with his Spirit, as the Master said:
love, joy and peace the wine of all our days,
    Christ and his life our true and living bread.

87 AS IN THAT UPPER ROOM YOU LEFT YOUR SEAT

As in that upper room you left your seat
and took a towel and chose a servant's part,
so for today, Lord, wash again my feet,
who in your mercy died to cleanse my heart.

I bow before you, all my sin confessed,
to hear again the words of love you said;
and at your table, as your honoured guest,
I take and eat the true and living bread.

So in remembrance of your life laid down
I come to praise you for your grace divine;
saved by your cross, and subject to your crown,
strengthened for service by this bread and wine.

88 GOD GIVES A NEW BEGINNING

God gives a new beginning
   to those who hear his call,
who turn from self and sinning
     to Christ as all-in-all:
to know him still more clearly
     their over-arching aim;
to follow him more nearly,
     and learn to love his Name.

In songs and celebration,
     in penitence and prayer,
we come with adoration
     the bread and wine to share:
to hear his truth expounded,
     before his cross to bend,
and, by his saints surrounded,
     to find in him a friend.

May we, his Name confessing,
     unwearied run the race,
and daily seek his blessing,
     his gifts of truth and grace:
his word our souls to nourish,
     his Spirit from above,
whose promised fruit shall flourish
     in joy and peace and love.

89 THE LORD IS HERE

T he Lord is here!
His promised word
is evermore the same,
    himself to be
    where two or three
are gathered in his Name.

The Lord is here!
Where Christ is come
his Spirit too is there,
    with all who raise
    the song of praise
or breathe the voice of prayer.

The Lord is here!
He comes in peace
with blessings from above,
    by pledge and sign
    of bread and wine
to fold us in his love.

The Lord is here!
To every soul
this gift of grace be given,
    to walk the way
    of Christ today,
and share the life of heaven.

90 WE COME AS GUESTS INVITED

We come as guests invited
    when Jesus bids us dine,
his friends on earth united
    to share the bread and wine;
the bread of life is broken,
    the wine is freely poured
for us, in solemn token
    of Christ our dying Lord.

We eat and drink, receiving
    from Christ the grace we need,
and in our hearts believing
    on him by faith we feed;
with wonder and thanksgiving
    for love that knows no end,
we find in Jesus living
    our ever-present friend.

One bread is ours for sharing,
    one single fruitful vine,
our fellowship declaring
    renewed in bread and wine:
renewed, sustained and given
    by token, sign and word,
the pledge and seal of heaven,
    the love of Christ our Lord.

3. Occasional and Annual Church Services

Certain texts which might have been listed here are classified under other headings, for example as metrical psalms or other Scriptures, metrical canticles and so on.

The Index of Themes and Subjects on page 544 contains entries under all the headings listed above, generally with a wider selection of suitable texts. 'Saints' is one example, though several hymns suitable for Saints days and festivals appear in this section. 'Bible' is another, while texts here listed as suitable for Bible Sunday often serve a wider purpose.

In general, texts are included here rather than in Section 9, 'Themes and Subjects', if they are particularly suitable for some special Service in the course of a local church's year, or for an 'Occasional Service' in the technical sense of a Baptism, Marriage and so on.

91 THIS CHERISHED CHILD OF GOD'S CREATION

T his cherished child of God's creation,
  heir to a world of joy and pain,
freely in thankful dedication,
    Father, we bring to you again.

Lord, as of old the children found you,
    when to your side with joy they pressed,
so may our children gather round you
    and in your loving arms be blessed.

Spirit of holiness, descending,
    grant them to grow, as years increase,
closer to Christ and his befriending,
    filled with your love and joy and peace.

God ever One, whose care unsleeping
    watches about your children's way,
take now this child within your keeping,
    whom here we dedicate today.

92 FATHER, NOW BEHOLD US

Father, now behold us
and this child, we pray:
in your love enfold us,
    wash our sins away.

Christ's eternal blessing
    for this life we claim:
faith, by ours, professing;
    signed in Jesus' Name.

By the Spirit tended,
    childhood grow to youth;
from all ill defended,
    full of grace and truth.

God of all creation,
    stoop from heaven's throne,
and by Christ's salvation
    make this child your own!

93 LORD JESUS, BORN A TINY CHILD

L ord Jesus, born a tiny child
and held in Mary's fond embrace,
who gravely looked at her, and smiled
    to see the joy upon her face,
        look with the same delight, we pray,
        upon this child we bring today.

Lord Jesus, when the children came
    your arms were wide to welcome all,
and for this child we ask the same,
    a heart responsive to your call.
        Receive and bless, O Lord, we pray,
        this child we here baptize today.

Lord Jesus, bearer of our sin,
    who died for us and rose again,
to make your children clean within
    and free from every sin and stain,
        so may this child be washed, we pray,
        whom with your cross we sign today.

Lord Jesus, reigning now as King,
    whose subjects serve for love alone,
let love enlist the life we bring
    and claim this child to be your own:
        in faith baptized, received, forgiven,
        to be by grace a child of heaven.

94 NOW TO THE LORD WE BRING
THE CHILD HE GAVE US

Now to the Lord we bring the child he gave us,
for rain or shine, for laughter and for tears;
pledged to his service, who was born to save us,
rich with the promise of the future years.

Into the threefold Name we here baptize you
as Jesus bids by water and the word;
fast in his grace, when Satan sifts and tries you,
child of the covenant of Christ the Lord!

True to believe and trust our living Master
from life's bright morning to the twilight dim,
firm in the face of evil or disaster,
Christ's faithful soldier, turned to follow him.

One with his church, though all the world deride you;
signed with his cross, who once was sacrificed;
strong in his strength, for Jesus walks beside you,
world without end, in company with Christ!

95 THIS CHILD FROM GOD ABOVE

This child from God above,
   the Father's gift divine,
to this new life of light and love
   we give his seal and sign;

To bear the eternal Name,
   to walk the Master's way,
the Father's covenant to claim,
   the Spirit's will obey;

To take the Saviour's cross,
   in faith to hold it fast;
and for it reckon all things loss
   as long as life shall last;

To tell his truth abroad,
   to tread the path he trod,
with all who love and serve the Lord,
   the family of God.

96 WHEN JESUS TAUGHT BY GALILEE

When Jesus taught by Galilee
  he called disciples to his side,
his friends and followers to be,
    to spread his gospel far and wide:
        the word of life we still proclaim,
        baptizing in the threefold Name.

That Name declares a Father's love,
    a covenant of grace and care,
an everlasting home above,
    a family on earth to share,
        beloved and precious in his sight,
        who walk as children of the light.

The Name of Christ becomes our own,
    our sovereign Lord and Saviour now,
to follow him, and him alone,
    whose sign is printed on our brow;
        his service share, his cause defend,
        and so continue to the end.

We bear the Holy Spirit's Name,
    who life and truth and power imparts,
who comes, as once in wind and flame,
    to make his home within our hearts;
        and daily in our lives increase
        his fruit of love, and joy and peace.

So in the threefold Name today
    baptized in faith from all our sins,
we turn to Christ, our Truth and Way,
    the Life in whom our life begins;
        to Christ who saves and sets us free,
        his followers and friends to be.

97 WE TURN TO CHRIST ALONE

We turn to Christ alone,
    the Son of God divine,
to bow the knee before his throne,
    to bear his Name and sign;
    to bear his Name and sign
      and walk the narrow way,
to make his love and glory known,
      his word and will obey.

We turn from self and sin
    in penitence and shame;
we trust, to make us clean within,
    the power of Jesus' Name;
    the power of Jesus' Name,
      whose cross is strong to save,
who gave his life our life to win
      from sin and death and grave.

We turn from every wrong,
    from every evil way,
who in the Spirit's strength are strong,
    as children of the day;
    as children of the day
      from dark to light we turn,
disciples who to Christ belong,
      his way of life to learn.

We turn to Christ as Lord
    who died and rose again,
as those whose hearts receive his word,
    as subjects of his reign;
    as subjects of his reign,
      who calls his servants friends,
our King of love to life restored,
      whose kingdom never ends.

98 WE TURN TO CHRIST ANEW

We turn to Christ anew
    who hear his call today,
his way to walk, his will pursue,
    his word obey.
To serve him as our King
    and of his kingdom learn,
from sin and every evil thing
    to him we turn.

We trust in Christ to save;
    in him new life begins:
who by his cross a ransom gave
    from all our sins.
Our spirits' strength and stay
    who when all flesh is dust
will keep us in that final day,
    in him we trust.

We would be true to him
    till earthly journeys end,
whose love no passing years can dim,
    our changeless friend.
May we who bear his Name
    our faith and love renew,
to follow Christ our single aim,
    and find him true.

99 AT CANA'S WEDDING, LONG AGO

for a marriage

At Cana's wedding, long ago,
they knew his presence by this sign,
a virtue none but Christ could show,
to turn their water into wine:
    and still on us his blessing be
    as in the days of Galilee.

What if the way be far to go
and life at times a weary load?
Yet may our hearts within us glow
as theirs on that Emmaus road:
    the risen Christ become our guest,
    with him to walk, in him to rest.

O Lord of all our life below,
O risen Lord of realms above,
eternal joy be theirs to know,
united in the bond of love:
    one in the faith, with one accord,
    one with each other and the Lord.

100 LORD, HEAR US AS WE PRAY

suitable for a marriage

L ord, hear us as we pray,
 a Father's blessing give,
that Christ be light upon our way
 and truth by which to live.

A faith in which to rest,
 a living hope, impart;
with charity of spirit blest
 in humbleness of heart.

The Spirit from above
 his gracious gifts increase,
that Christ be all our joy and love
 as Christ is all our peace.

101 LORD OF OUR LIVES, OUR BIRTH AND BREATH

suitable for a funeral

L ord of our lives, our birth and breath,
  the measure of our days,
to you alone, in life and death,
    we bring our prayer and praise.

For love of life and all its powers
    by sunlit memory stored,
for tasted joys and timeless hours,
    we praise our living Lord.

Within the love of Christ we rest
    whose cross is strong to save,
by whose eternal hand possessed
    we fear not death or grave.

So move our hearts, O God above,
    by whom all gifts are given,
that one in Christ with those we love
    we walk with him to heaven.

102 GIVE THANKS TO GOD, AND HONOUR THOSE

based on Ecclesiasticus 44.1-15

Give thanks to God, and honour those
    whose fame was spread abroad,
whose well-remembered lives disclose
    the glories of their Lord;
who held their just and gentle sway
    in trust beneath his hand,
and humbly sought to serve their day
    and work what God had planned.

His Name they lived to glorify
    who gives the poet's word,
the painter's all-discerning eye,
    the soul by music stirred;
and high among the human skills
    of wisdom, science, art,
a virtue grace alone instils,
    the pastor's patient heart.

For teacher's gift, for prophet's fire,
    for preachers of the word,
for all who still our souls inspire
    we praise your Name, O Lord;
we seek to follow where they trod,
    to reap what they have sown,
who spent themselves for love of God
    and sought his praise alone.

And some there be who take their rest
    in unremembered graves,
whose names are numbered with the blest
    whom Jesus loves and saves;
who kept the faith, who ran the race,
    whose work on earth is done:
may we, their children, know your grace
    until the crown is won.

103 HERE WITHIN THIS HOUSE OF PRAYER

H ere within this house of prayer
all our Father's love declare;
love that gave us birth, and planned
days and years beneath his hand:
    praise to God whose love and power
    bring us to this present hour!

Here, till earthly praises end,
tell of Christ the sinner's friend;
Christ whose blood for us was shed,
Lamb of God and living bread,
    life divine and truth and way,
    light of everlasting day.

Here may all our faint desire
feel the Spirit's wind and fire,
souls that sleep the sleep of death
stir to life beneath his breath:
    may his power upon us poured
    send us out to serve the Lord!

Here may faith and love increase,
flowing forth in joy and peace
from the Father, Spirit, Son,
undivided, Three-in-One:
    his the glory all our days
    in this house of prayer and praise!

104 IN THE NAME OF CHRIST REJOICING

In the Name of Christ rejoicing,
    share the song the angels cry,
every tongue his praises voicing:
    'Glory be to God on high!'
God who made us, sought us, found us,
    called and chose us from above,
cast a Father's arms around us,
    here unites us in his love.

Word of Christ, our hearts indwelling,
    be to life eternal sown;
Lord of love beyond our telling,
    let your love in us be shown.
On the cross of Christ relying,
    build your church in every place;
to a world where hope is dying
    holding forth the word of grace.

Kept by faith on Christ depending,
    learning still the power of prayer,
by our serving, teaching, tending,
    may your children know your care.
Grant us, Lord, the will to labour,
    teach us so in Christ to live,
that with all the world as neighbour
    all may share the gifts you give.

God of peace, our souls possessing,
    peace the risen Christ imparts,
through his lifted hands of blessing,
    reign in all our homes and hearts.
From a world of wars defend us,
    let your righteous rule increase;
tenants of the earth you lend us,
    teach us, Lord, to live in peace.

In the love of Christ united
    keep us to the end of days,
then shall every wrong be righted,
    every prayer be turned to praise.
When we close our earthly story,
    may we know as we are known,
one with all the saints in glory,
    one with Christ before the throne.

105 LORD, FOR THE YEARS YOUR LOVE HAS KEPT AND GUIDED

Lord, for the years your love has kept and guided,
    urged and inspired us, cheered us on our way,
sought us and saved us, pardoned and provided,
        Lord of the years, we bring our thanks today.

Lord, for that word, the word of life which fires us,
        speaks to our hearts and sets our souls ablaze,
teaches and trains, rebukes us and inspires us,
        Lord of the word, receive your people's praise.

Lord, for our land, in this our generation,
        spirits oppressed by pleasure, wealth and care;
for young and old, for commonwealth and nation,
        Lord of our land, be pleased to hear our prayer.

Lord, for our world; when we disown and doubt him,
        loveless in strength, and comfortless in pain;
hungry and helpless, lost indeed without him,
        Lord of the world, we pray that Christ may reign.

Lord, for ourselves; in living power remake us,
        self on the cross and Christ upon the throne;
past put behind us, for the future take us,
        Lord of our lives, to live for Christ alone.

106 TO GOD WE COME IN PRAYER AND PRAISE

To God we come in prayer and praise,
　　one people with one heart and voice;
the source and strength of all our days,
　　in God we trust, in him rejoice.

He spoke, and gave the planets birth,
　　the starry hosts of heaven above,
and formed for us a fertile earth
　　and loves us with a Father's love.

He reigns beyond the passing years,
　　by whom all thrones and kingdoms stand;
our life, with all its loves and fears,
　　is kept by his eternal hand.

Our Rock, our Refuge and our Tower,
　　our Hope while time itself shall last;
we celebrate this present hour
　　in thankfulness for mercies past.

To God, from age to age the same,
　　who came in Christ to make us free,
his will, his kingdom and his Name,
　　we consecrate the years to be.

107 WITH ALL WHO IN THIS HALLOWED PLACE

With all who in this hallowed place
their lifelong homage paid,
who sang of God's redeeming grace,
who worshipped here and prayed,
we come, as down the years they came,
and lift our hearts today
to Christ for evermore the same,
our new and living Way.

He comes to meet us in our need,
the Bread of life divine,
on him alone our spirits feed
in story, song and sign;
the Lord alike of age and youth,
the living Word is he,
the rock of everlasting Truth
who sets his people free.

Here may the Spirit's fruit be known
in peace and joy and love,
where all on whom his breath is blown
are born from God above;
in Christ from sin and death restored
and from the grave to rise,
we worship him, the living Lord,
the Life which never dies.

O God of grace, in this our day
may Christ his church renew,
to live his life, to walk his way,
and to his truth be true.
So send us out with hearts aflame
to tell his praise abroad,
and to a weary world proclaim
the love of Christ the Lord.

108 GIVE THANKS TO GOD ON HIGH

Give thanks to God on high
for saints of other days,
whose hope it was to live and die
in love's consuming blaze,
    for Christ and his kingdom,
his glory and his praise.

Their vision long-fulfilled,
our prayer is still the same:
upon their work of faith to build,
their word of truth proclaim,
    for Christ and his kingdom,
and for his holy Name.

New tasks today are ours
who serve a world in pain,
new calls to challenge all our powers
of heart and hand and brain,
    for Christ and his kingdom,
while life and breath remain.

Give thanks to God on high
for all the future sends,
in praise of Christ to live and die
who calls his servants friends,
    for Christ and his kingdom,
whose glory never ends!

For Europe and Africa: © Timothy Dudley-Smith
For the rest of the world including the USA and Canada: © 1985 Hope Publishing Company

109 THANKS BE TO GOD FOR HIS SAINTS OF EACH PAST GENERATION

Thanks be to God for his saints of each past generation,
one with us still in one body, one great congregation;
with them proclaim
Jesus for ever the same,
Author of life and salvation.

Thanks be to God for his blessings which daily surround us;
glory to Christ the Redeemer who sought us and found us,
who from the grave
rose, the almighty to save,
breaking the fetters that bound us.

Thanks be to God for the years that are yet in his keeping,
trusting each day to the care of a Father unsleeping,
on to the end,
Christ our companion and friend,
joy at the last for our weeping.

Thanks be to God who has called us and daily defends us,
who with the Son and the Spirit unchanging befriends us;
now in that Name,
Jesus for ever the same,
forth to his service he sends us.

110 WHEN JOHN BAPTIZED BY JORDAN'S RIVER

Jesus baptized by John

When John baptized by Jordan's river
　　in faith and hope the people came,
that John and Jordan might deliver
　　their troubled souls from sin and shame.
They came to seek a new beginning,
　　the human spirit's ageless quest,
repentance, and an end of sinning,
　　renouncing every wrong confessed.

There as the Lord, baptized and praying,
　　rose from the stream, the sinless one,
a voice was heard from heaven saying,
　　'This is my own beloved Son.'
There as the Father's word was spoken,
　　not in the power of wind and flame,
but of his love and peace the token,
　　seen as a dove, the Spirit came.

O Son of Man, our nature sharing,
　　in whose obedience all are blest,
Saviour, our sins and sorrows bearing,
　　hear us and grant us this request:
daily to grow, by grace defended,
　　filled with the Spirit from above;
in Christ baptized, beloved, befriended,
　　children of God in peace and love.

111 WHAT DEBT OF SIN THAT NONE CAN PAY

St Matthew the Evangelist

What debt of sin that none can pay
on Matthew's burdened conscience lay:
what longings deep within him stirred,
awakened at the Baptist's word,
to turn, and from his past be free,
when Jesus called him, 'Follow me!'

As in a dream, forsaking all,
he rose and answered Jesus' call.
By mountainside and shore and town
he set his Master's teaching down:
a coming kingdom, known of old,
and in the Scriptures long foretold.

And we with Matthew hear and see
and walk with Christ in Galilee,
the Son at last of David's line,
the promised Saviour, King divine,
by whom alone are sins forgiven,
whose throne is evermore in heaven.

So may we follow Christ today,
his work to do, his word obey,
the Lord on whom our sins are laid,
by whom our debt is freely paid,
who died and rose and lives again:
O Son of Man, return and reign!

112 PRAISE BE TO GOD FOR SERVANTS OF THE WORD

St Mark the Evangelist

Praise be to God for servants of the word,
  John Mark among them, held in high renown;
of all he witnessed, knew, received and heard,
  Mark in his gospel set the story down.

He tells of one who suffered for our sake,
  who in the paths of pain and sorrow trod,
that all-sufficient sacrifice to make,
  Saviour and Servant, Christ the Son of God.

Mark tasted hardship, failure too, and fears,
  yet from his weakness knew himself restored;
Mark learned of Peter, taught by bitter tears,
  how frail disciples still can serve their Lord.

All Mark bequeaths us from those earliest days
  we, who come after, thankfully receive.
For this his servant, we the Master praise.
  Mark shows us Jesus: seeing, we believe!

113 SAINT LUKE, BELOVED PHYSICIAN

St Luke the Evangelist

Saint Luke, beloved physician,
    with honour now recall,
who served his Master's mission,
    who ministered to Paul;
whose skill to distant ages
    bequeathed a gift unpriced,
a gospel in whose pages
    we see the face of Christ.

He tells for us the stories
    of Jesus here on earth,
the unsung pains and glories
    that marked the church's birth;
the Spirit's power in preaching,
    the contrite sinner freed,
the grace and mercy reaching
    our deepest human need.

For all who work our healing
    we lift our hearts in prayer,
the love of God revealing
    in science, skill and care:
his gifts be still imparted
    to those who make us whole,
like Luke the tender-hearted,
    physician of the soul.

114 IF ON OUR HEARTS THE LIGHT OF CHRIST HAS SHONE

St John the Evangelist

If on our hearts the light of Christ has shone
    and set our feet to follow where he trod,
then God be thanked for his Apostle John,
    a Son of Thunder born a child of God;
        seen through whose eyes the Lord of love appears,
        known still more clearly down the passing years.

John tells of Jesus, God's eternal Word,
    flesh of our flesh, yet Light and Life divine.
Death's power is broken where his voice is heard,
    bright in our darkness see his glories shine:
        the spotless Lamb of God, our risen Lord,
        the Way, the Truth, the Life to life restored.

Beloved disciple! From his pastor's heart
    he yearns that all believe and live and know;
and strong in faith from sin and self depart,
    in Christ abiding and in grace to grow;
        and in that home prepared by Christ above
        be there made like him, whom unseen we love.

115 GIVE PRAISE TO GOD FOR HIS APOSTLE PAUL

Give praise to God for his Apostle Paul,
once Saul of Tarsus, to whom Jesus showed
light, voice and vision, mercy, truth and call,
    bowed in the dust of that Damascus road.

Captive to Christ, his herald and his slave,
    Paul bore him witness, bold in every place:
Christ died and risen, Lord of death and grave,
    Christ who redeems us freely by his grace;

Christ the long hope of Israel's promised dream,
    come as fulfillment of their ancient law;
Christ for the nations, Paul's consuming theme,
    God's great Deliverer whom the prophets saw.

Paul paid the price in travel, toil and pain;
    he founded churches, faithful to his word:
'for me to live is Christ, to die is gain',
    if he might preach where none as yet had heard.

His course is run, to glory and a crown:
    still are his words the word of life for all.
We, who come after, hold him in renown,
    heirs to his gospel, blessing God for Paul.

116 O CHRIST THE SAME, THROUGH ALL OUR STORY'S PAGES

O Christ the same, through all our story's pages,
   our loves and hopes, our failures and our fears;
eternal Lord, the King of all the ages,
   unchanging still, amid the passing years:
O living Word, the source of all creation,
   who spread the skies, and set the stars ablaze,
O Christ the same, who wrought our whole salvation,
   we bring our thanks for all our yesterdays.

O Christ the same, the friend of sinners, sharing
   our inmost thoughts, the secrets none can hide,
still as of old upon your body bearing
   the marks of love, in triumph glorified:
O Son of Man, who stooped for us from heaven,
   O Prince of life, in all your saving power,
O Christ the same, to whom our hearts are given,
   we bring our thanks for this the present hour.

O Christ the same, secure within whose keeping
   our lives and loves, our days and years remain,
our work and rest, our waking and our sleeping,
   our calm and storm, our pleasure and our pain:
O Lord of love, for all our joys and sorrows,
   for all our hopes, when earth shall fade and flee,
O Christ the same, beyond our brief tomorrows,
   we bring our thanks for all that is to be.

117 GOD WHOSE LOVE IS EVERYWHERE

The orange,
representing
all the world.

God whose love is everywhere
made our earth and all things fair,
ever keeps them in his care;
    praise the God of love!
He who hung the stars in space
holds the spinning world in place;
    praise the God of love!

The sticks, fruit
& nuts, representing
the four seasons &
the fruit of the
earth.

Come with thankfulness to sing
of the gifts the seasons bring,
summer, winter, autumn, spring;
    praise the God of love!
He who gave us breath and birth
gives us all the fruitful earth;
    praise the God of love!

The red ribbon,
representing the
blood of Christ shed
for us.

Mark what love the Lord displayed,
all our sins upon him laid,
by his blood our ransom paid;
    praise the God of love!
Circled by that scarlet band
all the world is in his hand;
    praise the God of love!

The lighted candle,
representing Christ
the Light of the world.

See the sign of love appear,
flame of glory, bright and clear,
light for all the world is here;
    praise the God of love!
Gloom and darkness get you gone!
Christ the Light of life has shone;
    praise the God of love!

118 OUR FATHER GOD IN HEAVEN

suitable for Mothering Sunday

Our Father God in heaven
    on whom our world depends,
to you let praise be given
    for families and friends;
for parents, sisters, brothers,
    a home where love belongs,
but on this day for mothers
    we bring our thankful songs.

What wealth of God's bestowing
    for all the world to share!
what strength of heart outgoing
    to children everywhere!
Our deepest joys and sorrows
    a mother's path must trace,
and earth's unknown tomorrows
    are held in her embrace.

How well we know the story
    that tells of Jesus' birth,
the Lord of heaven's glory
    become a child of earth;
a helpless infant sleeping,
    yet King of realms above,
to find in Mary's keeping
    the warmth of human love.

Our Father God in heaven,
    to you we lift our prayer,
that every child be given
    such tenderness and care,
where life is all for others,
    where love your love displays:
for God's good gift of mothers
    let earth unite in praise!

119 ALL FLOWERS OF GARDEN, FIELD AND HILL

All flowers of garden, field and hill
this borrowed beauty find:
what Jesus taught they teach us still,
and bring our Lord to mind.

Where sheaves of Galilean corn
their whitened harvest yield,
where blue and purple robes adorn
the lilies of the field,

Where meadow grasses green and tall
await the reapers' hands,
or sheltered by the sunlit wall
a barren fig-tree stands,

We hear his voice; as in their turn
those first disciples heard:
in nature's picture-book we learn
to read the Master's word.

The thorn that scars a Saviour's head,
the palms the people wave,
the balsam wrapped about the dead,
the myrrh to mark his grave,

Or Joseph's plot where olives bloom
and tangled branches twine
to bear above the empty tomb
the true and living vine,

They speak of him; and with one voice
lift silent songs above:
'All creatures of our God, rejoice,
his saving Name is Love!'

120 FAITH AND TRUTH AND LIFE BESTOWING

F aith and truth and life bestowing,
 open now the Scriptures, Lord,
seed to life eternal sowing,
 scattered on the wind abroad.
Let not hearts, your word receiving,
 like a barren field be found,
choked with thorns and unbelieving,
 shallow earth or stony ground.

May the Spirit's power unceasing
 bring to life the hidden grain,
daily in our hearts increasing,
 bearing fruit that shall remain.
So in Scripture, song and story,
 Saviour, may your voice be heard.
Till our eyes behold your glory
 give us ears to hear your word.

121 GOD IN HIS WISDOM, FOR OUR LEARNING

God in his wisdom, for our learning
gave his inspired and holy word:
promise of Christ, for our discerning,
    by which our souls are moved and stirred,
finding our hearts within us burning
    when, as of old, his voice is heard.

Symbol and story, song and saying,
    life-bearing truths for heart and mind,
God in his sovereign grace displaying
    tenderest care for humankind,
Jesus our Lord this love portraying,
    open our eyes to seek and find.

Come then with prayer and contemplation,
    see how in Scripture Christ is known;
wonder anew at such salvation
    here in these sacred pages shown;
lift every heart in adoration,
    children of God by grace alone!

122 GOD OF OLD, WHOM SAINTS AND SAGES

God of old, whom saints and sages,
  priests and prophets, trembling heard,
at whose voice, in distant ages,
    hearts with dread and wonder stirred,
still to us in Scripture's pages
    speaks his true and living word.

Word of grace and peace, extending
    mercy to our souls' despair,
word of firm assurance, lending
    wings of faith to fervent prayer,
word of loving power, defending
    children of our Father's care.

Word of God in flesh declaring
    love that stoops to human aid,
Lamb of God our burden bearing
    till the price of sin was paid,
Son of God our nature sharing,
    in the Scriptures stand portrayed.

Gracious word of invitation,
    promised pledge of hope restored,
royal law for all creation,
    lamp of life and Spirit's sword,
tell of Christ, our souls' salvation,
    Christ the Scriptures' theme and Lord.

123 O GOD WHO SHAPED THE STARRY SKIES

O God who shaped the starry skies
and made the sun in splendour rise,
    whose love our life imparts,
still may that same creative word
which formless void and darkness heard
    be known within our hearts.

Teach us to see, as Moses saw,
your will revealed in perfect law,
    a covenant divine;
a word to make the simple wise,
a light of truth before our eyes,
    and on our souls to shine.

Move every heart in holy fear
the judgments of the Lord to hear,
    your word about our way;
and in that law let all rejoice
to find a loving Father's voice
    and his command obey.

So may we share for evermore
the sweetness of that golden store,
    and taste its rich reward;
and make the Scriptures our delight
and walk as pleasing in your sight,
    our great redeeming Lord.

124 OPEN OUR EYES, O LORD, WE PRAY

based on verses from Psalm 119

Open our eyes, O Lord, we pray,
　　enlighten heart and mind;
that as we read your word today
　　we may its treasures find.

Open our ears that, small and still,
　　your voice be clearly heard,
to guide our steps and cleanse our will
　　according to your word.

Open our lives to love's embrace,
　　our dear redeeming Lord:
your word of life and truth and grace
　　within our souls be stored.

Open our lips, O Lord, in praise
　　to tell what love imparts:
the work of grace about our ways,
　　your word within our hearts.

125 TEACH US TO LOVE THE SCRIPTURES, LORD

T each us to love the Scriptures, Lord,
    to read and mark and learn;
and daily in your written word
    the living Word discern.

Your purposes in us fulfil
    as we your promise claim,
who seek to know and do your will
    and learn to love your Name.

When in some dark and cloudy day
    beset by fears we stand,
your word be light upon our way,
    a sword within our hand.

As on your word our spirits feed
    through all its pages shine;
make known yourself to us who read,
    the Bread of life divine.

So shall the treasures of your word
    become as sacred ground;
teach us to love the Scriptures, Lord,
    where Christ is surely found.

126 TO GOD WHO GAVE THE SCRIPTURES

To God who gave the Scriptures
 we bring our thanks today
for light upon life's journey,
 a lamp to lead the way;
a sword to face the tempter,
 a seed of life divine,
a glimpse of heaven's glory
 upon our souls to shine.

To God who gave the Scriptures
 we sing salvation songs,
for laws of truth and judgment
 to right our human wrongs;
a word to stand for ever
 which faith and light imparts,
a fire of love unchanging
 to burn within our hearts.

To God who gave the Scriptures
 we come with love and praise
for all the gospel stories
 of Galilean days;
the words of grace and mercy,
 the cross and all its pains,
as now in risen splendour
 the King of glory reigns.

To God who gave the Scriptures
 we turn in faith to find
a taste of honeyed sweetness
 to nourish heart and mind;
the promise of salvation,
 the covenant restored,
the apostolic witness
 that Jesus is the Lord.

To God who gave the Scriptures
 we lift our souls in prayer,
for eyes the Spirit opens
 to find the treasures there;
that as we read and ponder
 one voice alone is heard,
the Christ of all the Scriptures,
 the true and living Word.

127 ETERNAL GOD, BEFORE WHOSE FACE WE STAND

suitable for Remembrance Sunday

E ternal God, before whose face we stand,
your earthly children, fashioned by your hand,
hear and behold us, for to you alone
all hearts are open, all our longings known:
  so for our world and for ourselves we pray
  the gift of peace, O Lord, in this our day.

We come with grief, with thankfulness and pride,
to hold in honour those who served and died;
we bring our hurt, our loneliness and loss,
to him who hung forsaken on the cross;
  who, for our peace, our pains and sorrows bore,
  and with the Father lives for evermore.

O Prince of peace, who gave for us your life,
look down in pity on our sin and strife.
May this remembrance move our hearts to build
a peace enduring, and a hope fulfilled,
  when every flag of tyranny is furled
  and wars at last shall cease in all the world.

From earth's long tale of suffering here below
we pray the fragile flower of peace may grow,
till cloud and darkness vanish from our skies
to see the Sun of Righteousness arise.
  When night is past and peace shall banish pain,
  all shall be well, in God's eternal reign.

128 GOD IS THE GIVER OF ALL THINGS THAT ARE

God is the giver of all things that are;
worlds without end were fashioned by his hand,
from earth's foundations to the furthest star,
    in splendour shining, countless as the sand.

God is the giver: from his love derive
    each conscious being, all our life and breath,
by whose sustaining care we live and thrive,
    our strong deliverer at the gates of death.

God is the giver, always, everywhere,
    through every harvest that the world affords;
so may we learn the gifts of God to share:
    we are but stewards, earth is still the Lord's.

God is the giver, for he gave his Son
    to bear with us our nature and our pain,
who on the cross our forfeit freedom won,
    who from the grave to glory rose again.

God is the giver: he it is who showers
    such gifts upon us, worthy of a King.
All things through Christ in life and death are ours;
    have we no gifts of thankfulness to bring?

O God the giver, in your hands we place
    our wealth, our time, and all we call our own.
Take now our love, transform us by your grace,
    for all we have and are is yours alone.

129 LOOK, LORD, IN MERCY AS WE PRAY

L ook, Lord, in mercy as we pray,
   on tasks as yet undone;
fire us anew to seek the day
   that makes our churches one:
heirs to one work of grace divine,
   one Spirit freely given,
one pledge in sacrament and sign,
   one cross the hope of heaven.

One living faith be ours to learn
   with saints in every age,
one timeless word of truth discern
   in Scripture's sacred page.
Make us, with new resolve, begin
   one common call to own;
to be one church one world to win,
   and make one Saviour known.

Hear us who join in praise and prayer
   one act of faith to bring,
children who own one Father's care,
   soldiers who serve one King:
your kingdom come, O Lord, we pray,
   your will on earth be done;
our sins and errors purge away
   and make our churches one.

For Europe and Africa: © Timothy Dudley-Smith
For the rest of the world including the USA and Canada: © 1984 Hope Publishing Company

130 LORD, GIVE US EYES TO SEE

based on Matthew 9.37, 38

L ord, give us eyes to see
in earth's unnumbered lands
today, as once in Galilee,
the ripening harvest stands.

Lord, give us ears to heed
and wills intent to share
that call to lay the harvest's need
before its Lord in prayer.

And give us hearts to pray
as you have taught us, Lord,
that God provide his church today
with servants of his word.

For Europe and Africa: © Timothy Dudley-Smith
For the rest of the world including the USA and Canada: © 1984 Hope Publishing Company

4. Metrical Psalms

based on the following

Psalm	2	131	Psalm	89.1–18	155
Psalm	8	132	Psalm	90	156
Psalm	10	133	Psalm	91	157
Psalm	16	134–135	Psalm	93	158
Psalm	19	136	Psalm	95	159
Psalm	20	137	Psalm	97	160
Psalm	25	138	Psalm	98	161
Psalm	26	139	Psalm	100	162
Psalm	27	140	Psalm	103	163
Psalm	32	141	Psalm	113	164
Psalm	34	142–143	Psalm	115	165
Psalm	40.1–3	144	Psalm	119.129–144	166
Psalm	41	145	Psalm	121	167
Psalm	56	146	Psalm	125	168
Psalm	60	147	Psalm	134	169
Psalm	63	148	Psalm	138	170–171
Psalm	65	149	Psalm	141	172
Psalm	67	150	Psalm	145	173
Psalm	69	151	Psalm	146	174
Psalm	72	152	Psalm	147	175
Psalm	73	153	Psalm	148	176
Psalm	84	154			

One or two texts which owe something to the Psalms are classified under other headings, for example in Section 3, 'Occasional and annual Church Services' under Bible Sunday.

The Index of Biblical and other Sources on page 499 contains a fuller list. Canticles drawn from the Psalms (e.g. the Venite, Psalm 95) are included above rather than in Section 6.

131 TO HEATHEN DREAMS OF HUMAN PRIDE

based on Psalm 2

To heathen dreams of human pride
rebellious nations cling:
the kindly rule of God defied,
and his anointed King.
'Throw off your fetters, burst your chain!'
the dreamers call; and call in vain.

For God enthroned above the skies
shall laugh his foes to scorn:
'On Zion's hill your King shall rise,
my Son a King is born;
before his sceptre none can stand
and all the world is in his hand.'

Let humble hearts this lesson learn
and bow before his throne;
in true and trembling homage turn,
and name him Lord alone.
O happy hearts, with wisdom blest,
who trust in him, and in him rest!

132 HOW GREAT OUR GOD'S MAJESTIC NAME

based on Psalm 8

How great our God's majestic Name!
His glory fills the earth and sky.
His praise the heavenly host proclaim,
eternal God and Lord most high.

His fingers set the moon in place,
the stars their Maker's hand declare;
in earth and sky alike we trace
the pattern of his constant care.

And what of us? Creation's crown,
upheld in God's eternal mind;
on whom he looks in mercy down
for tender love of humankind.

His praise the heavenly host proclaim
and we his children tell his worth:
how great is God's majestic Name,
his glory seen in all the earth!

133 IN MY HOUR OF GRIEF OR NEED

based on Psalm 10

In my hour of grief or need
when a friend is friend indeed,
now, when Satan walks abroad,
be not far from me, O Lord.

When the powers of evil ride
through the world in open pride,
flaunted sins and boasted shame
bring contempt upon your Name.

When the godless host are strong,
when their mouth is filled with wrong,
bitterness, deceit and fraud,
be not far from me, O Lord.

When the poor become their prey,
when the weak are led astray,
right is wrong and truth is lies,
then, O Lord our God, arise!

Powers of darkness bring to grief,
break the hold of unbelief,
sound anew the quickening word,
rise and come among us, Lord!

Then shall vice and falsehood fail,
truth and righteousness prevail,
all his ransomed people sing
God, their everlasting King!

134 LORD, WHEN THE STORMS OF LIFE ARISE

based on Psalm 16

Lord, when the storms of life arise
 be near to keep me yet,
my chosen portion and my prize
in whom alone my refuge lies,
 on whom my hope is set.

In God alone securely stand
 his saints for ever blest,
who shelter safe beneath his hand
as in a fair and pleasant land,
 and in his presence rest.

Lord of our life, our strength and stay,
 whom yet unseen we love,
uphold us in the narrow way
and guide our footsteps night and day
 with wisdom from above.

So shall the path of life be shown,
 the prayers of faith ascend;
until we know as we are known,
and sing before the Father's throne
 the songs that never end.

135 WITHIN THE LOVE OF GOD I HIDE

based on Psalm 16

Within the love of God I hide,
 on him my soul repose,
a tower of refuge fortified
 and safe from all my foes,
a haven from the stormiest tide
 and every wind that blows.

In him my true contentment lies
 with those who speak his praise,
who set his face before their eyes,
 his will about their ways;
the Lord my portion and my prize,
 his peace on all my days.

His everlasting Name I bless,
 in him my hope is stayed,
where death itself cannot distress
 nor leave my soul afraid,
for in his perfect righteousness
 my spirit stands arrayed.

Within my Father's purpose planned
 my path of life is plain,
until before his throne I stand
 and evermore remain
where pleasures wait at his right hand,
 and in his presence reign.

136 THE STARS DECLARE HIS GLORY

based on Psalm 19

The stars declare his glory;
    the vault of heaven springs
mute witness of the Master's hand
        in all created things,
and through the silences of space
        their soundless music sings.

The dawn returns in splendour,
        the heavens burn and blaze,
the rising sun renews the race
        that measures all our days,
and writes in fire across the skies
        God's majesty and praise.

So shine the Lord's commandments
        to make the simple wise;
more sweet than honey to the taste,
        more rich than any prize,
a law of love within our hearts,
        a light before our eyes.

So order too this life of mine,
        direct it all my days;
the meditations of my heart
        be innocence and praise,
my Rock, and my redeeming Lord,
        in all my words and ways.

137 THE LORD BE NEAR US AS WE PRAY

based on Psalm 20

T he Lord be near us as we pray
and help us, through the darkest day,
to find our spirits' strength and stay
　　in his most holy Name.
To him be heartfelt homage paid
and sacrifice of prayer be made;
in him we trust, and undismayed
　　his promised presence claim.

May God our dearest hopes fulfil
and move our hearts to seek his will,
rejoicing in his triumph still
　　and his prevailing Name;
who hears and answers all our prayers,
who knows the weight of human cares,
and in his Son our nature shares,
　　for evermore the same.

Let others trust in wealth and power
to save them in the evil hour,
we find our refuge and our tower
　　in God's eternal Name;
in him to stand, secure and strong,
believers who to Christ belong,
and with his saints in ceaseless song
　　his faithfulness proclaim.

138 ALL MY SOUL TO GOD I RAISE

based on Psalm 25

All my soul to God I raise;
Be my guardian all my days.
Confident in hope I rest,
Daily prove your path is best.
Ever work in me your will,
Faithful to your promise still.

Graciously my sins forgive;
Help me by your truth to live.
In your footsteps lead me, Lord,
Joy renewed and hope restored,
Knowing every sin forgiven,
Learning all the ways of heaven.

Mercies manifold extend,
Not as judge but faithful friend.
O my Saviour, hear my prayer,
Pluck my feet from every snare;
Quietude be mine at last,
Rest from all my guilty past.

Sheltered safe when troubles fret,
Trusting God I triumph yet!
Undismayed in him I stand,
Victor only by his hand.
Worship, homage, love and praise,
All my soul, to God I raise.

139 IN JUDGMENT, LORD, ARISE

based on Psalm 26

In judgment, Lord, arise,
　　draw near to take my part,
your tender love before my eyes,
　　your word within my heart.
Discern my thoughts, I pray,
　　discover all my mind,
and keep me in the narrow way
　　to innocence inclined.

To God I lift my voice,
　　his wondrous works confess;
let not their friendship be my choice
　　who love unrighteousness.
The praise of God above
　　my tongue unwearied tells;
his everlasting house I love
　　where endless glory dwells.

Sweep not my soul aside
　　to paths where sinners stray;
let love of truth my footsteps guide
　　and cast me not away.
So shall I stand unmoved
　　with all who love your word.
For mercy sure and promise proved
　　I bless your Name, O Lord.

140 WE SING THE LORD OUR LIGHT

based on Psalm 27

We sing the Lord our light;
    our strength, who walk his way;
though full of fears the night,
    though long and hard the day.
        His mercy kind
        we boldly claim
        who in his Name
    salvation find.

To him we make request;
    this prayer alone we bring:
that in his presence blest
    we may behold our King;
        by his free grace
        discern his will,
        and worship still
    before his face.

In trouble's darkest day
    his strength is near at hand;
in danger or dismay
    upon his rock we stand.
        O anxious heart,
        forsake your fear
        for God is here
    to take your part!

His love will still prevail,
    his mighty hand uphold,
though kith and kin may fail
    and dearest hearts grow cold;
        be patient yet!
        his kingdom own,
        in whom alone
    our hopes are set!

141 HAPPY ARE THOSE,
BEYOND ALL MEASURE BLESSED

based on Psalm 32

Happy are those, beyond all measure blessed,
who know their guilt is gone, their faults forgiven;
who taste the joys that come from sin confessed,
whose hearts are blameless in the sight of heaven.
Blessings are ours beneath a Father's hand;
by love made welcome, uncondemned we stand.

God is our strength when troubles flood the heart;
from his high throne he stoops to hear our prayer.
When trials come, the Lord shall take our part,
our Rock of refuge from the storms of care.
Safely enfolded in his keeping strong,
his sure salvation is our triumph-song.

God is our guide who watches all our way;
gently he teaches us our path to find.
Be not self-willed, like beasts that go astray,
God will direct our feet and form our mind:
mercy embraces us on every side
with God our joy, our Saviour, strength and guide.

142 ALL OUR DAYS WE WILL BLESS THE LORD

based on Psalm 34

All our days we will bless the Lord,
Bless and hallow his Name adored;
Call together to God most high,
Drawn to him who will hear our cry;
Ever look to him, Lord indeed,
Friend and Father to those in need.

God our refuge, our shield and sword,
He himself is our great reward.
In his service, with love and fear,
Joy be theirs who in faith draw near;
Known and cherished in all their ways,
Life possessing and length of days.

May no lies on our lips be heard,
No dishonouring deed or word;
Over all is the Lord above,
Peace bestowing and steadfast love,
Quick to answer and take our part,
Rich in mercy to heal the heart.

So delivered from hour to hour,
Trusting God and his sovereign power,
Uncondemned at his judgment throne,
Victors ever by grace alone,
We will publish his Name abroad:
All our days we will bless the Lord.

143 TELL HIS PRAISE IN SONG AND STORY

based on Psalm 34

T ell his praise in song and story,
　　bless the Lord with heart and voice;
in my God is all my glory,
　　come before him and rejoice.
Join to praise his Name together,
　　he who hears his people's cry;
tell his praise, come wind or weather,
　　shining faces lifted high.

To the Lord whose love has found them
　　cry the poor in their distress;
swift his angels camped around them
　　prove him sure to save and bless.
God it is who hears our crying
　　though the spark of faith be dim;
taste and see! beyond denying
　　blest are those who trust in him.

Taste and see! In faith draw near him,
　　trust the Lord with all your powers;
seek and serve him, love and fear him,
　　life and all its joys are ours:
true delight in holy living,
　　peace and plenty, length of days;
come, my children, with thanksgiving
　　bless the Lord in songs of praise.

In our need he walks beside us,
　　ears alert to every cry;
watchful eyes to guard and guide us,
　　love that whispers 'It is I.'
Good shall triumph, wrong be righted,
　　God has pledged his promised word;
so with ransomed saints united
　　join to praise our living Lord!

144 MY DAYS OF WAITING ENDED

based on Psalm 40.1–3

My days of waiting ended,
　　the Lord has heard my cry,
and in his grace befriended
　　a prisoner left to die.
The pit was all around me,
　　the mire and shifting sand,
but God in mercy found me
　　a rock on which to stand.

To God our strong salvation
　　eternal praise belongs,
with ceaseless celebration
　　and new triumphant songs.
Let all his saints adore him,
　　who trust in God alone;
lift high your hearts before him
　　and make his mercies known.

145 LORD, MAY OUR HEARTS WITHIN US BURN

based on Psalm 41

Lord, may our hearts within us burn
    and grant us grace to intercede,
to know compassion and concern
        for those in every kind of need,
            whose lives are seen as little worth,
            the poor and helpless of the earth.

In God alone his people stand,
    he keeps us in the evil day,
our lives are lived beneath his hand,
        his blessings lie about our way:
            in sin or sickness, hear our plea,
            'O Lord, be merciful to me.'

And when my days on earth shall end,
    should foes unite against my name,
or should my own familiar friend
        our lifelong bond of love disclaim,
            should hope decline and courage flee,
            O Lord, be merciful to me.

Our God shall not forsake his own,
    stronger than death his boundless grace.
When with the saints about his throne
        pardoned we stand before his face,
            'Glory to God', our song be then,
            'Glory to God, Amen, Amen.'

146 MERCIFUL AND GRACIOUS BE

based on Psalm 56

Merciful and gracious be,
O Most High, remember me.
When my enemies assail
may your grace and power prevail.
    Keep me in the day of fear
    firm in faith that God is near.

What though some should do me wrong,
plan my hurt the whole day long,
lie in wait about my way,
twist the very words I say,
    yet their time will soon be past;
    judgment comes to all at last.

Lord, you know my days and years,
all my wanderings, all my tears;
though the world should work me ill
God himself will keep me still
    in his light, through length of days,
    strong to stand and swift to praise.

147 WHEN TROUBLES COME AND HOPES DEPART

based on Psalm 60

When troubles come and hopes depart
    in mercy, Lord, arise;
the ruined landscape of my heart
    lies bare before your eyes.

Where human pride is humbled low
    and crushed beneath your hand,
your solace, Lord, again bestow
    and heal this broken land.

Though darkness seems to hide your face
    amid earth's sin and pain,
break through the clouds, O God of grace,
    restore my soul again.

The banner of your love unfurled
    proclaims a sheltering arm;
no foes in all this fallen world
    can bring your people harm.

In holiness your word goes forth
    from that eternal throne:
to east and west, to south and north,
    your glory rules alone.

Frail human strength is nothing worth
    beset by evil powers,
yet with the God of all the earth
    the victory is ours!

148 GOD IS MY GREAT DESIRE

based on Psalm 63

God is my great desire,
  his face I seek the first;
to him my heart and soul aspire,
    for him I thirst.
As one in desert lands,
    whose very flesh is flame,
in burning love I lift my hands
    and bless his Name.

God is my true delight,
    my richest feast his praise,
through silent watches of the night,
    through all my days.
To him my spirit clings,
    on him my soul is cast;
beneath the shadow of his wings
    he holds me fast.

God is my strong defence
    in every evil hour;
in him I face with confidence
    the tempter's power.
I trust his mercy sure,
    with truth and triumph crowned:
my hope and joy for evermore
    in him are found.

149 EVERY HEART ITS TRIBUTE PAYS

based on Psalm 65

Every heart its tribute pays,
every tongue its song of praise;
sin and sorrow, guilt and care,
brought to him who answers prayer;
there by grace may humankind
full and free forgiveness find;
called and chosen, loved and blest,
in his presence be at rest.

Ever while his deeds endure
our salvation stands secure;
he whose fingers spun the earth,
gave the seas and mountains birth,
tamed the ocean, formed the land,
spread the skies with mighty hand:
far-off shores revere his Name,
day and night his power proclaim.

Year by year, the seasons' round
sees the land with blessing crowned,
where caressed by sun and rain
barren earth gives life again;
sunlit valleys burn with gold,
nature smiles on field and fold,
byre and barn with plenty stored:
all things living, praise the Lord!

150 MERCY, BLESSING, FAVOUR, GRACE

based on Psalm 67

Mercy, blessing, favour, grace,
  saving power to us be shown;
brightness of the Father's face
  to the nations now be known.

Shout in triumph, sing in praise!
  Peoples all, proclaim his worth:
just and righteous are his ways,
  sovereign Lord of all the earth.

Harvests year by year proclaim
  blessings new in plenty poured;
all the earth shall fear his Name,
  all his people praise the Lord.

151 HELP ME, O GOD, AND HEAR MY CRY

based on Psalm 69

Help me, O God, and hear my cry,
　extend to me your saving hand,
the waters rise, the floods are high,
　　my feet have found no place to stand:
　　　　now, lest the depths become my grave,
　　　　O God of hosts, draw near and save.

My secret faults, my sin and shame,
　lie open, Lord, before your face,
yet in my heart I love your Name
　　and all my hope is in your grace:
　　　　Lord, in your mercy, think on me;
　　　　speak but the word, and set me free.

So shall I praise the God of love,
　with heaven and earth and sea and sky,
who hears us from his throne above
　　and lifts his ransomed people high,
　　　　to sound his praise in ceaseless song
　　　　where all who love his Name belong.

152 A KING ON HIGH IS REIGNING

based on Psalm 72

A King on high is reigning
　　whom endless ages bless,
from sea to sea sustaining
　　his rule of righteousness.
Beneath his strong defending
　　his people stand secure,
whose justice knows no ending
　　while sun and moon endure.

As rains that gently nourish
　　and bring the seed to birth,
his righteousness shall flourish,
　　his peace possess the earth;
her sceptred kings acclaim him,
　　before his feet they fall,
the nations kneel to name him
　　the sovereign Lord of all.

The poor are in his keeping,
　　he hears their bitter cry,
his watchfulness unsleeping
　　to answer every sigh;
the lonely and neglected,
　　the outcast and in need,
forsaken and rejected,
　　to him are dear indeed.

His Name endures for ever
　　who formed the fertile land;
the fruits of our endeavour
　　shall prosper in his hand.
With prayer and song and story
　　his praises sound again,
in all the earth his glory;
　　so be it, Lord! Amen!

153 WHAT BLESSINGS GOD BESTOWS

based on Psalm 73

W hat blessings God bestows,
   what gifts of grace imparts,
what loving-kindliness he shows
   to pure and upright hearts!
Yet still the world goes by
   in power and wealth and pride,
the lawless head is lifted high,
   the God of truth denied.

So sure the godless seem,
   secure in greed and gain,
with righteousness an idle dream
   and innocence in vain;
till that dread final day
   when judgment comes to all,
the powers of evil swept away,
   the dreams of darkness fall.

God is my strength and guide
   by his unchanging love:
whom have I, Lord, on earth beside,
   nor yet in heaven above?
My flesh and heart may fail,
   but God will constant be,
his grace and mercy still prevail
   to all eternity.

154 FOR GOD MY SPIRIT LONGS

based on Psalm 84

For God my spirit longs
    within his courts to come,
while in my heart I hear the songs
    that speak to me of home.

The sparrow builds her nest,
    the swallow lays her young:
may my long home be with the blest
    who hear God's praises sung.

My journey be with those
    whose pilgrim feet have trod
where water in the desert flows,
    a highway home to God.

To him, when life is past,
    my song shall still be praise;
our Sun and Shield while time shall last,
    and to eternal days.

155 TIMELESS LOVE! WE SING THE STORY

based on Psalm 89.1-18

Timeless love! We sing the story,
   praise his wonders, tell his worth;
love more fair than heaven's glory,
love more firm than ancient earth!
      Tell his faithfulness abroad:
      who is like him? Praise the Lord!

By his faithfulness surrounded,
north and south his hand proclaim;
earth and heaven formed and founded,
skies and seas, declare his Name!
      Wind and storm obey his word:
      who is like him? Praise the Lord!

Truth and righteousness enthrone him,
just and equal are his ways;
more than happy, those who own him,
more than joy, their songs of praise!
      Sun and Shield and great Reward:
      who is like him? Praise the Lord!

156 OUR GOD ETERNAL, REIGNING

based on Psalm 90

Our God eternal, reigning,
  creation's life sustaining,
    our refuge and our home;
enthroned, in light surrounded,
when earth was yet unfounded,
    the living God, to him we come.

We fade, a dream that passes,
like withered meadow grasses
    when summer's sun has shone.
Before that face all-seeing
of God who gave us being
    we pass away and we are gone.

O God of mercy, hear us,
in steadfast love draw near us,
    from age to age the same;
that we, by grace defended,
when earthly days are ended
    may live to praise a Saviour's Name.

157 SAFE IN THE SHADOW OF THE LORD

based on Psalm 91

Safe in the shadow of the Lord
  beneath his hand and power,
    I trust in him,
    I trust in him,
my fortress and my tower.

My hope is set on God alone
though Satan spreads his snare;
    I trust in him,
    I trust in him,
to keep me in his care.

From fears and phantoms of the night,
from foes about my way,
    I trust in him,
    I trust in him,
by darkness as by day.

His holy angels keep my feet
secure from every stone;
    I trust in him,
    I trust in him,
and unafraid go on.

Strong in the everlasting Name,
and in my Father's care,
    I trust in him,
    I trust in him,
who hears and answers prayer.

Safe in the shadow of the Lord,
possessed by love divine,
    I trust in him,
    I trust in him,
and meet his love with mine.

158 GOD IS KING! THE LORD IS REIGNING

based on Psalm 93

God is King! The Lord is reigning,
    might and majesty his robe;
to his seat on high ascended,
girded round with glory splendid,
there in time and space sustaining
        this our star-encircled globe.
Foreordained and founded fast,
evermore his throne shall last!

God is King! In storm and thunder
        wind and tide their warfare wage;
bursting seas and breakers towering,
pounding surge the rocks devouring,
lightning rending skies asunder,
        ocean's roar and tempest's rage.
Mightier far than sea or sky
stands the throne of God on high!

God is King! Let earth adore him,
        changeless still his sure decree;
throned beyond our mortal telling,
holiness and truth his dwelling,
come with trembling hearts before him,
        bow the head and bend the knee,
where the ransomed ever raise
God's imperishable praise!

159 COME, LET US PRAISE THE LORD

based on Psalm 95

Come, let us praise the Lord,
with joy our God acclaim,
his greatness tell abroad
and bless his saving Name.
Lift high your songs
before his throne
to whom alone
all praise belongs.

Our God of matchless worth,
our King beyond compare,
the deepest bounds of earth,
the hills, are in his care.
He all decrees,
who by his hand
prepared the land
and formed the seas.

In worship bow the knee,
our glorious God confess;
the great Creator, he,
the Lord our Righteousness.
He reigns unseen:
his flock he feeds
and gently leads
in pastures green.

Come, hear his voice today,
receive what love imparts;
his holy will obey
and harden not your hearts.
His ways are best;
and lead at last,
all troubles past,
to perfect rest.

160 THE EVERLASTING LORD IS KING

based on Psalm 97

T he everlasting Lord is King,
   let ocean find a voice,
her furthest shores his triumph sing
   and all the earth rejoice.

He comes in clouds with fire and flame
   to make his judgments known;
the mountains tremble at his Name
   and melt before his throne.

The sun and moon and starry sky
   his glories blaze abroad,
the one eternal God most high,
   the true and living Lord.

Defended by his hand divine
   his saints secure remain;
for them the light of life shall shine,
   the King of love shall reign.

161 SING A NEW SONG TO THE LORD

based on Psalm 98

Sing a new song to the Lord,
  he to whom wonders belong;
rejoice in his triumph and tell of his power,
  O sing to the Lord a new song!

Now to the ends of the earth
see his salvation is shown;
and still he remembers his mercy and truth,
  unchanging in love to his own.

Sing a new song and rejoice,
publish his praises abroad;
let voices in chorus, with trumpet and horn,
  resound for the joy of the Lord!

Join with the hills and the sea
thunders of praise to prolong;
in judgment and justice he comes to the earth,
  O sing to the Lord a new song!

162 LET THE EARTH ACCLAIM HIM

based on Psalm 100

L et the earth acclaim him,
　　 serve the Lord with gladness;
worship him, and name him
　　　　source of all our song.
　　　　　　He it is who made us,
　　sought us in our sadness,
　　　　　　and in joy arrayed us
　　who to him belong.

Come then with thanksgiving,
　　God on high confessing;
Lord of all things living,
　　　　fill his courts with praise.
　　　　　　Come in faith, securing
　　everlasting blessing:
　　　　　　loved by love enduring
　　to eternal days.

163 PRAISE THE LORD AND BLESS HIS NAME

based on Psalm 103

Praise the Lord and bless his Name,
life and peace in him are found;
all his benefits proclaim,
grace with love and mercy crowned:
    sins forgiven, strength restored!
    sing, my soul, and praise the Lord!

High as heaven's furthest star,
vaster than the shores of space,
so he bears our sins afar,
so he brings to us his grace.
    He who hears his children's prayer
    ever keeps us in his care.

Swifter than the winds that pass,
fading as the summer flowers,
what though all our days are grass?
faith and hope shall still be ours.
    God's unchanging love is sure
    and endures for evermore.

Praise the Lord of earth and heaven,
angel hosts about his throne,
sinners by his grace forgiven,
saints who his dominion own:
    God of all, by all adored!
    sing, my soul, and praise the Lord!

164 SERVANTS OF THE LIVING LORD

based on Psalm 113

Servants of the living Lord,
bend in awe before his throne,
tell his majesty abroad,
know and name him God alone.
    Join to praise the Lord of grace,
    all who stand before his face.

Age to age, his Name be blest,
Ancient of eternal days;
furthest bounds of east and west
echo his perpetual praise;
        ever-living Lord of grace,
        throned beyond all time and space.

Who like him in glory reigns
higher than the heavens are high?
He who world on world sustains,
sun and stars and sea and sky.
        He it is who, Lord of grace,
        hears from heaven, his dwelling-place.

Lord of grace! In him we trust,
by his love the lost are found,
lowly lifted from the dust,
happy homes with children crowned.
        All who stand before his face,
        praise, O praise, the Lord of grace!

165 NOT TO US BE GLORY GIVEN

based on Psalm 115

Not to us be glory given
but to him who reigns above:
Glory to the God of heaven
for his faithfulness and love!
What though unbelieving voices
hear no word and see no sign,
still in God my heart rejoices,
working out his will divine.

Not what human fingers fashion,
gold and silver, deaf and blind,
dead to knowledge and compassion,
having neither heart nor mind,
lifeless gods, yet some adore them,
nerveless hands and feet of clay;
all become, who bow before them,
lost indeed and dead as they.

Not in them is hope of blessing,
hope is in the living Lord:
high and low, his Name confessing,
find in him their shield and sword.
Hope of all whose hearts revere him,
God of Israel, still the same!
God of Aaron! Those who fear him,
he remembers them by name.

Not the dead, but we the living
praise the Lord with all our powers;
of his goodness freely giving,
his is heaven; earth is ours.
Not to us be glory given
but to him who reigns above:
Glory to the God of heaven
for his faithfulness and love!

166 THE WILL OF GOD TO MARK MY WAY

based on Psalm 119.129–144

The will of God to mark my way,
the word of God for light;
eternal justice to obey
in everlasting right,

Your eyes of mercy keep me still,
your gracious love be mine;
so work in me your perfect will
and cause your face to shine.

With ordered step secure and strong,
from sin's oppression freed,
redeemed from every kind of wrong
in thought and word and deed,

So set my heart to love your word
and every promise prove,
to walk with truth before the Lord
in righteousness and love.

167 I LIFT MY EYES

based on Psalm 121

I lift my eyes
to the quiet hills
in the press of a busy day;
    as green hills stand
    in a dusty land
so God is my strength and stay.

I lift my eyes
to the quiet hills
to a calm that is mine to share;
    secure and still
    in the Father's will
and kept by the Father's care.

I lift my eyes
to the quiet hills
with a prayer as I turn to sleep;
    by day, by night,
    through the dark and light
my Shepherd will guard his sheep.

I lift my eyes
to the quiet hills
and my heart to the Father's throne;
    in all my ways
    to the end of days
the Lord will preserve his own.

168 THE FAITHFUL ARE KEPT
AS THE MOUNTAINS THAT NEVER SHALL MOVE

based on Psalm 125

T he faithful are kept as the mountains that never shall move,
secure as the hills is the strength of the Lord and his love;
with joy they ascend, and encircled by mountains they come,
singing praises to God who is ever surrounding their home.

O Lord, our defender, be near in the enemy's hour,
protecting your people from evil's dominion and power:
as firm as the hills be our faith in the God we adore,
who are kept in his peace and surrounded by love evermore.

169 BLESS THE LORD AS DAY DEPARTS

based on Psalm 134

Bless the Lord as day departs,
   let your lamps be brightly burning,
lifting holy hands and hearts
   to the Lord till day's returning.

As within the darkened shrine,
   faithful to their sacred calling,
sons and priests of Levi's line
   blessed the Lord as night was falling;

So may we who watch or rest
   bless the Lord of earth and heaven;
and by him ourselves be blest,
   grace and peace and mercy given.

170 THE HEARTFELT PRAISE OF GOD PROCLAIM

based on Psalm 138

T he heartfelt praise of God proclaim
  by whom our prayers are heard,
who lifts on high his holy Name
  and his unchanging word.

To earth below, to heaven above,
  our thankful hearts confess
how sure his never-failing love,
  his steadfast faithfulness.

The kings of earth their homage yield
  before his word divine;
the King eternal there revealed,
  how great his glories shine!

For those who on his mercy call
  his arms he opens wide;
afar his eyes of judgment fall
  on arrogance and pride.

So sure his timeless promise stands,
  we journey unafraid;
the children whom almighty hands,
  the hands of love, have made.

171 WITH UNDIVIDED HEART AND CEASELESS SONGS

based on Psalm 138

With undivided heart and ceaseless songs
    give thanks to God.
To his high majesty all praise belongs:
    give thanks to God.
His love and truth proclaim,
his mercy still the same;
and for his holy Name
    give thanks to God.

Exalt his Name and his eternal word,
    he is our God.
Before his throne our every prayer is heard,
    he is our God.
Let kings declare his praise,
sing of his words and ways,
for through eternal days
    he is our God.

He reigns in glory from his throne above,
    he is the Lord:
and in our weakness meets us with his love,
    he is the Lord.
His purpose cannot fail;
though fears and foes assail
his love shall still prevail,
    he is the Lord.

172 COME QUICKLY, LORD, AND HEAR THE CRIES

based on Psalm 141

Come quickly, Lord, and hear the cries
    my heart and hands uplifted raise;
and let my prayer as incense rise,
      an evening sacrifice of praise.
          Guard now the lips that speak your Name,
          lest they, and I, be put to shame.

And if my steps should go astray
      and from the path of truth I move,
restore me to your narrow way
      and in your mercy, Lord, reprove;
          from love of self my soul defend,
          and wound me as a faithful friend.

When at the last, O Lord our God,
      we look to you alone to save,
the plough of judgment breaks the clod,
      and bones are scattered from the grave:
          our Rock, our Refuge and our Tower,
          protect us in the final hour.

We fix our eyes upon you, Lord,
      and tune our ears to hear your voice;
our hearts by faith receive your word
      and in your promises rejoice.
          Till morning breaks and night is gone,
          in God we trust, and journey on.

173 TO GOD OUR GREAT SALVATION

based on Psalm 145

To God our great salvation
    a triumph-song we raise,
with hymns of adoration
    and everlasting praise.
That Name beyond all naming
    from age to age adored,
we lift on high proclaiming
    the greatness of the Lord.

Declare in song and story
    the wonders we confess,
who hail the King of Glory
    the Lord our Righteousness.
In loving-kindness caring
    his mercies stand displayed,
forgiving and forbearing
    to all his hand has made.

His kingdom knows no ending,
    enthroned in light sublime,
his sovereign power extending
    beyond all space and time.
To us and all things living
    he comes in word and deed,
forbearing and forgiving,
    to meet us in our need.

The King of all creation
    is near to those who call;
the God of our salvation
    has stooped to save us all.
Lift high your hearts and voices,
    his praises sound again;
in God his earth rejoices
    for evermore. Amen!

174 PRAISE THE GOD OF OUR SALVATION

based on Psalm 146

Praise the God of our salvation,
    all life long your voices raise,
stir your hearts to adoration,
    set your souls to sing his praise!

Turn to him, his help entreating;
    only in his mercy trust:
human pomp and power are fleeting;
    mortal flesh is born for dust.

Thankful hearts his praise have sounded
    down the ages long gone by:
happy they whose hopes are founded
    in the God of earth and sky!

Faithful Lord of all things living,
    by his bounty all are blest;
bread to hungry bodies giving,
    justice to the long-oppressed.

For the strength of our salvation,
    light and life and length of days,
praise the King of all creation,
    set your souls to sing his praise!

175 FILL YOUR HEARTS WITH JOY AND GLADNESS

based on Psalm 147

Fill your hearts with joy and gladness,
    sing and praise your God and mine!
Great the Lord in love and wisdom,
    might and majesty divine!
He who framed the starry heavens
    knows and names them as they shine!

Praise the Lord, his people, praise him!
    Wounded souls his comfort know;
those who fear him find his mercies,
    peace for pain and joy for woe;
humble hearts are high exalted,
    human pride and power laid low.

Praise the Lord for times and seasons,
    cloud and sunshine, wind and rain;
spring to melt the snows of winter
    till the waters flow again;
grass upon the mountain pastures,
    golden valleys thick with grain.

Fill your hearts with joy and gladness,
    peace and plenty crown your days;
love his laws, declare his judgments,
    walk in all his words and ways;
he the Lord and we his children:
    praise the Lord, all people, praise!

176 PRAISE THE LORD OF HEAVEN

based on Psalm 148

Praise the Lord of heaven,
  praise him in the height;
praise him, all his angels,
  praise him, hosts of light.
Sun and moon together,
  shining stars aflame,
planets in their courses,
  magnify his Name!

Earth and ocean praise him;
  mountains, hills and trees;
fire and hail and tempest,
  wind and storm and seas.
Praise him, fields and forests,
  birds on flashing wings,
praise him, beasts and cattle,
  all created things.

Now by prince and people
  let his praise be told;
praise him, men and maidens,
  praise him, young and old.
He, the Lord of glory!
  We his praise proclaim!
High above all heavens
  magnify his Name!

5. *Other Metrical Scriptures*

based on the following

Certain texts which might have been listed here are included under other headings, for example as metrical psalms or canticles. In particular, the three New Testament canticles from Luke 1 & 2 (the Benedictus, the Magnificat and the Nunc Dimittis) will be found in Section 6, 'Metrical prayers, canticles and creed'. Canticles drawn from the Psalms, however, appear in Section 4 (for example, the Venite, Psalm 95). The Index of Biblical and other Sources on page 499 contains a fuller list.

177 O GOD WHO BROUGHT THE LIGHT TO BIRTH

based on Genesis 1–3

O God who brought the light to birth,
　　the moon and all the starry skies,
who set in space the globe of earth
　　　　and made the sun in splendour rise,
　　　　　　teach us to love the light, we pray,
　　　　　　and walk as children of the day.

A fertile earth, a sky and sea,
　　　　you filled with creatures great and small,
and fashioned humankind to be
　　　　your own vice-regents over all:
　　　　　　teach us your fragile world to tend,
　　　　　　and live as all creation's friend.

Delight and purpose, work and rest,
　　　　and innocence a garden made,
with human love and marriage blest,
　　　　before the flowers began to fade:
　　　　　　teach us your purpose to fulfil
　　　　　　and find delight within your will.

What sin was theirs who fell from grace
　　　　enslaved by one forbidden tree,
to found a fallen human race
　　　　no longer unashamed and free:
　　　　　　teach us to flee from Satan's power
　　　　　　and keep us in temptation's hour.

For Christ has crushed the serpent's head
　　　　to put an end to griefs and sins;
through him the powers of death are dead
　　　　and resurrection life begins:
　　　　　　teach us to make his triumphs plain,
　　　　　　and in him live, and rise, and reign.

178 THE GOD OF GRACE IS OURS

based on 1 Chronicles 29.10-14

T he God of grace is ours,
   eternally the same,
to him be glories, honours, powers,
   and blessings on his Name.

All worlds are in his hands,
   all heavens his domains,
for evermore his kingdom stands
   and over all he reigns.

Our good and gracious King,
   from him all bounty flows.
no other gift is ours to bring
   but what his love bestows.

From him our powers derive,
   upon his strength we call,
beneath his hand we live and thrive,
   most glorious Lord of all.

The God of grace is ours,
   his holy Name we praise;
to him be glories, honours, powers,
   through everlasting days.

179 GOD SHALL MY COMFORT BE

based on Isaiah 12

G od shall my comfort be,
   my consolation;
kept by his love I see
   no condemnation.
      I face without dismay
      that final judgment day,
      for wrath is turned away:
   he is salvation.

All thanks to God belong,
   praise past expressing,
salvation, strength and song
   in him possessing.
      Though all seems dead and dry
      no fear of want have I;
      the wells of life supply
   his joy and blessing.

Sing then what God has done,
   all songs excelling,
he gave his only Son,
   death's dread dispelling.
      Let all the earth proclaim
      his praise who overcame;
      the greatness of his Name
   for ever telling.

180 O COMFORT EACH BELIEVING HEART

based on Isaiah 40.1–11

O comfort each believing heart,
    our ancient bondage ends!
The Lord himself shall take our part
    and make, of sinners, friends.
Prepare for him a royal road,
    make smooth and straight his way,
who comes to bear our weary load,
    our ransom price to pay.

Our life is brief as summer grass,
    our days are but a sigh;
we wither at the winds that pass
    and fade and fall and die.
But safe in God's almighty hand
    our souls are kept secure:
for evermore his word shall stand,
    his covenant endure.

The very hills shall find a voice
    to make his tidings heard.
In God and in his grace rejoice,
    receive his promised word.
O comfort each believing heart
    where God in Christ has come!
The Lord himself shall take our part
    and lead his people home.

181 THE HEAVENS ARE SINGING, ARE SINGING AND PRAISING

based on verses from Isaiah 44 & 45

T he heavens are singing, are singing and praising,
the depths of the earth and the mountains rejoice;
the trees and the forests are raising, are raising
the song of creation in thunderous voice;
    for God has redeemed us,
    redeemed us and bought us,
remembered his people, and made us his choice!

The sun in his rising, his rising and setting,
the stars in their courses, their Maker proclaim.
We only, his children, forgetting, forgetting
the love of our Father, have turned to our shame;
    yet God has redeemed us,
    redeemed us and bought us,
remembered his people, and called us by name!

For he is the Father, the Father who made us,
who founded and fashioned the earth and the sky;
who stooped from his glory to aid us, to aid us
when yet we were sinners deserving to die;
    our God has redeemed us,
    redeemed us and bought us,
remembered his people, and lifted us high!

O Father eternal, eternally living,
resplendent in glory, the Lord on his throne,
we praise and adore you, forgiving, forgiving,
none other beside you, in mercy alone;
    for God has redeemed us,
    redeemed us and bought us,
remembered his people, and made us his own!

182 FROM ALL THE WIND'S WIDE QUARTERS

based on Isaiah 55

From all the wind's wide quarters
come, see the feast is spread,
of soul-sustaining waters,
of true and living bread;
of sorrows long-departed,
and joys beyond compare:
come, poor and humble-hearted,
the feast of life to share!

With mercy all-prevailing
God bids the wanderer come;
in grace and peace unfailing
he calls his children home;
with loving-kindness tender
he frees us from our sins,
in glory and in splendour
the feast of life begins!

Come, claim the promise spoken!
God's purpose stands secure.
His fruitful word unbroken
shall evermore endure.
All ancient bondage ended
to sin's corrupting powers,
forgiven, freed, befriended,
the feast of life is ours!

183 BELOVED IN CHRIST BEFORE OUR LIFE BEGAN

based on Jeremiah 29.11

Beloved in Christ before our life began,
and from our wayward wanderings restored,
God has for each a purpose and a plan:
    'I will fulfil my promise,' says the Lord.

Seek him and find him, then, with all your powers;
    good and not evil has the Lord in store.
A future hope, a destiny is ours,
    and, in his glory, life for evermore.

184 BEYOND ALL MORTAL PRAISE

based on Daniel 2.20–23

Beyond all mortal praise
God's Name be ever blest,
unsearchable his ways,
   his glory manifest;
      from his high throne
         in power and might
         by wisdom's light
      he rules alone.

Our times are in his hand
   to whom all flesh is grass,
while as their Maker planned
   the changing seasons pass.
      He orders all:
         before his eyes
         earth's empires rise,
      her kingdoms fall.

He gives to humankind,
   dividing as he will,
all powers of heart and mind,
   of spirit, strength and skill:
      nor dark nor night
         but must lay bare
         its secrets, where
      he dwells in light.

To God the only Lord
   our fathers' God, be praise;
his holy Name adored
   through everlasting days.
      His mercies trace
         in answered prayer,
         in love and care,
      and gifts of grace.

185 LET EVERY CHILD OF EARTH THAT SLEEPING LIES

based on Daniel 12.2,3

L et every child of earth that sleeping lies
　awake to hear what justice shall proclaim:
some to eternal life and light shall rise,
　　some to eternal shame.

Then shall they shine, for evermore the same,
　　the teachers of the faith, the true, the wise;
bright as the sunlit firmament aflame,
　　and as the starry skies.

186 OUR SAVIOUR CHRIST ONCE KNELT IN PRAYER

based on Mark 9.2-10, the Transfiguration

Our Saviour Christ once knelt in prayer
with none but three disciples there,
upon a lonely mountain high
beneath a blue expanse of sky:
> below them, far as eye could see,
> the little hills of Galilee.

There as he prays a radiance bright
transfigures all his form to light;
his robe in dazzling splendour shows
a purer white than sunlit snows,
> while on his countenance divine
> transcendent glories burn and shine.

So for a moment stands revealed
what human form and flesh concealed;
while Moses and Elijah share
in earth and heaven mingled there,
> with him whom prophecy foresaw,
> the true fulfiller of the law.

The shadowed summit, wrapped in cloud,
sounds to a voice that echoes loud:
'This is my true beloved Son,
listen to him, my chosen one.'
> The glory fades. With all its pains
> the road to Calvary remains.

Give to us, Lord, the eyes to see
as saw those first disciples three:
a teacher true, a friend indeed,
the risen Saviour sinners need,
> the Son whose praise eternal rings,
> the Lord of lords and King of kings!

187 O GOD OF EVERLASTING LIGHT

based on John 3.3-16

O God of everlasting light,
  whose boundless kingdom lies
beyond our world of sense and sight,
    unseen by mortal eyes;
we long to learn what Jesus taught
    that from this dust of earth
the seeking soul may still be brought
    a second time to birth.

Here may the springing waters flow
    to cleanse from every stain;
here may the Wind of heaven blow
    to stir to life again.
So freed from all the powers of death,
    from all our secret sins,
and quickened by the Spirit's breath,
    our life in Christ begins.

O God of love, your Son you gave,
    we see him lifted high;
your Son, who came to seek and save
    and on the cross to die.
We name him Lord of life and love
    with all our ransomed powers,
for born anew from God above
    eternal life is ours.

188 LIVING LORD, OUR PRAISE WE RENDER

based on Romans 6.5-11

L iving Lord, our praise we render!
His the blood for sinners shed.
In the Father's power and splendour
    Christ is risen from the dead.

Death's dominion burst and broken
    by that Life which no more dies;
we to whom the Lord has spoken,
    one with Christ, in freedom rise.

One with Christ, both dead and risen;
    dead to self and Satan's claim,
raised from death and sin's dark prison,
    life is ours through Jesus' Name.

189 BORN BY THE HOLY SPIRIT'S BREATH

based on Romans 8

Born by the Holy Spirit's breath,
loosed from the law of sin and death,
now cleared in Christ from every claim
no judgment stands against our name.

In us the Spirit makes his home
that we in him may overcome;
Christ's risen life, in all its powers,
its all-prevailing strength, is ours.

Children and heirs of God most high,
we by his Spirit 'Father' cry;
that Spirit with our spirit shares
to frame and breathe our wordless prayers.

One is his love, his purpose one:
to form the likeness of his Son
in all who, called and justified,
shall reign in glory at his side.

Nor death nor life, nor powers unseen,
nor height nor depth can come between;
we know through peril, pain and sword,
the love of God in Christ our Lord.

190 NOT FOR TONGUES OF HEAVEN'S ANGELS

based on 1 Corinthians 13

Not for tongues of heaven's angels,
　　not for wisdom to discern,
not for faith that masters mountains,
for this better gift we yearn:
　　may love be ours, O Lord.

Love is humble, love is gentle,
love is tender, true and kind;
love is gracious, ever patient,
generous of heart and mind:
　　may love be ours, O Lord.

Never jealous, never selfish,
love will not rejoice in wrong;
never boastful nor resentful,
love believes and suffers long:
　　may love be ours, O Lord.

In the day this world is fading
faith and hope will play their part;
but when Christ is seen in glory
love shall reign in every heart:
　　may love be ours, O Lord.

191 OUT OF DARKNESS LET LIGHT SHINE

based on 2 Corinthians 4.6

Out of darkness let light shine!
  Formless void its Lord obeyed;
at his word, by his design,
    sun and moon and stars were made.

Still his brightness shines abroad;
    darkened lives his light have known:
all the glories of the Lord
    in the face of Christ are shown.

New creation's second birth
    bids eternal night depart;
as the dawn of dawn on earth
    morning breaks within the heart.

Out of darkness let light shine,
    as it shone when light began;
earth be filled with light divine,
    Christ be light for everyman!

192 FRUITFUL TREES, THE SPIRIT'S SOWING

based on Galatians 5.22,23

Fruitful trees, the Spirit's sowing,
　　may we ripen and increase,
fruit to life eternal growing,
　　rich in love and joy and peace.

Laden branches freely bearing
　　gifts the Giver loves to bless;
here is fruit that grows by sharing,
　　patience, kindness, gentleness.

Rooted deep in Christ our Master,
　　Christ our pattern and our goal,
teach us, as the years fly faster,
　　goodness, faith and self-control.

Fruitful trees, the Spirit's tending,
　　may we grow till harvests cease;
till we taste, in life unending,
　　heaven's love and joy and peace.

193 BE STRONG IN THE LORD

based on Ephesians 6.10–18

Be strong in the Lord
　in armour of light,
with helmet and sword,
　　with shield for the fight;
on prayer be dependent,
　　be belted and shod,
in breastplate resplendent:
　　the armour of God.

Integrity gird
　　you round to impart
the truth of his word
　　as truth in your heart;
his righteousness wearing
　　as breastplate of mail,
his victory sharing,
　　be strong to prevail.

With eagerness shod
　　stand firm in your place,
or go forth for God
　　with news of his grace;
no foe shall disarm you
　　nor force you to yield,
no arrow can harm you
　　with faith as your shield.

Though Satan presume
　　to test you and try,
in helmet and plume
　　your head shall be high;
beset by temptation
　　be true to your Lord,
your helmet salvation
　　and Scripture your sword.

So wield well your blade,
　　rejoice in its powers,
fight on undismayed
　　for Jesus is ours!
Then in him victorious
　　your armour lay down,
to praise, ever glorious,
　　his cross and his crown.

194 THE BEST OF GIFTS IS OURS

based on Philippians 4.4–9

T he best of gifts is ours
within our Father's hand,
with joy and peace beyond the powers
of mind to understand.

Bid every anxious care
and wayward thought depart;
make known your need to God in prayer
and he will keep your heart.

Give love the highest place;
have all things good your goal.
Let truth and righteousness and grace
in peace possess your soul.

In honour take delight;
let justice mark your ways;
things innocent and pure and right
command your love and praise.

Become God's garden fair,
where virtue freely flowers;
and as the mind of Christ is there
the God of peace is ours.

195 PRAISE BE TO CHRIST IN WHOM WE SEE

based on Colossians 1.15–20

Praise be to Christ in whom we see
the image of the Father shown,
the first-born Son revealed and known,
the truth and grace of deity;
through whom creation came to birth,
whose fingers set the stars in place,
the unseen powers, and this small earth,
the furthest bounds of time and space.

Praise be to him whose sovereign sway
and will upholds creation's plan;
who is, before all worlds began
and when our world has passed away:
Lord of the church, its life and head,
redemption's price and source and theme,
alive, the first-born from the dead,
to reign as all-in-all supreme.

Praise be to him who, Lord most high,
the fullness of the Godhead shares;
and yet our human nature bears,
who came as man to bleed and die.
And from his cross there flows our peace
who chose for us the path he trod,
that so might sins and sorrows cease
and all be reconciled to God.

196 NO TEMPLE NOW, NO GIFT OF PRICE

based on Hebrews 10. 1–25

No temple now, no gift of price,
no priestly round of sacrifice,
  retain their ancient powers.
As shadows fade before the sun
the day of sacrifice is done,
  the day of grace is ours.

The dying Lord our ransom paid,
one final full self-offering made,
  complete in every part.
His finished sacrifice for sins
the covenant of grace begins,
  the law within the heart.

In faith and confidence draw near,
within the holiest appear,
  with all who praise and pray;
who share one family, one feast,
one great imperishable Priest,
  one new and living way.

For Christ is ours! With purpose true
the pilgrim path of faith pursue,
  the road that Jesus trod;
until by his prevailing grace
we stand at last before his face,
  our Saviour and our God.

197 FATHER OF LIGHTS, WHO BROUGHT TO BIRTH

based on James 1.17,18

Father of lights, who brought to birth
from waste of waters, ordered earth;
from void and darkness, sunlit day;
let there be light for us who pray.

Let there be light of faith and love,
perpetual radiance from above,
assuring faith that God is good
and love secure in Fatherhood.

He does not change; his splendour bright
no turning shadow fades to night.
His glories burn, his mercies shine,
one pure unvaried light divine.

Let there be light of heart and mind,
the narrow path of truth to find;
the Spirit's light that all obey
who walk with Christ in wisdom's way.

Father of lights, whose glory lies
in light unseen by mortal eyes,
let there be light for us who call
till Christ our light be all in all.

198 O CHRIST THE KING OF GLORY

based on 1 Peter 1

O Christ the King of glory
    who chose the way of loss,
to share our human story,
    to bear that bitter cross;
by loving self-surrender,
    by all the pains you bore,
you won for us the splendour
    of life for evermore.

May God, whose care unsleeping
    holds all beneath his hand,
enfold within his keeping
    the church in every land.
Through doubtings and denials,
    through grief to glory come,
through all their fiery trials
    he leads his children home.

O Lord of life, ascended
    to glory from the grave,
your grace be still extended
    to help and heal and save.
O Captain of salvation,
    in mercy bring to birth
your new redeemed creation
    from all the pains of earth.

To God alone be blessing
    and heartfelt ceaseless praise,
a love beyond expressing,
    to everlasting days.
Proclaim salvation's story,
    dominions, thrones and powers!
By cross and grave and glory
    a living hope is ours.

199 HE WALKS AMONG THE GOLDEN LAMPS

based on Revelation 1.12–18

He walks among the golden lamps
　　on feet like burnished bronze:
his hair as snows of winter white,
his eyes with fire aflame, and bright
his glorious robe of seamless light
　　　surpassing Solomon's.

And in his hand the seven stars
　　and from his mouth a sword:
his voice the thunder of the seas;
all creatures bow to his decrees
who holds the everlasting keys
　　　and reigns as sovereign Lord.

More radiant than the sun at noon,
　　who was, and is to be:
who was, from everlasting days;
who lives, the Lord of all our ways;
to him be majesty and praise
　　　for all eternity.

200 HEAVENLY HOSTS IN CEASELESS WORSHIP

based on Revelation 4 & 5

Heavenly hosts in ceaseless worship
'Holy, holy, holy' cry;
'he who is, who was and will be,
    God Almighty, Lord most high.'
Praise and honour, power and glory,
    be to him who reigns alone!
We, with all his hands have fashioned,
    fall before the Father's throne.

All creation, all redemption,
    join to sing the Saviour's worth;
Lamb of God, whose blood has bought us,
    kings and priests, to reign on earth.
Wealth and wisdom, power and glory,
    honour, might, dominion, praise,
now be his from all his creatures
    and to everlasting days!

201 THE GLORY OF OUR GOD AND KING

based on Revelation 15.3,4

The glory of our God and King,
    the splendour of his throne,
let heaven and earth unite to sing
    and all creation own.

The one eternal Father bless
    before whose state and crown,
whose reign of perfect righteousness,
    the nations all bow down.

His mercies shown, his triumphs won,
    unnumbered saints proclaim,
the deeds his mighty arm has done,
    his great and glorious Name.

In honour throned, in love adored,
    how just and true his ways:
of all the ages King and Lord,
    to everlasting days!

202 A CITY RADIANT AS A BRIDE

based on Revelation 21 & 22

A city radiant as a bride
    and bright with gold and gem,
a crystal river clear and wide,
    the new Jerusalem;
a city wrought of wealth untold,
    her jewelled walls aflame
with green and amethyst and gold
    and colours none can name.

A holy city, clear as glass,
    where saints in glory dwell;
through gates of pearl her people pass
    to fields of asphodel.
In robes of splendour, pure and white,
    they walk the golden floor,
where God himself shall be their light
    and night shall be no more.

A city ever new and fair,
    the Lamb's eternal bride;
no suffering or grief is there
    and every tear is dried.
There Christ prepares for us a place,
    from sin and death restored,
and we shall stand before his face,
    the ransomed of the Lord.

6. Metrical Prayers, Canticles and Creed

based on the following liturgical texts

Canticles are listed following the order in which they appear in the *Book of Common Prayer*. Certain texts which might have been listed here as prayers or canticles are classified under other headings; for example, as metrical psalms. In particular, for

The Index of Themes and Subjects on page 544 contains additional entries on a number of the themes included above, such as Penitence, Praise, Prayer, Faith and Thanksgiving.

203 FATHER WHO FORMED THE FAMILY OF MAN

based on the Lord's Prayer

Father who formed the family of man,
  high throned in heaven, evermore the same,
our prayer is still, as Christian prayer began,
    that hallowed be your Name.

Lord of all lords, the only King of kings,
    before whose countenance all speech is dumb,
hear the one song the new creation sings,
    your promised kingdom come.

Father of mercy, righteousness and love,
    shown in the sending of that only Son,
we ask on earth, as in the realms above,
    your perfect will be done.

Lord of the harvest and the living seed,
    the Father's gift from which the world is fed,
to us your children grant for every need
    this day our daily bread.

Father, whose Son ascended now in heaven
    gave once himself upon a cross to win
man's whole salvation, as we have forgiven,
    forgive us all our sin.

Lord of all might and majesty and power,
    our true Deliverer and our great Reward,
from every evil, and the tempter's hour,
    deliver us, good Lord.

Father who formed the family of man,
    yours is the glory heaven and earth adore,
the kingdom and the power, since time began,
    now and for evermore.

204 LIGHTEN OUR DARKNESS NOW THE DAY IS ENDED

based on the Collect for aid against all perils

Lighten our darkness now the day is ended:
  Father in mercy, guard your children sleeping;
from every evil, every harm defended,
    safe in your keeping;

To that last hour, when heaven's day is dawning,
    far spent the night that knows no earthly waking;
keep us as watchmen, longing for the morning,
    till that day's breaking.

205 LORD GOD ALMIGHTY, FATHER OF ALL MERCIES

based on the General Thanksgiving

L ord God Almighty, Father of all mercies,
   well-spring of goodness, fount of all things living,
we now your children, blest by loving kindness,
   come with thanksgiving.

Hear us who praise you, first for our creation,
   formed in your likeness, breath and being gaining;
then for our keeping, life in all its fullness
   daily sustaining.

But, above all things, for the gift of Jesus,
   love past comparing, source of our salvation;
humbly we bring you, for a world's redeeming,
   our adoration.

So in thanksgiving for the hope of glory,
   love, grace and mercy all our days attending,
more than our lips, Lord, let our living praise you,
   ages unending.

206 LIGHT OF THE MINDS THAT KNOW HIM

based on a prayer of St Augustine

Light of the minds that know him,
　　may Christ be light to mine!
my sun in risen splendour,
　　my light of truth divine;
my guide in doubt and darkness,
　　my true and living way,
my clear light ever shining,
　　my dawn of heaven's day.

Life of the souls that love him,
　　may Christ be ours indeed!
the living bread from heaven
　　on whom our spirits feed;
who died for love of sinners
　　to bear our guilty load,
and make of life's brief journey
　　a new Emmaus road.

Strength of the wills that serve him,
　　may Christ be strength to me,
who stilled the storm and tempest,
　　who calmed the tossing sea;
his Spirit's power to move me,
　　his will to master mine,
his cross to carry daily
　　and conquer in his sign.

May it be ours to know him
　　that we may truly love,
and loving, fully serve him
　　as serve the saints above;
till in that home of glory
　　with fadeless splendour bright,
we serve in perfect freedom
　　our strength, our life, our light.

207 O GOD OF OUR SALVATION

based on a prayer of St Chrysostom

O God of our salvation,
    we come with one accord
in common supplication
        to Christ the living Lord;
our Saviour's promise claiming
        that those who meet in prayer,
the Name of Jesus naming,
        will find his presence there.

As here we make petition,
        Lord, grant us our request,
and bring to full fruition
        what wisdom sees as best;
that we, the faith confessing,
        may lift our hearts in praise,
for life and truth and blessing
        to everlasting days.

208 GOD OF GODS, WE SOUND HIS PRAISES

based on the Te Deum

God of gods, we sound his praises,
　　highest heaven its homage brings;
earth and all creation raises
　　　glory to the King of kings.
　　　　　Holy, holy, holy name him,
　　　　　Lord of all his hosts proclaim him;
　　to the everlasting Father
　　　every tongue in triumph sings.

Christians in their hearts enthrone him,
　　tell his praises wide abroad;
prophets, priests, apostles own him
　　　martyrs' crown and saints' reward.
　　　　　Three-in-One his glory sharing,
　　　　　earth and heaven his praise declaring,
　　praise the high majestic Father,
　　　praise the everlasting Lord!

Hail the Christ, the King of glory,
　　he whose praise the angels cry;
born to share our human story,
　　　love and labour, grieve and die:
　　　　　by his cross his work completed,
　　　　　sinners ransomed, death defeated;
　　in the glory of the Father
　　　Christ ascended reigns on high.

Lord, we look for your returning;
　　teach us so to walk your ways,
hearts and minds your will discerning,
　　　lives alight with joy and praise:
　　　　　in your love and care enfold us,
　　　　　by your constancy uphold us;
　　may your mercy, Lord and Father,
　　　keep us now and all our days.

209 WE COME WITH SONGS OF BLESSING

based on the Te Deum

We come with songs of blessing,
    O Father, God Most High,
your Name on earth confessing
    to whom the angels cry;
by all the hosts of heaven
    continually adored,
to you all praise be given,
    the everlasting Lord.

The heavens show your glory,
    your greatness fills the earth;
the prophets tell your story,
    apostles praise your worth.
The saints and martyrs name you
    eternal Three-in-One,
and through the world acclaim you
    as Father, Spirit, Son.

O King for ever glorious,
    O Son for sinners slain,
O Christ who died victorious
    to rise and rule and reign:
the hosts on high enthrone you
    at God the Father's hand;
and wide, to those who own you,
    the gates of heaven stand.

In mercy, Lord, behold us,
    our God to whom we pray;
let Jesus' love enfold us
    against that final day;
no tale of sin confound us
    before the judgment throne;
his righteousness surround us,
    who trust in God alone.

For Europe and Africa: © Timothy Dudley-Smith
For the rest of the world including the USA and Canada: © 1997 Hope Publishing Company

210 BLESS THE LORD, CREATION SINGS

based on the Benedicite

B less the Lord, creation sings;
earth and sky his hand proclaim.
Praise him, all created things;
angel hosts, exalt his Name.

Bless the Lord! To heaven's throne
songs of endless glory rise;
in the clouds his praise be shown,
sun and moon and starry skies.

Bless the Lord with ice and snow,
bitter cold and scorching blaze,
floods and all the winds that blow,
frosty nights and sunlit days.

Bless the Lord in mist and cloud,
lightnings shine to mark his way;
thunders speak his Name aloud,
wind and storm his word obey.

Bless the Lord who brings to birth
life renewed by sun and rain;
flowing rivers, fruitful earth,
bird and beast on hill and plain.

Bless the Lord! From earth and sky,
ocean depths and furthest shore,
all things living bear on high
songs of praise for evermore.

Bless the Lord! His Name be blessed,
worshipped, honoured, loved, adored;
and with holy hearts confessed,
saints and servants of the Lord.

Bless the Lord! The Father, Son,
and the Holy Spirit praise;
high exalt the Three-in-One,
God of everlasting days!

211 OUR GOD AND FATHER BLESS

from the Benedictus, Luke 1.68–79

Our God and Father bless,
for by his sworn decree
he sends to us in power divine
the promised Lord of David's line,
fulfilling all his love's design
to save and set us free.

His ancient purpose stands,
unchanged for evermore,
that we and all who find a place
within his covenant of grace
may freely come before his face
to worship and adore.

Let truth prepare his path,
let righteousness increase!
that from the shade of nature's night
to dawn of heaven's glory bright
the ransomed children of the light
may walk the way of peace.

212 TELL OUT, MY SOUL,
THE GREATNESS OF THE LORD

based on the New English Bible
translation of the Magnificat, Luke 1.46-55

T ell out, my soul, the greatness of the Lord!
  Unnumbered blessings, give my spirit voice;
tender to me the promise of his word;
    in God my Saviour shall my heart rejoice.

Tell out, my soul, the greatness of his Name!
    Make known his might, the deeds his arm has done;
his mercy sure, from age to age the same;
    his holy Name, the Lord, the Mighty One.

Tell out, my soul, the greatness of his might!
    Powers and dominions lay their glory by.
Proud hearts and stubborn wills are put to flight,
    the hungry fed, the humble lifted high.

Tell out, my soul, the glories of his word!
    Firm is his promise, and his mercy sure.
Tell out, my soul, the greatness of the Lord
    to children's children and for evermore!

213 FAITHFUL VIGIL ENDED

*based on the New English Bible
translation of the Nunc Dimittis, Luke 2.29-32*

Faithful vigil ended,
  watching, waiting cease;
Master, grant your servant
    his discharge in peace.

All the Spirit promised,
    all the Father willed,
now these eyes behold it
    perfectly fulfilled.

This your great deliverance
    sets your people free;
Christ their light uplifted
    all the nations see.

Christ, your people's glory!
    watching, doubting cease:
grant to us your servants
    our discharge in peace.

214 ALL GLORY BE TO GOD ON HIGH

based on the Gloria in Excelsis

All glory be to God on high,
his peace on earth proclaim;
to all his people tell abroad
the grace and glory of the Lord,
and bless his holy Name.

In songs of thankfulness and praise
our hearts their homage bring
to worship him who reigns above,
almighty Father, Lord of love,
our God and heavenly King.

O Christ, the Father's only Son,
O Lamb enthroned on high,
O Jesus, who for sinners died
and reigns at God the Father's side,
in mercy hear our cry.

Most high and holy is the Lord,
most high his heavenly throne;
where God the Father, God the Son,
and God the Spirit, ever One,
in glory reigns alone.

215 GLORY TO GOD IN THE HIGHEST

based on the Gloria in Excelsis

Glory to God in the highest,
    rejoice in the praise of his worth!
Glory to God in the highest,
    all creatures of heavenly birth!
Glory to God in the highest,
    and peace to his people on earth!

Worship the Lord, the Almighty;
    devotion and thankfulness bring.
'Praise be to God for his glory
    and peace to his people', we sing;
'Glory to God in the highest,
    the Father and heavenly King.'

Jesus, the Christ, the Redeemer,
    the Son of the Father on high;
led as a lamb to the slaughter,
    the Lord who was willing to die;
God in the heavenly places,
    'Have mercy upon us', we cry.

Christ and he only is holy,
    the Lord whose dominion we own;
one with the Father and Spirit,
    most high, everlasting, alone;
reigning eternal in glory,
    the glory of God on his throne.

For Europe and Africa: © Timothy Dudley-Smith
For the rest of the world including the USA and Canada: © 1980 Hope Publishing Company

216 WE BELIEVE IN GOD THE FATHER

based on the Apostles' Creed

We believe in God the Father,
    God Almighty, by whose plan
earth and heaven sprang to being,
    all created things began.
We believe in Christ the Saviour,
    Son of God in human frame,
virgin-born, the child of Mary
    upon whom the Spirit came.

Christ, who on the cross forsaken,
    like a lamb to slaughter led,
suffered under Pontius Pilate,
    he descended to the dead.
We believe in Jesus risen,
    heaven's King to rule and reign,
to the Father's side ascended
    till as judge he comes again.

We believe in God the Spirit;
    in one church, below, above:
saints of God in one communion,
    one in holiness and love.
So by faith, our sins forgiven,
    Christ our Saviour, Lord and friend,
we shall rise with him in glory
    to the life that knows no end.

7. *The Lord Jesus Christ*

Most of the texts which might have been listed here are included under other headings, for example in Section 1, 'The Christian year' which contains hymns on Christ's Incarnation, Death and Resurrection and other 'seasonal' commemorations; or in Section 8 which includes hymns on such themes as 'The Call of God', 'Following Christ' and so on. The Index of Biblical and other Sources and the Index of Themes and Subjects on pages 499 and 544 contain fuller lists.

217 NAME OF ALL MAJESTY

Name of all majesty,
  fathomless mystery,
King of the ages
by angels adored;
> power and authority,
> splendour and dignity,
> bow to his mastery,
Jesus is Lord!

Child of our destiny,
God from eternity,
love of the Father
on sinners outpoured;
> see now what God has done
> sending his only Son,
> Christ the beloved One,
Jesus is Lord!

Saviour of Calvary,
costliest victory,
darkness defeated
and Eden restored;
> born as a man to die,
> nailed to a cross on high,
> cold in the grave to lie,
Jesus is Lord!

Source of all sovereignty,
light, immortality,
life everlasting
and heaven assured;
> so with the ransomed, we
> praise him eternally,
> Christ in his majesty,
Jesus is Lord!

218 SAVIOUR CHRIST, IN PRAISE WE NAME HIM

Saviour Christ,
in praise we name him;
all his deeds
proclaim him:

Lamb of God
for sinners dying;
all our need
supplying:

Risen Lord
in glory seated;
all his work
completed:

King of kings
ascended, reigning;
all the world
sustaining:

Christ is all!
Rejoice before him:
evermore
adore him!

219 CHRIST IS THE BREAD OF LIFE INDEED

based on the seven 'I am' passages in St John's Gospel

C hrist is the Bread of life indeed
 who nourishes the hungry soul,
the one on whom our spirits feed,
 who makes us whole.

Christ is the Door which open stands,
 the one who watch and ward will keep;
the Shepherd of the heavenly lands
 who knows his sheep.

Christ is the Light of all the earth,
 to end our night of sin and gloom;
the Resurrection-Life, whose birth
 has burst the tomb.

Christ is the living Vine, and we
 abide in him, who hear his call.
The Way, the Truth, the Life is he,
 and Lord of all.

220 CHRIST IS THE ONE WHO CALLS

C hrist is the one who calls,
 the one who loved and came,
to whom by right it falls
to bear the highest Name:
> and still today
> our hearts are stirred
> to hear his word
> and walk his way.

Christ is the one who seeks,
to whom our souls are known.
The word of love he speaks
can wake a heart of stone;
> for at that sound
> the blind can see,
> the slave is free,
> the lost are found.

Christ is the one who died,
forsaken and betrayed;
who, mocked and crucified,
the price of pardon paid.
> Our dying Lord,
> what grief and loss,
> what bitter cross,
> our souls restored!

Christ is the one who rose
in glory from the grave,
to share his life with those
whom once he died to save.
> He drew death's sting
> and broke its chains,
> who lives and reigns,
> our risen King.

Christ is the one who sends,
his story to declare;
who calls his servants friends
and gives them news to share.
> His truth proclaim
> in all the earth,
> his matchless worth
> and saving Name.

221 CHRIST THE ETERNAL LORD

Christ the eternal Lord
    whose promise here we claim,
whose gifts of grace are freely poured
    on all who name your Name;
with thankfulness and praise
    we stand before your throne,
intent to serve you all our days
    and make your glory known.

Christ the unchanging Word
    to every passing age,
whose timeless teachings still are heard
    set forth on Scripture's page;
transform our thought and mind,
    enlighten all who read,
within your word by faith to find
    the bread of life indeed.

Christ the redeeming Son
    who shares our human birth,
and by his death salvation won
    for every child of earth;
inspire our hearts, we pray,
    to tell your love abroad,
that all may honour Christ today
    and follow him as Lord.

Christ the unfading light
    of everlasting day,
our morning star in splendour bright,
    the Life, the Truth, the Way;
that light of truth you give
    to servants as to friends,
your way to walk, your life to live,
    till earth's brief journey ends.

Christ the ascended King
    exalted high above,
whose praise unending ages sing,
    whom yet unseen we love;
when mortal life is past
    your voice from heaven's throne
shall call your children home at last
    to know as we are known.

222 FREELY, FOR THE LOVE HE BEARS US

Freely, for the love he bears us,
God has made his purpose plain:
    Christ has died and Christ is risen,
    Christ will come again.

Christ has died, the world's Redeemer,
Lamb of God for sinners slain:
    Christ has died and Christ is risen,
    Christ will come again.

Christ is risen, high-ascended,
Lord of all to rule and reign:
    Christ has died and Christ is risen,
    Christ will come again.

Christ is coming, King of glory,
firmly then the faith maintain:
    Christ has died and Christ is risen,
    Christ will come again.

223 JESUS IS THE LORD OF LIVING

Jesus is the Lord of living,
all creation's bright array,
hearts for loving and forgiving,
ordered round of work and play:
Jesus is the Lord of living,
year by year and day by day.

Jesus is the Man for others,
love of God in man made plain.
Those whom God created brothers
now in Christ are one again:
Jesus is the Man for others,
ours the pardon, his the pain.

Jesus is the Prince of glory,
love and praise to him be shown;
love for our salvation's story,
praise for his eternal throne:
Jesus is the Prince of glory,
glory be to him alone.

224 WHO IS JESUS? FRIEND OF SINNERS

Who is Jesus? Friend of sinners,
    whom in love the Father gave;
born within a borrowed stable,
    laid within a borrowed grave,
Son of God and son of Mary,
    Son of Man to seek and save.

Who is Jesus? Man of sorrows!
    see his glory all put by;
Prince of life and sinners' ransom
    stumbles forth to bleed and die;
Lamb of God and Love immortal
    hangs upon the cross on high.

Who is Jesus? Risen Saviour!
    to his Father's throne restored,
firstborn of the new creation,
    sun and star and saints' reward:
Prince of glory, King of ages,
    Christ the ever-living Lord!

225 O COME TO ME, THE MASTER SAID

O come to me, the Master said,
my Father knows your need;
and I shall be, the Master said,
your bread of life indeed.
 By faith in him we live and grow
 and share the broken bread,
 and all his love and goodness know,
 for so the Master said.

Abide in me, the Master said,
the true and living vine;
my life shall be, the Master said,
poured out for you as wine.
 His body to the cross he gave,
 his blood he freely shed,
 who came in love to seek and save,
 for so the Master said.

Believe in me, the Master said,
for I have called you friends,
and yours shall be, the Master said,
the life that never ends.
 And so, with sin and sorrow past,
 when death itself is dead,
 the Lord shall raise us up at last,
 for so the Master said.

226 THE LOVE OF CHRIST WHO DIED FOR ME

T he love of Christ who died for me
 is more than mind can know,
his mercy measureless and free
 to meet the debt I owe.

He came my sinful cause to plead,
 he laid his glories by,
for me a homeless life to lead,
 a shameful death to die.

My sins I only see in part,
 my self-regarding ways;
the secret places of my heart
 lie bare before his gaze.

For me the price of sin he paid;
 my sins beyond recall
are all alike on Jesus laid,
 he died to bear them all.

O living Lord of life, for whom
 the heavens held their breath,
to see, triumphant from the tomb,
 a love that conquers death,

Possess my heart that it may be
 your kingdom without end,
O Christ who died for love of me
 and lives to be my friend.

227 LET HEARTS AND VOICES BLEND

L et hearts and voices blend
   the praise of Christ to sing;
our ever-living friend,
   our Saviour and our King;

Our Saviour and our King,
   who left his home on high,
for sinners life to bring,
   a sinner's death to die;

A sinner's death to die
   our rebel souls to save,
and at the last to lie
   within the silent grave.

Within the silent grave
   his risen power to claim;
eternal life he gave
   when forth to life he came;

When forth to life he came,
   whose kingdom knows no end:
to praise our Saviour's Name
   let hearts and voices blend!

228 LORD, WHO LEFT THE HIGHEST HEAVEN

Lord, who left the highest heaven
for a homeless human birth
and, a child within a stable,
came to share the life of earth,
with your grace and mercy bless
all who suffer homelessness.

Lord, who sought by cloak of darkness
refuge under foreign skies
from the swords of Herod's soldiers,
ravaged homes, and parents' cries,
may your grace and mercy rest
on the homeless and oppressed.

Lord, who lived secure and settled,
safe within the Father's plan,
and in wisdom, stature, favour
growing up from boy to man,
with your grace and mercy bless
all who strive for holiness.

Lord, who leaving home and kindred,
followed still as duty led,
sky the roof and earth the pillow
for the Prince of glory's head,
with your grace and mercy bless
sacrifice for righteousness.

Lord, who in your cross and passion
hung beneath a darkened sky,
yet whose thoughts were for your mother,
and a thief condemned to die,
may your grace and mercy rest
on the helpless and distressed.

Lord, who rose to life triumphant
with our whole salvation won,
risen, glorified, ascended,
all the Father's purpose done,
may your grace, all conflict past,
bring your children home at last.

229 O CHRIST, WHO TAUGHT ON EARTH OF OLD

the parables of Jesus

O Christ, who taught on earth of old,
and fashioned in the tales you told
of life and truth the hidden key,
and windows on eternity,
prepare our hearts, that in our turn
we too may read and mark and learn.

The world of nature, death and birth,
the secrets of the fertile earth,
the ripened field, the garnered grain,
the seed that dies to live again,
are doors in heaven, opened wide
upon your kingdom's countryside.

Of wedding-feasts and pearls and flowers,
of debts, and half-completed towers,
of sunny slopes where vineyards grow,
we read more wisely than we know;
for in your parables there shine
the images of things divine.

A beggar's bowl, a robber band,
foundations built on rock or sand,
we mark them all; but one imparts
a dearer hope to human hearts:
from that far country where we roam
a Father's welcome calls us home.

230 WHEN JESUS LIVED AMONG US HE CAME A CHILD OF EARTH

When Jesus lived among us he came a child of earth
to wear our human likeness, to share our human birth;
and after flight and exile, an alien refugee,
return in peace and safety at last to Galilee;
    through sunlit days of childhood a loving home to know;
    in wisdom and in favour with God and man to grow.

He came, the friend of sinners, to meet us in our need,
the gospel of his kingdom declare in word and deed,
to touch and cure the leper, the lost to seek and find,
to heal in signs and wonders the deaf and dumb and blind.
    The voice of their Creator the wind and waters heard;
    to those with ears to listen he spoke the living word.

'The Son of Man must suffer,' he taught by word and sign;
like bread his body broken, his blood poured out like wine.
His cross is for our pardon, our sacrifice for sins,
and by his resurrection our risen life begins.
    We come in faith to Jesus to follow where he trod;
    O Son of Man receive us, and make us sons of God.

231 KINGLY BEYOND ALL EARTHLY KINGS

Kingly beyond all earthly kings,
   Christ over all, his kingdom stands;
our world, all worlds, the sum of things,
   are held in being by his hands.

'King of the Jews', by Magi sought;
   'Blessed is he', the people cry;
crowned as a jest and set at nought,
   'King of the Jews' he hangs to die.

Lord of all life and power he rose,
   King of creation's wide domain,
soon shall the trump of God disclose
   Christ as the King who comes to reign.

Free from the bounds of time and space,
   yet of our inmost lives a part,
both King and kingdom find a place
   enshrined in each believing heart.

'Your kingdom come' in this our day:
   hear us, O Lord; make haste and bring
that reign of peace for which we pray,
   the righteous reign of Christ the King.

232 TO CHRIST OUR KING IN SONGS OF PRAISE

To Christ our King in songs of praise
lift every heart and mind;
unfading light of all our days,
    true life of humankind.

O Christ our light, draw near and fill
    this shadowed soul of mine;
renew my darkened heart and will
    to light and life divine.

O Christ our life, from death and sin
    my forfeit soul set free;
that life laid down, a world to win,
    be life indeed for me.

O Christ our King, to whom we give
    again the life you gave,
tell out by us that all may live
    through Christ who died to save.

May Christ, our light, our life, our King,
    make all our hearts his own,
join all our lives his praise to sing,
    and make his glories known!

233 FROM THE NIGHT OF AGES WAKING

From the night of ages waking
  morning comes to heart and mind,
day of grace in splendour breaking,
mists and shadows fall behind;
    in the brightness of his glory
Christ the Light of life has shined.

Christ in light immortal dwelling,
Word by whom the worlds were made;
Light of lights, our dark dispelling,
Lord of lords in light arrayed;
    in the brightness of his glory
see the Father's love displayed.

Risen Lord in radiance splendid,
Christ has conquered Satan's sway;
sin and shame and sorrow ended,
powers of darkness flee away;
    in the brightness of his glory
walk as children of the day.

Light to lighten every nation,
shining forth from shore to shore,
Christ who won the world's salvation
now let all the earth adore;
    in the brightness of his glory
Light of life for evermore.

234 CHRIST, OUR HUMAN LIKENESS SHARING

Christ, our human likeness sharing,
　　heaven's love on earth portrayed;
Christ the Shepherd, tending, caring,
　　in his death our ransom paid:
　　　　Christ the Saviour, Christ the Servant,
　　be your life in us displayed.

Hear the word that Christ has spoken,
　　help the weak, the hungry feed;
see the powers of darkness broken,
　　sinners pardoned, captives freed:
　　　　Christ the Saviour, Christ the Servant,
　　help us meet our neighbour's need.

Christ, in every congregation
　　build your temple, stone by stone,
with your word as firm foundation
　　for a faith matured and grown:
　　　　Christ the Saviour, Christ the Servant,
　　make in us your gospel known.

Come, O living Christ, renew us,
　　as of old in wind and flame;
with the Spirit's power endue us,
　　servants of your saving Name:
　　　　Christ the Saviour, Christ the Servant,
　　Christ whose kingdom we proclaim.

235 AS WATER TO THE THIRSTY

As water to the thirsty,
as beauty to the eyes,
as strength that follows weakness,
as truth instead of lies,
as songtime and springtime
and summertime to be,
  so is my Lord,
  my living Lord,
so is my Lord to me.

Like calm in place of clamour,
like peace that follows pain,
like meeting after parting,
like sunshine after rain,
like moonlight and starlight
and sunlight on the sea,
  so is my Lord,
  my living Lord,
so is my Lord to me.

As sleep that follows fever,
as gold instead of grey,
as freedom after bondage,
as sunrise to the day,
as home to the traveller
and all we long to see,
  so is my Lord,
  my living Lord,
so is my Lord to me.

236 CHRIST BE THE LORD OF ALL OUR DAYS

Christ be the Lord of all our days,
the swiftly passing years:
  Lord of our unremembered birth,
  heirs to the brightness of the earth;
Lord of our griefs and fears.

Christ be the source of all our deeds,
the life our living shares;
  the fount which flows from worlds above
  to never-failing springs of love;
the ground of all our prayers.

Christ be the goal of all our hopes,
the end to whom we come;
  guide of each pilgrim Christian soul
  which seeks, as compass seeks the pole,
our many-mansioned home.

Christ be the vision of our lives,
of all we think and are;
  to shine upon our spirits' sight
  as light of everlasting light,
the bright and morning star.

237 HE COMES TO US AS ONE UNKNOWN

He comes to us as one unknown,
  a breath unseen, unheard;
as though within a heart of stone,
or shrivelled seed in darkness sown,
    a pulse of being stirred.

He comes when souls in silence lie
    and thoughts of day depart;
half-seen upon the inward eye,
a falling star across the sky
    of night within the heart.

He comes to us in sound of seas,
    the ocean's fume and foam;
yet small and still upon the breeze,
a wind that stirs the tops of trees,
    a voice to call us home.

He comes in love as once he came
    by flesh and blood and birth;
to bear within our mortal frame
a life, a death, a saving Name,
    for every child of earth.

He comes in truth when faith is grown;
    believed, obeyed, adored:
the Christ in all the Scriptures shown,
as yet unseen, but not unknown,
    our Saviour and our Lord.

238 O CHANGELESS CHRIST, FOR EVER NEW

O changeless Christ, for ever new,
    who walked our earthly ways,
still draw our hearts as once you drew
    the hearts of other days.

As once you spoke by plain and hill
    or taught by shore and sea,
so be today our teacher still,
    O Christ of Galilee.

As wind and storm their Master heard
    and his command fulfilled,
may troubled hearts receive your word,
    the tempest-tossed be stilled.

And as of old to all who prayed
    your healing hand was shown,
so be your touch upon us laid,
    unseen but not unknown.

In broken bread, in wine outpoured,
    your new and living way
proclaim to us, O risen Lord,
    O Christ of this our day.

O changeless Christ, till life is past
    your blessing still be given;
then bring us home, to taste at last
    the timeless joys of heaven.

239 OUR LIVING LORD WHOSE NAME WE BEAR

Our living Lord whose Name we bear,
whose home was once in Galilee,
who called those first disciples there
  to rise and come and 'Follow me':
    we hear again your call today
    and follow where you lead the way.

Our friend and guide whose fruitful word
  is bread of life and living seed,
whose voice the people gladly heard,
  as one who knew their deepest need:
    we come to read and mark and learn,
    and in your word your will discern.

Our Saviour Christ who for our sake
  eternal glory laid aside,
and chose the path of pain to take,
  and on the cross for sinners died,
    may we, whose trust is in your Name,
    to all the world your love proclaim.

Our Prince of life who died and rose,
  and with the Father reigns above,
who by the Spirit lives in those
  whose hearts lie open to your love,
    your risen life be ours to share,
    our glorious King, whose Name we bear.

240 SO THE DAY DAWN FOR ME

So the day dawn for me,
so the day break,
Christ watching over me,
Christ as I wake.

Be the day shine to me,
be the day bright,
Christ my companion be,
Christ be my light.

Be the day dark to me,
be the day drear,
Christ shall my comfort be,
Christ be my cheer.

Be the day swift to me,
be the day long,
Christ my contentment be,
Christ be my song.

So the day close for me,
so the night fall,
Christ watching over me,
Christ be my all.

8. Christian Experience and Discipleship

Many texts which might have been included here are listed under other headings, for example in the sections on metrical psalms or other metrical Scriptures. The Index of Themes and Subjects on page 544 contains fuller lists under most of these headings and many others.

241 O GOD WHOSE THOUGHTS ARE NOT AS OURS

O God whose thoughts are not as ours,
  whose word can bring to birth
a universe of nature's powers,
    a green and ordered earth;
beyond the frame of time and space
    we lift our spirits' gaze,
and at the heart of all we trace
    the edges of your ways.

The God of thunder, fire and flame,
    whose voice the prophets heard;
creation trembles at his Name
    and bows before his word.
The sum of things is in his hands
    whom sun and stars confess;
beyond the clouds of heaven stands
    a throne of righteousness.

O God of love, whose love is shown
    to all your hand has made,
the likeness of your glory known
    when mists and shadows fade:
the light of God's eternal light
    in Christ be shed abroad,
to shine upon our mortal sight,
    the vision of the Lord.

242 CHRIST WHO CALLED DISCIPLES TO HIM

Christ who called disciples to him
from their nets beside the sea,
taught and trained the twelve who knew him
by the shores of Galilee,
still he calls us to his service,
saying 'Come and follow me.'

Christ whose touch was life and healing,
sight to blind and strength to lame,
deed and word alike revealing
mercy evermore the same,
still he calls us to his service,
strong in faith to bear his Name.

Christ in whom, for our salvation,
God's unchanging love is shown,
risen now in exaltation,
reigning from the Father's throne,
still he calls us to his service,
and to make his gospel known.

Christ whose calling knows no ending,
no reserve and no delays,
by his Spirit's power defending
those who follow in his ways,
we are come to be his servants,
faithful now and all our days.

243 O GOD OF GRACE, TO WHOM BELONGS

O God of grace, to whom belongs
　　the work that love eternal willed,
to right again our nature's wrongs,
　　to see our destinies fulfilled,
　　　　so still today your purpose proves
　　　　the end to which creation moves.

In every age your voice is heard,
　　the calling of your love divine,
by hearts responsive to your word
　　and sealed in covenant and sign.
　　　　Of old you led by cloud and flame:
　　　　we walk by faith in Jesus' Name.

The way of Christ who came to save
　　is born of love, and life laid down;
to go with him to death and grave,
　　who set the cross before the crown;
　　　　and so his path of life to tread
　　　　who rose in glory from the dead.

For evermore his kingdom stands
　　when earth itself is past and gone;
our future hopes are in his hands
　　who calls his church to journey on:
　　　　to work his will, to watch, and pray
　　　　'Your kingdom come in this our day.'

244 ABOVE THE VOICES OF THE WORLD AROUND ME

Above the voices of the world around me,
my hopes and dreams, my cares and loves and fears,
the long-awaited call of Christ has found me,
the voice of Jesus echoes in my ears:
    'I gave my life to break the cords that bind you,
    I rose from death to set your spirit free;
    turn from your sins and put the past behind you,
    take up your cross and come and follow me.'

What can I offer him who calls me to him?
Only the wastes of sin and self and shame;
a mind confused, a heart that never knew him,
a tongue unskilled at naming Jesus' Name.
    Yet at your call, and hungry for your blessing,
    drawn by that cross which moves a heart of stone,
    now Lord I come, my tale of sin confessing,
    and in repentance turn to you alone.

Lord, I believe; help now my unbelieving;
I come in faith because your promise stands.
Your word of pardon and of peace receiving,
all that I am I place within your hands.
    Let me become what you shall choose to make me,
    freed from the guilt and burden of my sins.
    Jesus is mine, who never shall forsake me,
    and in his love my new-born life begins.

245 JESUS MY BREATH, MY LIFE, MY LORD

Jesus my breath, my life, my Lord,
　　take of my soul the inmost part;
let vision, mind and will be stored
　　with Christ the Master of my heart,
my breath, my life, my Lord.

Jesus my Lord, my breath, my life,
　　my living bread for every day,
in calm and comfort, storm and strife,
　　Christ be my truth, as Christ my way,
my Lord, my breath, my life.

Jesus my life, my Lord, my breath,
　　the pulse and beat of all my years,
constant alike in life and death;
　　and when eternal day appears,
my life, my Lord, my breath.

246 O SAVIOUR CHRIST, BEYOND ALL PRICE

O Saviour Christ, beyond all price
the debt you paid for me,
the full, sufficient sacrifice
that sets the prisoner free:
    I come to plead your saving Name,
    to make your cross my prayer,
    to own my guilt and sin and shame,
    and find forgiveness there.

O Christ, the sure and certain guide
to where my pathway lies,
the patient teacher at my side
immeasurably wise,
    I come those richest gifts to find
    that love and grace impart,
    a humble and responsive mind,
    a true and willing heart.

O Christ, companion of the way
till life's long journey ends,
you cheer us through the darkest day
and call your servants friends:
    I come to follow where you lead,
    to trust, obey, adore;
    walk with me as my friend indeed
    this day and evermore.

O sovereign Christ, the Lord of all
in loftier worlds than ours,
before whose feet in homage fall
dominions, thrones and powers,
    I come in faith before your throne,
    your ransomed child, to bring
    my very self to be your own,
    my sovereign Lord and King.

247 LORD OF ALL LIFE AND POWER

Lord of all life and power
    at whose creative word
in nature's first primeval hour
    our formless being stirred,
you made the light to shine,
    O shine on us, we pray,
renew with light and life divine
    your church in this our day.

Lord of the fertile earth
    who caused the world to be,
whose life alone can bring to birth
    the fruits of land and sea,
teach us to use aright
    and share the gifts you give,
to tend the earth as in your sight
    that all the world may live.

Lord of the cross and grave
    who died and lives again,
who came in love to seek and save
    and then to rise and reign,
we share, as once you shared,
    in mortal birth and breath,
and ours the risen life that dared
    to vanquish sin and death.

Lord of the wind and flame,
    the promised Spirit's sign,
possess our hearts in Jesus' Name,
    come down, O Love divine!
Help us in Christ to grow,
    from sin and self to cease,
and daily in our lives to show
    your love and joy and peace.

Lord of the passing years
    whose changeless purpose stands,
our lives and loves, our hopes and fears,
    we place within your hands;
we bring you but your own,
    forgiven, loved and free,
to follow Christ, and Christ alone,
    through all the days to be.

248 NO WEIGHT OF GOLD OR SILVER

No weight of gold or silver
can measure human worth;
no soul secures its ransom
with all the wealth of earth;
no sinners find their freedom
but by the gift unpriced,
the Lamb of God unblemished,
the precious blood of Christ.

Our sins, our griefs and troubles,
he bore and made his own;
we hid our faces from him,
rejected and alone.
His wounds are for our healing,
our peace is by his pain:
behold, the Man of sorrows,
the Lamb for sinners slain!

In Christ the past is over,
a new world now begins;
with him we rise to freedom
who saves us from our sins.
We live by faith in Jesus
to make his glory known:
behold the Man of sorrows,
the Lamb upon his throne!

249 CHRIST BE MY LEADER BY NIGHT AS BY DAY

Christ be my leader by night as by day;
safe through the darkness for he is the way.
Gladly I follow, my future his care,
darkness is daylight when Jesus is there.

Christ be my teacher in age as in youth,
drifting or doubting, for he is the truth.
Grant me to trust him; though shifting as sand,
doubt cannot daunt me; in Jesus I stand.

Christ be my Saviour in calm as in strife;
death cannot hold me, for he is the life.
Nor darkness nor doubting nor sin and its stain
can touch my salvation: with Jesus I reign.

250 AFFIRM ANEW THE THREEFOLD NAME

Affirm anew the threefold Name
    of Father, Spirit, Son,
our God whose saving acts proclaim
    a world's salvation won.
In him alone we live and move
    and breath and being find,
the wayward children of his love
    who cares for humankind.

Declare in all the earth his grace,
    to every heart his call,
the living Lord of time and place
    whose love embraces all.
So shall his endless praise be sung,
    his teaching truly heard,
and every culture, every tongue,
    receive his timeless word.

Confirm our faith in this our day
    amid earth's shifting sand,
with Christ as Life and Truth and Way,
    a Rock on which to stand;
the one eternal Son and Lord
    by God the Father given,
the true and life-imparting Word,
    the Way that leads to heaven.

Renew once more the ancient fire,
    let love our hearts inflame;
renew, restore, unite, inspire
    the church that bears your Name;
one Name exalted over all,
    one Father, Spirit, Son,
O grant us grace to heed your call
    and in that Name be one.

251 BE WITH US, LORD, WHO SEEK YOUR AID

Be with us, Lord, who seek your aid
and give us eyes to see
the vision of our life remade
as you would have it be.

Renew in us that righteousness
your sovereign grace imparts:
may deed and word alike express
the worship of our hearts.

Defended by the Spirit's powers,
upheld by God alone,
a growing confidence be ours,
a strength beyond our own.

The praise of Christ, our living Lord,
let all our actions prove,
in lives surrendered to his word,
the vision of his love.

252 CHRIST THE WAY OF LIFE POSSESS ME

based on four images from the Book of Proverbs

C hrist the Way of life possess me,
　　lift my heart to love and praise;
guide and keep, sustain and bless me,
　　all my days.

Well of life, for ever flowing,
　　make my barren soul and bare
like a watered garden growing
　　fresh and fair.

May the Tree of life in splendour
　　from its leafy boughs impart
grace divine and healing tender,
　　strength of heart.

Path of life before me shining,
　　let me come when earth is past,
sorrow, self and sin resigning,
　　home at last.

253 FROM LIFE'S BRIGHT DAWN TO EVENTIDE

From life's bright dawn to eventide
shall faith and hope and love abide;
when earth and heaven shall fade and flee
there still shall stand these virtues three.

What though the road be steep and long,
yet faith in Christ shall tune my song;
my home in heaven seem faint and far,
yet hope in Christ be guiding star.

But more than these, this grace impart:
let love for Christ possess my heart,
until in heaven his face I see
who loved and gave himself for me.

254 MAY THE LOVE OF CHRIST ENFOLD US

May the love of Christ enfold us
    as we walk his way,
his eternal arms uphold us
    even as we pray;
strong in faith beneath his blessing,
every tongue his Name confessing,
every heart his peace possessing,
    this and every day.

May the word of Christ direct us
    as we walk his way,
and his providence protect us
    even as we pray.
May his Spirit's power defend us,
love and joy and peace attend us,
his companionship befriend us,
    this and every day.

May the living Christ renew us
    as we walk his way,
and with gifts of grace endue us
    even as we pray;
send us forth, his banner bearing,
all the truth of God declaring,
heaven's love for sinners sharing,
    this and every day.

255 THE PILGRIM CHURCH OF GOD

T he pilgrim church of God,
   we mount the narrow way,
we tread the path that Jesus trod,
his call obey:
> to whom God sent his Son,
> to whom the Spirit came,
> who in the faith of Christ are one
> and in his Name.

His word of life divine
shall light and truth impart,
and with immortal wisdom shine
for mind and heart.
> So may we live and grow,
> this grace upon us poured,
> with heart and mind alike to know
> and serve the Lord.

The work of grace fulfil
while life and strength shall last,
sustain your pilgrim people still
till earth be past;
> until what grace began
> shall win its final way,
> and God complete his perfect plan
> in endless day.

What though the way we tread
be dark, or faith be dim?
We look to Christ our risen Head
and walk with him.
> So lead your children on
> in love and truth and grace,
> to come where Christ himself has gone
> and see his face.

256 THOUGH PILGRIM STRANGERS HERE BELOW

Though pilgrim strangers here below,
we ask, as through the world we go,
to plant a flower, to pluck a weed,
to serve unsought a neighbour's need:
and to our children leave behind
a better world for humankind.

A friendlier world be theirs, we pray,
through lessons learned by us today;
where all shall cherish, all shall share,
the earth which God created fair:
where fear, disease and famine cease,
and peoples learn to live in peace.

O Prince of peace, whose reign on earth
brings freedom, light and hope to birth,
may we and all who name your Name
the love of God in Christ proclaim:
in Christ, by whom are sins forgiven,
the Life, the Truth, the Way to heaven.

257 WHEN THE WAY IS HARD TO FIND

When the way is hard to find,
  seeking first the Father's will,
Lord, your promise call to mind,
all your purposes fulfil:
    when the way is hard to find
    lead your pilgrim people still.

Dark beneath a starless sky,
tossing in the wind and tide,
when the seas of life are high,
lost upon an ocean wide,
    dark beneath a starless sky,
    Lord, we look to you to guide.

Wisdom from the living Word
shine upon us as we pray;
may the Spirit's voice be heard
in the dark and cloudy day:
    wisdom from the living Word
    be the light upon our way.

Faith be strong and doubt depart,
fear and unbelief be gone;
peace possess the anxious heart
where the light of Christ has shone:
    faith be strong and doubt depart,
    lead your pilgrim people on.

258 EYE HAS NOT SEEN, NOR EAR HAS HEARD

Eye has not seen, nor ear has heard,
　　nor can the mind conceive
what God has pledged within his word
　　for those he bids believe.

The secret things of God above
　　to faith by wisdom shown,
the sacred mysteries of love,
　　his Spirit now makes known.

Such love fulfilled its holiest part
　　when Christ was crucified:
the flower of love's eternal heart,
　　the Lord of glory died.

He died to do the Father's will,
　　he rose by love's design,
he ever lives, immortal still,
　　the Prince of life divine.

His immemorial purpose done,
　　what blessings yet unfold!
Shall he who gave his only Son
　　another gift withhold?

All things are ours! Our life restored
　　is one with Christ above:
and ours, for ever with the Lord,
　　the hidden depths of love.

259 LORD AND FATHER, FAITH BESTOWING

L ord and Father,
  faith bestowing,
    to our hearts draw near.
Love is ours beyond our knowing,
    God is here.

Christ our Saviour
come with blessing,
    bid our doubting cease.
Here may all, their sin confessing,
    find your peace.

Holy Spirit,
life instilling,
    breathe from God above;
come with power, our spirits filling,
    come with love.

God eternal,
grace unbounded,
    Three-in-One we praise;
keep us by your love surrounded
    all our days.

For Europe and Africa: © Timothy Dudley-Smith
For the rest of the world including the USA and Canada: © 1997 Hope Publishing Company

260 DRAW NEAR TO GOD, WHOSE STEADFAST LOVE

Draw near to God, whose steadfast love
no other gods can show,
in all the heights of heaven above,
in all the earth below.

His timeless truth is ever new,
his covenant secure,
his mercies as the morning dew,
while life and breath endure.

Fulfilling all his love's design,
embracing flesh and birth,
a nature human and divine,
he came in Christ to earth.

And he whose throne eternal stands
his Spirit's life imparts,
to share a house not made with hands,
a home within our hearts.

Have faith in God: his promise claim
who longs to hear our prayers;
who knows and loves our human frame,
who knows, and loves, and cares.

261 GOD OF ETERNAL GRACE

God of eternal grace
   in whom our spirits move,
we come to seek a Father's face,
   to rest within his love.

God of all truth and light
   from everlasting days,
who formed and lit the starry height,
   enlighten all our ways.

God of all joy and peace
   to whom all peace belongs,
our faith renew, our hope increase,
   and praise be all our songs.

God of all power and might,
   give us, whom Christ has freed,
the Spirit's strength to walk aright
   in thought and word and deed.

God of unchanging love
   who wears a Father's face,
we sing with all the saints above
   his glory and his grace.

262 ALMIGHTY LORD MOST HIGH DRAW NEAR

from the Prayer of Manasseh

Almighty Lord Most High draw near
whose awesome splendour none can bear;
eternal God, in mercy hear,
receive once more the sinners' prayer;
　　upon your word of grace we call
　　whose word of power has ordered all.

How measureless your mercies stand,
the hope and pledge of sins forgiven;
those sins, unnumbered as the sand,
that hide the very stars of heaven:
　　O God of grace, to us impart
　　a penitent and contrite heart.

From such a heart we bend the knee
and all our sin and shame confess.
Lord, your unworthy servants see,
and clothe us round with righteousness;
　　that loved and pardoned, healed and blest,
　　we taste your mercies manifest.

So lift on high the Saviour's praise
with all the hosts of heaven above,
and sing through everlasting days
the God of glory, grace and love.
　　The Lord of all let all adore,
　　for ever and for evermore!

263 O LORD, YOURSELF DECLARE

O Lord, yourself declare,
  our new and living way;
move all our hearts to love and prayer
and teach us how to pray:

In worship to be still,
in penitence confess,
to ask according to your will,
receive with thankfulness.

Your purposes to share,
your promises to claim,
move all our hearts to love and prayer
through faith in Jesus' Name.

264 THANKFUL OF HEART FOR DAYS GONE BY

T hankful of heart for days gone by,
  mirrored in memory's inward eye;
childhood and youth, their hopes and fears,
stored with the tale of all the years;
stilled from the storms of joy and pain
chiefly the sunlit hours remain.
    Come then, as Christian people should,
    give thanks to God, for God is good.

Thankful to welcome, day by day,
tokens of love about our way;
and from a Father's hand to trace
blessings of nature and of grace:
treasures on earth let time destroy!
Christ is our love, our peace, our joy.
    Come then, as Christian people should,
    rejoice in God, for God is good.

Thankful we look for days to be,
part of a purpose none foresee;
firm in the faith of sins forgiven,
Christ and his cross our hope of heaven;
Christ at the last our great reward,
Christ over all, ascended Lord!
    Come then, as Christian people should,
    hope still in God, for God is good.

265 FOR PEACE WITH GOD ABOVE

For peace with God above
and every sin forgiven,
for all our hope of heaven,
we lift our hearts in love.

The peace of God be ours
enfolding every part,
possessing thought and heart,
the will and all its powers.

The God of peace defend
and keep us all our days
unwearied in his praise,
whose peace shall never end.

266 'SET YOUR TROUBLED HEARTS AT REST'

'Set your troubled hearts at rest,'
hear again the word divine;
all our Father does is best;
    let his peace be yours and mine.

Trusting still in God above,
    set your troubled hearts at rest;
find within a Father's love
    comfort for a soul distressed.

When you come to make request
    know that God will answer prayer;
set your troubled hearts at rest,
    safe within a Father's care.

Be at peace, then, and rejoice,
    loved and comforted and blest;
hear again the Saviour's voice;
    'Set your troubled hearts at rest.'

9. *Themes and Subjects*

Many texts which might have been included here are listed under other headings, for example in Section 8 on Christian experience and discipleship, or in Section 3 because they relate to the Occasional or Annual Services of a local church's year. Hymns on Holy Communion, for example, will be found in Section 2 'Regular daily and weekly Church Services', while hymns on themes such as Stewardship or Unity are included in Section 3. The Index of Themes and Subjects on page 544 contains fuller lists under some of these headings, and many others.

267 THE GOD WHO SET THE STARS IN SPACE

The God who set the stars in space
   and gave the planets birth
created for our dwelling place
   a green and fruitful earth;
a world with wealth and beauty crowned
   of sky and sea and land,
where life should flourish and abound
   beneath its Maker's hand.

A world of order and delight
   God gave for us to tend,
to hold as precious in his sight,
   to nurture and defend;
but yet on ocean, earth and air
   the marks of sin are seen,
with all that God created fair
   polluted and unclean.

O God, by whose redeeming grace
   the lost may be restored,
who stooped to save our fallen race
   in Christ, creation's Lord,
through him whose cross is life and peace
   to cleanse a heart defiled
may human greed and conflict cease
   and all be reconciled.

Renew the wastes of earth again,
   redeem, restore, repair;
with us, your children, still maintain
   your covenant of care.
May we, who move from dust to dust
   and on your grace depend,
no longer, Lord, betray our trust
   but prove creation's friend.

Our God, who set the stars in space
   and gave the planets birth,
look down from heaven, your dwelling place,
   and heal the wounds of earth;
till pain, decay and bondage done,
   when death itself has died,
creation's songs shall rise as one
   and God be glorified!

268 THE LORD IN WISDOM MADE THE EARTH

based on Proverbs 8

The Lord in wisdom made the earth,
  our sky and sea and land,
and gave the furthest stars their birth,
unnumbered as the sand:
    beyond all worlds, all stars and skies,
    he reigns all-loving and all-wise.

Beneath his hand the seasons turn,
he rules the wind and tide;
for him the fires of nature burn,
the cells of life divide:
    creation moves as he decrees
    and wisely works its mysteries.

By him the lamps of reason shine,
the laws of life are told;
within his purposes divine
our destinies unfold:
    in love and wisdom, Lord, fulfil
    and work in us your perfect will.

So make us wise, in Christ to trust,
in truth to walk his ways,
the wise, the righteous and the just
from everlasting days:
    redeeming Son, eternal Word,
    the power and wisdom of the Lord.

269 WHAT COLOURS GOD HAS MADE

What colours God has made
in flower and field and tree!
From springing green of leaf and blade
I learn his love for me.

The summer's yellow sand,
the blue of sky and sea,
they tell of God their Maker's hand,
and all his love for me.

The turning autumn leaves,
the fruit so full and free,
the golden glow of harvest sheaves,
declare his love for me.

He frames the winter skies,
his silver stars I see;
he makes the sun in splendour rise,
the God who cares for me.

So sing my Father's praise,
the living God is he,
whose colours brighten all our days,
who loves and cares for me.

270 THE LORD MADE MAN, THE SCRIPTURES TELL

The Lord made man, the Scriptures tell,
  to bear his image and his sign;
yet we by nature share as well
    the ancient mark of Adam's line.

In Adam's fall falls every man,
  with every gift the Father gave:
the crown of all creation's plan
    becomes a rebel and a slave.

Herein all woes are brought to birth,
  all aching hearts and sunless skies:
brightness is gone from all the earth,
    the innocence of nature dies.

Yet Adam's children, born to pain,
  by self enslaved, by sin enticed,
still may by grace be born again,
    children of God, beloved in Christ.

In Christ is Adam's ransom met;
  earth, by his cross, is holy ground;
Eden indeed is with us yet;
    in Christ are life and freedom found!

For Europe and Africa: © Timothy Dudley-Smith
For the rest of the world including the USA and Canada: © 1984 Hope Publishing Company

271 AS FOR OUR WORLD WE LIFT OUR HEARTS IN PRAISE

As for our world we lift our hearts in praise,
for gifts unnumbered from our childhood days,
  now, in God's Name
stir our compassions; give us eyes to see
the orphaned child, the starved and refugee,
  the sick and lame:
for sad and needy children everywhere,
for this our world, we lift our hands in prayer.

As for our world we lift our hearts in praise,
the joy of home with lights and hearth ablaze,
  the welcome plain;
so we recall the homeless and the cold,
the destitute, the prisoners, and the old
  who lie in pain:
for all who grieve, for all who know despair,
for this our world, we lift our hands in prayer.

As for our world we lift our hearts in praise,
recount the blessings that our life displays
  in every part,
so look in mercy, Lord, where shadows rest,
the ravaged homes by want and wars oppressed,
  the sick at heart,
with burdens more than we were meant to bear:
for this our world, we lift our hands in prayer.

As for our world we lift our hearts in praise,
the love of God on all our works and ways,
  so we commend
all those who loveless live and hopeless mourn,
who die at last uncomforted, forlorn,
  without a friend;
who own no Saviour's love, no Father's care,
for this our world we lift our hands in prayer.

As for our world we lift our hearts in praise,
so with our songs of thankfulness we raise
  this ageless plea,
that darkened souls who have no song to sing
may find in Christ the living Lord and King
  he came to be,
and in his cross and resurrection share:
for this our world we lift our hands in prayer.

For Europe and Africa: © Timothy Dudley-Smith
For the rest of the world including the USA and Canada: © 1968 Hope Publishing Company

272 BEHOLD A BROKEN WORLD, WE PRAY

Behold a broken world, we pray,
  where want and war increase,
and grant us, Lord, in this our day,
  the ancient dream of peace:

A dream of swords to sickles bent,
  of spears to scythe and spade,
the weapons of our warfare spent,
  a world of peace remade;

Where every battle-flag is furled
  and every trumpet stilled,
where wars shall cease in all the world,
  a waking dream fulfilled.

No force of arms shall there prevail
  nor justice cease her sway;
nor shall their loftiest visions fail
  the dreamers of the day.

O Prince of peace, who died to save,
  a lost world to redeem,
and rose in triumph from the grave,
  behold our waking dream.

Bring, Lord, your better world to birth,
  your kingdom, love's domain;
where peace with God, and peace on earth,
  and peace eternal reign.

273 O GOD, WHO GIVES THE FERTILE SEED

O God, who gives the fertile seed,
   the life by which the world is fed,
with mercy look on those in need
      of hearth and home and daily bread.

In flood and famine, drought and dearth,
      a world where want and wars increase,
behold the helpless of the earth
      who cry for justice and for peace.

Help us to bridge the world's divide,
      to share the healing gifts you gave,
for all earth's children stem the tide
      of sore disease and infant grave.

Teach us to put the past behind
      and seek this broken earth restored:
one equal home for humankind,
      a better world where Christ is Lord.

274 REMEMBER, LORD, THE WORLD YOU MADE

Remember, Lord, the world you made,
for Adam's race to find
the life of heaven on earth displayed,
a home for humankind.

A home of peace: but war and strife
and hatred we confess;
where death is in the midst of life
and children fatherless.

A home of freedom: yet the flame
burns low for liberty;
and few will serve in Jesus' Name
that all men may be free.

A home of plenty: clothed and fed
our sturdy children play;
while other children cry for bread
not half the world away.

Renew our love, O Lord, and touch
our hearts to feel and care
that we who seem to have so much
so little seem to share.

For those who have no prayers to say,
who in despair are dumb,
teach us to live as well as pray
'O Lord, your kingdom come!'

275 MOST GLORIOUS GOD, FOR BREATH AND BIRTH

Most glorious God, for breath and birth
  receive our thankful prayer,
that we, as children born of earth,
    your life and image share.

We praise for all your grace imparts,
    the human spirit's powers,
to sense and know within our hearts
    the love that wakens ours.

While in this fallen world we move,
    a world estranged, self-willed,
our weakness and our frailty prove
    God's purpose unfulfilled.

Yet God in Jesus loves and cares,
    and makes his promise known;
the Wounded Healer feels and shares
    the griefs we call our own.

For out of death shall life arise,
    and glory spring from loss,
when all shall see with wondering eyes
    the triumphs of the cross.

As with the dawn the dreamer wakes
    from earthbound sin and pain,
so resurrection morning breaks
    on Christ's unclouded reign.

276 O LORD, WHOSE SAVING NAME

O Lord, whose saving Name
is life and health and rest,
to whom the children came
and in your arms were blest,
we seek your face;
your love be shown,
your presence known,
within this place.

That love be ours to share
with tenderness and skill,
with science, faith and prayer,
to work your sovereign will;
we praise you, Lord,
for banished pain,
for strength again,
for health restored.

When deepest shadows fall
to quench life's fading spark,
be near us when we call,
walk with us through the dark,
our Light and Way,
by grief and loss
and bitter cross,
to endless day.

In God our hope is set,
beneath whose rule alone
is peace from fear and fret,
and strength beyond our own.
His kingdom stands,
and those this day
for whom we pray
are in his hands.

Join every heart to bring
our praise to God above,
whom children's voices sing
and whom unseen we love.
O God of grace,
for evermore
your blessings pour
upon this place.

For Europe and Africa: © Timothy Dudley-Smith
For the rest of the world including the USA and Canada: © 1997 Hope Publishing Company

277 WHEN TO OUR WORLD THE SAVIOUR CAME

When to our world the Saviour came
the sick and helpless heard his Name,
and in their weakness longed to see
the healing Christ of Galilee.

That good physician! Night and day
the people thronged about his way;
and wonder ran from soul to soul,
'The touch of Christ has made us whole!'

His praises then were heard and sung
by opened ears and loosened tongue,
while lightened eyes could see and know
the healing Christ of long ago.

Of long ago: yet living still,
who died for us on Calvary's hill;
who triumphed over cross and grave,
his healing hands stretched forth to save.

His sovereign purpose still remains
who rose in power, and lives and reigns;
till every tongue confess his praise,
the healing Christ of all our days.

278 O GOD, WHOSE ALL-SUSTAINING HAND

suitable for a Civic Service

O God, whose all-sustaining hand
is over this and every land,
whose laws from age to age have stood,
sure guardians of our common good,
    may love of justice rule our days
    and ordered freedom guide our ways.

Be near to those who strive to see
our homes from harm and terror free,
who live their lives at duty's call
and spend themselves in serving all:
    receive for them your people's prayer,
    uphold them by your constant care.

Teach us to serve our neighbour's need,
the homeless help, the hungry feed,
the poor protect, the weak defend,
and to the friendless prove a friend;
    the wayward and the lost reclaim
    for love of Christ and in his Name.

So may our hearts remember yet
that cross where love and justice met,
and find in Christ our fetters freed,
whose mercy answers all our need:
    who lives and reigns, our risen Lord,
    where justice sheathes her righteous sword.

279 WE BRING YOU, LORD, OUR PRAYER AND PRAISE

We bring you, Lord, our prayer and praise
    that every child of earth
should live and grow in freedom's ways,
    in dignity and worth.

We praise for such a task begun
    to serve each other's need,
for every cause of justice won,
    for every fetter freed.

Our prayers are for a world in pain
    where force and fear prevail,
the plough becomes the sword again,
    and hope and harvests fail.

Alike our prayer and praise express
    the wants of humankind,
that those in bondage and distress
    their larger freedoms find.

So may we still maintain the fight
    till earth's oppressions cease
before the universal right
    to liberty and peace.

In Christ we learn to love and care
    and spread his truth abroad;
and in his Name we lift our prayer:
    'Your kingdom come, O Lord.'

280 BEFORE THE WORLD'S FOUNDATION

a celebration of the word

Before the world's foundation,
 before the stars and sun,
to summon all creation
 God spoke and it was done;
the life of earth and oceans
 to breath and being stirred,
the planets in their motions
 were ordered at his word.

His Name we come declaring
 who reigns enthroned above,
the Word incarnate, sharing
 God's inmost life of love.
To us for our discerning
 the ways of God are shown
where, written for our learning,
 his word is read and known.

Baptize, O Lord, and christen
 their culture and their creed
who speak where many listen,
 who write what many read;
till by the Spirit's striving
 the heart and conscience find
a word of truth, deriving
 from God's eternal mind.

Affirm again the glory
 of this, your church's call,
to tell the Saviour's story
 and publish him to all;
his word of grace and healing
 that speaks of sins forgiven,
his word of promise, sealing
 our longed-for hope of heaven.

May all our faithful teaching
 exalt, O Lord, your Name;
our foolishness of preaching
 the cross of Christ proclaim.
In words of wisdom's lending
 inspire the songs we raise,
who look for life unending
 where all our words are praise.

281 FATHER ON HIGH TO WHOM WE PRAY

Father on high to whom we pray
and lift our thankful hearts above,
for all your mercies day by day,
for gifts of hearth and home and love:
protect them still beneath your care;
Lord in your mercy, hear our prayer.

O Christ who came as man to earth,
and chose in Egypt's land to be
a homeless child of alien birth,
an exile and a refugee:
for homeless people everywhere,
Lord in your mercy, hear our prayer.

Spirit divine, whose work is done
in souls renewed and lives restored,
strive in our hearts to make us one,
one faith, one family, one Lord:
till at the last one home we share,
Lord in your mercy, hear our prayer.

282 LORD OF THE CHURCH,
WE PRAY FOR OUR RENEWING

L ord of the church, we pray for our renewing:
   Christ over all, our undivided aim.
Fire of the Spirit, burn for our enduing,
   wind of the Spirit, fan the living flame!
We turn to Christ amid our fear and failing,
   the will that lacks the courage to be free,
the weary labours, all but unavailing,
   to bring us nearer what a church should be.

Lord of the church, we seek a Father's blessing,
   a true repentance and a faith restored,
a swift obedience and a new possessing,
   filled with the Holy Spirit of the Lord!
We turn to Christ from all our restless striving,
   unnumbered voices with a single prayer:
the living water for our souls' reviving,
   in Christ to live, and love and serve and care.

Lord of the church, we long for our uniting,
   true to one calling, by one vision stirred;
one cross proclaiming and one creed reciting,
   one in the truth of Jesus and his word.
So lead us on; till toil and trouble ended,
   one church triumphant one new song shall sing,
to praise his glory, risen and ascended,
   Christ over all, the everlasting King!

283 THE CHURCH OF GOD ON EARTH, WE COME

T he church of God on earth, we come
to him whose love has sought us,
a people lost and far from home,
    in Christ he came and bought us.
For all in faith's allegiance sworn
God's new community is born,
    to live as Jesus taught us.

And still the call of God is heard
    that summons all creation.
He sends his Spirit and his word,
    the word of our salvation;
and as the seed of life is sown
so love's community is known
    in every generation.

Within the bond of love and peace,
    the grace of Christ possessing,
we sing the songs that never cease,
    our God and King confessing:
eternal praise unite our powers
for Christ's community is ours,
    and everlasting blessing!

284 GOOD NEWS OF GOD ABOVE

Good news of God above
is ours to tell abroad,
the Father's everlasting love
in Christ the risen Lord.
For neighbours near and far
the seed of life is sown;
then spread the seed
by word and deed
to make the Saviour known.

The love of Christ proclaim
who left his home on high;
to live our human life he came,
our human death to die.
The Father's only Son
became the sinners' friend,
our lot to share,
our sin to bear,
and death's dominion end.

The Lord of glory lives!
From cross and death and grave
his own abundant life he gives
to those he died to save.
His righteousness and peace
declare from sea to sea;
his praises sound
the world around
for Christ has made us free.

Hear now the Master's word
to those who bear his Name:
'So send I you,' till all have heard,
'make known, declare, proclaim!'
Go forth in all the earth,
embrace the path he trod,
with Christ beside
as friend and guide,
to bring good news of God.

285 'HOW SHALL THEY HEAR,' WHO HAVE NOT HEARD

'How shall they hear,' who have not heard
news of a Lord who loved and came;
nor known his reconciling word,
    nor learned to trust a Saviour's Name?

'To all the world,' to every place,
    neighbours and friends and far-off lands,
preach the good news of saving grace;
    go while the great commission stands.

'Whom shall I send?' Who hears the call,
    constant in prayer, through toil and pain,
telling of one who died for all,
    to bring a lost world home again?

'Lord, here am I:' your fire impart
    to this poor cold self-centred soul;
touch but my lips, my hands, my heart,
    and make a world for Christ my goal.

Spirit of love, within us move:
    Spirit of truth, in power come down!
So shall they hear and find and prove
    Christ is their life, their joy, their crown.

NOTES ON THE HYMNS

The hymn number shown against each first line is the same as the number of the page on which the text appears in the previous part of the book.

In these Notes, versions of the Bible are referred to by the following abbreviations:

AV *Authorized Version,* 1611, also known as the *King James Version*
RV *Revised Version,* 1881-5
RSV *Revised Standard Version,* 1946-52
JBP *J.B.Phillips,* 1958
JB *Jerusalem Bible,* 1958
NEB *New English Bible,* 1970
NIV *New International Version,* 1979
REB *Revised English Bible,* 1989
NRSV *New Revised Standard Version,* 1990

Coverdale refers to the translation by Miles Coverdale, 1535
Knox refers to the translation by Ronald A. Knox, 1946-9
Gelineau refers to the translation arranged for singing to the psalmody of Joseph Gelineau, 1963

Note also:
ASB *Alternative Service Book, 1980*
BCP *Book of Common Prayer*
DNB *Dictionary of National Biography*
OED *Oxford English Dictionary*

1 AWAKE, AS IN THE SKIES ABOVE

86 86 (CM)

Theme	Advent; the return of Christ
Written	at Ford, November 2000
Suggested tune	ST MAGNUS by Jeremiah Clarke
	ST STEPHEN by William Jones

The season of Advent has been part of the Christian church's calendar since at least the 6th century; a time of preparation for the coming of Christ which we celebrate at Christmas and for his coming again at the Last Day. The *Book of Common Prayer* gives as the Epistle of Advent Sunday the words of Paul's letter to the Romans (13. 12), telling of how 'the night is far spent' and that it is 'time to awake out of sleep', thoughts echoed in the Collect. The same passage is used in Year A of the current Church of England Calendar for Advent Sunday, and explains the imagery of darkness and light, night and daybreak, of verses 1 and 2 of this text.

The remaining verses turn our thoughts to Christ's second coming, and the imagery of Romans 14.11, drawing on Isaiah 45.23; and of Philippians 2.11 coupled with Revelation 1.7, 'every eye will see him.' The four verses therefore express in turn expectation, anticipation, preparation and adoration.

2 FROM THE FATHER'S THRONE ON HIGH

77 77

Based on	Mark 13. 24–27
Theme	Advent; the return of Christ in glory
Written	at Bramerton, January 1986
Suggested tune	LAUDS by John W. Wilson
	MONKLAND by John Antes
	ORIENTIS PARTIBUS (French traditional)
Published in	*Carol Praise*, 1987 to MONKLAND

The *Book of Common Prayer* takes as the Gospel reading for the second Sunday in Advent the comparable passage to this one, from St Luke. The 1997 Calendar for the Church of England now includes this passage from St Mark as the Gospel set for the First Sunday in Advent, Year B, at the Principal Service.

The opening verse of this text makes reference to both the first and second Advents of Christ as Redeemer and as Judge; while the final verse looks back to Christ's part in the creation of the world (John 1.3), and forwards to his inauguration of the new age.

3 HERE ON THE THRESHOLD OF A NEW BEGINNING

11 10 11 10 D

Theme	Advent; New Year; anniversary; dedication and renewal
Written	at Killay, Swansea, May and June 1977; revised at Ford, May 1998
Suggested tune	ADVENIT by Malcolm Archer
	NEW MILLENNIUM by Michael A. Baughen

SALVATOR MUNDI by Kenneth W. Coates

Published in	*Worship 2000!*, 1999 to NEW MILLENNIUM
	New Start Hymns and Songs, 1999 to ADVENIT
	Supplement 99 (USA), 1999 to NEW MILLENNIUM
	Sing Glory!, 1999 to NEW MILLENNIUM
	Complete Anglican Hymns Old & New, 2000 to ADVENIT
	Praise!, 2000 to NEW MILLENNIUM

In 1997 Nassau Presbyterian Church, Princeton, advertised for a text on the theme of 'New Beginnings' to mark the arrival of a new pastor. This text was written and submitted, short-listed but not finally chosen. However, a year or two later, it appeared in one or two collections as a hymn suitable for singing at the millennium; though this is not included under 'Theme' above since it will be some time before such an occasion occurs again! But from time to time most local churches find themselves starting a new chapter, possibly but not necessarily at Advent or New Year, and may find this text expresses what they wish to say.

Verse 2 is a reminder that for the Christian family, 'new beginnings' must look wider than our domestic affairs; and the final stanza recognizes that it is Scripture which shapes a church. Romans 8.17 speaks of God's believing people as 'heirs': indeed 'joint heirs with Christ'.

The stress pattern of the metre is an unusual one, and both tunes NEW MILLENNIUM and ADVENIT were written for this text.

4 HIGH PEAKS AND SUNLIT PRAIRIES   76 76 D

Theme	Advent; Christmas and Epiphany
Written	at Ruan Minor, August 1974
Suggested tune	CRÜGER by Johann Crüger
	MUNICH from *Gesangbuch,* Meiningen, 1693

These verses appeared on our family Christmas card in 1974; and perhaps they are more in the nature of a Christmas poem than of a hymn. The three verses speak in succession of our natural world and the universe to which it belongs; then of the living creatures, among whom the 'absent Lord' is content to be numbered; and finally of ourselves, men and women who are the crown of all God's creative work, for whose redemption God comes to earth.

See Index 6.

5 WHEN HE COMES   3 3 11 8 8 11 and refrain

Based on	1 Thessalonians 4.14–17
Theme	Advent; the return of Christ
Written	June 1967
Suggested tune	THORNTON by J.D. Thornton
Translated into	German

Published in   *Youth Praise 2*, 1969 to THORNTON
Sing to God, 1971 to THORNTON
Keswick Praise, 1975 to THORNTON
Preist Ihn (Germany), 1978 to THORNTON in a translation by
    Brigitte Mayer
Jesus Praise, 1982 to a traditional tune arranged by Norman
    Warren (using as a first line the third line of each verse; and so
    indexed as 'We shall see the Lord in glory').
The Singing Church (USA), 1985 to THORNTON
Seventh-day Adventist Hymnal (USA), 1985 to DAVID by Wayne
    Hooper
Sing Joyfully (USA), 1990 to THORNTON

This text, which began as something I sang tunelessly to myself on a car-journey, found a place in *Youth Praise 2;* and in a number of song-books or collections for young people since then. Paul's phrase in 1 Thessalonians 4.17 is 'Then we which are alive and remain shall be caught up....' and this text is written from the viewpoint of those who are alive when the Lord returns at his second Advent. The 'alleluias' are an inference of my own; but Paul says we are to 'encourage one another' with what he here tells us; and 'Alleluia' seems a fitting accompaniment to this encouragement!

6 WHEN THE LORD IN GLORY COMES   77 77 77 D

Theme   Advent; the return of Christ
Written   at Sevenoaks, January 1967
Suggested tune   GLORIOUS COMING by Michael A. Baughen
Translated into   German
Published in   *Youth Praise 2*, 1969 to GLORIOUS COMING
Family Worship, 1971 (words only)
Renewal Songbook, 1971 (words only)
Thirty Hymns, 1972 (words only)
Keswick Praise, 1975 to GLORIOUS COMING
Anglican Hymn Book Supplement, 1978 (words only)
Preist Ihn (Germany), 1978 to GLORIOUS COMING in a
    translation by Brigitte Mayer
Partners in Praise, 1979 to GLORIOUS COMING
Hymns for Today's Church, 1982 to GLORIOUS COMING
Hymnal Supplement (USA), 1984 to GLORIOUS COMING
Junior Praise, 1986 to GLORIOUS COMING
Mission Praise 2, 1987 to GLORIOUS COMING
The Worshiping Church (USA), 1990 to GLORIOUS COMING
Mission Praise Combined, 1990 to GLORIOUS COMING
Anthem (USA), 1993 by Bob Moore
Gather, 2nd edition (USA), 1994 to ST JOHN'S by Bob Moore
Songs for the People of God (USA), 1994 to MORNING TRUMPET
    from *The Southern Harmony*, 1835
RitualSong (USA), 1996 to ST JOHN'S
Junior Praise Combined, 1997 to GLORIOUS COMING

Recorded on   *A Tribute to Youth Praise*, 1969 to GLORIOUS COMING
                When the Lord in Glory Comes (USA), 1993 to ST JOHN'S
                The Hymn Makers: 'Tell out, my soul', 1996 to GLORIOUS
                     COMING
                Junior Praise Combined 19, 1999 to GLORIOUS COMING
                Twenty Favourite Hymns 3, 2000 to GLORIOUS COMING

When in the 1960s *Youth Praise 2* was in preparation, and the editors were seeking more material in a 'youth idiom', I happened to hear on television one evening a song with a very pronounced beat, an emphatic rhythm which stayed in my head. Taking a late-night stroll round the streets near my home, I found the beginning of this text coming into my mind as I walked. I sent the words to Michael Baughen in Manchester, who telephoned me to ask if I had any *tune* in mind. I did attempt to give some indication of the beat that had been running in my head, but I think entirely unsuccessfully. Michael Baughen, however, produced the tune which was included in *Youth Praise 2;* and which later became known as GLORIOUS COMING. The metre shown, 77 77 77 D, is that of the tune: in singing, the last two lines of the text are repeated.

Verse 3, line 2 contains a conscious echo of a famous description from Shakespeare. See *Julius Caesar*, Act 1, scene 2, line 134.

7 A NEW SONG GOD HAS GIVEN   76 76 D

Theme   Christmas and Epiphany

Written   at Ford, August 1992

Suggested tune   CRÜGER by Johann Crüger
                 MORNING LIGHT by George J. Webb
                 ST THEODULPH by Melchior Teschner

Published in   *Beneath a Travelling Star*, 2001 to CRÜGER

The 'new song' , which is a favourite theme of Scripture, is here linked to the 'new thing' God has done in sending Jesus, the new-born baby greeted by the new-found star. It is his birth on that 'new-made morning' which ushers in the 'new world' (see 2 Corinthians 5.17, NEB) of God's new creation; leading on to the new heaven and the new earth of Revelation 21, and the 'new song' of Revelation 5 and 14.

Charles Wesley noted in his journal how this thought of the 'new song' was among the three Scriptures that spoke to him on that fateful 21 May 1738:

'I rose and looked into the Scripture. The words that first presented were, "And now Lord, what is my hope? truly my hope is even in thee." I then cast down my eye, and met, "He hath put a new song in my mouth, even a thanksgiving unto our God. Many shall see it, and fear, and shall put their trust in the Lord".'

See also the text and Note on 144 'My days of waiting ended', based on Psalm 40.

The text was written with our 1992 Christmas card in mind, but in the event it carried instead 20 'Exult, O morning stars aflame'.

Theme	Christmas and Epiphany
Written	at Ruan Minor and Porthoustock, August 1978
Suggested tune	ALFORD by John B. Dykes
Published in	*Hymns for Today's Church*, 1982 to
	(1) CHERRY TREE CAROL (English traditional)
	(2) HOLY APOSTLES by David G. Wilson
	A Song was Heard at Christmas (USA), 1983 to ALFORD
	Hymnal Supplement (USA), 1984 to ALFORD
	Praise God Together, 1984 to CHERRY TREE CAROL
	Covenant Carols (Australia), 1984 to ALFORD
	Carols for Christmas, 1985 (words only)
	Carols for Today, 1986 to HOLY APOSTLES
	Anthem (USA), 1987 by Cindy Johnson
	Anglican Praise, 1987 to HOLY APOSTLES
	Carol Praise, 1987 to HOLY APOSTLES
	Together at Christmas (Australia), 1987 to CHERRY TREE CAROL
	New Hymns and Songs - a Sampler (USA), 1987 to ALFORD
	A Song at Christmas, 1991 (words only)
	The Penguin Book of Carols, 1999 (words only)
	Beneath a Travelling Star, 2001 to ALFORD

These verses were the subject of extensive re-working from the original draft, 'A star there was at Christmas'. There are not now many texts of which I can remember the time of writing in any detail, since they tend to run together in one's mind. But I have clear recollections of picking early blackberries while turning over this text in the process of revision, on a path by the Porthoustock quarry in Cornwall during our family holiday.

Verse 3 begins the progression from Christmas to Calvary. 'Tree' from Deuteronomy 21.23 is so quoted in the New Testament (Galatians 3.13) and the word is used in the apostolic preaching of Peter and Paul (Acts 5.30; 10.39; 13.29). 'Tinsel' is used here not in the common sense of 'mean and tawdry finery', but from its original derivation as 'the sparkling'; applied, for example, by Milton to the goddess of the sea. As such, it helps to throw into stark and dreadful contrast the tree of Christmas, and the tree of shame become the tree of glory.

This hymn was first printed on the official Christmas card of the Lord Mayor of Norwich, Dr J.P. English, in 1978; and because of this did not appear on our family card.

See Index 6.

9 A STONE TO BE THE LINTEL 76 76 D

Theme	Christmas and Epiphany; 'a carol for a carpenter'
Written	at Ford, August 1993
Suggested tune	TYROL (Tyrolean traditional)
	WOODWAY by David W. Music
Published in	*Christian Herald,* 2 December 1995 (words only)
	Supplement '96 (USA), 1996 to WOODWAY
	Anthem (USA), 2001 by Steven R. Janco

Like many other texts, this was nearly discarded in the course of the writing. It was intended for, and used on, our family Christmas card, 1993. No music was in mind when I wrote it (and in the original draft a slightly different metre) so that I was fortunate to find the carol suited to Martin Shaw's tune. Part of the problem lay in the text's strong affinities with Rudyard Kipling's poem 'Cold Iron' *('Gold is for the mistress - silver for the maid -/Copper for the craftsman cunning at his trade...'),* the more so because the original metre was even closer to his.

I later discovered by chance that there is a 'Woodworker's Ballad' by H.E. Palmer in the 1939 edition of the *Oxford Book of English Verse,* which describes how Jesus 'was born in a wooden stable, /and He died on a wooden tree'.

From the Christmas scene of verse 1 the carol moves to the village life of Nazareth; the fields, the hearth and home, the workshop: but all against a background of Roman occupation. Verse 3 speaks of the entry into Jerusalem and the Passion, while the final verse carries us to the theme of resurrection where even the 'wood' which is central to the text is no longer the dead tree felled for timber, but the 'Tree of Life' (Revelation 22.2), symbol of the new creation which is ours in Christ.

10 CAROLS TO CHRIST BE SUNG   664 6664

Theme	Christmas and Epiphany
Written	at Ford, June 2001
Suggested tune	MOSCOW by Felice de Giardini

The gaiety (as it seems to me) of the tune MOSCOW made me wish to use it for a Christmas hymn; and this was written for our 2001 Christmas card. Luke 2 is, of course, the main inspiration, with Matthew 2 for verse 3. Following my usual custom, the text moves in the last verse from New Testament days to our present experience of Jesus risen and ascended.

The line 'Saviour and Son alone' speaks of the uniqueness of Christ, with reference to the repeated 'only begotten' of John, 1 John and Hebrews, literally 'alone begotten', and to verses such as Acts 4.12 following the miracle at the Beautiful Gate.

The final line is intended as a climax to the whole hymn, all of which is framed between the opening and the closing lines with their reference to Christ by name.

11 CHILD OF MARY, NEWLY BORN   77 77 D

Theme	Christmas and Epiphany
Written	at Ruan Minor, August 1990
Suggested tune	ABERYSTWYTH by Joseph Parry LYNCH'S LULLABY from J.P. Lynch's *Melodies of Ireland* (c.1845) arranged by Donald Davison
Translated into	Danish
Published in	*New Songs of Praise 6,* 1991 to LYNCH'S LULLABY (with the suggestion of ABERYSTWYTH as an alternative) *The Popular Carol Book,* 1991 to LYNCH'S LULLABY *Anthem* (USA), 1991 by Austin Lovelace

Anthem (USA), 1993 in *Three Carols for Christmas* by Gordon
    Lawson
Anthem (Denmark), 1994 to LYNCH'S LULLABY in a translation
    by Beata Højlund
Anthem (USA), 1999 by Raymond Guiao
Anthem (USA), 2000 by Bob Moore
Beneath a Travelling Star, 2001 to LYNCH'S LULLABY

Recorded on   *This is Our Joy and This is Our Feast* (USA), 1999 to the music of
    Bob Moore

The tune LYNCH'S LULLABY was published in *Irish Church Praise* (APCK/Oxford 1990)
to a text of mine, 266 'Set your troubled hearts at rest', in an arrangement by Dr Donald
Davison, one of the music editors of the book. On hearing it, and noting the name LUL-
LABY, it seemed appropriate to borrow the tune in writing a hymn for our 1990 family
Christmas card, on which Dr Davison and the publishers allowed me to print the music
with the words.

    The themes of the text are Christ as Light (verse 1); Christ as the incarnate Word (verse 2);
the glory of Christ's cross and resurrection (verse 3): and Christ as our peace (verse 4), one
with us and God with us, bringing joy in reconciliation.

12 CHILD OF THE STABLE'S SECRET BIRTH   89 99 98

Theme	Christmas and Epiphany
Written	at Sevenoaks, February 1969
Suggested tune	FOYE by Valerie Ruddle
	MORWENSTOW by Christopher Dearnley
	NEWTOWN ST LUKE by Anthony Caesar
Published in	*Crusade* magazine, December 1969 (words only)
	English Praise, 1975 to MORWENSTOW
	Christmas Carols, 1978 (words only)
	Hymns for Today's Church, 1982 to (1) MORWENSTOW
	(2) SECRET BIRTH by Norman L. Warren
	A Song was Heard at Christmas (USA), 1983 to MORWENSTOW
	Hymns and Psalms, 1983 to (1) MORWENSTOW (2) FOYE
	The New English Hymnal, 1986 to NEWTOWN ST LUKE
	King New-Born, 1986 to a setting by Anthony Caesar, based on
	NEWTOWN ST LUKE
	Carols for Today, 1986 to (1) MORWENSTOW (2) SECRET BIRTH
	Anthem, 1990 by Valerie Ruddle
	The Penguin Book of Carols, 1999 (words only)
	Praise!, 2000 to FOYE
	Common Praise, 2000 to NEWTOWN ST LUKE
	Beneath a Travelling Star, 2001 to NEWTOWN ST LUKE
Recorded on	*Christmas Music,* 1975 to MORWENSTOW
	The New English Hymnal: Hymns for the Church's Year, 1987 to
	NEWTOWN ST LUKE

Originally written as a poem for our family Christmas card with no thought of a musical setting, this text was noticed by Christopher Dearnley, at that time organist of St Paul's Cathedral, and set to his arrangement of MORWENSTOW, before I was aware that it might become a hymn or carol. It was included in *English Praise,* of which he was himself one of the editors, and recorded by his choir in a selection of Christmas carols. I like to think that had I been aware of this possibility earlier, I might have tidied up the metrical consistency of the verses! My MS shows that verse 2 was written first, and indeed contains the original 'vision' of the text.

See Index 6.

13 CHILL OF THE NIGHTFALL   55 54 D

Theme	Christmas and Epiphany
Written	at Bramerton, December 1979
Suggested tune	BUNESSAN (Gaelic traditional)
	PRIOR LAKE by David Haas
Published in	*The Hymn* (USA), July 1980
	(words only)
	Anthem (USA), 1982 by Hal Hopson
	Anthem (USA), 1982 by Robert Kircher
	Anthem (USA), 1982 by John Horman
	Son of the Highest (USA), 1983 to a tune by Robert Kircher
	A Song was Heard at Christmas (USA), 1983 to BUNESSAN
	Anthem (USA), 1983 by Robert E. Frey
	To be Your Bread (USA), 1985 to PRIOR LAKE
	Gather (USA), 1988 to PRIOR LAKE
	Anthem (USA), 1990 by Gary James
	Christmas Praise (USA), 1991 to a tune by Waldo Beach
	Anthem (USA), 1994 by Hal Hopson
	Gather, 2nd edition (USA), 1994 to PRIOR LAKE
	Anthem (USA), 1977 'Carol of the Stable' by Richard Jeffrey
	Anthem (USA), 1999 by Tom Kendzia
	Rejoice in God (USA), 2000 to CAMILLA by K. Lee Scott
	Beneath a Travelling Star, 2001 to BUNESSAN
Recorded on	*Son of the Highest* (USA), 1983 to the tune by Robert Kircher
	arranged by Dick Bolks
	To be Your Bread (USA), 1986 to PRIOR LAKE
	Singing Assembly (USA), 1988 to PRIOR LAKE
	Breath of Life (USA), 1998 to PRIOR LAKE
	Star Child (USA), 1999 to PRIOR LAKE

Written over the Christmas holiday of 1978, the opening lines place the hymn firmly in the Northern Hemisphere! The rhyming scheme varies in texts sung to the tune BUNES-SAN, and it will be seen that in the second half of each verse it is lines 5 and 6 that here carry the rhyme, rather than (as in 'Morning has broken' or 'Praise and thanksgiving') lines 5 and 7. Though intended to be sung to BUNESSAN the publication of the text in *The Hymn* resulted in a number of anthem settings, and the text continues to attract the attention of (mainly American) composers. The words first appeared on our family

Christmas card in 1979, with a picture of Rectory Meadow, which was then our home. (For the tune RECTORY MEADOW see 33 'O Prince of peace whose promised birth', from the same period.)

14 CHOIRS OF ANGELS, TELL ABROAD   77 77 D

Theme	Christmas and Epiphany
Written	at Ford, May 1996
Suggested tune	RILEY by Martin Shaw
	SALZBURG by Jakob Hintze
	ST EDMUND by Charles Steggall
	ST GEORGE'S WINDSOR by George J. Elvey

This text was written for our family Christmas card, 1996. Unusually, the rhyming scheme provides a different pattern in the two halves of each verse: aabb for lines 1–4; and abab for lines 5–8. Imposed on this is the repetition of the word 'Christ' to begin lines 5, 6 and 7 in each verse, underlining the fact that Christmas is about Christ himself. The final verse carries this repetition into every line.

The theme is familiar, with the emphasis in succeeding verses on the characteristic and contrasting elements of the nativity story: heavenly and human, natives and foreigners, familiar and mysterious, keepers of sheep and watchers of stars. In verse 1 the angels are the heralds, both 'abroad' and 'on high'; they contrast with the earthly 'manger'; with the divine Son; and with the experience of incarnation, a human nature different from their own. The shepherds (verse 2) are the human heirs of the prophetic word; they too are citizens of 'David's town'; they remind us of Christ the Shepherd, Christ the Lamb. The Magi (verse 3) are representatives of the wise, come in search of Wisdom, of kings (by tradition; the New Testament does not say so) in search of a King, of those who follow light to find the Light of the world. Their scientific wisdom, their learning and treasure, contrast with Mary's lullaby. Verse 4, in praise of Christ, is for all of them, and for all of us as well.

15 CHRIST FROM HEAVEN'S GLORY COME   77 77 77

Theme	Christmas and Epiphany
Written	at Ruan Minor, August 1983
Suggested tune	ARFON (Welsh traditional)
	ENGLAND'S LANE (English traditional)
	PETRA by Richard Redhead
Published in	*The Christmas Road: an anthology*, 1986 (words only)

Written for our family Christmas card in 1983, this text sprang from the familiar comparison of Christ unwelcomed and rejected, with those who experience disadvantage and rejection in our world today. But the note, almost of satire, which emerges in this text was certainly not in my mind when I sat down to begin work on it. I include it here for three reasons, even though it seems unlikely to find a place in ordinary congregational worship: (a) because it might make an effective choir or group item, perhaps with an antiphonal 'echo' taking the alternate lines; (b) because the theme is a serious one, easily overlooked in our traditional inheritance of Christmas praise; and (c) because I am conscious that some of my own Christmas hymn-writing is self-contained in its biblical images; and not immediately related to the world we live in. I do not regret this; but items like this present one, and like 228 'Lord, who left the highest heaven' (written more than forty years ago) show the other side of the coin.

Verse 1 is a picture of Bethlehem, verse 2 of Egypt (hence the reference to 'alien race'). In verse 4, the three quotations come from Matthew 21.37, John 19.7, and the words and actions of Pontius Pilate in John 18.38 and Matthew 27.24.

The asterisks between verses 4 and 5 mark, of course, a change of mood (which might well be emphasized by a pause) and in the final verse ironic emphases should be replaced by sincerity of prayer and purpose.

16 CHRIST IS COME! LET EARTH ADORE HIM 87 87 D

Theme	Christmas and Epiphany
Written	at Ruan Minor, August 1989
Suggested tune	ABBOT'S LEIGH by Cyril V. Taylor
	HYFRYDOL by Rowland H. Pritchard
	LUX EOI by Arthur S. Sullivan
Published in	*Anthem* (USA), 1998 by Austin Lovelace
	Beneath a Travelling Star, 2001 to LUX EOI

The three verses of this hymn provide a natural progression from the 'good news' announced in verse 1, to the call to put our trust in Christ (verse 2) and to experience him (verse 3) as Saviour, King and Friend. 'Word' in verse 1 refers to the Word made flesh of which the New Testament declares that 'we beheld his glory' (John 1.14) and yet he 'made himself nothing' (Philippians 2.7, REB), as the last three lines of verse 1 describe.

The text was written for our family Christmas card, 1989, and sung at the 'Farewell Service' in Norwich Cathedral on 20 December 1991, to mark my retirement.

17 COME NOW WITH AWE, EARTH'S ANCIENT VIGIL KEEPING 11 10 11 10 11 10

Theme	Christmas and Epiphany
Written	at Ruan Minor, August 1975
Suggested tune	FINLANDIA by Jean Sibelius
Published in	*The Church of England Newspaper*, 12 December 1975 (words only)
	A Song was Heard at Christmas (USA), 1983 to FINLANDIA
	Carol Praise, 1987 to FINLANDIA
	Mission Praise Supplement, 1989 to FINLANDIA
	Mission Praise Combined, 1990 to FINLANDIA
	A Song at Christmas, 1991 (words only)
	Complete Mission Praise, 1999 to FINLANDIA
	Beneath a Travelling Star, 2001 to FINLANDIA

This text was intended for our 1975 family Christmas card though actually written in August, on our summer holiday, about a verse a day, over three or four days. Line 3 of verse 1 has been criticized as inconsistent with Luke 2.16, 'They came with haste...', but in my own mind I saw the picture of the shepherds feeling their way along a rough and stony track, lit only by the stars; country-dwellers will not, I think, find the description 'creeping' untrue to experience. Peter Cutts wrote a tune to these words to which he gave the name RUAN MINOR, the village of our Cornish holidays.

18 COME, WATCH WITH US THIS CHRISTMAS NIGHT 86 86 D (DCM)

Theme	Christmas and Epiphany
Written	at Ruan Minor, August 1988
Suggested tune	COE FEN by Ken Naylor
	KINGSFOLD (English traditional)
	NOEL (English traditional)
Published in	*Christian Music*, Autumn 1989, to CHRISTMAS NIGHT
	by Robin Sheldon
	Mission Praise Combined, 1990 to a tune by Phil Burt
	Complete Mission Praise, 1999 to the tune by Phil Burt
	Merrily on High, 1999 to a setting by Malcolm Archer
	Beneath a Travelling Star, 2001 to KINGSFOLD

The text is based on a simple structure of: watch with the shepherds; wonder with the wise men; rejoice with the angels; worship with all creation. It was written for our family Christmas card, 1988. The tune NOEL already has associations almost exclusively with Christmas (to 'It came upon the midnight clear') so I was pleased to have two new tunes written to this text (see above). But it would be good to discover a strong under-used tune, already known to congregations; since inevitably Christmas hymns, sung at annual intervals, afford little opportunity to learn new tunes.

19 DONKEY PLOD AND MARY RIDE 77 77 77

Theme	Christmas and Epiphany
Written	at Bramerton, January 1976
Suggested tune	ARFON (Welsh traditional)
	ENGLAND'S LANE (English traditional)
	LUX PRIMA by Charles F. Gounod
	NICHT SO TRAURIG harmonized by J.S. Bach
	PETRA by Richard Redhead
Published in	*The Novello Book of Carols*, 1986 to a tune adapted from THE
	PATH TO THE MOON by Eric H. Thiman, arranged by
	William Llewellyn
	A Song at Christmas, 1991 (words only)
	Beneath a Travelling Star, 2001 to ENGLAND'S LANE

A number of these texts begin with a line or couplet, arrived at with difficulty, sadly rejected and returned to as more satisfying than it had first appeared. This is one such instance. The hymn took its shape round the third line of each verse, linking an eternal truth which is our present possession to some part of the Christmas story that belonged especially to one group of participants. It was written in the days immediately following Christmas, and verse 1 had originally the two lines which now conclude it as part of the verse (i.e. as lines 3 and 4) in the form 'In your hearts draw near to them/On the road to Bethlehem'. The rest of the hymn followed when, on New Year's Day, the line 'Come away to Bethlehem' at last appeared as the key. The text was printed on our family Christmas card for 1976.

20 EXULT, O MORNING STARS AFLAME

888 6

Theme	Christmas and Epiphany
Written	at Ford, August 1992
Suggested tune	CHILDHOOD from *A Student's Hymnal*, 1923
	SAFFRON WALDEN by Arthur H. Brown
Published in	*Deo*, winter 1993, (words only)
	Glory Be (New Zealand), 2000 to SAFFRON WALDEN

This was the carol on our family Christmas card, 1992. An invocation of the morning stars appears in verse 2 of Phillips Brooks' 'O little town of Bethlehem'. The reference comes from Job 38.7 which tells of how when the Lord laid the foundations of the earth 'the morning stars sang together and all the sons of God shouted for joy'.

The text is based on five titles of the Lord Jesus Christ which are emphasised by the use of capital letters: the Child of Bethlehem, the Man of Galilee, the Lamb of Calvary, the Christ in Majesty, and the Prince of Peace.

CHILDHOOD, one of the few successful tunes written by a committee, appears to have been composed by a group of students of the University of Wales under the guidance of Sir Walford Davies, Professor of Music, and to have been first published in *A Student's Hymnal* (Sir Walford Davies, ed., University of Wales 1923).

21 GOLD FOR A MANGER BED

65 65 66 65

Theme	Christmas and Epiphany
Written	at Ford, December 1999
Suggested tune	MONK'S GATE (English traditional adapted by R. Vaughan Williams)

The familiar contrast is stated in the opening lines of the first and last verses: the child in the manger under the stars, and the High King of Ages, reigning eternally in his glory. In between we visit a different contrast; between the King who is also Creator and the incarnate Saviour and seeking Shepherd (Luke 19.10; John 10.11, 15, 16). These titles 'Prince' and 'Potentate' refer to Acts 5.31 ('Prince and Saviour'), Revelation 1.5 ('Prince of the kings of the earth', hence the adjective 'High'), and 1 Timothy 6.15, 'the blessed and only Potentate'; of whom Paul writes (as the closing lines of this text remind us) that he 'alone has immortality' and therefore reigns eternal.

Theme	Christmas and Epiphany
Written	at Iwerne Minster, Dorset in the 1940s; and completed at Sevenoaks in November 1969
Suggested tune	ELLERS by Edward J. Hopkins
	JULIUS by Martin Shaw
	SURSUM CORDA by Alfred M. Smith
Translated into	Chinese
Published in	*News Extra*, December 1976 (words only)
	Songs of Worship, 1980 to SURSUM CORDA
	Hymns for Today's Church, 1982 to SURSUM CORDA
	Carols for Today, 1986 to BEACON HILL by Peter White
	Come Rejoice!, 1989 to BEACON HILL
	The Roy Hopp Hymnary (USA), 1990 to SHANTY CREEK by Roy Hopp
	Sounds of Grace (Hong Kong), 1991 to BEACON HILL (with a Chinese translation)
	Hymns for the People, 1992 to (1) ROUNDHAY by Christopher Norton (2) ELLERS
	Preparing for Worship, 1995 (words only)
	Anthem (USA), 1999 by Bret Heim
	Beneath a Travelling Star, 2001 to ELLERS
Recorded on	*Carols for Today*, 1987 to BEACON HILL by Peter White

This text has its origins earlier than any other in the collection. Two of the three verses were written as a poem, in the late 1940s; and used, I think, as part of a talk. I came across it in 1969; and brought it to completion with the addition of an extra verse. It appeared on our Christmas card that year, but otherwise remained unpublished in any hymnal until 1980, more than thirty years from its inception.

23 HE COMES, THE WAY THAT ALL MAY TREAD
88 86 86

Theme	Christmas and Epiphany
Written	at Ford, December 2000
Suggested tune	BLAIRGOWRIE by Robert. G. Thompson
	DUNSTAN by Joseph Barnby

It was the attractive tune BLAIRGOWRIE which suggested the form of this text, a tune commissioned by the editors of *The Methodist Hymn Book* (1933) as a setting for Edward Shillito's celebration of Spring, 'Away with gloom, away with doubt', to form an Easter carol. Here the same lightness of touch is transferred to Christmas in a carol based on the three titles of John 14.6 which was originally intended for our family Christmas card for 2001. I think myself that (perhaps because of the 'alleluias') it sings better than it reads on the printed page, so that in the event I wrote an alternative, 10 'Carols to Christ be sung', and it was this which appeared on our Christmas card that year.

24 HEAR HOW THE BELLS OF CHRISTMAS PLAY

88 44 88 and Alleluias

Theme	Christmas and Epiphany
Written	at Ruan Minor, August 1985
Suggested tune	LASST UNS ERFREUEN (or EASTER SONG) from *Geistliche Kirchengesang*, Cologne, 1623
Published in	*Carol Praise*, 1987 to EASTER SONG
	Beneath a Travelling Star, 2001 to LASST UNS ERFREUEN

This stirring and historic melody, with its exuberance and rejoicing, seemed to me a good tune for a Christmas hymn. Although at certain times and places the liturgical alleluia ('Praise the Lord') has been especially associated with Easter, it also seems highly appropriate for the nativity. The third and sixth lines are often intended as more than an interjection, so that they become part of the construction of the verse. It is what the bells proclaim (verse 1), what our voices sing (verse 2), what the angels heard (verse 3) and what nature expresses (verse 4).

25 HERE IS THE CENTRE: STAR ON DISTANT STAR

10 10 10 10 10 10

Theme	Christmas and Epiphany
Written	at Bramerton, August 1991
Suggested tune	SONG 1 by Orlando Gibbons
	YORKSHIRE by John Wainwright
Published in	*New Song No 7*, September 1992 to ASHLANDS by Charles Cleall
	Deo, Winter 1993, to ASHLANDS
	Anthem (USA), 1994 'A Carol for Christmas' to HERE AND NOW by Russell Schulz-Widmar
	Sing to the Lord, vol. 4, part 2, 1997 to music by Kevin Norbury
	Sing Glory, 1999 to YORKSHIRE
	Beneath a Travelling Star, 2001 to SONG 1

Written for our 1991 family Christmas card (during the first August for 22 years that we were not at Ruan Minor), the theme of this text is the incarnation of Christ as pivotal in space and time—as indeed the use of the division between BC and AD shows it to be pivotal in human history. Verse 1 has space in mind, with the whole of God's created universe attending to the stable at Bethlehem. Verse 2 takes the same image, but in terms of time-span. Verse 3 celebrates the event, and verse 4 calls us to appropriate rejoicing.

Both the contemporary tunes listed seem to have been written on or soon after reading the text on our Christmas card. HERE AND NOW was sung at the University Church, Austin, Texas on Christmas Eve 1991; and ASHLANDS (named after our new home) was composed in Scotland about a week earlier.

26 HOLY CHILD, HOW STILL YOU LIE

77 77

Theme	Christmas and Epiphany
Written	at Sevenoaks, September 1966

Suggested tune	HOLY CHILD by Michael A. Baughen
	THE CALL by R. Vaughan Williams
Translated into	Chinese; Welsh
Published in	*News Extra*, December 1969 (words only)
	Youth Praise 2, 1969 to HOLY CHILD
	Hear the Bells of Christmas (Manila), 1975 to HOLY CHILD
	Merrily to Bethlehem, 1978 to HOLY CHILD
	Christmas Carols, 1978 (words only)
	Hymns for Today's Church, 1982 to (1) FAIRMILE by David Peacock (2) HOLY CHILD
	A Song was Heard at Christmas (USA), 1983 to HOLY CHILD
	Praise God Together, 1984 to HOLY CHILD
	Covenant Carols (Australia), 1984 to HOLY CHILD
	Carols for Christmas, 1985 (words only)
	Carols for Today, 1986 to (1) RUXLEY by Brian Hoare (2) HOLY CHILD
	Carol Praise, 1987 to (1) HOLY CHILD (2) FAIRMILE
	Church Family Worship, 1988 to (1) HOLY CHILD (2) RUXLEY (3) FAIRMILE
	Hymns & Songs for Worship, 1988 to RUXLEY
	Christmas Carols and their Stories, 1988 (words only)
	Come Rejoice!, 1989 to RUXLEY
	Mission Praise Supplement, 1989 to HOLY CHILD
	Carolling, 1989 (words only)
	Mission Praise Combined, 1990 to HOLY CHILD
	Gaudeamus!, 1990 to HOLY CHILD
	A Song at Christmas, 1991 (words only)
	The Popular Carol Book, 1991 to HOLY CHILD
	Sounds of Grace (Hong Kong), 1991 to HOLY CHILD (with a Chinese translation)
	Hymns for the People, 1993 to HOLY CHILD
	Mission Praise Carol Leaflet, 1995 (words only)
	Supplement '96 (USA), 1996 to RUXLEY
	Youth Challenge Chorus Book (Ireland), 1998 (words only)
	Songs of Fellowship 2, 1998 to HOLY CHILD
	Anthem, (USA), 1998 to HOLY CHILD, arranged by Kurt E. von Kampen
	Singing Faith, 1998 to RUXLEY
	Songs of Victory (Scotland), 1998 to HOLY CHILD
	Complete Mission Praise, 1999 to HOLY CHILD
	Praise!, 2000 to HOLY CHILD
	Beneath a Travelling Star, 2001 to HOLY CHILD
Recorded on	*Christmas Praise*, 1976 to HOLY CHILD
	Covenant Carols (Australia), 1985 to HOLY CHILD
	Gaudeamus, 1992 to HOLY CHILD
	Glorify the Lord (Hong Kong), 1992 to HOLY CHILD (sung in Chinese)
	The Hymn Makers: 'Tell out, my soul', 1996 to HOLY CHILD

If an author is allowed favourite texts, this is one of mine. I recall writing it in the days following the birth of our youngest child; and it appeared on our family Christmas card that same year. No doubt much of its popularity is due to the tune that Michael Baughen wrote for these words.

Besides the anthem listed above, the various hymnals shown include arrangements by David Wilson, Noël Tredinnick, David Iliff, Phil Burt and Michael Paget.

In singing the hymn, a change of mood should be emphasised as between verse 5 and verse 6, where the thought moves from the cross to the resurrection. If a choir is singing, a slight pause is then effective, before the gentle reprise of the final verse.

See Index 6.

27 HOW FAINT THE STABLE-LANTERN'S LIGHT   86 86 (CM)

Theme	Christmas and Epiphany
Written	at Bramerton, December 1979
Suggested tune	BALLERMA by François H. Barthélémon
	ST BOTOLPH by Gordon A. Slater
	THIS ENDRIS NYGHT (English traditional)
	WINCHESTER OLD from Thomas Este's *The Whole Book of Psalmes*, 1592
Published in	*A Song was Heard at Christmas* (USA), 1983 to THIS ENDRIS NYGHT
	The Keys of Bethlehem, 1990 to LANTERN'S LIGHT by Michael Paget
	A Song at Christmas, 1991 (words only)
	Beneath a Travelling Star, 2001 to THIS ENDRIS NYGHT

This text was written, two days before Christmas, round a single word. A few years later, reading an edition of Cecil Beaton's *Diaries* (ed. Richard Buckle, London 1979, p.91), I came across an entry which reminded me of the experience:

'Lunch with Cecil Day Lewis who talked about the way he writes poetry: gets a clue line, writes it in a notebook. Later, when he has a stomach-ache that denotes it is time for him to deliver, the poem is evolved round this line.'

Apart from the stomach-ache, that accurately describes this text; the word was 'candle' in a line originally written a 'A candle through the night' with a note '(better, dark?)'.

28 HOW SILENT WAITS THE LISTENING EARTH   86 86 D (DCM)

Theme	Christmas and Epiphany
Written	at Ford, August, 1995
Suggested tune	COE FEN by Ken Naylor
	KINGSFOLD (English traditional)
	LADYWELL by William H. Ferguson
Published in	*Songs for the Manger* (USA), 1996 to music by Richard Proulx
	New Carols for Christmas (USA), 1997 to music by Richard Proulx

Anthem (USA), 2000 'The Listening Carol' by K. Lee Scott
Beneath a Travelling Star, 2001 to COE FEN

Written for our family Christmas card, the carol is centred on the traditional and yet mysterious participants in the first Christmas, the angel choir, the shepherds of the Bethlehem fields, and the wise men from the East. Angels remind us that our earthly praise of Christ is a tiny part of the eternal worship in the heavens, which is his by right. The shepherds are unaware that the Christmas Child is both Shepherd and Lamb: in verse 2 the Lamb who is our sacrifice, and in verse 4 the Lamb who reigns for ever and ever. The Magi, following Jeremiah 9.23, submit their wisdom and devote their riches to One who is himself both the Word and the Wisdom of God (John 1.1; 1 Corinthians 1.24).

Finally the narrative shifts in time from the first Christmas to that which we celebrate as we sing the carol. By faith, Jesus is more truly known to us than to those who 'bowed to the ground in homage to him' (Matthew 2.11, NEB) and 'opened their treasures and offered him gifts'. As we take upon our lips the Name which is above every name we come 'with every created thing in heaven and on earth and under the earth and in the sea' to pay homage before the throne of God and of the Lamb (Revelation 5.13; 22.3).

The phrase in the opening line, the 'listening earth' comes, though I did not consciously remember it at the time of writing, from a poem by John Meade Falkner. Milton in *Paradise Lost* has listening planets, but Falkner's poem 'After Trinity' concludes:

> 'Kneel with the listening earth,
> Behind the Advent trumpets
> They are singing Emmanuel's birth.'

29 HUSH YOU, MY BABY   55 65 D

Theme	Christmas and Epiphany
Written	at Sevenoaks, June 1968
Suggested tune	HUSHABY by Michael A. Baughen
Published in	*Crusade* magazine, December 1969 (words only)
	Youth Praise 2, 1969 to HUSHABY
	Hear the Bells of Christmas (Manila), 1975 to HUSHABY
	Carols (USA), 1978 to music by H.M. Huffman
	A Song was Heard at Christmas (USA), 1983 to HUSHABY
	Anthem (USA), 1984 by Carlton E. Young
	The Novello Book of Carols, 1986 to music by William Llewellyn
	Carol Praise, 1987 to UPTON VALE by David Peacock
	Anthem (USA), 1998 by Scott M. Hyslop
	Anthem (USA), 1998 by Paul A. Tate
	Beneath a Travelling Star, 2001 to HUSHABY
Recorded on	*Joy to the World: Carols from Worcester Cathedral*, 1989 to the music by William Llewellyn
	Anno Domini: a musical whirlwind tour of the history of Christianity to celebrate the Millennium, 2000 to music by Raymond Smith

Originally written on the back of a Christmas card bearing the words of 26 'Holy child, how still you lie', both texts have obvious similarities in their treatment of a Christmas theme, looking forward through the coming years at the life, and death, of Christ.

Though I have been a reader of Kipling since childhood, it was only in the course of preparing these notes in 1983 that I became conscious of his poem, used as a chapter heading for 'The White Seal' in the *Jungle Book,* beginning 'Oh! hush thee, my baby, the night is behind us.' I must have read it more than once; and lodged it in my unconscious mind. Later still, I heard a recording of the traditional Scottish lullaby, 'Dream Angus', which has the words 'Hush you, my baby, and sleep without fear.'

The tune by Michael Baughen, arranged by David Wilson, had no title in the earliest publication above, but was named HUSHABY in *A Song was Heard at Christmas,* 1983 and I have used this for the tune throughout.

The text appeared on our family Christmas card for 1968.

30 IN OUR DARKNESS LIGHT HAS SHONE   77 77 & Alleluias or 74 74 D

Based on	selected verses from John 1
Theme	Christmas and Epiphany
Written	at Killay, Swansea, June 1997
Suggested tune	EASTER HYMN from *Lyra Davidica,* 1708
	GWALCHMAI by Joseph D. Jones
	LLANFAIR by Robert Williams
Published in	*Evangelicals Now,* December 1997 (words only)
	Supplement 99 (USA), 1999 to LUX by Austin C. Lovelace
	Sing to the Lord, 2000 to MILLER by Ronald Turner
	Beneath a Travelling Star, 2001 to GWALCHMAI

Written for our family Christmas card, 1997, this text takes up some of the thoughts from the Prologue to St John's Gospel: the light in the darkness (verse 5); the creative Word made flesh (verse 3; verse 14); his 'splendour' (J.B. Phillips), full of grace and truth (verse 14). Stanza 3 returns to the promise of John 1.12,13, the 'name and nature' being our inheritance as children (cf. also 2 Peter 1.4).

In the Prologue, the reference is to Christ in his adult manhood (cf. John's testimony, verse 15); so the final stanza of my carol draws on the other Gospels for Christ's infancy, but on John 1.1,2 for Christ as 'God's eternal Word'. The Revised English Bible has in verse 14 'he made his home among us'; and it is in contrast with this that the last line of the carol looks forward to our eternal home with him.

'Alleluia' is a very early liturgical expression of rejoicing, from the songs of the saints in glory (Revelation 19.1,3,4,6). Though more usually linked with Easter and the resurrection, it seems entirely appropriate for Christmas and the incarnation with its message of 'great joy... to all people' (Luke 2.10).

GWALCHMAI, now largely associated with 'Let all the world in every corner sing', was in use in Wales for fifty years before being set to George Herbert's text in the *English Hymnal,* 1906.

The other tunes suggested are both sung primarily at Eastertide, and can well bear introduction at Christmas also.

31 NOT IN LORDLY STATE AND SPENDOUR   87 87 87

Theme	Christmas and Epiphany
Written	at Bramerton, January 1977
Suggested tune	GRAFTON (French traditional) PICARDY (French traditional) RHUDDLAN (Welsh traditional)
Published in	*Carols* (USA), 1978 to PICARDY *The Hymn* (USA), January 1980 to PICARDY *A Song was Heard at Christmas* (USA), 1983 to PICARDY *Covenant Carols* (Australia), 1984 to PICARDY *Carols for Today*, 1986 to RHUDDLAN *A Song at Christmas*, 1991 (words only) *Beneath a Travelling Star*, 2001 to PICARDY
Recorded on	*Covenant Carols* (Australia), 1985 to PICARDY

This text appeared on our family Christmas card in 1997, eleven months after it was written. PICARDY, originally a French carol tune of the 17th century and described in Percy Dearmer's *Songs of Praise Discussed* (Oxford 1933) as 'dignified and ceremonious', well matches the mood of the words. In my own mind I see a break between the note of glory and triumph which concludes verse 3, and the repetition of verse 1 (slightly changed) to close the carol by a return to the stable at Bethlehem.

'Storied' is used here in more than one sense, to convey sumptuousness, grandeur and dignity. Technically it has at least three meanings: divided into storeys (as in a great house), ornamented with scenes from history or legend (paintings, tapestries, etc.), and celebrated or recorded in history or legend.

'Panoplied', literally 'clad in complete armour', is a transliteration of the Greek word in Ephesians 6.11, superbly used by Charles Wesley in his lines from 'Soldiers of Christ, arise':

> 'and take to arm you for the fight
> the panoply of God.'

'Sceptred sway' is a direct borrowing from Portia's famous speech beginning 'The quality of mercy...' in Shakespeare's *Merchant of Venice*. It has remained with me since I played the part in a school production at the age of twelve!

32 O CHILD OF MARY, HARK TO HER   86 86 D (DCM)

Theme	Christmas and Epiphany
Written	at St Anthony-in-Meneage and Ruan Minor, August 1981
Suggested tune	FOREST GREEN (English traditional) KINGSFOLD (English traditional) ST MATTHEW by William Croft
Published in	*Country Way*, Autumn 1998 (words only) *Beneath a Travelling Star*, 2001 to THE AULD HOOSE (Scottish traditional)

This text, which appeared on our family Christmas card in 1982, was begun on a family picnic at St Anthony, a natural tidal harbour in South Cornwall. Line 3 of verse 1, obvious enough in itself, was nevertheless the nucleus about which the rest began to grow. I had in my mind a picture of the child Jesus growing up in a foreign country, and hearing from his mother, even before he was old enough to understand, the songs of home.

Originally the text was conceived in three verses, looking in turn at the son of Mary (humanity), the Son of Man (suffering) and the Son of God (triumph). All that remains of this pattern is the final couplet of verse 3. 'The shadow of a sword' is a reference to the Song of Simeon in Luke 2.35; while in the final lines the sword is seen as a symbol of victory and kingship.

Those who know the poems of Sir John Betjeman will recollect his use of the epithet 'resin-scented' from which mine must have been unconsciously (or at most half-consciously) derived. I read his *Collected Poems* (a number of them Cornish in theme and setting) every summer holiday; and the word comes there at least twice: 'Resin-scented rain' is from 'Love in a Valley' and 'resin-scented air' in 'The Town Clerk's Views'. Robert Frost has pointed out in E.C. Latham, ed., *Interviews with Robert Frost* (London 1967), that in general the intention (which was not mine here) to make use of a special word borrowed from another poet is fraught with danger:

> 'Words that are the product of another poet's imagination cannot be passed off again. They have done their work. One of my abominations is the word "immemorial", which every poet for years has pulled in whenever he has need of a long word. They can't get away with it.'

But I am unrepentant, and indeed pleased with the word in this context, where I believe it is at home.

33 O PRINCE OF PEACE WHOSE PROMISED BIRTH   irregular

Theme	Christmas and Epiphany; the peace of the world
Written	at Bramerton, December 1978
Suggested tune	RECTORY MEADOW by Erik Routley
Published in	*The Hymn* (Hymn Society of America), July 1980 (words only)
	Hymns for Today's Church, 1982 to RECTORY MEADOW
	Word & Music, October/December 1982 to RECTORY MEADOW
	A Song was Heard at Christmas (USA), 1983 to RECTORY MEADOW
	Carols at Christmas, 1985 (words only)
	Carols for Today, 1986 to RECTORY MEADOW
	Carol Praise, 1987 to music by Mary Chandler
	Beneath a Travelling Star, 2001 to RECTORY MEADOW
Recorded on	*Christmas with Haven* (USA), 1988 to music by Walt Harrah

'Prince of Peace' and 'Prince of Life' are both biblical titles, the one of the Messiah who was to come, in Isaiah 9.6; the other of the Lord Jesus Christ who came and died and rose, in Peter's sermon in Acts 3.15. This text employs the word 'Peace' as a salutation, indeed as a prayer, fifteen times from start to finish, and perhaps it is worth quoting the following passage from R.C. Trench's *The Study of Words* (London 1851) to set this in context:

> 'The innermost distinctions between the Greek mind and the Hebrew reveal themselves in the several salutations of each, in the "Rejoice" of the first, as

contrasted with the "Peace" of the second. The clear, cheerful, world-enjoying temper of the Greek embodies itself in the first; he could desire nothing better or higher for himself, nor wish it for his friend, than to have *joy* in his life. But the Hebrew had a deeper longing within him and one which finds utterance in his "Peace". It is not hard to perceive why this latter people should have been chosen as the first bearers of that truth which indeed enables truly to *rejoice*, but only through first bringing *peace*; nor why from them the word of life should first go forth.'

The text was half-written before the device which gives it its special character, the cumulative lines before the final line, began to appear; and when it was printed in *The Hymn* for July 1980 there was still no tune to which it could possibly be sung. Erik Routley, with characteristic generosity, sent me a tune in MS which he had himself composed, and it is to this that the text was set in *Hymns for Today's Church*. The tune is called, as its author called it on his original MS, RECTORY MEADOW: the name of our home in Bramerton, near Norwich, where Erik Routley was once, for a single evening, our guest. The house is indeed a former rectory, and we coined the name *Rectory Meadow* because of the glebe field in front of it. The text appeared on our family Christmas card for 1980, with a reference to Erik Routley's tune.

Frank Colquhoun's collection, *New Parish Prayers* (London 1982) includes a prayer (No. 82) based on this hymn.

34 PEACE BE YOURS AND DREAMLESS SLUMBER   8 33 6

Theme	Christmas and Epiphany
Written	at Ruan Minor, August 1989
Suggested tune	THANET by Joseph Jowett
Published in	*News of Hymnody,* October 1989 (words only)
	Songs of the Manger, 1996 to music by Norman L. Warren
	New Carols for Christmas, 1997 to music by Norman L. Warren
	Beneath a Travelling Star, 2001 to THANET

'Blessings without number' is a phrase used by Isaac Watts in his 'Cradle Hymn', which first appeared in the eighth edition (1727) of *Divine Songs*, his celebrated collection for children first published in 1715. Here too the rhyme is with 'slumber'. I mention this because it is, I think, all that remains of a first draft which read like a direct plagiarism of Watts—though quite unconsciously. I had wanted to write to the tune THANET (commended by Erik Routley) and felt the particular metre and style of the tune very suitable for a Christmas lullaby. My opening line was therefore 'Hush you, Child, lie still and slumber'. I finished the text and put it away.

Ten days later, sitting on the beach on holiday and dipping into my battered copy of the *Oxford Book of English Verse,* I turned to the index to see what, if anything, Quiller-Couch had included of Watts and Wesley. There is in fact in the 1918 edition no Wesley and only two Watts (the 1939 edition does better). One of these is the 'Cradle Hymn' which begins 'Hush! my dear, lie still and slumber...' and continues 'Heavenly blessings without number...'. No doubt I had read it before; but I had no inkling that what I had written was anything but original.

As can be seen, both the metre and the theme of this text differ from 'A Cradle Hymn' (which is a nursery song of some fourteen verses, addressed to any child at bedtime). But the episode remains in my mind as an illustration of how a line that 'sounds right' may in fact do so because it is already in use elsewhere. The final line of verse 2 is an allusion to Philippians 2.7.

35 SEE, TO US A CHILD IS BORN 7 7 or 77 77 or 77 77 D

Based on	Isaiah 9.6, 7
Theme	Christmas and Epiphany
Written	at Ruan Minor, August 1982
Suggested tune	INNOCENTS from William H. Monk's *The Parish Choir*, 1850
	LAUDS by John Wilson
Published in	*A Song was Heard at Christmas* (USA), 1983 to INNOCENTS
	On the Move (Australia), July 1983 (words only)
	Hymnal Supplement (USA), 1984 to INNOCENTS
	Covenant Carols (Australia), 1984 to CARRAMAR by
	M.L. Hemingway
	The Novello Book of Carols, 1986 to LAUDS with an alternative
	arrangement by William Llewellyn
	Anthem (USA), 1987 by Gary Matheny
	Carol Praise, 1987 to REBECCA by David Peacock
	The Baptist Hymnal (USA), 1991 to INNOCENTS
	Twenty New Carols, 1991 to THETFORD by Alan Ridout
	Carols Old and New, 1991 and 1992 to THETFORD
	Junior Praise 2, 1992 to INNOCENTS
	Anthem, 1992 by Alan Ridout
	Catholic Book of Worship III (Canada), 1994 to music by David Haas
	Junior Praise Combined, 1997 to INNOCENTS
	Beneath a Travelling Star, 2001 to INNOCENTS
Recorded on	*The Welkin Rings*, 1991 to THETFORD
	Junior Praise Combined 31, 2000 to INNOCENTS

The plan to try a hymn text based on Isaiah 9 came to me at Christmas 1981; and I entered into my MS book translations of Isaiah 9.6, 7 from the RSV, Knox, the Jerusalem Bible, the Good News Bible, and the RV. AV and NEB would be available to me when I came to write.

Originally planned as a hymn upon the titles of the Messiah in that passage, the text as written took shape quickly, and assumed 'antiphonal' form almost of its own accord, a pattern of singing notably rooted in Old Testament worship (cf. Nehemiah 12.8, 9).

Because the text is in eight couplets, there is a wide variety in the way they can be combined to make verses of 2, 4 or 8 lines each. It is not of course necessary to sing the lines antiphonally, though to do so serves to convey some sense of the complementarity of odd and even lines.

Theme	Christmas and Epiphany; 'a carol for Christmas pilgrims'
Written	at Ruan Minor, August 1986
Suggested tune	See below
Published in	*Carol Praise,* 1987 to THE MARCH OF THE CHRISTMAS PILGRIMS by Michael Paget
	Anthem (USA), 1987 by John Carter
	Lift High your Songs!, 1988 to THE MARCH OF THE CHRISTMAS PILGRIMS
	Anthem (USA), 1988, 'A Carol for Christmas Pilgrims', by Alec Wyton
	The Keys of Bethlehem, 1990 to THE MARCH OF THE CHRISTMAS PILGRIMS
	New Song No 1, September 1990 to BEALL by John Carter

First printed on our family Christmas card for 1986, this text proved popular as a challenge to composers, and I have on file a number of tunes in MS. Though for simplicity I prefer to use first lines rather than titles to identify hymn texts, the title which this acquired, 'A carol for Christmas pilgrims', serves to draw the mind on from the events of Christmas to the demands of everyday discipleship at the start of a new year. This is brought home especially by the concluding verse and the repeated refrain, not now addressed to Mary and Joseph, or to the Magi, but to ourselves.

37 STARS OF HEAVEN, CLEAR AND BRIGHT 77 77 D

Theme	Christmas and Epiphany
Written	at Ruan Minor, August 1983
Suggested tune	MAIDSTONE by Walter B. Gilbert
	SALZBURG by Jakob Hintze
	ST GEORGE'S WINDSOR by George J. Elvey
Published in	*Carols for Today,* 1986 to CUXHAM by John Barnard
	A Song at Christmas, 1991 (words only)
	Beneath a Travelling Star, 2001 to SALZBURG
Recorded on	*Carols for Today,* 1987 to CUXHAM

Written for our family Christmas card, 1983, the key to this text is in the repeated final line of each verse. It is this thought of the contrast between earth and heaven, a gulf nevertheless bridged by the nativity, which unites the whole. In verse 1, it is introduced in terms of the comparison between the stars, which seem to us so unchanging and yet are temporal, and the permanent realities of the eternal world; and also between Bethlehem's stable and the courts of heaven. Verse 2 takes up the same contrast in each of the three couplets. In verse 3 it is seen in the first couplet ('shepherds... angels') and the third ('immortal... earthly'); while in verse 4 the paradox is contained in individual single lines.

In the light of the preoccupation of this text with earth and heaven, I add the derivations of these words from R.C. Trench's *The Study of Words* (London 1861):

'"Heaven" is only the perfect of "to heave" and is so called because it is "heaved" or "heaven" up, being properly the sky as it is raised aloft; while the "earth" is that which is "eared" or ploughed.'

I think myself that the attempt to demythologize religious language (of a kind, for example, which looks 'up' to heaven), whatever logic it may have on its side, is dealing with matters that are more deep-seated in human tradition (and in the human heart, even?) than we care to recognize; and risks destroying our appreciation of those truths which such language manages mysteriously to preserve.

'Enmities' in verse 5 looks to, e.g. Romans 5.10 or Colossians 1.21.

38 THE DARKNESS TURNS TO DAWN   66 86 (SM)

Based on	selected verses of Scripture (see below)
Theme	Christmas and Epiphany
Written	at Sevenoaks, May 1970
Suggested tune	CARLISLE by Charles Lockhart
	SAIGON by Norman L. Warren
	SANDYS (English traditional)
Published in	*Crusade* magazine, December 1971 (words only)
	Psalm Praise, 1973 to SAIGON
	Hymns II (USA), 1976 to SAIGON
	Carols (USA), 1978 to SAIGON
	Hymns for Today's Church, 1982 to SAIGON
	A Song was Heard at Christmas (USA), 1983 to SAIGON
	Anthem (USA), 1985 by John F. Wilson
	Carols for Christmas, 1985 (words only)
	Carols for Today, 1986 to (1) SAIGON (2) SANDYS
	Carol Praise, 1987 to (1) SAIGON (2) SANDYS
	Sing Glory, 1999 to SAIGON
	Grace Praise (New Zealand), 1999 (words only)
	Praise!, 2000 to SAIGON
	Beneath a Travelling Star, 2001 to SANDYS

This text was written for *Psalm Praise* as a 'Christmas Canticle' to echo familiar (and less familiar) words and phrases from a number of New Testament passages describing the incarnation.

In manuscript form, it carried one or more Bible references in the margin beside almost every line as follows:

verse 1: line 1, Isaiah 9.2; line 2, Luke 1.78; lines 3 and 4, Isaiah 9.6
verse 2: line 1, Luke 1.32; line 2, Proverbs 8.22; line 3, Isaiah 7.14; line 4, Luke 19.10
verse 3: lines 1 and 2, John 1.11; line 3, Hebrews 1.3; line 4, Isaiah 7.14
verse 4: lines 1 and 2, 2 Corinthians 8.9; line 3, Philippians 2.7; line 4, John 1.4
verse 5: lines 1 and 2, Philippians 2.7; lines 3 and 4, 1 Peter 2.24
verse 6: lines 1 and 2, Philippians 2.8; lines 3 and 4, Hebrews 1.3
verse 7: line 1, Romans 5.5; line 2, 1 John 4.10; line 3, Luke 2.11; line 4, Luke 1.33

'Dayspring' in line 2 is now admittedly archaic (we should say daybreak) but the OED cites examples from 1300 to 1875, and it retains some familiarity from the translation of Luke 1.78 in the AV and the *Book of Common Prayer*.

The text first appeared on our family Christmas card for 1970.

39 THE HUSH OF MIDNIGHT HERE BELOW   86 88 6

Theme	Christmas and Epiphany
Written	at Ford, December 1998
Suggested tune	HUSTAD by Ronald Turner
	REPTON by C. Hubert H. Parry
Published in	*Hymn Sampler 2000* (USA), 2000 to HUSTAD
	Anthem, 2000 by Valerie Ruddle
	Beneath a Travelling Star, 2001 to REPTON

Written for our family Christmas card, 1999, a year in advance, this text returns to the familiar angels, shepherds and Magi of the Christmas story and seeks to convey something of the mystery and stillness of that 'night of wonder long ago'.

'Immanuel' is a transliteration of the Hebrew, 'with us is God ', and appears in Isaiah 7.14 and 8.8. In the New Testament the word appears only once, in Matthew 1.23, usually (following the Greek) in the form 'Emmanuel' but in J.B. Phillips and in the NIV 'Immanuel' is retained, reflecting the Hebraic origin.

40 THE KING OF GLORY COMES TO EARTH   86 86 D (DCM)

Theme	Christmas and Epiphany
Written	at Ruan Minor, August 1987
Suggested tune	KINGSFOLD (English traditional)
	TYROL (Tyrolean traditional)
Published in	*A New Hymnal for Colleges and Schools* (USA), 1992 to JORDAN
	by William Billings
	Beneath a Travelling Star, 2001 to LADYWELL by William H.
	Ferguson

The title 'King of glory' is familiar to us from the Psalter (24.8, 9, 10) and the hymn book. George Herbert's 'King of glory, King of peace' published as a poem in 1633, found its way, much altered, into an early hymnal of John Wesley's (1737); and, in the form we know it, into the *Yattendon Hymnal* in 1899. But 'Lord of glory' is used by Paul (1 Corinthians 2.8) and James (2.1) as a title for the Lord Jesus Christ; and 'King of glory' is surely legitimate. As in others of my Christmas texts, much use is made of contrasts, detailed in verses 1 and 2, summed up in the first line of verse 3.

The carol was written in the summer of 1987 at Seacroft and used on our family Christmas card the same year.

41 THE LIGHT OF GLORY BREAKS

66 66 88

Theme	Christmas and Epiphany
Written	at Ford, November 2001
Suggested tune	DARWALL'S 148TH by John Darwall
	GOPSAL by G.F. Handel
	MILLENNIUM (source unknown)
	ST GODRIC by John B. Dykes

Written for our Christmas card in 2002, this simple text takes again the three sets of characters of the familiar story of Christmas and Epiphany, the angels, the shepherds and the Magi. Each of the first three verses contains a reference to one of these in turn; and the final verse invites the singers to join them and all creation in praise of what God has done:

> 'Glory to God in the highest,
> and on earth peace...'

I have chosen to personify the wise men as 'Wisdom' in verse 3, not in the usual biblical sense of the divine Wisdom, but to underline the significance of their treasures, presumably far beyond what they themselves could know.

In so far as I had any tune in mind while writing the text, it would be GOPSAL; but I was delighted later to discover the more lively MILLENNIUM, and this is now my personal preference.

42 THE SHINING STARS UNNUMBERED

76 76 887 87

Theme	Christmas and Epiphany
Written	at Ruan Minor, August 1976
Suggested tune	See below
Published in	*A Song was Heard at Christmas* (USA), 1983 to SONG OF THE HOLY SPIRIT (Dutch traditional)
	A Song at Christmas, 1991 (words only)

The text owes its origin to the attractions of the metre, which I first met in *English Praise*, the 1975 supplement to the *English Hymnal*, published in preparation for the *New English Hymnal* some ten years later. The text, 'Upon that Whitsun morning', was by G.B. Timms, chairman of the editorial committee, but neither text nor tune found a place in the *New English Hymnal*; possibly because at that time the term 'Whit-Sunday', used for centuries by the *Book of Common Prayer*, was being superseded by the more biblical but less traditional 'Pentecost'. The tune, DUTCH MELODY, seems to have been published in 1880 by Edmund Sedding to a Christmas carol; and though I know of nothing else to this metre, it is interesting to see what a variety of metres can be found to tunes whose first four lines are 76 76. David Perry's *Hymns and Tunes Indexed* (Croydon 1980) lists more than thirty such, from 76 76 with a chorus (as in ALL THINGS BRIGHT AND BEAUTIFUL) to 76 76 88.

The text first appeared on our family Christmas card, 1978.

Theme	Christmas and Epiphany; the Lord Jesus Christ
Written	at Ford, July 1998
Suggested tune	HANOVER attributed to William Croft
	LAUDATE DOMINUM by C. Hubert H. Parry
Published in	*Beneath a Travelling Star,* 2001 to HANOVER

The text was written for our 1998 family Christmas card. The opening verses draw on passages usually read at Carol Services; but the text moves on to the theme of a suffering Messiah (as in Isaiah 53) and so to the identification of the Promised One with our Lord Jesus Christ. 'Bethlehem' provides a bridge between such prophecies and the gospel accounts (see Micah 5.2; Matthew 2.1), which verse 5 carries forward to our Lord's resurrection and ascension. 'The child of our story' is thus set forth in terms both of the Old Testament and of the New; with the fitting Christmas themes of rejoicing and proclaiming by way of conclusion.

Printed in the form 10 10 11 11, the text contains internal rhymes; but it could equally well be printed as 5 5 6 6 D. The difference can be seen by comparing the text 'O praise ye the Lord' by Sir Henry Baker, as set in *Ancient and Modern New Standard* (No. 203) and in the *New English Hymnal* (No. 427). One effect of the rhyme is to ensure that the caesura falls in the identical place within each line.

---

44 TO THIS OUR WORLD OF TIME AND SPACE 886 D

Theme	Christmas and Epiphany
Written	at Ford, October 1994
Suggested tune	CORNWALL by Samuel S. Wesley
	INNSBRUCK NEW based on Heinrich Isaak
Published in	*Supplement '96* (USA), 1996 to WELLSHIRE by Austin C. Lovelace
	Beneath a Travelling Star, 2001 to CORNWALL

This text was written originally in August 1994 for our family Christmas card; but revised and re-cast that Autumn. The repetition of lines 3 and 6 in every verse is intended to emphasize a sense of destiny (cf. Galatians 4.4), the fulfilling of an eternal purpose, which is the central theme of the hymn, set forth in the opening verse. Incarnation and redemption form the substance of the middle two verses, and resurrection and glory of the last. Here the text depends on a sensitive and distinctive singing of the repeated affirmation, 'to die for us and rise again', to bring home to our hearts that destiny of eternal joy of which Christmas is a foretaste and pledge.

---

45 WHERE DO CHRISTMAS SONGS BEGIN? 77 77 D

Theme	Christmas and Epiphany
Written	at Poldhu Cove and Ruan Minor, August 1984

Suggested tune	ABERYSTWYTH by Joseph Parry
	MAIDSTONE by Walter B. Gilbert
	ST EDMUND by Charles Steggall
	ST GEORGE'S WINDSOR by George J. Elvey

Published in   *Carol Praise*, 1987 to MOUNTAIN HEIGHTS (source unknown)
                    arranged by David Peacock
                Lift High your Songs!, 1988 to THE STREETS OF BETHEHEM by
                    Michael Paget
                Light the Candles round the World, 1989 to THE STREETS OF
                    BETHLEHEM
                Baptist Praise and Worship, 1991 to MOUNTAIN HEIGHTS
                Anthem (USA), 1994 by Bob Moore
                Anthem (USA), 1996 by Malcolm Archer
                Beneath a Travelling Star, 2001 to ST EDMUND

Hymn singers often find themselves asking questions. William Blake's 'Jerusalem' has at least four questions in its opening verse. We sing with Samuel Crossman 'Why, what hath my Lord done ?'; with John Mason, 'How shall I sing that majesty ?'; with Frances Cox, 'Who are these like stars appearing?' and with Benjamin Hanby, 'Who is he in yonder stall ?'. This text sets out to ask the Where, the Who and the Why of the Christmas story. It might have appeared on our family Christmas card for 1984 but was displaced by 15 'Christ from heaven's glory come'.

46 WITHIN A CRIB MY SAVIOUR LAY   888 7

Theme	Christmas and Epiphany; the Lord Jesus Christ
Written	on Arnside Knott, August 1968
Suggested tune	EWHURST by Cecil J. Allen
	GREENWELL by William J. Kirkpatrick
	LORD OF LOVE by Norman L. Warren
Published in	*Youth Praise 2*, 1969 to LORD OF LOVE
	Hymns for Today's Church, 1982 to LORD OF LOVE
	Carol Praise, 1987 to LORD OF LOVE
	Trinity Hymnal, revised edition (USA), 1990 to LORD OF LOVE
	Anthem (USA), 1991 by Walt Harrar
	A Song at Christmas, 1991 (words only)
	Anthem (USA), 1992 'All Glory be to Jesus' by Jeffrey Honoré
	Beneath a Travelling Star, 2001 to EWHURST
Recorded on	*Christmas with Haven* (USA), 1988 to music by Walt Harrah
	A Treasury of Christmas Music (USA), 1994 to music by Walt Harrah

Arnside Knott, where this text originated, is one of my special places. It is a celebrated tree-crowned hillside overlooking the estuary of the river Kent, with fine views of the hills of the Lake District on the distant skyline. I was walking there when *Youth Praise 2* was in preparation, turning over in my mind a number of ideas for hymn texts, including the well-known trio of the crib, the cross and the crown. This simple text was the result.

47 CHRIST OUR REDEEMER KNEW TEMPTATION'S HOUR 10 10 10 10

Based on	Matthew 4.1–11; Luke 4.1–13
Theme	Lent; the Lord Jesus Christ; temptation
Written	at Ford, August 1995
Suggested tune	ELLERS by Edward J. Hopkins
	ST AGNES by James Langran
Published in	*Sing Glory*, 1999 to CARSON NEWMAN by Noël Tredinnick
	Praise!, 2000 to HUNTINGDON by S. Wellens

Although primarily a narrative hymn based on the gospel accounts (which can only have come from the Lord himself), the story, and so the hymn text, carries lessons for the life of the believer: the power of the Scriptures (verses 1 and 2), the life of faith (verse 3) and worship as response to God 's revelation of himself (verse 4).

Verse 1 concludes with a double description of the 'word' which the Lord deploys against his adversary: God's word written (cf. the threefold 'It is written...' of Matthew 4.4, 6, 10) but also retained in the memory (cf. Psalm 119.11 'Thy word have I hid in mine heart, that I might not sin against thee').

The opening lines of verse 2 are meant to provoke thought. Why would the Lord not make bread out of a stone, when he was willing soon afterwards to turn water into wine? I would offer at least a threefold answer: because it is Satan who suggests it; because it would be done for himself and not another; and (chiefly, perhaps) because it would be to contradict the nature God has given to a stone. By contrast, it is in the nature of water to be made wine. God does it every day in every vineyard!

John Betjeman in a gentle criticism offered to two schoolboy poets gave his opinion that 'Tower and hour are not to my nice ear, true rhymes...' (Candida Lycett Green, ed., *John Betjeman: Letters, Volume One 1926–1951*, London 1994, p.416): even so, he occasionally allowed himself similar rhymes in his lesser poems. However Robert Bridges, to take an example from an earlier Poet Laureate, was not afraid to use such a rhyme in one of the Yattendon hymns (with 'power' as the third of the trio); and many other hymn writers have done the same.

48 O CHRIST, WHO FACED IN DESERTS BARE 88 88 88

Theme	Christ the Good Shepherd; Lent; pilgrimage
Written	at Ford, November 2001
Suggested tune	GIESSEN from Gauntlett's *Comprehensive Tune Book*, 1851
	MELITA by John B. Dykes
	ST CATHERINE by Henri F. Hemy

Towards the end of 2001 the episcopal Church of the Good Shepherd, Austin, Texas, commissioned ten new hymns on the theme of Jesus the Good Shepherd, taking account of the cycle of the Christian year. Their Director of Music, Dr Russell Schulz, asked if I would write such a hymn text, with the season of Lent in mind.

The Lenten theme appears most clearly in the opening verse of this text looking back to Christ's temptation, which in the *Book of Common Prayer* and many lectionaries is read traditionally on the first Sunday in Lent. But pilgrimage is also a Lenten theme and can be found in most of the verses of the hymn. Verse 1, besides the allusion to Matthew 4, borrows imagery from Psalm 23. 'The voice', in verse 2, is taken from John 10.3; and the 'other sheep' of the next verse from the same chapter ('scattered' is the word used in Ezekiel 34.12; note also John 1.36 and 14.6). In verse 4, the 'Good Shepherd' is from John 10.15; the 'Great Shepherd' from the closing ascription of the Letter to the Hebrews (13.20) with its reference to the blood of the eternal covenant, coupled with Matthew 20.28. In the final verse, for 'rest' see Hebrews 4; and for 'home at last', Psalm 23.6.

49 NO TRAMP OF SOLDIERS' MARCHING FEET   86 86 D (DCM)

Based on	Luke 19.35–40
Theme	Palm Sunday; the triumphal entry
Written	at Ruan Minor, August 1979
Suggested tune	KINGSFOLD (English traditional)
	LADYWELL by William H. Ferguson
Published in	*Rugby School Service Book and Hymnal,* 1992 to O.B.S. by Peter Crook
	Worship Together (USA), 1995 (words only)
	Hymnal Supplement 1998 (USA), 1998 to KINGSFOLD

Christ's 'triumphal entry' into Jerusalem is recorded by all four evangelists, a fulfilment of Zechariah's prophecy in Zechariah 9.9. The militaristic expectations of verse 1 of this text are an echo of the disciples' bewilderment, as indicated in John 12.16: 'His disciples did not understand this at first; but when Jesus was glorified, then they remembered that this had been written of him and had been done to him'. The phrase 'King of glory' in this context (line 4 of each verse) is a reference to Psalm 24.9. The other repeated line, 'Behold, your King', refers again to Zechariah 9.9, quoted by both Matthew and John ('Behold, thy King cometh unto thee...'), and also, in verse 3 of this text, to John 19.5, the 'Ecce Homo' of much religious painting. Pilate there presents Jesus to the crowd beaten and bleeding and wearing a crown of thorns, in mockery of his kingship, with the words 'Behold, the man!'.

The form 'strown' is recognized by the *Oxford English Dictionary* (1991 ed.) but with the hint that it suggests archaism and dialect. I use it here to facilitate the rhyme, as (I suppose) did A.E. Housman in his celebrated 'In summertime on Bredon' *(A Shropshire Lad,* XXI) where 'strewn' appears in an early draft, but was later rejected.

Line 3 of verse 4 is a direct reference to Philippians 2.7, and the 'Hosanna' of line 5 to the greetings of the crowd in Matthew 21.9.

50 IN THE SAME NIGHT IN WHICH HE WAS BETRAYED   10 10 10 10 10 10

Based on	Luke 22.39–62
Theme	Passiontide; Maundy Thursday
Written	at Ford, December 1997
Suggested tune	SONG 1 by Orlando Gibbons
	UNDE ET MEMORES by William H. Monk
Published in	*Cantate Domino,* 2000 to TRAITOR'S KISS by Martin Setchell
	The Poetic Bible, 2001 (words only)

This text originates in a request from William Llewellyn, composer, editor and friend. He was writing what he called 'Lenten Music', a cantata for passiontide using Luke's Gospel, and interweaving passages of narrative with spirituals such as 'Were you there when they crucified my Lord?' and with a number of hymns and verses on this theme taken from my *Lift Every Heart* and subsequent collections. He found himself in need of a metrical solo or congregational hymn to come at the end of Luke's account of Gethsemane and of Peter's denial, and asked if I would write one. This is the text that resulted from my meditation.

As can be seen the first three stanzas are narrative, visually imagined. There is a break following them, since all those who hear them will know very well what happened in the courtyard, and can reflect upon it rather than be given words in which to recount the sad story. When the verse resumes it is no longer narrative but prayer, recognizing Peter's position as our own; with the recognition leading to line 4 (a deliberate echo, for those who care to recognize it, from Tennyson's 'In Memoriam') and so to line 6—the only possible conclusion.

51 A PURPLE ROBE, A CROWN OF THORN   86 86 (CM)

Theme	Passiontide; the cross of Christ
Written	at Sevenoaks, October 1968
Suggested tune	A PURPLE ROBE by David G. Wilson
Translated into	Chinese
Published in	*Youth Praise 2*, 1969 to A PURPLE ROBE
	Thirty Hymns, 1972 (words only)
	Anglican Hymn Book Supplement, 1978 (words only)
	A Purple Robe, 1982 to A PURPLE ROBE (five choral settings in Chinese, translated and arranged by S. Y. Suen)
	The Singing Church (USA), 1985 to MARTYRDOM by Hugh Wilson
	The Lion Easter Book, 1987 (words only)
	Supplement to Lutheran Hymnal (Australia), 1987 to MY SAVIOUR by Joanna Booth
	Lift High your Songs!, 1988 to MARCH OF TRIUMPH by Michael Paget
	Songs of Rejoicing (USA), 1989 to GRAND VALLEY by Roy Hopp
	Come Rejoice, 1989 to A PURPLE ROBE
	The Worshiping Church (USA), 1990 to A PURPLE ROBE
	The Roy Hopp Hymnary (USA), 1990 to GRAND VALLEY
	The Baptist Hymnal (USA), 1991 to SERENITY by William V. Wallace
	Sounds of Grace (Hong Kong) 1991 to A PURPLE ROBE (with a Chinese translation)
	Worship Songs Ancient & Modern, 1992 to A PURPLE ROBE
	Junior Praise 2, 1992 to A PURPLE ROBE
	Hymns for the People, 1993 to A PURPLE ROBE
	Sing we Merrily, 1995 to BANGOR from William Tans'ur's *Harmony of Syon*, 1735
	Remember Jesus, 1995 (words only)
	Worship Together (USA), 1995 to A PURPLE ROBE

The Covenant Hymnal (USA), 1996 to A PURPLE ROBE
Junior Praise Combined, 1997 to A PURPLE ROBE
Anthem (USA), 1997 to music by Bret Heim
Sing Glory, 1999 to A PURPLE ROBE
Complete Anglican Hymns Old & New, 2000 to A PURPLE ROBE
Praise!, 2000 to A PURPLE ROBE
Spring Harvest Praise, 2001 to A PURPLE ROBE
Worship & Rejoice (USA), 2001 to A PURPLE ROBE
Methodist Hymns Old & New, 2001 to A PURPLE ROBE

Recorded on   Here is Youth Praise, 1975 to A PURPLE ROBE
Hymns for Today's Church, 1982 to A PURPLE ROBE
Glorify the Lord (Hong Kong), 1992 to A PURPLE ROBE
    (sung in Chinese)
The Rock Communion, 1994 to A PURPLE ROBE
Junior Praise Combined 21, 1999 to A PURPLE ROBE

This simple passiontide text was written for *Youth Praise 2*, where David Wilson contrived a tune which takes account of the change in the metrical stresses which occur in verse 3, so making this a point of transition between the Via Dolorosa and Christ's death for sinners. Some books have found it better to omit that verse (where the tune A PURPLE ROBE may be better suited to a choir than a congregation), and indeed with some tunes it is essential to do so; others omit it to avoid the reference to the generic 'man', but David Wilson's tune has stood the test of time; and I naturally prefer to see the text printed and sung as a whole.

See Index 6.

52 APPROACH WITH AWE THIS HOLIEST PLACE   86 86 88

Theme   Passiontide; the cross of Christ
Written   at Ruan Minor, 1984
Suggested tune   AUCH JETZT MACHT GOTT from Koch's *Choralbuch*, 1816
                   CONQUEST by Donald S. Barrows
                   PALMYRA by Joseph Summers
Published in   *Grace Praise* (New Zealand), 1999 (words only)
                   Praise!, 2000 to PALMYRA

The 'empty cross, empty grave', of verse 5, line 5, I owe to Dr J.A. Motyer's book *The Message of Philippians* (Leicester 1984) quoting some words of Bishop Handley Moule who wrote to a nephew in 1919:

'I have often prayed that daily, and to the end, I may live as in a tent pitched between the Cross and the Grave of our Lord—the *empty* Cross, symbol and seal of His finished work of sacrifice and redemption, the *empty* grave, likewise the evidence and pledge of His eternal victory for us over the last enemy, death, and of our life hid with Him in God.'

53 BEHOLD, AS LOVE MADE MANIFEST 86 86 (CM)

Theme	Passiontide; the cross of Christ; grace
Written	at Ruan Minor, August 1983
Suggested tune	BALLERMA by François H. Barthélémon
	BELMONT from William Gardiner's *Sacred Melodies*, 1812
	ST MAGNUS by Jeremiah Clarke

The theme of this text is what the cross of Christ *reveals,* though this is inseparably linked with the fact that it *redeems.* These two emphases come together in the words 'sacrifice' and 'sign' which conclude the first and the last verses. Starting from John the Baptist's 'Behold, the Lamb of God...' (John 1.36), the significance of the cross in terms of grace, love, mercy and victory forms the subject of the four central verses, returning to the declaration of 1 John 4.10 (AV) 'Herein is love...'

Verse 2 contains an allusion to the prayer 'O Jesus, Master Carpenter of Nazareth, who on the cross through wood and nails didst work man's whole salvation...' It appears in a number of collections, but I do not know its original source.

54 DEAR LORD, WHO BORE OUR WEIGHT OF WOE 86 86 (CM)

Theme	Passiontide; penitence
Written	at Bramerton, October 1976
Suggested tune	BANGOR from William Tans'ur's *Harmony of Syon*, 1735
	BELMONT from William Gardiner's *Sacred Melodies*, 1812
	KILMARNOCK by Neil Dougall
Published in	*Anthem*, 1995 by Ian Kellam

This hymn was written at the request of the Roman Catholic International Commission on English in the Liturgy, who were seeking hymns to accompany their revision of the *Rite of Penance.* It did not in the event prove to be what they wanted; and verse 4 has always stood for me as an illustration of how difficult it is for a writer to be his own critic. I find the verse satisfying; and the parallelism and inversion of the first two lines meaningful. But I know this is not a general view, as compared, for example with the directness of the final two lines of the text. Whatever the merits of the hymn, the truths of which it speaks seem to me the most precious, and the nearest to the heart, of our Christian faith.

55 UPON A TREE THE SIN OF MAN 86 86 (CM)

Theme	Passiontide
Written	at Iwerne Minster, April 1949
Suggested tune	BANGOR from William Tans'ur's *Harmony of Syon*, 1735
	STRACATHRO by Charles Hutcheson
Published in	*British Weekly*, 22 November 1951 (words only)
	All Things are Thine, 1992 to music by Alan Ridout

This text, among the earliest in this collection, belongs to the days when I thought hymn writing a closed book to me, since I was (and remain) so unmusical. It was simply one of a number of poems on Christian themes which I wrote throughout my student days, and published in journals during my curacy to supplement a slender income. It can be found in *Lift Every Heart* in the section of 'Early Poems', and it was from here that Alan Ridout discovered the text and used it as the basis of an anthem 'for choirs which are short of men'. Like some other texts which are closer in style to anthems or cantatas rather than to congregational hymns, there are not many occasions when this would find usefulness as a hymn. It is included here because it happened to attract the attention of an established composer.

56 WE TURN IN FAITH TO CHRIST THE LAMB OF GOD — 10 4 10 4 10 10

Theme	Passiontide; redemption; response to the gospel
Written	at Bramerton, August 1991
Suggested tune	ALBERTA by William H. Harris
	SANDON by Charles H. Purday

This text owes its general theme and structure to the *Agnus Dei*, in the version written by the late Dr J.G. Cuming for the International Consultation on English Texts. It differs by being in the form of statement or declaration rather than petition, until the final stanza. The prayer for peace with which the *Agnus Dei* concludes is here amplified to include explicitly that peace with God which is the fruit of Christ's finished work; as well as peace with neighbours and inner peace, all of which are bound up in 'the life of heaven'.

57 ALL SHALL BE WELL — 46 46 or 10 10

Theme	Eastertide
Written	at Ruan Minor and St Anthony-in-Meneage, April 1976
Suggested tune	SONG 46 by Orlando Gibbons
Published in	*News Extra*, April 1977 (words only)
	Hymns for Today's Church, 1982 to (1) SONG 46 (2) EASTER SKIES by John Marsh
	Anglican Praise, 1987 to SONG 46
	Supplement to Lutheran Hymnal (Australia), 1987 to JESUS ALIVE by Joanna Booth
	The Worshiping Church (USA), 1990 to SONG 46
	Baptist Praise and Worship, 1991 to EASTER SKIES
	Breaking Bread (USA), 1993 to music by John Foley
	Hymns for the People, 1993 to SONG 46
	Breaking Bread (USA), 1994 to music by John Foley
	Journeysongs (USA), 1994 to music by John Foley
	Breaking Bread (USA), 1995 to music by John Foley
	Today's Missal, Holy Week/Triduum (USA), 1996 (shortened) to music by John Foley

Today's Missal, Easter/Pentecost (USA), 1996 (shortened) to music
    by John Foley
Breaking Bread (USA), 1997 to music by John Foley
Glory and Praise (USA), 1997 to music by John Foley
Today's Missal, Easter/Pentecost (USA), 1998 (shortened) to music
    by John Foley
Common Praise (Canada), 1998 to SONG 46
Breaking Bread (USA), 1999 to music by John Foley
Sing Glory, 1999 to SONG 46

This text was written in Easter week on holiday in Cornwall, much of it walking beside Carne Creek, an estuary of the Helford River. The words echo a meditation of the Lady Julian of Norwich in the thirty-first chapter of her *Revelations of Divine Love*: 'All shall be well, and all shall be well, and all manner of thing shall be well'—though they are not there applied specifically to Christ's resurrection. I accept the comment that the hymn might read (and indeed, sing) better in 10 10 rather than in 4 6 4 6, but I prefer to print it as it appears, emphasizing the repetition of the key line which appears in every verse.

For 'Sun of Righteousness' see Malachi 4.2; for verse 4 see Romans 6.9 and 2 Timothy 1.10.

See Index 6.

58 AND SLEEPS MY LORD IN SILENCE YET   88 88 88

Theme	Eastertide; especially Easter Eve
Written	at Durgan and Ruan Minor, August 1982
Suggested tune	EISENACH by Johann H. Schein
	MOZART by W. A. Mozart
	SUSSEX CAROL (English traditional)
Published in	*News of Hymnody,* January 1983 (words only)
	Word & Music, January/February/March 1984, to EISENACH
	Word & Music, March/April 1985, to WAKEHURST by Norman
	L. Warren

A number of hymns begin with the word 'And' (for example, Charles Wesley's 'And can it be' or William Bright's 'And now, O Father') and this seems to have been one of the starting points of this text. Durgan is a tiny cluster of houses in a little bay on the Helford River; and the first four lines—in a rather different form—came into my head over a picnic supper on the beach. The device of question rather than affirmation, and the picture of the Lord still within the tomb, makes the text specially appropriate for Easter Eve; but the final verse requires a note of triumph and assurance suitable for other Easter occasions.

59 BY LOVING HANDS THE LORD IS LAID   86 88 6

Theme	Eastertide
Written	at Bramerton, March 1975
Suggested tune	REPTON by C. Hubert H. Parry

Published in   *News Extra,* April 1976 (words only)

My original fair copy is dated 29 March 1975; and the text was first published under the title EASTER in the parish magazine inset *News Extra.* Lines 3 and 4 of verse 2 then read:

> 'With none to see their footsteps pass
> As cold as dew across the grass...'

I have been sorry to lose the impression of the icy dew of early morning, while believing that the present version (revised at the request of the editor of a hymnal as yet unpublished) is the better.

See Index 6.

60 CHRIST IS RISEN AS HE SAID   77 77

Theme	Eastertide
Written	at Ruan Minor, August 1987
Suggested tune	CHRIST IS RISEN AS HE SAID by John Carter
	INNOCENTS from William H. Monk's *The Parish Choir,* 1850
Published in	*Songs of Rejoicing* (USA), 1989 to SWEETLY JOIN by Deborah Holden-Holloway
	Anthem (USA), 1991 by John Carter
	Church Hymnary (Ireland), 2000 to CHRIST IS RISEN AS HE SAID
Recorded on	*The Hymn Makers: 'Tell out, my soul',* 1996 to CHRIST IS RISEN AS HE SAID
	Church Hymnal: love of God, life of faith (Ireland), 2000 to CHRIST IS RISEN AS HE SAID

In August, 1982 I wrote a Christmas antiphon in this metre, 35 'See, to us a child is born'; and this is intended as a companion piece. It is suggested that alternate lines might be sung by choir or soloist, with the following line by the congregation; to enhance the effect, these pairs of lines begin with the same word. Besides the resurrection accounts in the Gospels, biblical allusions include Colossians 1.18, Revelation 17.14, Philippians 2.10,11, Romans 8.2, 2 Corinthians 2.14, Luke 19.10.

61 COME AND SEE WHERE JESUS LAY   77 77 D

Based on	Matthew 28.6,7
Theme	Eastertide; mission and evangelism
Written	at Poldhu and Ruan Minor, August 1986
Suggested tune	EVERLASTING LOVE by James Mountain
	ST EDMUND by Charles Steggall
	ST GEORGE'S WINDSOR by George J. Elvey

Published in   *Songs of Rejoicing* (USA), 1989 to WHERE JESUS LAY by Don
                      Robinson
                      Praise!, 2000 to SIGNIFER by A. M. Goodhart

The structure of this hymn empasizes the two imperatives of verses 6 and 7 in Matthew
28. 'Telling' is to be based on first-hand evidence of 'seeing'. John Stott has vividly
described (in *Basic Christianity,* second edition, Leicester 1971, p.53) three characteristics
of these discarded graveclothes:

> 'First he saw the cloths "lying". The word is repeated twice, and the first time
> it is placed in an emphatic position in the Greek sentence. We might translate,
> "He saw, as they were lying (or collapsed), the linen cloths." Next, the head
> napkin was "not... with the linen cloths but... in a place by itself". This is
> unlikely to mean that it had been bundled up and tossed into a corner. It lay
> still on the stone slab, but was separated from the body cloths by a noticeable
> space. Third, this same napkin was "not lying... but wrapped together...". This
> last word has been translated "twirled". The Authorized Version "wrapped
> together" and the Revised Standard Version "rolled up" are both unfortunate
> translations. The word aptly describes the rounded shape which the empty
> napkin still preserved.'

This is the image which informs lines 5 and 6 of the first verse of the hymn.

62 FROM AFAR A COCK IS CROWING   885 D

Theme	Eastertide
Written	at Ruan Minor, August 1983
Suggested tune	see below

The text arose from a desire to write on the theme of Easter, and to experiment with short
lines containing internal rhyme. There are 15 rhyming pairs in these 3 verses, six with a
feminine rhyme. The first couplet (now lines 4 and 5 of verse 1) set the shape for the
whole.

Line 3 of verse 2 is a reference to our Lord's numerous prophecies to his disciples of
his own resurrection (e.g. Matthew 20.19, though more are recorded in Mark and Luke).

Line 5 of verse 3 takes up the references in Colossians (2.12; 3.1) to the people of God
as 'risen with Christ'. Line 6 is based on 2 Timothy 2.12 and numerous references in the
book of Revelation.

Although there seems to be no existing hymn-tune to the metre 885 D (in striking contrast to 886 D) I still hope that one may be written which will catch an editor's eye.

63 JESUS, PRINCE AND SAVIOUR   65 65 D and refrain

Theme	Eastertide; the Lord Jesus Christ
Written	at Ruan Minor, August 1974
Suggested tune	ST GERTRUDE by Arthur S. Sullivan
Translated into	Chinese, French, Spanish

Published in	*News Extra,* March 1975 (words only)
	Songs of Worship, 1980 to ST GERTRUDE
	Declare His Glory, 1981 to ST GERTRUDE
	A Supplement to Congregational Praise, 1982 (words only)
	Making Melody, 1983 to ST GERTRUDE
	Hymns for Praise and Worship (USA), 1984 to WYE VALLEY by James Mountain
	Mission Praise 2, 1987 to ST GERTRUDE
	Mission Praise Combined, 1990 to ST GERTRUDE
	Songs of Celebration, 1991 to ST GERTRUDE (with translations into French by Ann Maouyo and into Spanish by Felicity Houghton)
	Sounds of Grace (Hong Kong), 1991 to BARN RISE by Daniel K.L. Chua (with a Chinese translation)
	Junior Praise 2, 1992 to ST GERTRUDE
	Hymns Old and New, 1996 to ST GERTRUDE
	New Hymns and Worship Songs, 1996 to ST GERTRUDE
	Junior Praise Combined, 1997 to ST GERTRUDE
	Songs of Victory (Scotland), 1998 to ST GERTRUDE
	Complete Mission Praise, 1999 to ST GERTRUDE
	Sing Glory, 1999 to ST GERTRUDE
	Complete Anglican Hymns Old & New, 2000 to ST GERTRUDE
	Praise!, 2000 to ARMAGEDDON (German traditional)
	New Hymns and Worship Songs, 2001 to ST GERTRUDE
	Methodist Hymns Old & New, 2001 to ST GERTRUDE
Recorded on	*King Forever,* 1987 to NORFOLK PARK by Sir Henry Coward
	Junior Praise Combined 28, 1999 to ST GERTRUDE

This text was written from the conviction that Easter is the most suitable time for Christian triumph; and that in Sir Arthur Sullivan's ST GERTRUDE we have a tune of stirring power, wedded to words by Sabine Baring-Gould whose 'militarism' sometimes limits their usefulness. Both tune and words have stern critics as well as stalwart advocates.

'Onward, Christian soldiers,' written in 1864, was first sung to a tune by Haydn from his 'Imperial' Symphony. ST GERTRUDE was published in 1871, named after the hostess (Mrs Gertrude Clay-Ker-Seymer) in whose house Sullivan was staying at the time he wrote it. Tune and words, therefore, were not always as inseparably linked as they appear today.

The phrase 'Prince and Saviour' comes from Acts 5.31 when Peter and the apostles are bearing witness to the high priest about the resurrection and exaltation of Christ.

Lines 3 and 4 of the last verse embody the ancient Easter greeting of the Church. I have sometimes thought how effectively they might be sung by giving line 3 to be sung by, say, choir only; with line 4 as a congregational response.

Three lines in verse 1 which had in practice proved confusing have been changed in this definitive version.

See Index 6.

Based on	John 21
Theme	Eastertide; the lakeside
Written	at Poldhu Cove and Ruan Minor, August 1981
Suggested tune	ALL SAINTS (German traditional) IRBY by Henry J. Gauntlett
Published in	*Symphony,* Spring/Summer 1983 (words only) *Moravian Book of Worship* (USA), 1995 to IRBY *Hymnal Supplement 1998* (USA), 1998 to ALL SAINTS

Jesus' resurrection appearance to the disciples at the lakeside, on the shore of the Sea of Galilee, occupies the whole of the final chapter of St John's Gospel. It is a story of which Professor Tasker has written 'Few passages in the New Testament have a more numinous quality, or are so haunting in their beauty; and there can be few readers who remain insensitive to the awe and mystery which pervade it' (see R.V.G. Tasker, *The Gospel according to St John,* London 1960, p.229). It is a passage to which I return year by year in the days after Easter; and one on which I had wanted to write a hymn for some years before completing this text.

The hymn is narrative in form for the first three verses; and in the last two it relates the experience of the disciples to our own experience of Christ's presence today, finding in him forgiveness for the past (surely the fire on the beach must have reminded Peter of the fire in the High Priest's courtyard), bread for the new day, a renewed call to work for him, and the assurance of his continuing friendship. Indeed, I recall the pleasure with which I found a final couplet to conclude the hymn and to sum up the meaning of this story of dawn on the beach, with its message of resurrection life. For me, this chapter fitly concludes John's Gospel by opening a door between his day and our own.

65 NOW IS CHRIST RISEN FROM THE DEAD   88 44 88 and Alleluias

Theme	Eastertide
Written	at Ford, April 1992
Suggested tune	LASST UNS ERFREUEN (EASTER SONG) from *Geistliche Kirkengesang,* Cologne 1623
Published in	*Honour His Name,* 1993 to music by Alan Ridout *Anthem* (USA), 1995 'An Easter Hodie' by Donald Hustad *New Mission Praise,* 1996 to LASST UNS ERFREUEN *Complete Mission Praise,* 1999 to LASST UNS ERFREUEN

'Alleluia', translated as 'Praise the Lord', comes in a number of the Psalms, and four times in Revelation 19 as part of the heavenly song. Because it expresses joy, the Christian church has long linked its use in liturgy with Eastertide. EASTER SONG (also known as LASST UNS ERFREUEN and as ST FRANCIS) with its repeated Alleluias was originally associated with an Easter text; and more recently has been set to others on the same theme, for example to 'I know that my Redeemer lives' by Samuel Medley, or to 'Light's glittering morn bedecks the sky', a translation from the Latin by J. M. Neale. These texts come to us from the 18th and 19th centuries respectively, whereas the tune itself is 17th century.

The opening line of each stanza will have a familiar ring to those who recognize it as a direct quote from the AV version of 1 Corinthians 15.20, the opening of the set lesson at the Order for the Burial of the Dead in the *Book of Common Prayer*.

I have marked the text as 88 44 88, to fit EASTER SONG. But the Alleluias are not an integral part of the sense and meaning (as they are, for example, in 24 'Hear how the bells of Christmas play') and the text can therefore be sung, without the Alleluias, to tunes in Long Metre.

66 OUR RISEN LORD, OUR KING OF KINGS   888 and Alleluias

Theme	Eastertide; the Lord Jesus Christ
Written	at Ford, August 1995
Suggested tune	VICTORY adapted by William H. Monk
	VULPIUS from M. Vulpius's *Gesangbuch,* 1609
Published in	*Glory Be* (New Zealand), 2000 to O FILII ET FILIAE
	(French traditional)
	Anthem (USA), 2001 by Bob Moore

The metre lends itself to the theme of Christ's triumph over death, as in John Mason Neale's translation from the French, 'O sons and daughters, let us sing!' or Francis Pott's translation from the Latin, 'The strife is o'er, the battle done.' It was also used by Cyril Alington for his 'Good Christian men, rejoice and sing!' which was written for *Songs of Praise,* 1925. It may be, therefore, that VULPIUS (to which these words were written) should now give place, for a new text such as this, to a new and 21st-century tune. The structure of the hymn is designed to begin with praise of the risen Lord, and then to rehearse his incarnate life using titles which relate to his birth (verse 2), his life and ministry (verse 3), his death and burial as the one, perfect and sufficient sacrifice (verse 4), and his rising to be with his people always. Alleluia!

67 WHO IS THERE ON THIS EASTER MORNING   98 98 98

Based on	John 20.1–18
Theme	Eastertide
Written	at Ruan Minor, August 1980
Suggested theme	FRAGRANCE (French traditional)
	NEUMARK by Georg Neumark
Published in	*On the Move* (Australia), October 1981 (words only)
	Songs of Rejoicing (USA), 1989 to FRAGRANCE
	Voices United (Canada), 1996 to FRAGRANCE
	Common Praise (Canada), 1998 to QUELLE EST CETTE ODEUR
	(FRAGRANCE)

In December 1979 at a Carol Service in Norwich Cathedral it occurred to me that the tune FRAGRANCE would lend itself to words rooted more strongly in the doctrine of the incarnation than is the traditional text, 'Whence is that goodly fragrance flowing'. When

I examined this thought again, I realized that this is what Frank Houghton had done with his carol 'Thou who wast rich beyond all splendour'. Unwilling to leave the tune, I turned instead to the theme of Easter, and especially to John 20.1–18.

The hymn was first sung in May 1983, in Westminster Abbey, during one of their regular lunch-hour Services entitled 'Come and Sing'.

68 CHRIST HIGH-ASCENDED, NOW IN GLORY SEATED   11 11 11 6

Theme	Ascensiontide; mission and evangelism
Written	Ruan Minor, August 1983
Suggested tune	CHRISTE SANCTORUM (French traditional)
Published in	*The Worshiping Church* (USA), 1990 to CHRISTE SANCTORUM
	Daily Office, Community of the Holy Name, 1990 (words only)
	Christian Worship: a Lutheran Hymnal (USA), 1993 to CHRISTE SANCTORUM
	Moravian Book of Worship (USA), 1995 to CHRISTE SANCTORUM
	Worship & Rejoice (USA), 2001 to CHRISTE SANCTORUM

I went on holiday in August 1983 hoping to write a hymn suitable for Ascensiontide, having consulted the Biblical passages in Acts and the Gospels, and in 1 Corinthians, Ephesians, Colossians and 1 Peter, as well as certain Old Testament references. The subject is one not over-represented in some hymnals, particularly for churches which wish to observe both Ascension Day and (as in the Church of England calendar) the Sunday after Ascension.

Ascensiontide is inseparable from the giving of the Great Commission and the promise of the Spirit. The first is recognized in the five-times-repeated final line which ends each verse, as well as more specifically in verses 2 and 3. The final verse looks forward to Pentecost.

The first line of verse 5 refers expressly to the final verse of St Luke's Gospel with its surprising testimony that after 'he was parted from them' they returned 'with great joy'—so exactly the contrary to what, by any human reckoning, the circumstances would suggest.

The tune suggested, CHRISTE SANCTORUM, is metrically 11 11 11 5; however, it will be found suitable for this text by allowing two full syllables in the penultimate bar.

69 HEAVEN'S THRONE ASCENDING   665 665 786

Theme	Ascension; Eastertide
Written	at Ford, April 1994
Suggested tune	JESU, MEINE FREUDE by Johann Crüger
Published in	*New Mission Praise*, 1996 to JESU, MEINE FREUDE
	Complete Mission Praise, 1999 to JESU, MEINE FREUDE

The Hymn Society in the United States and Canada instituted a 'hymn search' during 1994 to find new texts to the tune JESU, MEINE FREUDE with its unusual metre. I was writing at Eastertime, which accounts for the choice of theme.

Romans 6.9 speaks of death as 'having no more dominion'. Hebrews 1.3 emphasizes Christ seated in glory, after the work of redemption is done. 'Bought with a price' (verse 1, line 9) is the theme of e.g. 1 Corinthians 6.20; while Ephesians 6.12 speaks of 'powers' of evil, and Colossians 1.13 of the 'power' of darkness. Finally Isaiah 42.7, a Messianic prophecy, links the ending of darkness with release from prison.

70 RISEN LORD IN SPLENDOUR SEATED 87 87 87

Theme	Ascensiontide
Written	at Ford, January 2000
Suggested tune	REGENT SQUARE by Henry T. Smart
	RHUDDLAN (Welsh traditional)
	WESTMINSTER ABBEY adapted from an anthem by Henry Purcell
Published in	*Cantate Domino,* 2000 to MAGISTER by Martin Setchell

Shortly after my time among them came to an end, the trustees of the Jerusalem Trust invited me to write a new hymn for the occasion of a major Christian festival, to be sung at a Service of Thanksgiving for the work of the trust.

I was drawn to the tune RHUDDLAN, not least because of the emphasis given to the final couplet of each verse; and I originally planned to use an identical fifth line throughout: 'Christ for ever high ascended.'

Christ's parting promises in Matthew 28.20, and the thought of Christ's intercession for his people in Hebrews 7.25, appear in verses 2 and 3 respectively; while the titles 'Son' and 'Saviour' sprang naturally out of the pictures of Jesus set out in the first verse.

As with many hymns written with ascensiontide in mind, this text is not confined to that season; but can serve as a more general hymn of praise to the Lord Jesus Christ, his person and his work.

71 BE PRESENT, SPIRIT OF THE LORD 86 88 6

Theme	Pentecost; the Holy Spirit
Written	at Bramerton and Ruan Minor, April and August, 1984
Suggested tune	BINNEY'S by Eric H. Thiman
	NEWCASTLE by Henry K. Morley
	REPTON by C. Hubert H. Parry
	REST by Frederick C. Maker
Published in	*Daily Office, Community of the Holy Name,* 1990 (words only)
	Anthem (USA), 1991 by Mary Kay Beall
	Eleven New Anthems, 1997 to music by Malcolm Archer
	The Anthems of Malcolm Archer, 2000 to music by Malcolm Archer
	The Young Choir Songbook, 2001 to music by Malcolm Archer

This invocation of the Spirit is not, by its theme, confined to Pentecost but can be used on any occasion when a congregation seek a fuller commitment to Christ and a new enduing with his Spirit. Verse 2 echoes Isaiah 11.1,2, while 'an understanding heart' is from

Solomon's prayer in 1 Kings 3.9, among other Old Testament instances. Similarly, 'dew' as a metaphor of blessing is found through much of the Bible, from Genesis 27.28 onwards; in Hosea 14.5 God declares that he himself will 'be as the dew to Israel'. It does not seem to be a picture repeated in the New Testament; but is familiar to Anglicans from the 'Prayer for Clergy and People' in the Services of Morning and Evening Prayer from the *Book of Common Prayer,* which asks God to 'pour upon them the continual dew of thy blessing.'

72 SPIRIT OF FAITH, BY FAITH BE MINE   888 6

Theme	Pentecost; the Holy Spirit
Written	at Ruan Minor, August 1985
Suggested tune	LITTLE STANMORE by John Barnard
	SAFFRON WALDEN by Arthur H. Brown
Published in	*Worship Songs Ancient & Modern,* 1992 to LITTLE STANMORE
	Hymns for the People, 1993 to LITTLE STANMORE
	Songs for the People of God (USA), 1994 to LAWNDALE by Keith Landis
	Supplement 99 (USA), 1999 to SPIRITUS FIDEI by Carl L. Stam
Recorded on	*Worship Songs Ancient & Modern,* 1992 to LITTLE STANMORE

Ian Bradley in his study of Victorian hymnody, *Abide with me* (London 1997), lists five qualities which John Ellerton, acknowledged as a master hymn writer, identified as the marks of a good hymn. Among them is brevity; which sounds as if it should not present problems, but in practice often does: look, for example, at 'Soldiers of Christ, arise' as it left Charles Wesley's pen in sixteen eight-line verses! This text follows Ellerton's advice while invoking God's Holy Spirit in terms of eight titles drawn from Scripture. The RSV Biblical references are:

Spirit of faith - 2 Corinthians 4.13

Spirit of truth - John 14.17

Spirit of holiness - Romans 1.4

Spirit of Jesus - Philippians 1.19

Spirit of life - Romans 8.2

Spirit of grace - Hebrews 10.29

Spirit of glory - 1 Peter 4.14

73 SPIRIT OF GOD WITHIN ME   76 86 86 86

Theme	Pentecost; the Holy Spirit; dedication and renewal
Written	at Sevenoaks, June 1968
Suggested tune	ALFORD by John B. Dykes
	LIVING FLAME by Norman L. Warren
	RUACH by David McCarthy
Translated into	Chinese, German

Published in	*Youth Praise 2,* 1969 to SPIRIT OF GOD WITHIN ME by Michael Baughen
	Keswick Praise, 1975 to SPIRIT OF GOD WITHIN ME
	Preist Ihn (Germany), 1978 to SPIRIT OF GOD WITHIN ME in a translation by Brigitte Mayer
	Hymns for Today's Church, 1982 to LIVING FLAME
	Hymns and Psalms, 1983 to RUACH
	Anthem (USA), 1985 by Michael Joncas
	Come and Journey (USA), 1985 to WILLOW RIVER by Michael Joncas
	Worship III (USA), 1986 to ESCAMBIA by Randolph Currie
	Today's Missal: Music Issue 1987 (USA), 1986 to WILLOW RIVER
	Breaking Bread: Music Issue 1988 (USA), 1988 to WILLOW RIVER
	Gather (USA), 1988 to SCHOLA by Martin Willett
	Rejoice and Sing, 1991 to DEBEN by Gordon Hawkins
	Baptist Praise and Worship, 1991 to LIVING FLAME
	Sounds of Grace (Hong Kong), 1991 to LIVING FLAME (with a Chinese translation)
	Celebration Hymnal for Everyone, 1994 to SCHOLA
	Songs for the People of God (USA), 1994 to CALVERT by Keith Landis
	RitualSong (USA), 1996 to WILLOW RIVER
	Lambeth Praise, 1998 to DEBEN
	Laudate, 1999 to WILLOW RIVER
	Sing Glory, 1999 to GULLIMAN'S WAY by Norman L. Warren
	Complete Anglican Hymns Old & New, 2000 to DEBEN
	Common Praise, 2000 to ALFORD
	Methodist Hymns Old & New, 2001 to RUACH
Recorded on	*Come and Journey* (USA), 1985 to WILLOW RIVER
	Glorify the Lord (Hong Kong), 1992 to LIVING FLAME sung in Chinese

This hymn to the Holy Spirit was written for *Youth Praise 2.* Verses 1 and 4 make reference to the Spirit seen in wind and flame at Pentecost; verse 2 to 2 Corinthians 4.4 and John 8.32,36; verse 3 to 1 Corinthians 13.7; verse 4 to 2 Corinthians 5.1, echoing (perhaps) Job 4.19. In verse 1, line 5, it should be noted that 'Strive' is still addressed to the Holy Spirit (cf. Genesis 6.3); and that the word 'lost' need not be pressed to mean more than 'lost in its perfection'. Charles Hodge in his *Systematic Theology* quotes the Lutheran view that 'The image of God... was that which was lost by the fall, and is restored by redemption' (Vol. II, p. 97 of the 1875 edition), and it is in that general sense that the words here may be understood. Charles Wesley twice used the couplet

> 'Come, Father, Son and Holy Ghost,
> Restorer of thine image lost ...'

in his *Hymns on the Trinity* (Bristol 1767), though in differing metrical forms: see Nos. XIV and XXX.

'New minted' (verse 1, line 6) is an epithet drawn from coinage, as in Matthew 22.20; with an echo of A.E. Housman's justly famous line *(A Shropshire Lad,* No. XXIII):

> 'They carry back bright to the coiner the mintage of man'

—a line that takes account of creation in God's image, but not of our fallen nature.
See Index 6.

Based on	Acts 2
Theme	Pentecost; the Holy Spirit, mission and evangelism
Written	at Ruan Minor, August 1977
Suggested tune	VINEYARD HAVEN by Richard W. Dirksen
Published in	*Anglican Hymn Book Supplement*, 1978 (words only)
	Songs of Worship, 1980 to SOUND OF WIND by Robin Sheldon
	Making Melody, 1983 to SOUND OF WIND
	Worship III (USA), 1986 to VINEYARD HAVEN
	The New Redemption Hymnal, 1986 to REPLETUS SPIRITU by Robert H. Williams
	Anglican Praise, 1987 to CARDINGTON by Paul C. Edwards
	Irish Church Praise (Ireland), 1990 to (1) MALONE by W. Donald Davison; (2) LIMERICK by Edward F. Darling
	GIA Hymnal Supplement 1991 (USA), 1990 (words only)
	The Worshiping Church (USA), 1991 to VINEYARD HAVEN
	Christian Worship: a Lutheran Hymnal (USA), 1993 to FRANKLIN by Bruce R. Backer
	Songs for the People of God (USA), 1994 to MURRAY by Keith Landis
	RitualSong (USA), 1996 to VINEYARD HAVEN
	Church Hymnal (Ireland), 2000 to LIMERICK
Recorded on	*More Hymns from Irish Church Praise* (Ireland), 1993 to LIMERICK

In June 1977, on the one occasion that Erik Routley stayed at our home, he addressed a small number of invited friends on his impressions of hymnody in America; and introduced us to Richard Dirksen's tune, VINEYARD HAVEN, of which he had a number of copies with him. I felt at the time that Dean Plumptre's accompanying words 'Rejoice, ye pure in heart' (written for a cathedral festival over a century before) had begun to date; and perhaps because of this I wrote two texts later that summer with this metre in mind (the other is 85 'This day above all days'). As can be seen, in both of them I incorporated what Plumptre uses as a chorus into the body of the text, retaining only an identical fifth line to link the verses together.

Almost all that is referred to in this text is drawn directly from Acts 2, including the verses describing the life of the Christian community; with the exception of the final line of verse 3, which draws on Galatians 5.22.

75 GOD AND FATHER, EVER GIVING 87 87 77

Theme	The Holy Trinity; praise and worship
Written	at Ruan Minor, August 1987
Suggested tune	ALL SAINTS (German traditional)
	IRBY by Henry J. Gauntlett

The Trinitarian address of the first three verses is echoed in the threefold reference to 'the life we share': in our creation by the Father (Genesis 2.7); and in union with Christ the Son (2 Corinthians 5.17); and in the indwelling of the Spirit (Romans 8.11). The wind and fire of verse 3 is an allusion to Acts 2, the Day of Pentecost, just as 'dust of earth' in verse 1 is a reminder of the creation of Adam in Genesis 2.7.

76 GOD IS NOT FAR, WHOSE THREEFOLD MERCIES SHINE
10 10 10 10

Theme	The Holy Trinity; praise and worship
Written	at Bramerton, June 1989; and at Ruan Minor, August 1990
Suggested tune	JULIUS by Martin Shaw
	OLD 124TH (TOULON) from the *Genevan Psalter,* 1551
	WOODLANDS by Walter Greatorex

In May 1989 I was asked by the Hobart High School, Loddon, Norfolk, to write the words for a short cantata, to be sung in the parish church of Holy Trinity, Loddon to celebrate its 500th anniversary. The cantata, with music by Derek Scott, is entitled *Stone on Stone* (Stainer & Bell, London 1991) and is about a stylized encounter between the builders of a great church, and various members of the community around them. This text, and its companion 77 'God lies beyond us, throned in light resplendent', are both derived from this cantata, celebrating respectively God's immanence and his transcendence.

The present text takes its middle verse almost directly trom the cantata; and verses 1 and 3 were written a year later on holiday in Ruan Minor. Note in verse 1 the allusion to the Trinitarian words of 'the Grace' from 2 Corinthians 13.14.

77 GOD LIES BEYOND US, THRONED IN LIGHT RESPLENDENT
11 11 11 11

Theme	The Holy Trinity; Christian experience and discipleship; work
Written	at Bramerton, June 1989; and at Ruan Minor, August 1990
Suggested tune	NOAH'S SONG by Norman L. Warren
Published in	*Sing Glory,* 1999 to NOAH'S SONG

The origin of this text is described in the note above to the companion piece 76 'God is not far, whose threefold mercies shine'.

In this case, the first three verses come from *Stone on Stone,* where they are sung respectively (with minor changes, as from singular to plural) by a Watcher of the Heavens, the Tillers of the Fields, and the Searcher of the Soul. The final verse was written to bind the three into a corporate hymn celebrating our own experience of the Triune God, perceived in different ways and at different times as 'beyond', 'beside' and 'within us'.

78 THE EVERLASTING FATHER REIGNS
86 86 D (DCM)

Theme	The Holy Trinity; praise and worship
Written	at Ford, December 2001

Suggested tune	COE FEN by Ken Naylor
	KINGSFOLD (English traditional)
	LADYWELL by William H. Ferguson

In the late autumn of 2001, Trinity Church on the Green, New Haven, Connecticut, were looking for hymns based upon the theme of the Holy Trinity as part of the celebrations for their forthcoming 250th anniversary. Though in the event this was not one of the texts they chose, it was their search that lay behind the writing of the hymn.

The form is typical of many Trinitarian hymns: a verse on each of the three Persons, and a concluding verse on the Three as One. Various Scriptural references can be identified. Line 6 of verse 1 draws on Revelation 1.4, 8, the missing present tense (as in Alpha and Omega) being implied by the opening lines of the verse. The following line represents the worship of heaven from Revelation 4.6, looking back to Isaiah 6.3. In verse 2, line 5 is taken from Revelation 1.5 in the RV (RSV, NIV have 'freed us') and 'abundant' in the next line from our Lord's words in John 10.10. In the following verse, the phrase 'harbinger of heaven' is used to express the 'earnest' (AV), 'guarantee' (RSV), 'pledge' (NEB) of 2 Corinthians 1.22. Knox uses 'foretaste' and harbinger means a forerunner: probably the best known use of the word in hymnody is in John Milton's hymn, 'The Lord will come and not be slow'. Line 7 of verse 3 is a reference to the work of the Spirit in Romans 8.26. In the final verse, the love of the Father, the grace of our Lord Jesus Christ, and the fellowship of the Spirit are from Paul's Trinitarian salutation in, e.g. 2 Corinthians 13.14.

79 IN ENDLESS EXULTATION
76 76 D

Theme	Praise and worship; creation
Written	at Ruan Minor, August 1980
Suggested tune	CRÜGER by Johann Crüger
	ELLACOMBE (German traditional)
	EWING by Alexander Ewing
Published in	*On the Move* (Australia), October 1981 (words only)

Successive drafts of this hymn are entered in my MS book under the title *The Song of the Earth,* which rightly indicates the starting place of the text. Perhaps in consequence the first verse 'wrote itself'. The second half of the hymn proved much more intractable.

The thought of earth rejoicing is a recurring theme in Scripture—for example in Isaiah 44.23: 'Sing, O heavens... shout, O depths of the earth...' Luke 19.40 and Psalm 96.11 exemplify the ideas which end verse 1; and the wind and storm of verse 2 is from Psalm 148.8 in the Prayer Book version. The ending owes, I think, a debt to the last line of several verses of Charles Wesley's 'Come, O thou Traveller unknown'.

80 LET US SING THE GOD OF GLORY WHO HAS SET THE STARS IN PLACE
15 15 15 6 and refrain

| Theme | Praise and worship; rejoicing, thanksgiving |
| Written | at Ford, August 1994 |

Salisbury Cathedral, whose spire is almost visible from my study window, has for several years run a successful series of 'Workshop Days for Schools' when 9–11 year olds, mainly from the Church Schools of the diocese, pay an extended visit to the cathedral and learn something of its history and the faith and worship which it represents. Mrs Patricia Hellewell, then Visitors' Officer of the cathedral, and a member of our local church, asked me if I would write a hymn which these children might sing towards the close of their visit in the final Service; perhaps in procession. It needed to be a tune which was well-known, and would go with a swing. BATTLE HYMN, to which so far I had not attempted a text, seemed a suitable choice.

The resulting text includes five verses (it takes some time to process round Salisbury Cathedral!), praising in turn the God of glory, beauty, bounty, mercy, and finally God in Christ; with a Trinitarian reference in the final verse which offers a challenge to recognize the call and claim of God upon the life of every individual, and the response to God's love in the worship of the redeemed community.

81 REJOICE IN GOD! LET TRUMPETS SOUND 4486 8886

Theme	Praise; anniversary; thanksgiving; the dedication of a church; rejoicing
Written	at Ford, July 1996
Suggested tune	BANNER OF HOPE by Norman L. Warren
	MT GRETNA by K. Lee Scott
Published in	*Supplement 99* (USA), 1999 to BANNER OF HOPE
	Sing Glory, 1999 to BANNER OF HOPE
	Rejoice in God (USA), 2000 to MT GRETNA

Visiting Israel in 1995, I met on the same party the Reverend John W. Banner, vicar of Christ Church, Tunbridge Wells, in Kent. He told me of his plans to demolish the old Christ Church, now quite unsuitable and in a poor state, and rebuild both the physical structure and the congregation. His vision that this was God's call to him dated back some twenty years, long before moving to Tunbridge Wells; and it was not to be fulfilled without, in his own words 'heartache and struggle, trials, testing and tears'.

But by the time we met, plans were well under way; and he asked if I would write a hymn for the Dedication Service of his new church, to which Norman Warren, then Archdeacon of Rochester, would write a tune. 'The mood', he wrote later, 'should clearly be triumphant...' Hence the trumpets in the opening verse! The text looks to the experience of the people of Christ Church through these years, proving the faithfulness of God as he led them forward. It offers thanksgiving and praise, rehearses the central truths of God's salvation through grace, and looks to the 'living temple' which was part of the original vision, borrowing words the Psalmist uses to describe Jerusalem, the City of God, from Psalm 48.2. In the final verse, thanksgiving becomes the springboard for mission.

Theme	Praise and worship; the Holy Trinity
Written	at Ford, June 1993
Suggested tune	THE SILVER ARROW by P. C. Buck
Published in	*St Peter's College, Radley, Hymn Book,* revised and enlarged 1993, to THE SILVER ARROW

When in 1993 Radley College was preparing a new hymn book for use in chapel, the editors wished to include this rousing tune, set to the words of a Christian hymn. This text is the result, prepared in consultation with Robert Gower, Director of Music (whose idea it was to use this tune) and the College Chaplain, the Reverend David Coulton.

The original words include a verse to be sung softly, even regretfully; and the tune provides for this. This text expects a similar treatment in verse 2, lines 1–5. The structure of the three verses follows a simple Trinitarian pattern of God's hand seen in creation, his love in redemption, and our response in praise and discipleship.

The tune, THE SILVER ARROW, is from *Harrow School Songs;* and the composer, Percy Buck, was a former Director of Music at the school. The original words, by C.J. Maltby, begin 'We sing the praise of the olden days...' and continue in the same vein.

Theme	Morning; work
Written	at Ruan Minor, August 1980
Suggested tune	LITTLE CORNARD by Martin Shaw SAMUEL by Arthur S. Sullivan
Published in	*Hymns for Today's Church,* 1982 to SAMUEL *Anglican Praise,* 1987 to SAMUEL *Rejoice!* (Australia), 1987 to SAMUEL *Trinity Hymnal, revised edition* (USA), 1990 to SAMUEL *Today's Missal: Music Issue 1998* (USA), 1997 to HOLY VINE by Stephen Dean *Laudate,* 1999 to HOLY VINE *Breaking Bread: Jubilee 2000* (USA), 1999 to HOLY VINE *Common Praise,* 2000 to LITTLE CORNARD *Praise!,* 2000 to LITTLE CORNARD *Glory Be* (New Zealand), 2001 to LAWES' PSALM 47 by Henry Lawes

This text arose from the combination of tune (a desire to try my hand at a text to LITTLE CORNARD) and theme (I had already three texts on the theme of evening; nothing on morning).

LITTLE CORNARD was written originally for Charles Oakley's 'Hills of the North, rejoice'; and apart from the change of rhythm in the final lines of each verse, it is unusual in the stress that falls on the opening word in each of the first four lines. Few texts in the metre of 66 66 88 are suitable therefore.

Here, verse 1 asks for a heart turned towards God from the beginning, knowing his forgiveness, protection and guidance, so as to live to his glory. Verse 2 thinks of daily work and life in community, and the interdependence of the human family; our days filled with the fruit of the Spirit (Colossians 3.2; Galatians 5.22). Verse 3 asks for strength, direction, safety and sustenance; and for continual thankfulness (Ephesians 5.20). The change in line 2 between verse 1 and verse 4 provides the keynote of the text.

84 LORD, FOR THE GIFT OF THIS NEW DAY   88 84

Theme	Morning
Written	at Bramerton, August 1991
Suggested tune	ALMSGIVING by John B. Dykes
	ES IST KEIN TAG by Johann D. Meyer

The structure of the text is drawn from line 3 of the first verse, 'think and do and say', echoed in the following verses which take the themes of mind, action and speech, drawing on Colossians 3.2 and Philippians 4.8f.

'Doubly blessed' in the final verse refers to the privilege both of walking the pilgrim way, and of doing so in the company of Christ; but it can be applied also to God's blessing resting both upon ourselves and upon those we meet.

85 THIS DAY ABOVE ALL DAYS   66 86 66

Theme	Sunday; Eastertide
Written	at Ruan Minor, August 1977
Suggested tune	CARDINGTON by Paul C. Edwards
	VINEYARD HAVEN by Richard W. Dirksen
Published in	*Songs of Worship*, 1980 to SOUND OF WIND
	Hymns for Today's Church, 1982 to CARDINGTON
	Anthem (USA), 1985 by Douglas E. Wagner
	The New Redemption Hymnal, 1986 to SURREXIT CHRISTUS by Robert H. Williams
	Songs for the People of God (USA), 1994 to MURRAY by Keith Landis

For the origin of this and a companion text to the tune VINEYARD HAVEN, see the note on 74 'When God the Spirit came'. The text is intended, not just for the Easter season, but for any Sunday, being 'the first day of the week' on which Christians celebrate anew Christ's resurrection.

'Prince of life' (verse 3) is a title given to Jesus in Peter's sermon at Solomon's porch (Acts 3.15). 'Death's dominion' (verse 2) is a reference to Romans 6.9; 'Christ being raised from the dead dieth no more; death hath no more dominion over him.'

86 AN UPPER ROOM WITH EVENING LAMPS ASHINE   10 10 10 10

Theme	Holy Communion
Written	at Ruan Minor, August 1987
Suggested tune	ELLERS by Edward J. Hopkins
	EVENTIDE by William H. Monk
	FARLEY CASTLE by Henry Lawes
Published in	*Anthem* (USA), 1989 by David W. Music
	Chalice Hymnal (USA), 1995 to EVENTIDE
	Worship & Rejoice (USA), 2001 to EVENTIDE

The final verse begins with a conscious echo of the closing prayer of the Service of Holy Communion in the *Alternative Service Book 1980* of the Church of England which was superseded by *Common Worship* in 2000. The prayer is retained unaltered in 'Order One' (p. 182); and 'Order One (Traditional)' includes the same petition that God will 'send us out in the power of thy Spirit to live and work to thy praise and glory' (p.226).

87 AS IN THAT UPPER ROOM YOU LEFT YOUR SEAT   10 10 10 10

Theme	Holy Communion
Written	at Ford, April 1992
Suggested tune	MORESTEAD by Sydney Watson
	SONG 22 by Orlando Gibbons
	SURSUM CORDA by Alfred M. Smith
Published in	*Remember Jesus*, 1995 (words only)
	Wonder, Love and Praise (USA), 1997 to (1) SURSUM CORDA
	(2) CHAPPELL by Carol Haywood
	Cantate Domino, 2000 to ST MAUGHAN by Robert Jones
	Sing to the Lord no Threadbare Song (USA), 2001 to CLENACLE
	by Alfred V. Fedak

The text moves from the Last Supper and the foot washing, to 'the washing of regeneration' (Titus 3.5) in the final line of verse 1. In this sense, every Service of Holy Communion looks back to the full and free forgiveness that is promised to all those who turn to Christ in faith; and at the same time includes elements of confession and forgiveness for the stains of the daily journey in a fallen world (John 13.10).
    'True and living bread' refers to John 6.32, 51.

88 GOD GIVES A NEW BEGINNING   76 76 D

Theme	Holy Communion; growth in grace
Written	at Ford, August 2000
Suggested tune	AURELIA by Samuel S. Wesley
	MORNING LIGHT by George J. Webb
	NYLAND (Finnish traditional)

In the General Thanksgiving, Anglicans thank God 'for the means of grace', all those things God has provided to help us on our spiritual journey towards maturity, 'the measure of the stature of the fullness of Christ', as Paul describes it in Ephesians 4.13. This hymn is about some of those things: music and worship, prayer and fellowship, the Scriptures and the Lord's Supper. All these spring from our 'new beginning' in conversion to Christ and God's regenerating work within us (there are echoes of the Anglican liturgy in turning from self and sin and turning to Christ), and the new direction, discipline and motivation which follow. In the final verse they are seen in the light of the indwelling Spirit of God without whom spiritual life, let alone spiritual growth in Christ, would be vain.

Verse 1 borrows from the 13th century prayer of St Richard of Chichester (to know, to follow and to love); while the concluding lines of the hymn are a reminder of the fruit of the Spirit in Galatians 5.22. 'Saints' in the second verse has the New Testament meaning of our fellow-believers in the local congregation.

89 THE LORD IS HERE   446 D or 86 86 (CM)

Theme	Holy Communion; praise and worship
Written	at Ruan Minor, August 1985
Suggested tune	CRIMOND (Scottish traditional)
	DUNDEE (Scottish traditional)
	STRACATHRO by Charles Hutcheson
Published in	*Lift High your Songs!*, 1988 to HOLY PRESENCE
	by Michael Paget
	The Worshiping Church (USA), 1990 to CRIMOND
	Anthem (USA), 1992 by John Carter
	Worship Songs Ancient & Modern, 1992 to SIBFORD FERRIS
	by John Barnard
	New Songs of Rejoicing (USA), 1994 to GRAHAM by Keith Landis
	Songs for the People of God (USA), 1994 to GRAHAM
	Moravian Book of Worship (USA), 1995 to ST ANNE
	by William Croft
	Sing We Merrily, 1995 to KONOMICHI by Christopher Dearnley
	Glory Be (New Zealand), 2000 to BANGOR from William
	Tans'ur's *Harmony of Syon*, 1735

The words 'The Lord is here' marked the beginning of Rite A in Order for Holy Communion, or of the Eucharistic Prayer itself, in the *Alternative Service Book, 1980* of the Church of England. *Common Worship*, the book which superseded it in 2000, retains these words as a versicle at the start of each of the ten alternative Eucharistic Prayers of Order One. The response, 'His Spirit is with us', can be seen in the second verse of the text. The 'promised word' of verse 1 is Matthew 18.20.

90 WE COME AS GUESTS INVITED   76 76 D

Theme	Holy Communion
Written	at Ruan Minor, August 1975

Suggested tune	AURELIA by Samuel S. Wesley
	NYLAND (Finnish traditional)
	PASSION CHORALE harmonized by J.S. Bach
Translated into	Chinese
Published in	*Songs of Worship*, 1980 to PASSION CHORALE
	A Supplement to Congregational Praise, 1982 (words only)
	Making Melody, 1983 to PASSION CHORALE
	The Singing Church (USA), 1985 to PASSION CHORALE
	Mission Praise 2, 1987 to PASSION CHORALE
	Hymns for Today's Church (enlarged second edition), 1987 to PASSION CHORALE
	Church Family Worship, 1988 to (1) PASSION CHORALE (2) CRÜGER by Johann Crüger
	Anthem (USA), 1988 by Judy Hunnicutt
	Sing Joyfully, 1990 to PASSION CHORALE
	Irish Church Praise (Ireland), 1990 to KING'S LYNN (English traditional)
	The Presbyterian Hymnal (USA), 1990 to WIE LIEBLICH IST DER MAIEN by Johann Steurlein
	The Worshiping Church (USA), 1990 to PENLAN by David Jenkins
	Mission Praise Combined, 1990 to PASSION CHORALE
	Sounds of Grace (Hong Kong), 1991 to CRÜGER (with a Chinese translation)
	Hymns for the People, 1993 to CRÜGER
	Anthem (USA), 1993 by Austin Lovelace
	Glory to God (Ireland), 1994 to PASSION CHORALE
	Journeysongs 1994-5 Annual Supplement (USA), 1994 to music by James Walsh
	Breaking Bread 1995 (USA), 1994 to music by James Walsh
	Chalice Hymnal (USA), 1995 to WIE LIEBLICH IST DER MAIEN
	Worship Together (USA), 1995 to PASSION CHORALE
	Breaking Bread 1997 (USA), 1996 to music by James Walsh
	The Book of Praise (Canada), 1997 to NYLAND
	Today's Missal: Music Issue 1998 (USA), 1997 to music by James Walsh
	Peculiar Honours, 1998 to CRÜGER
	Laudate, 1999 to music by James Walsh
	Complete Mission Praise, 1999 to PASSION CHORALE
	Church Hymnal (Ireland), 2000 to KING'S LYNN
	Praise!, 2000 to PASSION CHORALE
	Worship & Rejoice (USA), 2001 to WIE LIEBLICH IST DER MAIEN
Recorded on	*Songs of Worship*, 1980 to PASSION CHORALE
	The Hymn Makers: 'Tell out, my soul', 1996 to PASSION CHORALE

The phrase 'guests invited' is a reference to the recorded words of Jesus as they came to us in St Luke: 'Do this in remembrance of me' (Luke 22.19). In verse 2, lines 3 and 4 incorporate the final words of administration from the *Book of Common Prayer*: 'Feed on him in your hearts by faith with thanksgiving.' The three verses move from the recital of what is taking place, into our own participation and experience of Christ, and so to the united family receiving together the gifts of love.

Theme	The dedication of a child
Written	at Ruan Minor, August 1986
Suggested tune	LES COMMANDEMENS DE DIEU by Louis Bourgeois
	SPIRITUS VITAE by Mary Hammond
Published in	*New Songs of Praise 3,* 1987 to SPIRITUS VITAE
	Lift High your Songs!, 1988 to DEDICATION CAROL by Michael Paget

Written in response to the Oxford University Press search for hymns on this theme for inclusion in *New Songs of Praise 3,* the hymn is intended for use in a Service of Dedication, either in churches which do not practise infant baptism, or where dedication is preferred, as in the 'Thanksgiving for the Gift of a Child' in *Common Worship,* 2000. The problem of gender ('him/her') has been avoided by casting verses 2, 3 and 4a into the plural. Note the Trinitarian address of verses 1–3, summed up in verse 4 with the words 'God ever One'. I owe the adjective 'cherished' to Derek Kidner.

Theme	The baptism of a child
Written	at Poldhu Cove and Ruan Minor, August 1980
Suggested tune	CASWALL by Friedrich Filitz
	GLENFINLAS by Kenneth G. Finlay
	PASTOR PASTORUM by Friedrich Silcher
Published in	*On the Move* (Australia), October 1981 (words only)
	Hymns for Today's Church, 1982 to NORTH COATES by T.R. Matthews
	Church Family Worship, 1988 to NORTH COATES
	Songs of Rejoicing (USA), 1989 to NEWARK by Roy Hopp
	Irish Church Praise (Ireland), 1990 to GLENFINLAS
	The Roy Hopp Hymnary (USA), 1990 to NEWARK
	Church Hymnal (Ireland), 2000 to GLENFINLAS

In the summer of 1980 we happened to sing at a Service in my local church T. B. Pollock's hymn 'Faithful Shepherd, feed me' to the tune PASTOR PASTORUM. In its simplicity it struck me as a specially suitable tune for a hymn intended for use at the baptism of a child; and I tried my hand at one on holiday that summer. This is the result.

Baptism—especially infant baptism—is a large subject, and by no means simple. The text can only allude to various aspects, as indicated by the use of verbs: loving, washing, blessing, claiming, believing, signing, beginning, growing, saving, belonging. Verse 2 has a compressed, even elliptical, reference to the place of parents, godparents and sponsors who declare their faith and repentance 'in the name of this child'; and verse 3 echoes both the traditional confirmation prayer of the Church of England ('Defend, O Lord, this thy Child...') and the description of the Word made flesh in John 1.14.

93 LORD JESUS, BORN A TINY CHILD   88 88 88

Theme   The baptism of a child
Written   at Ford, August 1994
Suggested tune   MELITA by John B. Dykes
                         ST MATTHIAS by William H. Monk
                         SURREY by Henry Carey

In March 1994 I received a letter on behalf of the Liturgical Commission of the Church of England, pointing out the need for new hymns on the theme of Christian initiation: 'a recurring gap in our studies concerns baptismal hymnody'.

Accordingly, I wrote three texts on the theme of baptism (with confirmation also in mind) during the summer of 1994:

    93   'Lord Jesus, born a tiny child' (for infants)

    97   'We turn to Christ alone' (for adult baptism and confirmation)

    96   'When Jesus taught by Galilee' (for any Service of baptism and confirmation)

My aim here is to offer a text which is firmly biblical, but accessible to parents with little church background: those, for example, who are being drawn to faith through baptismal preparation. Verse 2 takes up the story of how Jesus welcomed children, from Mark 10, the gospel reading in the *Book of Common Prayer* for the Baptism of Infants; while verse 3 unfolds the thought of washing from sin and the symbolism of the signing of the cross.

Where more than one is to be baptized, the words 'each child' may replace 'this child'.

94 NOW TO THE LORD WE BRING THE CHILD HE GAVE US   11 10 11 10

Theme   The baptism of a child
Written   at Ruan Minor, August 1976
Suggested tune   O PERFECT LOVE by Joseph Barnby

Among biblical echoes might be the presentation of Samuel in the temple (which can stand as a type of other presentations, including that of our Lord)—see 1 Samuel 1.28. The Name, the word and the water come from Matthew 28.19, the 'sifting' from Luke 22.31. 'Covenant' refers to the theological basis of infant baptism as I understand it: the successor to the 'covenant of circumcision' (Acts 7.8), the sign of the 'new covenant' (Hebrews 8. 10) which would be not of the flesh, but of the mind and heart. 'Believe and trust' is an echo of the *Common Worship* Baptism Service of the Church of England, as is the word 'turn'; while 'Christ's faithful soldier' echoes the traditional words of baptism in the *Book of Common Prayer*. Verse 4 speaks of three of the consequences of baptism: membership, discipleship, companionship.

The hymn took its origin from a Saturday morning walk on the beach at Poldhu Cove, Cornwall.

Theme	The baptism of a child
Written	at Ruan Minor, April 1974
Suggested tune	ST MICHAEL adapted by William Crotch
	WINDERMERE by Arthur Somervell
Published in	*Partners in Praise*, 1979 to EGHAM attributed to W. Turner
	Songs for the People of God (USA), 1994 to GOLDEN HILL from
	The Missouri Harmony, 1820
	Hymns for Prayer and Praise, 1996 to (1) MARIANDYRYS by John
	Harper (2) ST MICHAEL
	Church Hymnal (Ireland), 2000 to WINDERMERE

This text reflects the view that (as with circumcision, the sign of the old covenant) baptism with water in the threefold Name is the appointed means whereby a child of believing parents receives the sign of the new covenant, carrying with it obligations to discipleship, obedience, witness and membership of Christ's church. It includes the expectation that the repentance and faith expressed on behalf of the child will be personally appropriated and renewed in future years. The word 'divine' in verse 1 is a reference to the quality of the giving; a royal gift, for example, is one we receive at royal hands, or which reflects the royal nature of the giver. Verse 3 refers to Mark 8.34 and to Philippians 3.8 where the phrase 'reckon all things loss' is quoted also in Charles Wesley's 'And are we yet alive' which has been used for over two centuries to open the Methodist Conference.

Theme	Baptism and confirmation; the Holy Trinity
Written	at Ford, August 1994
Suggested tune	ST CHRYSOSTOM by Joseph Barnby
	ST PETERSBURG by D.S. Bortniansky
	SURREY by Henry Carey
Published in	*Church Hymnal* (Ireland), 2000 to SURREY

For the origin, see the note on 93 'Lord Jesus, born a tiny child'. The structure of the text is based upon the threefold Name into which Christians are baptized (see verse 1, line 6). The following three verses speak in turn of Father, Son and Holy Spirit; while the final verse links this threefold Name with the 'baptism into Christ' of e.g. Romans 6.3 and Galatians 3.27 and the 'turning to Christ' of the Baptism Service, interpreted in terms of John 14.6, Christ the Way, the Truth and the Life. The text contains other echoes of the Church of England Services of Baptism and of Confirmation; for example, in the sign of the cross and in prayers for continuance and for daily increase in the Holy Spirit. See also Matthew 28.19; Ephesians 5.8 and similar references; Acts 2.2,3; Galatians 5.22; John 8.36.

Theme	Adult baptism; confirmation; dedication and renewal
Written	at Ford, August 1994
Suggested tune	DIADEMATA by George J. Elvey
	ICH HALTE TREULICH STILL attributed to J.S. Bach
	LEOMINSTER by George W. Martin
	OLIVA SPECIOSA (Italian traditional)
Published in	*Supplement '96* (USA), 1996 to UNIVERSITY HILLS
	New Mission Praise, 1996 to DINBYCH by Joseph Parry
	Complete Mission Praise, 1999 to DINBYCH

For the origin, see the note on 93 'Lord Jesus, born a tiny child'.

The structure of the text seeks to follow the three questions put to the candidate in the Services both of Baptism and of Confirmation in the *Alternative Service Book, 1980* of the Church of England and in other similar liturgies including those of *Common Worship*:

'Do you turn to Christ?

Do you repent of your sins?

Do you renounce evil?'

Note that 'to turn' is the root meaning of the word 'repent'. The final verse echoes the traditional prayer that the newly-baptized into Christ 'shall continue his faithful *soldiers* and *servants* to the end of your lives'. Where the Service includes the giving of a baptismal candle, verse 3 can be seen as making reference to this.

The repeated fourth line arose during the writing of the text, and lends strength. It is a device used to great effect in Richard Wilbur's poem 'A stable lamp is lighted'; though not every setting of his text as a carol does justice to this. An earlier example, with an adjustment for its DCM metre, is found in Rudyard Kipling's 'Our Lord, Who did the ox command...'

OLIVA SPECIOSA is little published; but can be found as No. 49 in the Appendix to the *English Hymnal*, 1933.

---

98 WE TURN TO CHRIST ANEW   66 84 D

Theme	Confirmation; adult baptism; discipleship; dedication and renewal
Written	at Ruan Minor, August 1982
Suggested tune	LEONI (from a Synagogue melody)
Published in	*Anglican Praise*, 1987 to LEONI
	Irish Church Praise (Ireland), 1990 to LEONI
	Moravian Book of Worship (USA), 1995 to LEONI
	Anthem, 1995 by Ian Kellam
	Church Hymnal (Ireland), 2000 to LEONI

For some years I had wanted to write a confirmation hymn; and the fact that as a bishop I found myself conducting many Confirmation Services strengthened this desire. I had hoped to write an alternative to 'O Jesus, I have promised'; and while I do not think this text serves just that purpose, I see it none the less as particularly suitable for use at confirmation. The three 'T's of the opening lines (echoed in the final lines) of the three verses refer to different parts of the Service: the renewal of baptismal vows; the affirmation of faith, with the repeated 'Do you believe and trust...?'; and the traditional prayer that those confirmed 'may continue yours for ever'.

Though closely built around confirmation the hymn is not tied to it. Turning to Christ, trusting him, and living true to him, are basic parts of Christian experience in any church. Moreover, the word 'anew' in the first line indicates that though a 'turning to Christ' may be a once-for-all never-to-be-repeated moment of conversion, nevertheless in another sense all discipleship is a daily 'turning to him anew' in obedience, loyalty and service.

99 AT CANA'S WEDDING, LONG AGO 88 88 88

Based on	John 2.1–11 and Luke 24.13f.
Theme	Marriage
Written	at Ruan Minor, August 1976
Suggested tune	STELLA (English traditional)
	WYCH CROSS by Erik Routley
Published in	*Common Praise*, 2000 to STELLA

As with many wedding hymns, there is an ambiguity about how far the words are for the couple and how far for the congregation. Yet there seems no logical reason why the congregational 'us' and 'our' of verses 1 and 2 should not become the intercessory 'their' of verse 3. It may be worth adding that commentators have suggested (there is no kind of evidence) that the second of the two disciples (Luke 24.13) was Cleopas's wife; making the Emmaus walk, along with the wedding at Cana, a favourite passage for wedding addresses.

Perhaps three names from the geography of the Gospels are too much for today? And yet one should not underestimate the evocative power of the proper name, not only in rooting the allusion within the gospel history, but in less expected ways. In his inaugural lecture, *The Victorian Hymn* (University of Durham 1981), Professor J.R. Watson described how D.H. Lawrence once confessed :

> 'To me the word Galilee has a wonderful sound. The Lake of Galilee! I don't want to know where it is. I never want to go to Palestine. Galilee is one of those lovely, glamorous words, not places, that exist in the golden haze of a child's half-formed imagination. And in my man's imagination it is just the same. It has been left untouched ...'

There are losses as well as gains to be reckoned with in that account, of course. But the 'wonderful sound' of Galilee here receives testimony from an unexpected source.

'Virtue' in verse 1 is here used in the sense of 'strength, power and efficiency': see Henry Bett, *The Hymns of Methodism* (London, 3rd edition 1945), p.44.

100 LORD, HEAR US AS WE PRAY

66 86 (SM)

Theme	Peace and blessing; marriage
Written	at Ruan Minor, August 1990
Suggested tune	DONCASTER by Samuel Wesley
	FRANCONIA adapted by William H. Havergal
	ST MICHAEL adapted by William Crotch
Published in	*Songs for the People of God* (USA), 1994 to TEACHER'S FAREWELL from *The Original Sacred Harp*, 1911

The short hymn has a valued place in congregational worship, as can be seen by the use-fulness, for example, of Christopher Wordsworth's 'Lord, be thy Word my rule' or the eight lines (out of 56) now sung as Joseph Hart's 'How good is the God we adore'. I did not begin this text with a marriage hymn in mind; but the three triplets (way, truth, life; faith, hope, charity; love, joy, peace) together with the Trinitarian reference, seem to make it suitable as a hymn to ask God's blessing on a marriage.

101 LORD OF OUR LIVES, OUR BIRTH AND BREATH

86 86 (CM)

Theme	The Christian hope; death; a funeral
Written	at Ruan Minor, August 1990
Suggested tune	BELMONT from William Gardiner's *Sacred Melodies*, 1812
	CAITHNESS (Scottish traditional)
	CONTEMPLATION by Frederick A.G.Ouseley
Published in	*New Songs of Praise 6*, 1991 to THEOC by Gordon Lawson

A previous text was designated as 'suitable for a marriage' and with that in mind I sought soon afterwards to write a companion piece, 'suitable for a funeral'. I would be glad to think it might be sung at mine.

The thought moves from an acknowledgment of God as our Creator and Sustainer in whose hands we rest, and to whom we bring our prayers and praises, through a thank-ful recollection of life past and an affirmation of Christian assurance. It concludes with a prayer for ourselves, the worshippers, in the days that are left to us. The hymn was first sung in the BBC TV programme 'Songs of Praise' in January 1991 from Cheadle, Cheshire, in their Festival of New Hymns.

102 GIVE THANKS TO GOD, AND HONOUR THOSE

86 86 D (DCM)

Based on	Ecclesiasticus 44.1–15
Theme	Commemoration; anniversary; thanksgiving
Written	at Ford, March 1998
Suggested tune	FOREST GREEN (English traditional)
	RESIGNATION (American traditional)
	SELFLESS LOVE by Andrew Maries
	THE AULD HOOSE (Scottish traditional)

Published in   *Supplement 99* (USA), 1999 (words only)

The text originated from a request by the Reverend Paul Conrad, parish priest of Christ Church, Hampstead Square, London, for a hymn to be sung at a commemoration of Bishop Edward Henry Bickersteth, for thirty years vicar of that parish (1855-1885) and then Bishop of Exeter. He was a poet, winning medals and prizes at Oxford and later publishing books of poetry, one of which *(To-day and For Ever: a poem in twelve books,* 1886) went into seventeen editions: the DNB says of it:

> 'It supplied evangelicals with poetry that did not offend their piety, and took for them the place held by Keble's *Christian Year* among another school of churchmen.'

It is doubtful how far one can reconcile a proper use of hymnody with too specific a commemoration of an individual life; and hence the hymn is general in its references and draws on the famous passage in the Apocryphal book of Ecclesiasticus to give some structure, and some familiar echos of thought and phrase. Those who know something of Bickersteth's life can find allusions to his episcopal oversight, his pastoral care, his teaching and preaching, his poetry (and, by implication, his hymnody: he was perhaps best known as the editor of *The Hymnal Companion to the Book of Common Prayer,* London 1870) and his devotional writing, as well as his strong missionary concern.

But I publish the text here in the hope that it may prove not unsuitable in other contexts—a memorial Service or a celebration of another individual, or of alumni, for example; or in the anniversary of a church or a college with a strong Christian tradition.

103 HERE WITHIN THIS HOUSE OF PRAYER   77 77 77

Theme	Anniversary, thanksgiving or special occasion; the Holy Trinity
Written	at Bramerton, January 1978
Suggested tune	DIX by Conrad Kocher ENGLAND'S LANE (English traditional)
Published in	*Hymns for Today's Church,* 1982 to (1) ASHBURTON by Robert Jackson (2) DIX *Anglican Praise,* 1987 to ENGLAND'S LANE *Anthem* (USA), 1991 by Richard Proulx

About the end of 1977, Canon Frank Colquhoun, then Vice-Dean of Norwich Cathedral, asked if I would write a hymn for the Installation of David Edwards as Dean of Norwich, on 8 April 1978. Norwich Cathedral is dedicated to 'the Holy and Undivided Trinity'; so that a Trinitarian form seemed right. The first verse is designed to indicate a landmark or a milestone, without specifying at all closely the nature of the occasion thus celebrated. Verse 2 speaks of Christ as central to the ministry of both Word and Sacrament; and the final line of verse 3 is a deliberate echo of the concluding prayer at every Service of Holy Communion (in one of the modern alternatives): 'Send us out in the power of your Spirit to live and work to your praise and glory.' By the end the hymn, it will be seen that prayer has been lifted into praise.

Theme	Festivals, the call of God; unity; mission, service
Written	at Ford, March 1998
Suggested tune	HYFRYDOL by Rowland H. Pritchard
Published in	*Cantate Domino*, 2000 to HUNTLEY by Alan Viner

The text contains echoes of Colossians 3.12–17, since this was one of the readings at the Service for which the hymn was written. It arose from a request by the Mothers' Union of the Winchester diocese for a new hymn to sing in the Cathedral at an international Festival Service, in preparation for their World Wide Council at York. This is held every ten years, in the weeks preceding the Lambeth Conference. The Diocese of Winchester traditionally acts as host for this Service since it was in one of the parishes of that diocese that the MU was first begun in 1876.

The theme of the Service was 'united in love'—drawn from Colossians 3.14; and the text takes this thought for the concluding line of the first verse and the first line of the concluding verse. For the rest, the MU's special concerns for family and home can be read into the brief reference to home and children; but also into the prayer that runs through the middle verses for the needs of the world, both spiritual and physical, not least for freedom from war.

If the hymn is used in a different context, the reference to 'children' in verse 3 can be taken easily enough in the biblical sense of 'God's children' rather than as a reference to human childhood (cf. Luke 16.8, AV).

Theme	Anniversary; thanksgiving; dedication
Written	in February 1967
Translated into	Chinese, Norwegian, Welsh
Suggested tune	LORD OF THE YEARS by Michael A. Baughen
	O PERFECT LOVE by Joseph Barnby
Published in	*Youth Praise 2*, 1969 to LORD OF THE YEARS
	Family Worship, 1971 (words only)
	Thirty Hymns, 1972 (words only)
	*Keswick Praise,*1975 to LORD OF THE YEARS
	Anglican Hymn Book Supplement, 1978 (words only)
	Partners in Praise, 1979 to LORD OF THE YEARS
	Songs of Worship, 1980 to LORD OF THE YEARS
	A Supplement to Congregational Praise, 1982 (words only)
	Hymns for Today's Church, 1982 to LORD OF THE YEARS
	A Service for Remembrance Sunday, 1982 (words only)
	Making Melody, 1983 to LORD OF THE YEARS
	Mission England Praise, 1983 to LORD OF THE YEARS
	Hymnal Supplement (USA), 1984 to LORD OF THE YEARS
	Hymns Old & New (Anglican Edition), 1986 to LORD OF THE YEARS
	The New Redemption Hymnal, 1986 to LORD OF THE YEARS
	Anglican Praise, 1987 to LORD OF THE YEARS

Church Family Worship, 1988 to (1) LORD OF THE YEARS
   (2) O PERFECT LOVE
Let's Praise!, 1988 to LORD OF THE YEARS
The Wedding Book, 1989 to LORD OF THE YEARS
Irish Church Praise, 1990 to MARLBOROUGH PARK by
   W. Donald Davison
Mission Praise Combined, 1990 to LORD OF THE YEARS
Rejoice and Sing, 1991 to LORD OF THE YEARS
Baptist Praise and Worship, 1991 to LORD OF THE YEARS
Sounds of Grace (Hong Kong), 1991 to LORD OF THE YEARS
   (with a Chinese translation)
Ring of Praise (Australia), 1991 to LORD OF THE YEARS
100 Hymns of Hope (USA), 1992 to LORD OF THE YEARS
Hymns for the People, 1993 to LORD OF THE YEARS
Anthem (USA), 1994 by Allen Pote
Glory to God (Ireland), 1994 to LORD OF THE YEARS
Sing we Merrily, 1995 to LORD OF THE YEARS
Worship Together (USA), 1995 to LORD OF THE YEARS
Hymns Old & New, 1996 to LORD OF THE YEARS
New Hymns and Worship Songs, 1996 to LORD OF THE YEARS
Sing Hallelujah, 1997 to LORD OF THE YEARS
Design your own Wedding Ceremony, 1997 (words only)
BBC Songs of Praise, 1997 to LORD OF THE YEARS
The Source, 1998 to LORD OF THE YEARS
Youth Challenge Chorus Book (Ireland), 1998 (words only)
Songs of Fellowship 2, 1998 to LORD OF THE YEARS
Lambeth Praise (USA), 1998 to LORD OF THE YEARS
Spring Harvest Praise, 1998 to LORD OF THE YEARS
   (with a translation by Hywel M. Griffiths in the Welsh edition)
Common Ground (Scotland), 1998 to LORD OF THE YEARS
Songs of Victory (Scotland), 1998 to LORD OF THE YEARS
Worship 2000!, 1999 to LORD OF THE YEARS
Spring Harvest Praise 99, 1999 to LORD OF THE YEARS
New Start Hymns and Songs, 1999 to LORD OF THE YEARS
Laudate, 1999 to LORD OF THE YEARS
Complete Mission Praise, 1999 to LORD OF THE YEARS
Sing and Praise, 1999 to LORD OF THE YEARS
Sing Glory, 1999 to LORD OF THE YEARS
Grace Praise (New Zealand), 1999 (words only)
Complete Anglican Hymns Old and New, 2000 to LORD OF THE
   YEARS
Common Praise, 2000 to LORD OF THE YEARS
Keswick Songbook, 2000 to LORD OF THE YEARS
Church Hymnal (Ireland), 2000 to LORD OF THE YEARS
Praise!, 2000 to LORD OF THE YEARS
Sing to the Lord, 2000 to LORD OF THE YEARS
The Bridge, 2001 to LORD OF THE YEARS
Worship Today, 2001 to LORD OF THE YEARS
New Hymns and Worship Songs, 2001 to LORD OF THE YEARS
Worship & Rejoice (USA), 2001 to LORD OF THE YEARS
Methodist Hymns Old & New, 2001 to LORD OF THE YEARS

Salmer Underveis (Norway), 2001 to LORD OF THE YEARS in a
translation by Sven Aasmundtveit

Recorded on

Here is Youth Praise, 1975 to LORD OF THE YEARS
Centenary Praise, 1987 to LORD OF THE YEARS
Keswick Praise 4, 1989 to LORD OF THE YEARS
Irish Church Praise (Ireland), 1990 to MARLBOROUGH PARK
Ascribe Greatness, 1994 to LORD OF THE YEARS
O God, your Praise we Sing, 1994 to LORD OF THE YEARS
The Hymn Makers: 'Tell out, my soul', 1996 to LORD OF THE
YEARS
Lord of all Hopefulness, 1997 to LORD OF THE YEARS
The Songs of Fellowship Collection 1, 1999 to LORD OF THE
YEARS
Heavenly Music for Earthly Use, 1999 to LORD OF THE YEARS
Christ Triumphant (The English Hymn 1), 1999 to LORD OF THE
YEARS
Songs of Praise, 2001 to LORD OF THE YEARS

In 1867 a remarkable organization called 'the Children's Special Service Mission' was founded, following the visit to England of an American, Payson Hammond, who conducted a number of children's missions. Twelve years later a children's 'Scripture Union' was begun under the same auspices. Today the name 'Scripture Union' is the one commonly used, but the organization continues, grows and flourishes, undertaking a huge variety of Christian work among young people. In 1967 I was asked to try my hand at a hymn for the centenary service, which would be held at St Paul's Cathedral. As I recall, the tune FINLANDIA was suggested because it was available with orchestral parts.

Owing much to the Scripture Union in my own spiritual pilgrimage, I agreed to try; and I recall writing this text on a train, travelling home from Nottingham to London in the early evening. It was sung at the Service, and included in *Youth Praise 2* a couple of years later. Dr George Carey chose it for his Enthronement Service as Archbishop of Canterbury in 1991. It proved popular at Services to mark 50 years from the end of the Second World War, and a few years later to celebrate the millennium. It is also requested surprisingly often for weddings, and indeed was sung at the weddings of both our daughters.

For verse 2, see Philippians 2.16, Luke 24.32, 2 Timothy 3.16: for verse 3, line 2, see Luke 8.14: for verse 5, see Galatians 5.24 and Colossians 3.3.

Towards the end of 2001 I was asked by 'Churches Together in England' to write an additional verse to this text with the Queen's Golden Jubilee in mind, which they might circulate with other liturgical material to local churches and those preparing Orders of Service to celebrate the event. Their feeling was that the hymn was sufficiently well known, and already included references which chimed with the themes of the Jubilee. In the event, I wrote a new hymn with the Jubilee in mind (see 106 'To God we come in prayer and praise') but offered also the further verse they had requested, though not as a permanent part of the hymn. Both hymns were included in *Worship Material for the Queen's Jubilee* (Churches Together in Britain and Ireland, London 2002).

See Index 6.

106 TO GOD WE COME IN PRAYER AND PRAISE 88 88 (LM)

Theme	Celebration; anniversary; thanksgiving
Written	at Ford, December 2001
Suggested tune	CHURCH TRIUMPHANT by James W. Elliott
	PUER NOBIS NASCITUR adapted by Michael Praetorius

The previous Note explains how in November 2001 I was approached about a hymn for the Queen's forthcoming Golden Jubilee: in the first instance, an additional verse to 'Lord, for the years'. This I dutifully wrote, with a strong feeling at the back of my mind that I was putting a new patch on an old garment; and at the same time offered to attempt a new hymn with the Jubilee in mind. The themes 'flowing from the Palace', I was told, were thanksgiving, service, community, and looking forward as well as back.

After a period when inspiration seemed totally lacking, this is the hymn I submitted, affirming our united trust in the God of our creation and our history, with thankfulness for the past, celebration for the present, and dedication for the future. Rock, Refuge and Tower are taken from the Psalms (e.g. 18.2, where AV has 'high tower') and from Proverbs 18.10; and God our Hope from e.g. Psalm 71.5; see also Proverbs 8.15 for verse 3, line 2. Line 3 of verse 5 draws on the prayer that Jesus taught us (Matthew 6.9,10) and so implies our service to God and to each other which is one of the given themes.

Both hymns, 105 and 106, together with 116, were sung on the Sunday before the Jubilee in a number of local churches across the United Kingdom and the Commonwealth.

107 WITH ALL WHO IN THIS HALLOWED PLACE 86 86 D (DCM)

Based on	John 14.6
Theme	Anniversary; dedication and renewal
Written	at Ford, July 1996
Suggested tune	ST MATTHEW by William Croft
	ST MICHAEL'S from W. Gawler's *Hymns and Psalms,* 1789
	THE AULD HOOSE (Scottish traditional)
Published in	*Cantate Domino,* 2000 to HOLDERNESS by Andrew Wright
	Sing to the Lord no Threadbare Song (USA), 2001 to VAN ZOEREN by Alfred V. Fedak

When St John's Church, Nevilles Cross, Durham, was preparing to celebrate its centenary, the Reverend Michael Rusk, the Vicar, approached me for a hymn of celebration, to which David Lee, their Director of Music who had set a number of my texts, would write a tune. In the event, the text worked out as DCM, and may therefore also be sung to existing DCM tunes.

Michael Rusk asked for something which would reflect the dedication of the church to St John; and this accounts for the use of John 14.6; Christ the Way, the Truth and the Life, as a connecting link between the stanzas. Verse 1 looks back over the past (in the case of St John's Church, over the past century), the middle verses are concerned with the church of the present in its living experience of Christ today; and the conclusion looks ahead to a church renewed for mission in preparation for its next 100 years.

Johannine references, in addition to John 14.6, include the Bread of life, the living Word, freedom through the truth, and the new birth.

Theme	Thanksgiving; anniversary; dedication; saints and forerunners
Written	at Ruan Minor, August 1984
Suggested tune	CHRISTO ET REGNO by Daniel Horn
	VINEYARD HAVEN by Richard W. Dirksen
Published in	*Gather* (USA), 1988 to BALDWIN by James J. Chepponis
	Songs of Rejoicing (USA), 1989 to LUDY by Howard M. Edwards
	Daily Office, Community of the Holy Name, 1990 (words only)
	The Collegeville Hymnal (USA), 1991 to CEOLA by Edward J.
	McKenna
	The Yes of the Heart (USA), 1993 to LUDY
	Give Thanks to God on High: the Choral Music of Peter Cutts, 1993 to
	WOOLLEY by Peter Cutts
	Christian Worship: a Lutheran Hymnal (USA), 1993 to FRANKLIN
	by Bruce R. Backer
	Gather, 2nd edition (USA), 1994 to BALDWIN
	RitualSong (USA), 1996 to BALDWIN
	Rejoice in God (USA), 2000 to BLUFF PARK by K. Lee Scott
	Anthem (USA), 2001 by K. Lee Scott
Recorded on	*Give Thanks to God on High*, 1985 to CHRISTO ET REGNO

This text was requested by Wheaton College, Illinois, for their 125th anniversary. As it happened I was in Wheaton in 1984, after paying my first visit to the annual conference of the Hymn Society of America, now The Hymn Society in the United States and Canada. Hope Publishing Company had mounted a major symposium on hymns and hymn singing among evangelicals, 'Hymns '84', in the Billy Graham Center at Wheaton College over two days at the end of July. Walking through the college grounds and pondering their request for a hymn, I was struck to see the college motto prominently displayed, 'For Christ and his kingdom'—and this became the main thrust of the text. Daniel Horn, a member of the Wheaton College Conservatory of Music, composed the tune CHRISTO ET REGNO, and the hymn was first sung at the Anniversary Convocation on 9 January 1985 in the Edman Memorial Chapel.

109 THANKS BE TO GOD FOR HIS SAINTS OF EACH PAST GENERATION

                                                                14 14 4 7 8

Theme	Anniversary; thanksgiving; saints
Written	at Ford, May 1996
Suggested tune	LOBE DEN HERREN by Johann Crüger
Published in	*Sing Glory*, 1999 to LOBE DEN HERREN
	Sing to the Lord, 2000 to LOBE DEN HERREN

Christ Church, Winchester, owes its foundation to William Carus, sometime Fellow and Senior Dean of Trinity College, Cambridge; but chiefly remembered as curate to Charles Simeon and editor of Simeon's memoirs: the church was founded 'almost as a Simeon memorial'. In 1995 Archdeacon E.S. Shirras, Vicar of Christ Church, wrote asking for a hymn which might be sung following a total re-ordering of the church then in progress, and which would include celebration and personal rededication, looking forward to the millennium and beyond. He added 'A strong theme would be "Jesus Christ the same yesterday, and today, and for ever" from Hebrews 13.8.'

The text takes this theme explicitly in line 4 of verses 1 and 4; but also in its structure, where succeeding verses look to the past, the present and the future. The 'great congregation' of verse 1 echoes a number of psalms; while the final line draws on Hebrews 5.9 in the AV; and on the prayer at the heart of the Marriage Service in the *Book of Common Prayer* where God is addressed as 'the Author of everlasting life'. 'Joy at the last' (verse 3) again brings to mind the psalms (30.5; 126.5) but more especially the vision of Revelation 7.17.

The tune LOBE DEN HERREN, to which the text was written, is described by Erik Routley in the *Companion to Congregational Praise*, 1953 as 'one of the finest of the ancient chorales'. It is almost invariably set to Catherine Winkworth's translation, 'Praise to the Lord, the Almighty, the King of creation'; few later texts have been written for it, as far as I am aware, beyond Herbert O 'Driscoll's hymn on the Scriptures, 'God who hast caused to be written thy word for our learning'. 'Praise to the Lord' is clearly a hymn for the start of worship ('now to his temple draw near') whereas this is more suitable as a concluding hymn, ending on the note of 'Forth to his service...'

---

110 WHEN JOHN BAPTIZED BY JORDAN'S RIVER   98 98 D

Based on	The gospel accounts in Matthew 3, Mark 1 and Luke 3
Theme	John the Baptist; the baptism of Jesus; baptism and confirmation
Written	at Ruan Minor, August 1979 and 1982
Suggested tune	RENDEZ À DIEU by Louise Bourgeois
Published in	*Worship III* (USA), 1986 to RENDEZ À DIEU
	Hymnal for the Hours (USA), 1989 to RENDEZ À DIEU
	The Song Goes On (USA), 1990 to RENDEZ À DIEU
	Celebration Hymnal for Everyone, 1994 to RENDEZ À DIEU
	Catholic Book of Worship III (Canada), 1994 to RENDEZ À DIEU
	Moravian Book of Worship (USA), 1995 to RENDEZ À DIEU
	The Covenant Hymnal (USA), 1996 to RENDEZ À DIEU
	RitualSong (USA), 1996 to RENDEZ À DIEU
	Laudate, 1999 to RENDEZ À DIEU
	Worship & Rejoice (USA), 2001 to RENDEZ À DIEU

In December 1978 I received a letter from the Reverend Dirk van Dissel of South Australia, asking if I had written a hymn upon the Baptism of Christ. He pointed out that there is not much on this subject in the older hymnals, and that 'recent Supplements have done little to supply the dearth'; while adding that all the revised Calendars and Liturgies include the Baptism of Christ as a feast on the First Sunday after Epiphany. This is the case, for example, in the Church of England *Common Worship*, 2000. I see from Fred Pratt Green's *Hymns and Ballads* (Carol Stream and London 1982) that his hymn on the same theme, 'When Jesus came to Jordan', sprang from a similar correspondence.

Accordingly, I tried my hand in the summer of 1979; and achieved two versions of an opening verse. I returned to the text in 1981, making no further progress; but in 1982 things 'came together' based on the abortive efforts of previous years. Once the mental block that had held me up for two years was broken, the text took shape in a single day, partly on the beach at Poldhu. I should like to think that its usefulness is not confined to

Services which have the Baptism of Christ as their theme, but that it could be sung at Services of baptism, and indeed of confirmation. The final prayer of verse 3 would be specially appropriate here, echoing as it does the traditional confirmation prayer of the Church of England.

The baptism of Jesus by John is traditionally celebrated at Epiphany; and John's birth and death on 24 June and 29 August respectively.

111 WHAT DEBT OF SIN THAT NONE CAN PAY

88 88 88

Theme	St Matthew; the Bible; Christ the King
Written	at Ford, November 2000
Suggested tune	PATER OMNIUM by Henry J.E. Holmes
	ST PETERSBURG by D.S. Bortniansky

This is one of a set of four hymns, which follow in consecutive order, each to a different metre, on the four Evangelists. They are intended not only for the particular saints' days, but to accompany reading of the Scriptures, perhaps before the Gospel at Holy Communion. Each text tries to relate to the individual writer, including some aspect of his life and what is distinctive in his work.

Matthew the tax collector, it is conjectured, may well have come under the influence of John the Baptist, preparing him to respond so immediately to the call of Jesus (Matthew 9.9). Because this is no more than a probability, I have referred to it in the form of a question; though the words in verse 2, 'as in a dream' are a conjecture (I hope a legitimate one) of my own. Stephen Motyer points out in *Men with a Message* (Grand Rapids 1994) what importance Matthew attaches to the forgiveness of sins, which therefore finds mention in more than one verse of this text; and how (with his commercial background) the concept of debt is a very real one to him: witness Matthew 6.12 where debts and debtors feature in his version of the Lord's Prayer, or the story of the unforgiving debtor (18.23–35) which he alone records. It seemed appropriate, therefore, to begin and end this hymn with that theme. Another concern of Matthew's, from his Jewish background, is Christ's fulfilment of the Old Testament as the promised King of the House of David; and indeed the whole concept of kingship, and the kingdom of heaven. And it is Matthew, of course, who brings us the Sermon on the Mount, and other substantial passages of the teaching of Jesus not found in Mark (see line 4 of my verse 2); among these are well-known references to the coming of the Son of Man in glory, the note on which the hymn concludes (see, e.g. 16.27; 19.28; 24.30; 25.31).

The Festival of St Matthew, Apostle and Evangelist, traditionally falls on 21 September.

112 PRAISE BE TO GOD FOR SERVANTS OF THE WORD

10 10 10 10

Theme	St Mark; the Bible; Passiontide
Written	at Ford, November 2000
Suggested tune	FARLEY CASTLE by Henry Lawes
	SONG 22 by Orlando Gibbons
	ST AGNES (LANGRAN) by James Langran

For a general introduction to these four hymns built round the writers of the four Gospels, see the note on 111 'What debt of sin that none can pay'.

A number of references in the New Testament tell us something of John Mark, to give him his fuller name (Acts 12.12). Other traditions, though generally accepted, are less certain; for example that Mark 14.51,52 is a self-portrait; or that Mark was the first to write a 'gospel' and in Christian terms the originator of the form. Verse 1 of the text therefore refers to Mark the Evangelist, without specifically claiming his priority, just as verse 3 refers to his 'fears', without affirming that these are the fears that prompted flight from the Garden of Gethsemane. It seems likely that the move from the comfort of his mother's house in Jerusalem to the work of a pioneer missionary was bound to mean 'hardship'; while his failure and restoration to ministry can be seen by comparing Acts 15.38 with Philemon 24. Indeed, the frailty of the disciples is a thread that runs throughout his Gospel; and there is a strong tradition (to put it no higher) that in writing it, Mark was recording what he had often heard in Peter's preaching (see 1 Peter 5.13, 'my son Mark...').

Verse 2 in the text is a reminder that Mark's Gospel is the record of Christ the Suffering Servant, while the whole Gospel is written from the outset as good news of 'Jesus Christ, the Son of God' (Mark 1.1), and could be said to culminate in the centurion's testimony at the foot of the cross (Mark 15.39).

'Ministers (that is, servants) of the word' is a phrase used by St Luke to describe those from whose information he wrote his Gospel (Luke 1.2). It seems likely enough that John Mark was high among them, but in any event, as one of the four Evangelists, he has a right to be counted among the 'servants of the word' for whom we praise God. The Festival of St Mark the Evangelist traditionally falls on 25 April.

113 SAINT LUKE, BELOVED PHYSICIAN   76 76 D

Theme	St Luke; the Bible; health and healing
Written	at Ford, November 2000
Suggested tune	AURELIA by Samuel S. Wesley
	NYLAND (Finnish traditional)
	PENLAN by David Jenkins

For a general introduction to these four hymns built round the writers of the four Gospels, see the note on 111 'What debt of sin that none can pay'.

It was Paul (Colossians 4.14) who gave to St Luke the title 'Beloved Physician' and his name has always been associated with health and healing as well as a 'concern for people on the margins', including women and children. When we think of Christ's expression as compassionate, we owe much of that to Luke. Dante described him as recording 'the gentleness of Christ'. Luke wrote not only his Gospel, but also the Book of Acts, sharing with Paul a first-hand experience of those 'pains and glories' to which the hymn refers. These included constant opportunities to see the power of God at work in 'the foolishness of preaching'; and for Luke the power of the Holy Spirit is a recurring theme in both his books, bearing witness to Christ the universal Saviour. It is Luke, too, who gives us the picture of the contrite sinner returning to his waiting father in Luke 15.21, and of the poor woman 'bound for eighteen years' and freed by Christ (Luke 13.16).

Luke has been shown to have a special interest in prayer, so it is fitting that the final verse of the hymn should begin with a prayer and be related to health and wholeness today. 'Physician of the soul' is borrowed from the Collect of St Luke the Evangelist in the *Book of Common Prayer*, a phrase retained in *Common Worship*, 2000.

The Festival of St Luke the Evangelist traditionally falls on 18 October.

Theme	St John; the Bible; growth in Christ
Written	at Ford, November 2000
Suggested tune	FINLANDIA by Jean Sibelius
	SONG 1 by Orlando Gibbons
	UNDE ET MEMORES by William H. Monk

For a general note on these four hymns built round the writers of the four Gospels, see the note on 111 'What debt of sin that none can pay'.

The Gospel of John is markedly different from the other three. It is generally thought to be the last of the Gospels, perhaps written in old age, presenting a picture of Jesus remembered and matured by long reflection. This is the intended significance of the final couplet of verse 1 of the text, a verse which also makes reference to John's themes of love (one of his key words) and of re-birth from above (John 3). Verse 2 picks up the famous Prologue, and the ideas of Christ as Light and Life (John 1.4,9; 8.12). Death's power broken is seen in the raising of Lazarus in John 11, while John alone of the Evangelists uses the title Lamb of God. The final line of verse 2 is taken from John 14.6, the same chapter which describes 'that home prepared by Christ' in verse 3, line 5. 'Beloved disciple' is not, I think, a direct biblical quote (Luke and Timothy are both called 'beloved', as are many others: e.g. Romans 16.8, 9, 12) but refers to John's threefold references to himself in chapters 20 and 21 as 'the disciple whom Jesus loved'.

In the final verse John's letters do more than his Gospel to shape the hymn. Line 2, though taken from the Gospel ('believe and live', John 20.30) adds the purpose John gave for his first letter (1 John 5.13) where his aim is to help his readers to an assurance of salvation—that is, to *know*; and to urge them to show their faith and love in obedience. 'Abiding in Christ' comes from the famous image of the vine in chapter 15 of the Gospel; but also from 1 John 2. 27, 28. The final line of the hymn depends upon the promise in 1 John 3.2.

The Festival of St John, Apostle and Evangelist, traditionally falls on 27 December.

115 GIVE PRAISE TO GOD FOR HIS APOSTLE PAUL   10 10 10 10

Theme	St Paul; the Bible; commitment to Christ
Written	at Ford, May 2001
Suggested tune	WOODLANDS by Walter Greatorex

Paul features with outstanding frequency in both liturgy and preaching. Half the Book of Acts tells his story; and of the letters which make up so much of the New Testament, the greater part are from his pen. In the most recent Calendar of the Church of England his conversion is remembered in January and his Apostolate in June.

In this hymn, verse 1 speaks of Paul's conversion experience, as recounted three times over in Acts, chapters 9, 22 and 26. Each of the six characteristics named in line 3 appear in each account, mercy being implicit (but see, e.g., 1 Corinthians 7.25) and truth understood as the truth about Jesus of Nazareth; the call is described most fully by Paul to Agrippa in Acts 26. Other references to, or echoes from, Paul's preaching and writing are included: 'Captive' or 'slave', Ephesians 3.1; 'herald', 1 Corinthians 1.23, where 'preach' or 'proclaim' equates to 'herald'; 'bold', Philippians 1.20; 'died and risen', Acts 17.3; 'Lord of death and grave', 1 Corinthians 15.55-57; 'freely by his grace', Romans 3.24; 'Deliverer',

Romans 11.26; 'paid the price', 2 Corinthians 11.24f; 'to live... to die', Philippians 1.21; 'none... had heard', Romans 15.20; 'course...crown', 2 Timothy 4.7,8; 'word of life', Philippians 2.16; 'heirs', Ephesians 3.6; 'my gospel', Romans 2.16; 'blessing God', Ephesians 1.3. 'Nations' in verse 3 is an equivalent translation for 'Gentiles', in contrast to 'Israel' of the opening line.

The Festival of Paul's conversion falls traditionally on 25 January. Peter and Paul, Apostles, are commemorated on 29 June.

116 O CHRIST THE SAME, THROUGH ALL OUR STORY'S PAGES   11 10 11 10 D

Theme	New year; anniversary; thanksgiving
Written	at Sevenoaks, September 1971
Suggested tune	LONDONDERRY AIR (Irish traditional)
Published in	*Hymns for Today's Church*, 1982 to SALVATOR MUNDI by Kenneth W. Coates
	The New English Hymnal, 1986 to LONDONDERRY AIR
	Irish Church Praise (Ireland), 1990 to LONDONDERRY AIR
	The Quarterly Review of the Churches' Fellowship for Psychical and Spiritual Studies, Autumn 1993 (words only)
	Anthem (USA), 1995 by Michael Connolly
	With One Voice (USA), 1995 to LONDONDERRY AIR
	Anthem (USA), 2000 by Craig Courtney
	Complete Anglican Hymns Old & New, 2000 to LONDONDERRY AIR
	Church Hymnary (Ireland), 2000 to LONDONDERRY AIR
	Praise!, 2000 to MOORDOWN by Linda Mawson
	Worship & Rejoice (USA), 2001 to LONDONDERRY AIR
Recorded on	*Lord of all Hopefulness*, 1997 to LONDONDERRY AIR

This hymn was written on request, to be sung at the Service to mark the opening of the new premises of the Cambridge University Mission in Bermondsey (now the Salmon Youth Centre), in November 1972. The Mission had been my home, in a tiny flat at the top of three old terrace houses, during the two years I spent as Head of the Mission from 1953 to 1955.

The starting point of the text is Hebrews 13.8, 'Jesus Christ the same, yesterday, today and for ever'; and this is worked out in the three verses with their emphasis on thanksgiving for past, present and future.

The titles given to Christ in this hymn are drawn directly, or by implication, from Scripture as follows: eternal Lord, from Deuteronomy 33.27 (eternal God) and 1 Timothy 1.17 (King eternal); King of ages (cf. Ephesians 3.21; Psalm 145.13); living Word (John 1.14); friend of sinners (Matthew 11.19); Son of Man (e.g. Matthew 8.20 and throughout the four Gospels); Prince of life (Acts 3.15); Lord of love (cf. Ephesians 5.2).

The text has been placed in some hymnals as suitable for the start of a new year; and has also been used for Remembrance Sunday (see lines 1 and 2 of verse 3). It was sung in St Paul's Cathedral on 4 June 2002 at 'A Service of Celebration and Thanksgiving on the occasion of the Golden Jubilee of Her Majesty the Queen' with the combined choirs of the Cathedral and Her Majesty's Chapels Royal.

117 GOD WHOSE LOVE IS EVERYWHERE   7775 775

Theme	Christingle
Written	at Ruan Minor and at Poldhu Cove, September 1988
Suggested tune	CHRISTINGLE PRAISE by John Barnard
	FALLING FIFTHS by Noël Tredinnick
Published in	*Two New Hymns in Celebration of Christingle*, 1989 to FALLING FIFTHS
	New Songs of Praise 5, 1990 to FALLING FIFTHS
	The Promise of His Glory, 1990 (words only)
	Junior Praise 2, 1992 to FALLING FIFTHS
	Sing to the Lord, volume 4, 1997 to music by Kevin Norbury
	Junior Praise Combined, 1997 to FALLING FIFTHS
	New Start Hymns and Songs, 1999 FALLING FIFTHS
	Supplement 99 (USA), 1999 to CHRISTINGLE PRAISE
	Sing Glory, 1999 to FALLING FIFTHS
	Common Praise, 2000 to CHRISTINGLE PRAISE
Recorded on	*Junior Praise Combined 24*, 1999 to FALLING FIFTHS

The word 'Christingle' is said to mean 'Christ-light'. Christingle Services have achieved considerable popularity in England through the work of the Church of England Children's Society, who have linked the old Moravian tradition of Christingle to the work they are doing for young people in need. The theme of the Service is thankfulness, and as the congregation offer their gifts to help bring the light of Christ to darkened lives, they each receive in return a 'Christingle' as a sign of God's love and goodness to them. The Christingles are made with an orange, to which fruit and nuts are secured with wooden sticks. Around the orange is placed a red ribbon, and a small lighted candle surmounts it. The significance of each part can be seen from the commentary beside each verse of the text. The words were written in response to a request for hymns on this theme for *New Songs of Praise 5*. The fifth line of the final verse may call to mind Henry Vaughan's 'Death and darkness, get you packing', written 300 years ago.

118 OUR FATHER GOD IN HEAVEN   76 76 D

Theme	Mothering Sunday; the Virgin Mary
Written	at Ford, January 2000
Suggested tune	ST THEODULPH by Melchior Teschner
	WOLVERCOTE by William H. Ferguson
Published in	*Cantate Domino*, 2000 to SARA by Christopher Tambling

Mothering Sunday has become a significant occasion in the life of many local churches. The *Alternative Service Book, 1980* recognized it by lectionary readings for the fourth Sunday in Lent; and *Common Worship* goes further with liturgical provision. But in our day family life is in flux. A hymn for congregational use has to take account of the sensitivities of a variety of personal circumstances. One cannot ask everyone, not even every child, in a large congregation to thank God without reservation for their own mother. They may never have known her, nor even who she was. Their memories may be of neglect and desertion. Yet many, and one may hope most, of those present will be genuinely thankful for mothers, perhaps beside them in the pew, or far away, or long dead; and will want to express gratitude to God for them, as I do myself.

I hope this text manages to walk such a tightrope without giving the impression that it is treading delicately. The metre and style have family services in mind, and I have tried to avoid the 'cringe-factor', the mawkish or over-sentimental. The limitation on its use suggested by line 7 of verse 1 is deliberate, but not finally exclusive for other occasions, such as the commemoration of Mary, the mother of the Lord.

Verse 4 lifts our eyes beyond our personal circumstances to 'every child' in our global village; and adds, I hope, a note of sobering realism to our personal thanksgiving.

119 ALL FLOWERS OF GARDEN, FIELD AND HILL   86 86 (CM)

Theme	Flower festival; harvest; nature; creation
Written	at Ruan Minor and at Stopham, Sussex, August 1977
Suggested tune	BEATITUDO by John B. Dykes
	UNIVERSITY by Charles Collignon
Published in	*Country Way,* Winter/Spring 1999 (words only)

Flower festivals are a feature of country churches in many parts of England. This text sets out to evoke some of the ways in which the Lord Jesus Christ used the natural world around him in his teaching; or in which plants and flowers remind us of the gospel story.

Unusually, as can be seen by the concluding commas, verses 2 and 3 find their main verb only in verse 4; and verses 5 and 6 in verse 7. A well-established example of such a delayed main verb can be seen in the opening verse of Isaac Watts' 'O God, our help in ages past'.

120 FAITH AND TRUTH AND LIFE BESTOWING   87 87 D or 87 87

Based on	The parable of the sower, Matthew 13.3–9
Theme	Harvest; the Bible; parables
Written	at Ford, August 1996
Suggested tune	BEECHER by John Zundel
	MEAD HOUSE by Cyril V. Taylor
	RUSTINGTON by C. Hubert H. Parry
Published in	*Country Way,* Spring/Summer 1998 to CHISELBURY by R.C. Fielding
	Sing Glory, 1999 to HOPE PARK by Ian Sharp
	Sing to the Lord, 2000 to LLANSANNAN (Welsh traditional)

Since each four-line stanza of this text is complete in itself, it can be sung to 87 87 tunes; but I prefer it as two verses of eight lines each. It is primarily, as can be seen, a hymn to sing before the Scriptures are read or taught: a short hymn before the sermon, or perhaps a Gradual hymn (the name means simply 'step' and originally referred to portions of psalms sung between the Epistle and Gospel at Holy Communion from the chancel step). Alan Dunstan, in his admirable small book *These are the Hymns* (London 1973), writes,

'A hymn about the Holy Scriptures is also appropriate at this point—but unfortunately only two or three hymns on this theme exist in most Anglican collections. The congregation was not unnaturally rather bored in a church where part of 'Lord, thy word abideth' was always sung at this point...'

The opening line has in mind Paul's words in Romans 10.17 ('faith comes from what is heard', RSV); while 'fruit that shall remain' is borrowed from John 15.16. The final line is a prayer based on the Lord's exhortation which concludes the parable of the sower, 'He who has ears, let him hear'; or, in J.B. Phillips' phrase 'The man who has ears to hear should use them!'

121 GOD IN HIS WISDOM, FOR OUR LEARNING   98 98 98

Theme	The Bible
Written	at Ford, August 1995
Suggested tune	FRAGRANCE (French traditional)
Published in	*New Daylight*, January-April 1997 (words only)
	Guidelines to the Bible, January-April 1997 (words only)
	Praise!, 2000 to FRAGRANCE

The year 1997 saw the 75th anniversary of the Bible Reading Fellowship, and this text is one of two written at the request of Sue Doggett, commissioning editor of BRF (for the second, see 125 'Teach us to love the Scriptures, Lord'). FRAGRANCE was a tune specially requested and the text was written to it.

Line 1, 'for our learning' is an immediate reminder for Anglicans of the Collect of Bible Sunday, Advent 2 or the last Sunday after Trinity. Line 2 is drawn from 2 Timothy 3.16 and line 5 takes us to the Emmaus Road and the experience of Cleopas and 'another disciple' (Luke 24.32). Verse 2 rehearses some of the many forms in which God's word is known. 'Symbol' suggests, perhaps, the bow in the cloud (Genesis 9.13), or the brazen serpent (Numbers 21), and so on through many such examples to the bread and wine of the Last Supper, or the Tree of Life of Revelation 22. 'Story' might equally be the historical books of the Old Testament, the gospel narratives or the Acts of the Apostles. 'Songs' come pre-eminently in the Psalms and 'sayings' in Proverbs. In all this, the word is 'life-bearing' (cf. seed, Luke 8.11) and 'truth' (John 17.17), with God's fatherly care displayed in all his dealings with humanity, and portrayed in the person of his Son. 'Open our eyes' is the prayer of the Psalmist (e.g. Psalm 119.18), and 'Christ in Scripture' the theme of the BRF prayer, following Luke 24.27.

122 GOD OF OLD, WHOM SAINTS AND SAGES   87 87 87

Theme	The Bible
Written	at Bramerton, May 1979
Suggested tune	REGENT SQUARE by Henry T. Smart
	RHUDDLAN (Welsh traditional)

Published in   *On the Move* (Australia), April 1980 (words only)
                Declare His Glory, 1981 to REGENT SQUARE
                Bible Sunday Hymns, 1989 (words only)

The text was written for the Norwich celebration of the centenary of the Scripture Union, to be sung to REGENT SQUARE. Verse 3 points to 'Christ in all the Scriptures' from the opening chapter of John's Gospel, portrayed as Word of God (John 1.1), Lamb of God (John 1.29), and Son of God (John 1.34). The same thought is continued in the last stanza, where the invitation (Matthew 11.28), the promise or pledge (Acts 2.39), the royal law (James 2.8), the lamp (Psalm 119.105), and the Spirit's sword (Ephesians 6.17) all in their own way 'tell of Christ'.

123 O GOD WHO SHAPED THE STARRY SKIES   886 D

Based on	Psalm 19.7–11
Theme	The Bible
Written	at Ford, August 1993
Suggested tune	CORNWALL by Samuel S. Wesley INNSBRUCK NEW based on Heinrich Isaak
Published in	*Praise!*, 2000 to INNSBRUCK NEW *The Poetic Bible*, 2001 (words only)

The main thrust of the text, as of that part of Psalm 19, is that the 'same creative word' which brought forth our world at the beginning may be at work in the new creation of the Christian heart.

This text follows the RSV in its use of 'law', 'fear' and 'commandments'; 'covenant' is related to the 'testimony' of verse 7, while 'word' stands for 'precept(s)', and 'judgments' for 'ordinances'.

124 OPEN OUR EYES, O LORD, WE PRAY   86 86 (CM)

Based on	Verses from Psalm 119
Theme	The Bible
Written	at Ford, June 1993
Suggested tune	BEATITUDO by John B. Dykes RICHMOND adapted from Thomas Haweis
Published in	*Prayers & Hymns for Bible Sunday*, 1993 (words only) *New Mission Praise*, 1996 to BISHOPTHORPE by Jeremiah Clarke *Complete Mission Praise*, 1999 to BISHOPTHORPE *Anthem* (USA), 1999 by Jeffrey Honoré *Glory Be* (New Zealand), 2000 to RICHMOND

In June 1993 Canon W.H. Andrew, the Communications Director of the Bible Society, wrote to tell me of their plans to use Psalm 119 as the suggested passage for 'Bible Sunday' 1993, with the thought of 'treasure' as a continuing theme.

Looking again at the psalm, especially verse 18 (long familiar as the Scripture Union prayer) a pattern of God's 'openings' began to appear, not all of them in this psalm. The 'open ear' is in Psalm 40.6; 'open lips' in Psalm 51.15; while for the 'open lives' of verse 3 of this text we have to look to Acts 16.14 and the story of Lydia 'whose heart the Lord opened'; or to the 'any man' of Revelation 3.20. Perhaps in today's speech a life open to love is more meaningful than would be the use of the word 'heart'; which finds its place in verse 4, following Psalm 119.11.

The same idea finds expression in two or three contemporary worship songs; for example, 'Open our eyes, Lord, we want to see Jesus' by Robert Cull, or 'Open your eyes, see the glory of the King' by Carol Tuttle. Finally Prebendary Colin C. Kerr's brief biblical chorus from Psalm 119, 'Open thou mine eyes', continues to find a place—for example in successive editions of *Mission Praise*, 1990.

125 TEACH US TO LOVE THE SCRIPTURES, LORD   86 86 (CM)

Theme	The Bible
Written	at Ford, August 1995
Suggested tune	CONTEMPLATION by Frederick A.G. Ouseley DUNDEE (Scottish traditional) ST HUGH by Edward J. Hopkins
Published in	*New Daylight*, January-April 1997 (words only) *Guidelines to the Bible*, January-April 1997 (words only)

This text is one of two written at the request of the Bible Reading Fellowship for their 75th Anniversary in January 1997 (see also 121 'God in his wisdom, for our learning'). The opening verse echoes the *Book of Common Prayer* Collect for Advent 2, which prays that the written word of Scripture may lead us, as we read, to the living Word, Jesus Christ himself. This thought, which is repeated in the final couplet of the text, forms the basis of the BRF prayer:

> 'We bless you, Lord,
> For all who teach us
> To love the Scriptures
> And for all who help us
> To understand them;
> Grant that in
> The written word
> We may encounter
> The Living Word,
> Your Son, our Saviour, Jesus Christ.
> Amen.'

The second verse of this text thinks prayerfully of the Scriptures as revealing God's will and purpose, his promises and 'Name'—that is, his character and person. Verse 3 takes up the theme of light on our path (Psalm 119.105) and the sword of the Spirit (Ephesians 6.17); and includes in the opening line a phrase from Ezekiel 34.12, AV, the 'cloudy and dark day' when the sheep are scattered and the Shepherd searches for them. Finally verses 4 and 5 remind us that the word of God is sustenance (cf. 1 Peter 2.2) and treasure (e.g. Psalm 119.162; Colossians 3.16); and that Christ himself is to be found 'in all the Scriptures' (Luke 24.27).

Theme	The Bible
Written	at Ruan Minor, August 1990
Suggested tune	ELLACOMBE (German traditional)
	EWING by Alexander Ewing
	NYLAND (Finnish traditional)
Published in	*Celebrate the Growing* (Australia), 1991 to CRÜGER
	Bible Society Hymns, 1991 (words only)
	Moravian Book of Worship (USA), 1995 to NYLAND

In March 1990 the publishing manager of Scripture Union, Australia, invited me to attempt a hymn to accompany the launch of a new initiative in Bible-reading notes, planned for 1991. This text is the result.

It contains a variety of allusions to, or echoes of, the text of Scripture. For example 2 Timothy 3.16; Psalm 119.105; Ephesians 4.12; Matthew 4.4; Luke 8.11; Psalm 119.18; 1 Peter 1.25; Romans 10.17; Jeremiah 23.29; Luke 24.32; Luke 4.22; 1 Corinthians 15.3,4; Psalm 19.10; Ezekiel 3.3; Psalm 119.162; John 5.39; Luke 24.27.

127 ETERNAL GOD, BEFORE WHOSE FACE WE STAND 10 10 10 10 10 10

Theme	Remembrance Sunday; the peace of the world
Written	at Ford, January 1999
Suggested tune	SONG 1 by Orlando Gibbons
	UNDE ET MEMORES by William H. Monk
Published in	*Country Way*, Autumn 2000 (words only)
	Cantate Domino, 2000 to REMEMBRANCE by Colin Mawby
	Twelve Hymns, 2001 to CHURCH STRETTON by Maurice Bevan

Canon Charles Stewart, Precentor of Winchester Cathedral, approached me in November 1998 'in the aftermath of this year's Remembrance Sunday' to ask if I would write a hymn for Remembrance Sunday in the Cathedral the following year. It is a Cathedral with strong military associations.

Unusually, I began by searching for a tune. It had to be reasonably familiar, not over-used, solemn but not mournful. UNDE ET MEMORES, composed a hundred years ago for William Bright's 'And now, O Father, mindful of the love', seemed to set the mood and is already published to other texts.

The hymn seeks to couple the twin themes of remembrance, and the search for peace in our time; a remembrance which moves us to action, a peace which in the last resort is peace with God through Jesus Christ.

There is an echo in verse 1, line 4, of the Collect for Purity from the *Book of Common Prayer*. In verse 4 'the flower of peace' is borrowed from Henry Vaughan's lyric, 'My soul, there is a country/Far beyond the stars...' to which he gave the title 'Peace'. Three hundred years earlier in his *Piers Plowman* (the greatest poem of the Middle Ages) William Langland described Love as 'the plant of peace'.

128 GOD IS THE GIVER OF ALL THINGS THAT ARE   10 10 10 10

Theme	Stewardship; thanksgiving
Written	at Ford, September 1998
Suggested tune	ANIMA CHRISTI by William Maher
	EVENTIDE by William H. Monk
	ST AGNES (LANGRAN) by James Langran
Published in	*First Fruits: a Worship Anthology on Generosity and Giving*, 2001 (words only)

In the summer of 1998 the Anglican Stewardship Association approached me about a projected publication on Giving and Worship, asking whether I would be prepared to write a hymn for them. The Association aims to assist parishes, deaneries and dioceses to address issues of money and wealth-handling in the interests of mission. Adrian Mann of their Board of Governors wrote: '...hymns are needed which are relevant to the subject of giving (and which do not always avoid the subject of money itself).'

The text is concerned to emphasize that it is God who is the giver: giver in creation; giver of love and care through both life and death; giver and sustainer; giver and redeemer; giver of all things, to whom our giving is but a response. The reference to money may not loom particularly large in the final verse, but it is firmly there, among our time, our love, 'and all we call our own'.

129 LOOK, LORD, IN MERCY AS WE PRAY   86 86 D (DCM)

Theme	Church unity
Written	at Ruan Minor and Poldhu Cove, August 1980
Suggested tune	CHRISTMAS CAROL by H. Walford Davies
	ELLACOMBE (German traditional)
	LADYWELL by William H. Ferguson
Published in	*Church of England Newspaper*, 2 January 1981 (words only)
	Hymns for Today's Church, 1982 to CHRISTMAS CAROL
Recorded on	*Festival of Praise*, Methodist Conference, 1987 to LLOYD by C. Howard

I believe that the prayer of this text is one which more people find in their hearts today than in most previous generations. It is still true of us and our churches, in the telling phrase, 'that our scandalous divisions are by no means always the most scandalous thing about us'; but there is an unwillingness to settle merely for Christian co-operation; and a sense that to maintain unity (Ephesians 4.3) means to maintain it visibly. In that context, this hymn offers a prayer for motivation ('fire us anew'); and a reminder of the things we hold in common, on the foundation of Scripture. In the words of Cranmer's prayer for the church militant, our prayer is still that 'they that do confess thy holy Name may agree in the truth of thy holy Word, and live in unity...'

Moreover (verse 2, lines 7, 8) unity is for mission, just as (verse 3, line 7) it is 'our sins and errors' which inhibit it.

130 LORD, GIVE US EYES TO SEE

66 86 (SM)

Based on	Matthew 9.37, 38
Theme	Embertide; the ordained ministry
Written	at Sevenoaks, May 1966
Suggested tune	DOMINICA by Herbert S. Oakeley
	FESTAL SONG by William H. Walter

Ember days, originally associated with seed-time, harvest and autumn vintage, are now traditionally periods of prayer for the church's ministry, and especially for forthcoming ordinations.

This text was written, in its earlier form, following a suggestion put to me by the then Recruitment Secretary of the Advisory Council for the Church's Ministry, that there was a lack of hymns on this theme. The revision of 1998 was to take account of the ordination of women in the Church of England.

The opening line (I later discovered) echoes one of James Montgomery's, where verse 2 of his hymn 'Lord, give us ears to hear' (cf. my verse 2, line 1) begins with just these words.

See Index 6.

131 TO HEATHEN DREAMS OF HUMAN PRIDE

86 86 88

Based on	Psalm 2
Theme	The rule of God
Written	at Bramerton, July 1982
Suggested tune	AUCH JETZT MACHT GOTT from Koch's *Choralbuch*, 1816
	PALMYRA by Joseph Summers

This is one of a small number of metrical psalms written in the summer of 1982. Having no Hebrew, I tend to work from a variety of English translations; and usually with Derek Kidner's commentary at my side *(Psalms 1–72* and *Psalms 73–150,* London 1973 and 1975). In this instance, the text has a number of echoes from the New English Bible, while the thought of 'dreamers' comes from the *Liturgical Psalter* (Collins 1977) which has as its first verse:

> 'Why are the nations in tumult:
> and why do the peoples cherish a vain dream?'

Indeed, my original opening line was

> 'To what vain dream of human pride'

later changed to read 'To what fond dreams...' But the traditional 'Why do the heathen rage?' of both AV and the Coverdale version persuaded me to retain 'heathen' in the opening line.

132 HOW GREAT OUR GOD'S MAJESTIC NAME 88 88 (LM)

Based on	Psalm 8
Theme	Praise and worship; God the Father, the living God; creation
Written	at Ruan Minor and Poldhu Cove, August 1989
Suggested tune	EISENACH by Johann H. Schein
	PUER NOBIS NASCITUR adapted by Michael Praetorius
Published in	*The Baptist Hymnal* (USA), 1991 to DUKE STREET attributed to John Hatton

The word 'majestic' in the first line follows the RSV translation.

Verse 2 is an attempt to suggest (following Derek Kidner: see Note above) that the right inference from God's ordered heaven 'is not his remoteness but his eye for detail... he planned no meaningless and empty universe but a home for his family.' Hence in reply to 'What is man?' it is proper to answer, not 'a few random atoms' but 'creation's crown'.

133 IN MY HOUR OF GRIEF OR NEED 77 77

Based on	Psalm 10
Theme	Deliverance
Written	at Sevenoaks, March 1970
Suggested tune	see below, by Michael A. Baughen
	HEINLEIN by Martin Herbst
	NUN KOMM, DER HEIDEN HEILAND from *Enchiridia*, 1524
Published in	*Psalm Praise*, 1973 to music by Michael A. Baughen
	Grace Hymns, 1975 to THEODORA by G.F. Handel
	Rejoice! (Australia), 1987 to VIENNA by J.H. Knecht
	Psalms for Today, 1990 to HEINLEIN
	Praise!, 2000 to ABERAFON by J.H. Roberts

I believe this to be one of my first 'metrical psalms', written especially for *Psalm Praise*. If memory serves, I wrote much of it on a train journey to Chipping Campden.

Psalm Praise provides for the repetition of verse 1 as the conclusion of the hymn; which does something to secure the balance of the verses (pivoting, as they do, about the final line of verse 4). Notations in hymnals about how individual lines should be sung are rightly out of fashion; my own choice would be for verse 1, if repeated as verse 7, to signal a change of mood from the triumphalism of verses 5 and 6 to the realities of present temptation, by being sung softly and prayerfully.

See Index 6.

134 LORD, WHEN THE STORMS OF LIFE ARISE 86 88 6

Based on	Psalm 16
Theme	God our strength; pilgrimage
Written	at Ford, December 1992

Suggested tune	REPTON by C. Hubert H. Parry
	GATESCARTH by Caryl Micklem
Published in	*Mission Praise Combined*, 1996 to REPTON
	Complete Mission Praise, 1999 to REPTON

The thought of 'taking shelter' from the storms of life is derived from the Jerusalem Bible translation of this psalm. 'Portion' (verse 1) is Coverdale; and 'chosen' means 'allotted' (REB) or 'appointed' (*The Liturgical Psalter*), chosen *for* me rather than chosen by me. The theme of the psalm has been described as 'single-mindedness'; it lies behind one of Charles Wesley's happiest and most serviceable hymns, 'Forth in thy Name, O Lord, I go', on the theme of 'Before Work', the approach to the new day. But the psalm is also plainly Messianic (see Acts 2.29f, Peter's sermon on the Day of Pentecost), and yet speaks of the blessings of every believer. 'Fair and pleasant' combines the epithets of two translations of verse 6 of the psalm. Verse 3 carries echoes of 1 Peter 1.8, Matthew 7.14 and James 3.17; with a reference in verse 4 to 1 Corinthians 13.12.

For another hymn based on this psalm, see 135 'Within the love of God I hide'.

135 WITHIN THE LOVE OF GOD I HIDE   86 86 86

Based on	Psalm 16
Theme	Testimony; confidence; hope
Written	at Ruan Minor, August 1984
Suggested tune	BROTHER JAMES' AIR by James L. Bain
Published in	*Lift High Your Songs!*, 1988 to MEDITATION by Michael Paget

C.H. Spurgeon writes of how this psalm has been called 'golden' or 'David's jewel'; and in his *Treasury of David* (London 1869) chooses to call it 'the psalm of the precious secret'. It is not surprising, therefore, that I should have twice tried to write a metrical version (see 134 'Lord, when the storms of life arise') with eight years between them; Isaac Watts did the same in his *Psalms of David*, 1719. As with a number of psalms, it is Messianic in the sense that, as Peter tells us (Acts 2.25), it refers to the Lord Jesus Christ; but at the same time it can be read as 'a believer's testimony regarding both his present faith and his future hope'.

136 THE STARS DECLARE HIS GLORY   76 86 86

Based on	Psalm 19
Theme	Creation; God's providential order; the Bible; praise and worship
Written	at Sevenoaks, April 1970
Suggested tune	see below, by Michael A. Baughen and Elisabeth Crocker
	ALDINE by Richard Proulx
Published in	*Psalm Praise*, 1973 to music by Michael A. Baughen and Elisabeth Crocker
	Anthem (USA), 1981 by Hal H. Hopson
	The Hymnal 1982 (USA), 1985 to ALDINE

Worship III (USA), 1986 to ALDINE
Sing Alleluia (Australia), 1987 to ASTRO by Lawrence Bartlett
Hymnal Supplement II (USA), 1987 to PSALM 19 by Alec Wyton
Gather (USA), 1988 to DEERFIELD by David Haas
GIA Hymnal Supplement 1991 (USA), 1991 to ALDINE
A New Hymnal for Colleges and Schools (USA), 1992 to ALDINE
Christian Worship: a Lutheran Hymnal (USA), 1993 to ALDINE
Songs for the People of God (USA), 1994 to ST JUDE by Keith
    Landis
Gather, 2nd edition (USA), 1994 to DEERFIELD
RitualSong (USA), 1996 to ALDINE
Common Praise (Canada), 1998 to GIBSON by Patrick Wedd
Sing Glory, 1999 to EYTHORNE by John Barnard
Anthem (USA), 1999 by Austin C. Lovelace

Recorded on	Light and Peace (USA), 1986 to DEERFIELD
	Poems of Grace (USA), 2000 (words only)

This text was written for *Psalm Praise;* and if an author is allowed favourites among his texts, this is one of mine. In re-reading it (I seldom hear it sung) I recall the solution of a number of technical problems in a manner more satisfying than one can often hope for. The psalm itself is a celebration of nature and Scripture, and the opening verses are the basis of Addison's famous hymn 'The spacious firmament on high'. The thought of 'order' in the final verse may be going beyond the immediate meaning of the psalmist; but it is not, I think, inconsistent to ask that he who orders the heavens and gives the stars their laws will also direct and order the lives of his children. See also 123 'O God who shaped the starry skies'.

137 THE LORD BE NEAR US AS WE PRAY   888 6 D

Based	Psalm 20
Theme	Trust in God
Written	at Killay, Swansea, and at Ford, November 1996
Suggested tune	FRAMLINGHAM by John Barnard
Published in	Supplement 99 (USA), 1999 to TRUSTING GOD by Hal. H. Hopson
	Praise!, 2000 to BROOKSHILL by John Barnard

In 1995 the editors of *Praise!* began work on 'a new and comprehensive book of psalms, hymns and songs for Christian worship' a book which would reflect the language of today and be faithful to Scripture; and which would aim to include at least one modern version representing each biblical psalm.

In October 1996 the chairman of the group at work on the psalms for *Praise!* wrote to me asking for new metrical versions of five psalms, 20, 32, 41, 69 and 73. I was spending part of that autumn with my daughter in Killay, Swansea, which accounts for the place of writing. The triple use of the 'Name', as line 4 of each stanza, echoes the psalmist; Coverdale (followed by most other translations) has this repetition in verses 1, 5 and 7 of the psalm. Stanza 2, lines 6, 7 and 8, introduces a deliberately Christian perspective on the 'mighty victories' (JB, RSV) of the Lord, transposing them into our knowledge of God in Christ, with particular reference to 1 Peter 3.12, Hebrews 4.15 and Hebrews 2.16.

'Wealth and power' in stanza 3 is taken as a contemporary paraphrase for 'chariots and horses': weaker, perhaps, for being an abstraction, but stronger for its freedom of contemporary application.

138 ALL MY SOUL TO GOD I RAISE   77 77 77

Based on	Psalm 25
Theme	Trust in God
Written	at Ruan Minor, August 1982
Suggested tune	WELLS by D.S. Bortniansky
Published in	*Psalms for Today*, 1990 to ST PETERSBURG by D.S. Bortniansky
	Praise!, 2000 to NORICUM by Frederick James

Psalm 25, which has been called 'an alphabet of entreaty', is a Hebrew acrostic (a device used also in Psalm 34). Each verse starts with a successive letter of the Hebrew alphabet, in order. Few translations attempt to transpose this framework into the English version (one who does is R. A. Knox; and I have followed him to the extent of omitting the letters X, Y and Z; indeed the Hebrew scheme is not wholly regular) and there is a very real danger that an attempt to do so will sacrifice too much to this particular constraint—one found in English almost exclusively in comic verse. My notes suggest that I did not at first intend to try to follow the acrostic pattern, but over the three days in which the first draft was being written, it seemed to become possible to try. A hymn of 24 lines, without the three final letters of the alphabet, clearly needed one repetition; and I have come full circle to my opening line, re-punctuated to fit the syntax.

139 IN JUDGMENT, LORD, ARISE   66 86 D (DSM)

Based on	Psalm 26
Theme	Trust in God; God our strength
Written	at Ford, March 1998
Suggested tune	LEOMINSTER by George W. Martin
	OLIVA SPECIOSA (Italian melody)
	PARADOXY by Donald Hustad
	REVIVE THY WORK, O LORD by William H. Doane
Published in	*Praise!*, 2000 to LEOMINSTER

For the circumstances behind this text, see the note on 137 'The Lord be near us as we pray'. It would not be easy to put into the mouths of a present-day congregation the opening words of the psalm: 'I have led a blameless life...' (NIV); 'I have lived my life without reproach...' (NEB); 'I walk in the path of perfection...' (Gelineau): in an Anglican Service of Morning Prayer it would fit uneasily with the words of the General Confession. When sung as a psalm we can meditate on the words, and at the same time transpose them before applying them exactly to our own condition. This is what this hymn seeks to do, making a prayer or an aspiration of some of what the psalmist affirms.

The text can be sung in six verses to SM metre, which widens considerably the choice of tune: each fourth line, as can be seen, ends a sentence with a full stop. I have chosen to cast it into DSM, however, partly because DSM is a little less common in our hymnals; and partly because the eight lines which comprise each stanza in DSM seem to belong naturally to one another.

140 WE SING THE LORD OUR LIGHT 66 66 44 44

Based on	Psalm 27
Theme	God our strength; the love of God
Written	at Ruan Minor, August 1982
Suggested tune	DARWALL's 148TH by John Darwall

In the 1980s, when I was at work on some metrical psalms for a projected publication, Derek Kidner was still acting as my mentor and critic. An illustration of the way in which I valued his comments lies in line 2 of verse 2 of this text. As I sent it to him in draft, the line read 'one prayer alone we bring'. He wrote: 'Verse 2 troubles me a little (or am I getting hypercritical?) since the Psalm (and even your verse 2 itself) contains more than "one prayer alone". The meaning, in the Psalm, is evidently "Above all else". Can you somehow convey this sense?'

It is the kind of point easily overlooked by a writer preoccupied in searching for the apt phrase. Alexander Pope in his *Essay on Criticism* (lines 243f) declared that the perfect judge (or critic) would 'survey the whole, nor seek slight faults to find'. But what constitutes 'a slight fault'? If by pointing out a weakness, the critic can help a metrical version to keep even a little closer to the original, he is doing the writer (and perhaps, too, the worshipper) a real service.

'Father and mother' of verse 12 presented a metrical problem; 'parents' besides being (to my ear) indefinably unsuitable was little better. 'Kith and kin', with a respectable Old English etymology, seems a resolution of the problem.

141 HAPPY ARE THOSE, BEYOND ALL MEASURE BLESSED 10 10 10 10 10 10

Based on	Psalm 32
Theme	Forgiveness; God our strength; guidance
Written	at Killay, Swansea, and at Ford, November 1996
Suggested tune	SONG 1 by Orlando Gibbons
	YORKSHIRE (STOCKPORT) by John Wainwright
Published in	*Supplement 99* (USA), 1999 TO (1) BEATI SUNT by Carl L. Stam
	(2) FALERA by David Iliff
	Sing Glory, 1999 to FALERA
	Praise!, 2000 to HILASTERION by David G. Preston

For the circumstances behind this text, see the note on 137 'The Lord be near us as we pray'.

Psalm 32 is much-loved. It speaks to the troubled conscience. God's forgiveness is considered under a number of different images; hence the fourfold repetition in stanza 1 of guilt gone, faults forgiven, hearts blameless, and uncondemned. The phrase 'faults forgiven' is from Knox, followed by the Jerusalem Bible.

The first line of stanza 2 looks to Coverdale's 'greate water floudes'. 'Songs of deliverance' in verse 8 of the psalm (BCP) was a phrase borrowed to form the title of an earlier collection of these hymn texts: in this version of the psalm, it becomes 'triumph-song', again following Knox.

The 'beasts that go astray' in stanza 3 are those 'who will not keep with you' (RSV) rather than likely to attack you (BCP). For 'I will counsel you' (RSV), stanza 3 speaks of the formation of a Christian mind to accompany God's directing of our feet 'in the way you should go' (REB).

The last line but one of the final stanza comes direct from the BCP; while the concluding line looks back over the whole psalm, reflecting on God as joy (verse 1), Saviour (verses 5,7) strength (verse 7) and guide (verse 8).

142 ALL OUR DAYS WE WILL BLESS THE LORD   88 88 88

Based on	Psalm 34
Theme	Confidence and peace; praise and worship
Written	at Ruan Minor, August 1990
Suggested tune	see below

Psalm 34 is one of the greatest treasures of the psalter. A much earlier metrical version, 'Through all the changing scenes of life', is among the most enduring of the Tate and Brady paraphrases, first published 1696.

In the Hebrew this psalm is an acrostic, based on the initial letters of the Hebrew alphabet; and I have sought to follow this device. The text can be regarded as a companion piece to 138 'All my soul to God I raise' which follows the acrostic pattern of Psalm 25. Though these two texts both have four stanzas, each of six lines, and both omit the letters X, Y and Z, returning to A for the final line, yet they were written eight years apart and in different metres.

C.H. Spurgeon in his monumental *Treasury of David* (London 1869) regrets that of the nine psalms based on acrostics, only one (119) is so identified in the King James version of the Scriptures; and adds 'I do think that the existence of such a remarkable style of composition ought to be indicated in one way or another, and that some useful purposes are served by it being actually reproduced in the translation.' In our own day this has been done in the R. A. Knox version.

Though the metrical form is regular, the stress seems to mean that no suitable tune is available.

For another hymn based on this psalm, see 143 'Tell his praise in song and story'.

143 TELL HIS PRAISE IN SONG AND STORY   87 87 D

Based on	Psalm 34
Theme	Praise and testimony

Written	at Ruan Minor, August 1976
Suggested tune	EBENEZER by Thomas J. Williams
	PLEADING SAVIOUR from Leavitt's *Christian Lyre,* 1830
Published in	*Hymns for Today's Church,* 1982 to WEALDSTONE by John Barnard
	The Book of Praises, 1986 to AVE VERUM CORPUS by Edward Elgar
	Psalms for Today, 1990 to ALLELUIA by Samuel S. Wesley
	The Worshiping Church (USA), 1990 to HOLY MANNA, attributed to William Moore
	Baptist Praise and Worship, 1991 to EBENEZER
	Grace Praise (New Zealand), 1999 (words only)
	Complete Anglican Hymns Old & New, 2000 to ABBOT'S LEIGH
	Praise!, 2000 to HYFRYDOL by Rowland H. Pritchard

Written too late for inclusion in *Psalm Praise,* this text takes a favourite psalm for its basis: one which lies behind the familiar 'Through all the changing scenes of life' adapted from Tate and Brady's *New Version of the Psalms of David,* 1696.

Verse 1, line 3, uses an expression from Psalm 62.7; while line 7 has a direct borrowing from Bunyan's 'Who would true valour see' in part two of *The Pilgrim's Progress.*

There is an intentional reference to the gospel incident in verse 4, line 4; where the Lord's words, 'It is I', addressed to the terrified and troubled disciples alone on the lake (Matthew 14.27) provide a New Testament fulfilment of the psalmist's confidence in God.

For another hymn based on this psalm see 142 'All our days we will bless the Lord'.

144 MY DAYS OF WAITING ENDED 76 76 D

Based on	Psalm 40.1–3
Theme	Deliverance; testimony; praise and worship
Written	at Ruan Minor and Poldhu Cove, August 1989
Suggested tune	MUNICH from *Gesangbuch,* Meiningen, 1693
	PENLAN by David Jenkins

Psalm 40, verse 3 was among three passages of Scripture that met the eye of Charles Wesley at the time of his conversion to Christ on May 21st, 1738. 'I rose and looked into the Scripture' he wrote in his journal, followed by 'I now found myself at peace with God, and rejoiced in the hope of loving Christ.'

145 LORD, MAY OUR HEARTS WITHIN US BURN 88 88 88

Based on	Psalm 41
Theme	Trust in God; the world's need
Written	at Killay, Swansea and at Ford, November 1996
Suggested tune	HOLY FAITH by George C. Martin
	ST CATHERINE by Henri F. Hemy

Published in   *Supplement 99* (USA), 1999 to ST CATHERINE
                      Praise!, 2000 to STELLA (English traditional)

For the circumstances behind this text, see the note on 137 'The Lord be near us as we pray'.

Though the word 'intercede' is commonly used of prayer, its root meaning is to come between, to interfere or intervene; and I use it in stanza 1 to indicate action as well as prayer (or, better, the prayer that leads to action). 'Sin or sickness' (stanza 2) are linked together in the thought of the psalmist in his verses 3 and 4; while his 'enemies' of verses 2 and 5 appear in the metrical version more generally as 'the evil day', or (stanza 3) as death, the last enemy. Here the unremembered name is linked with the unfaithful friend, as hope and courage ebb in the face of death. So the prayer for mercy from verses 4 and 10 of the psalm is similarly repeated at the end of stanzas 2 and 3.

The final stanza picks up the confident faith of verse 11, 'By this I know...' and here that last enemy is forced to yield (cf. the strong man armed, of Luke 11.21). The 'innocence' of verse 12, a translation that goes back to Coverdale, is represented in the last stanza by the full salvation of the redeemed ('pardoned we stand...'), sealed with the repeated 'Amen' of the psalmist.

146 MERCIFUL AND GRACIOUS BE   77 77 77

Based on	Psalm 56
Theme	Trust in God
Written	September 1970 at Sevenoaks, revised 1998 at Ford
Suggested tune	DIX by Conrad Kocher
	RATISBON from Werner's *Choralbuch*, 1815
Translated into	French
Published in	*Psalm Praise*, 1973 to MERCIFUL AND GRACIOUS
	by Norman L. Warren
	Songs of Worship, 1980 to MERCIFUL AND GRACIOUS
	Rejoice! (Australia), 1987 to HEATHLANDS by Henry T. Smart
	Songs of Celebration, 1991 to MERCIFUL AND GRACIOUS (with
	a French translation by Ann Maouyo)
	Praise!, 2000 to MOUNT ZION by Arthur S. Sullivan

This is one of a number of early metrical psalms written for *Psalm Praise*. In seeking to be faithful to the text (verse 7, AV, 'In thine anger cast down the people, O God') I concluded my second stanza with the couplet:

> 'wither them beneath your frown;
> in displeasure cast them down.'

In this form, it attracted the unfavourable attention of the *Church Times* reviewer; and when collecting my texts for *Lift Every Heart* (1984) I consulted Derek Kidner, who offered me wise words about metrical psalmody: 'In singing the actual psalms, one sings them with allowance for their context, and adjusts their thrust accordingly, but I would have thought that in turning a psalm into a hymn one ought to bring it explicitly into the completed context of the gospel, where one prays *for* one's enemies and slanderers.'

By this time the text had appeared in *Psalm Praise* and in *Songs of Worship* (1980); but I did not include it in *Lift Every Heart*. However, when the editors of *Praise!* wanted to include this text among their metrical psalms, I revised it to its present form.

See Index 6.

147 WHEN TROUBLES COME AND HOPES DEPART   86 86 (CM)

Based on	Psalm 60
Theme	Trust in God; Christian experience and discipleship
Written	at Ford, December 1997
Suggested tune	BELMONT from William Gardiner's *Sacred Melodies*, 1812
	ST MAGNUS by Jeremiah Clarke
	ST PETER by Alexander R. Reinagle
Published in	*Praise!*, 2000 to ST MAGNUS

For the circumstances behind this text, see the note on 137 'The Lord be near us as we pray'.

The earthquake imagery of the psalmist's second verse has here been internalized, with God as its witness; and this seems in keeping with the inward confusion evident in the psalm. The banner of the psalmist's verse 4 seems to be a rallying-point in the thick of the battle—there is some difference of opinion as to whether for advance or for retreat—but I have linked it with the famous 'banner' of the Song of Solomon (2.4); a sign of the Lord's sheltering presence, not here in the banqueting-house but on the battlefield.

If Isaac Watts could write in the Preface to his *Hymns and Spiritual Songs in Three Books* (London 1707), 'The names of Ammon and Moab may be properly chang'd into the names of the Chief Enemies of the Gospel... Judah and Israel may be called England and Scotland...' then perhaps it may be right to omit the historical geography proper to the psalmist on the occasion of his writing, in favour of the worldwide inclusiveness of my stanza 4.

148 GOD IS MY GREAT DESIRE   66 84 D

Based on	Psalm 63
Theme	Love for God; God our strength
Written	at Ruan Minor, August 1982
Suggested tune	LEONI (from a Synagogue melody)
Published in	*Worship III* (USA), 1986 to LEONI
	The Book of Praises, 1986 (words only)
	Lift High your Songs!, 1988 to QUANTOCK HILLS by Michael Paget
	Psalms for Today, 1990 to LEONI
	The Worshiping Church (USA), 1994 to LEONI
	Celebration Hymnal for Everyone, 1994 to LEONI
	Renew! (USA), 1995 to LEONI
	Laudate, 1999 to LEONI
	Liturgical Hymns Old & New, 1999 to LEONI
	Catholic Supplement, 1999 to LEONI

Grace Praise (New Zealand), 1999 (words only)
Complete Anglican Hymns Old & New, 2000 to LEONI
Praise!, 2000 to COVENANT by John Stainer
New Hymns and Worship Songs, 2001 to LEONI
Hymns of Heritage and Hope (USA), 2001 to LEONI

This is one of a small number of metrical psalms written at the request of David G. Preston, the compiler of a projected collection. As with the others, I had Derek Kidner's *Tyndale Commentary* (London 1973) open beside me; and the threefold division, with its headings of desire, delight and defence I owe to him.

In an early draft, line 3 of verse 1 ends with the word 'afire'—which is indeed true to the thought of the psalmist; perhaps nearer his meaning than the text as it stands. But in a hymn for congregational use one must not put into the mouths of those who sing the words sentiments which are so far beyond our experience as to be quite unreal. I judge that many of us can speak (or sing) of a desire for God, and of aspirations towards him; whereas few, for any length of time together, can honestly sing that their heart is 'afire' with thirst for the Divine.

While other sounds are repeated in places, s and t (sometimes as st) echo through every verse. No doubt this was part of the attraction of 'trust' in the final verse of the text. The combination st comes, I think, eight times in these 24 lines; while s and t appear in the same word on at least five other occasions. This of course is something I only discovered after the text was written.

149 EVERY HEART ITS TRIBUTE PAYS   77 77 D

Based on	Psalm 65
Theme	Praise and worship; creation; harvest
Written	at Ruan Minor, August 1979
Suggested tune	MAIDSTONE by Walter B. Gilbert
	ST GEORGE'S WINDSOR by George J. Elvey
Published in	*On the Move* (Australia), April 1980 (words only)
	The Book of Praises, 1986 to BRAMERTON from a melody by J.G. Ebeling
	Lift High your Songs!, 1988 to IVYTHORN HILL by Michael Paget
	Evangelicals Now, October 1997, to music by Ian Parker
	Grace Praise (New Zealand), 1999 (words only)
	Praise!, 2000 to SYRIA, *Union Tune Book*, 1842

Originally planned in verses of six lines rather than eight, it proved impossible to do justice to the theme of verse 2 in only six lines; and I believe that the final two lines of verse 1 are not such as fall under John Wesley's condemnation (in his famous preface to the Collection of 1780) '...no doggerel; no botches; nothing put in to patch up the rhyme; no feeble expletives'. The final verse was completed late at night, after a drive to Zennor along the high cliff road from St Ives, and is (to my mind) enhanced by the double alliteration of 'field and fold, byre and barn'. The psalm, and so this text, gives praise to God under the threefold division of the General Thanksgiving of the *Book of Common Prayer*; in which the Lord is recalled as the God of our creation, our preservation amid the blessings of this life, and of our salvation through Christ.

See Index 6.

Based on	Psalm 67, Deus Misereatur
Theme	The blessing of God; harvest
Written	at Sevenoaks, July 1971
Suggested tune	MONKLAND by John Antes
	IMPACT (MONKSGATE) by David G. Wilson
	BINSCOMBE (PSALM 67) by Alan Davies
Published in	*Psalm Praise,* 1973 to (1) IMPACT (2) PSALM 67
	Grace Hymns, 1975 to (1) PSALM 67 (2) ST BENEDICT by John Stainer
	Hymns II (USA), 1976 to MONKSGATE
	Hymnal Supplement (USA), 1984 to MONKSGATE
	The Wedding Book, 1989 to (1) BINSCOMBE (2) IMPACT (3) URCHFONT by John Barnard
	Psalms for Today, 1990 to URCHFONT

Psalm 67, of which this is a metrical version, is one of the canticles set for the Service of Evening Prayer in the *Book of Common Prayer.* It is of course well served by the metrical version 'God of mercy, God of grace' by H.F. Lyte; though Professor J.M. Barkley in his *Handbook to the Church Hymnary* (Oxford 1979) rightly calls that 'not really a paraphrase of the psalm but a hymn based upon it'. The same is true of this text.

I am not now taken with the opening couplet of the hymn. It is perhaps an example of a text which found its way too early into print; and was thereby placed beyond the reach of substantial revision. In the light of its inclusion in current hymnals, I have not withdrawn it; but I hope one day to attempt a better version.

David Wilson prefers the title IMPACT for his tune to this text, listed above.

151 HELP ME, O GOD, AND HEAR MY CRY 88 88 88

Based on	parts of Psalm 69
Theme	Patience; love for God; deliverance
Written	at Ford, December 1996
Suggested tune	MELITA by John B. Dykes
	PATER OMNIUM by Henry J.E. Holmes
	ST CHRYSOSTOM by Joseph Barnby
Published in	*Praise!,* 2000 to AD ASTRA by Henry G. Ley

This is not, I think, a psalm which I would have chosen, left to myself, as the basis of a metrical version intended for Christian worship. For an account of how I came to attempt it, see the note on 137 'The Lord be near us as we pray'.

These three stanzas, though based on the psalmist's experience, are deliberately selective. They do not attempt to enter into the psalm's pre-figuring of the sufferings of Christ; and they do not draw upon those parts of the psalm which call down judgment and seek for vindication, if not indeed for vengeance. My guide here, as so often, has been Derek Kidner, who very early in our association helped me to see that it is no rejection of Scripture to feel that not all is suited for the corporate worship of a Christian congregation. He writes in his *Tyndale Commentary* (London 1973):

'To the question, Can a Christian use these cries for vengeance as his own? the short answer must surely be No; no more than he should echo the curses of Jeremiah or the protests of Job. He may of course translate them into affirmations of God's judgment, and into denunciations of 'the spiritual hosts of wickedness' which are the real enemy. As for the men of flesh and blood who 'live as enemies of the cross of Christ' or who make themselves our enemies, our instructions are to pray not against them but for them; to turn them from the power of Satan to God; to repay their evil with good; and to choose none of their ways.'

What is offered here, from Psalm 69, is the timeless cry of those who call upon God in trouble of circumstance or conscience, and find him faithful to his promise.

152 A KING ON HIGH IS REIGNING   76 76 D

Based on	Psalm 72
Theme	Praise and worship; the living God; the Lord Jesus Christ
Written	at Ford, September 1997
Suggested tune	AURELIA by Samuel S. Wesley
	GOSTERWOOD (English traditional)
Published in	*Supplement 99* (USA), 1999 to REX CARROLL by Hal H. Hopson
	Praise!, 2000 to LE MAIRE by G. le Maire Barnes

This royal psalm is generally seen as Messianic, translating 'the terms of earthly Israelite empire into those of Christ's dominion'. Admirable metrical versions have long been in use which freely make this transition: James Montgomery's 'Hail to the Lord's anointed' written as a hymn of eight stanzas, each of eight lines, in 1821; and Isaac Watts' very familiar 'Jesus shall reign' from his *The Psalms of David* a century before. It would be more accurate to say that parts of 'Jesus shall reign' are very familiar; it must be a long time since a congregation was asked to sing his version of the biblical places to which the psalmist refers:

> 'Behold the Islands with their kings,
> And Europe her best tribute brings:
> From North to South the princes meet
> To pay their homage at his feet.
>
> There Persia, glorious to behold,
> There India shines in eastern gold,
> And barbarous nations at his word
> Submit and bow and own their Lord.'

This hymn was written for the editors of *Praise!* (see note on 137 'The Lord be near us as we pray') and the fact that I have passed by the place-names is a reminder that metrical psalms (at least in my hands) are not translations, not always even paraphrases, but hymns 'based on' the original psalm. This is surely the tradition which has given us most of the 'metrical psalms' to be found in our hymn books; and it has this advantage, that the metrical version cannot be seen as a *substitute* for the original Scripture in private reading or congregational worship.

Based on	Psalm 73
Theme	Love of God; God our strength
Written	at Ford, December 1996
Suggested tune	ICH HALTE TREULICH STILL attributed to J.S. Bach
	LEOMINSTER by George W. Martin
	TERRA BEATA (English traditional)
Published in	*Praise!,* 2000 to GOBAITH by Tom Price

For the circumstances behind this text, see the Note on 137 'The Lord be near us as we pray'.

These three verses take as their theme the riddle which perplexed the psalmist, as it has troubled so many observers of the human condition; but he prefaces all that follows with a great affirmation of faith in the goodness of God. Verse 2 of my text provides the contrast between temporal prosperity, the theme of the evocative description in verses 4–9 of the psalm, and the reminder (which came to the writer when he went into God's sanctuary and turned his mind to eternal things) that this life is not the ultimate reality.

And what if the godless prosper in their own terms? God's presence, his sustaining, guiding and welcoming to glory, far outweigh 'the worldling's treasure'; and through all our struggles with our human frailty God remains for the Christian, as for the psalmist, 'the strength of my heart and my portion for ever'.

Based on	Psalm 84
Theme	Love for God
Written	at Ford, August 1995
Suggested tune	CARLISLE by Charles Lockhart
	FRANCONIA adapted by William H. Havergal
	ST THOMAS from Aaron Williams' *New Universal Psalmodist,* 1770

Derek Kidner in his *Tyndale Commentary* (London 1975) entitles Psalm 84 'The pull of home'. He writes. 'Longing is written all over this psalm' and it is that sense of longing which, within the confines of so brief a text, I am seeking to convey. The phrase 'long home' in verse 2 borrows the adjective from Ecclesiastes 12.5 (AV) which in RSV and NIV is translated 'eternal home'. The word comes in each of the first three verses of the hymn.

Henry Lyte wrote two metrical versions of this psalm, of which the better-known is 'Pleasant are thy courts above', published in his *Spirit of the Psalms* in 1834. It was included in *Hymns Ancient & Modern* almost from the beginning, and was in every new edition up to and including 1950. Its omission from *Ancient & Modern New Standard* (1983) and then from *Common Praise* (2000), as from most other contemporary mainstream hymnals, suggests that it may have begun to outlive what has been its undoubted usefulness.

155 TIMELESS LOVE! WE SING THE STORY							87 87 77

Based on	Psalm 89.1–18
Theme	Love of God; praise and worship
Written	at Sevenoaks, April 1970
Suggested tune	ALL SAINTS (German traditional)
	IRBY by Henry J. Gauntlett
	TIMELESS LOVE by Norman L. Warren
Translated into	Chinese
Published in	*Psalm Praise*, 1973 to (1) TIMELESS LOVE (2) ALL SAINTS
	Hymns for Today's Church, 1982 to (1) PATRIXBOURNE by John Barnard (2) TIMELESS LOVE
	Hymns and Psalms, 1983 to (1) TIMELESS LOVE (2) ALL SAINTS
	Mission England Praise, 1983 to TIMELESS LOVE
	Praise and Thanksgiving, 1985 to BODAFON FIELDS by William Llewellyn
	Rejoice! (Australia), 1987 to TIMELESS LOVE
	Church Family Worship, 1988 to (1) ALL SAINTS (2) TIMELESS LOVE
	Psalms for Today, 1990 to PATRIXBOURNE
	Mission Praise Combined, 1990 to TIMELESS LOVE
	With Almost Every Voice, 1991 to TIMELESS LOVE
	Sounds of Grace (Hong Kong), 1991 to TIMELESS LOVE (with a Chinese translation)
	Songs for the People of God (USA), 1994 to GOOD SHEPHERD by Keith Landis
	With Almost Every Voice, 1997 to music by Norman L. Warren
	Fifty New Anthems for Mixed Voices, 1999 to music by Norman L. Warren
	Complete Mission Praise, 1999 to TIMELESS LOVE
	Anthems Old and New for SA Men, 1999 to music by Norman L. Warren
	Sing Glory, 1999 to (1) PATRIXBOURNE (2) TIMELESS LOVE
	Grace Praise (New Zealand), 1999 (words only)
	Short Anthems for Small Choirs, 2000 to music by Norman L. Warren
	Common Praise, 2000 to ALL SAINTS
	Methodist Hymns Old & New, 2001 to TIMELESS LOVE
Recorded on	*Here is Psalm Praise*, 1975 to TIMELESS LOVE

Among the earlier texts written for *Psalm Praise*, this hymn looks only at a small part of one of the longer psalms; and the description 'based on' is not meant to claim any very exact correspondence with the text. 'Timeless' in the first line is an echo of the repeated 'for ever', 'to all generations', of the opening verses of the psalm. 'North and South' I take to be symbolic of the universal sway of God (as one might say 'from East to West') as indicated even more widely in verse 11 of the psalm, with its reference to the heavens and the earth. In the final couplet, 'Shield' is drawn directly from verse 18 of the psalm; 'Sun and Shield' as a pair are drawn from Psalm 84.11 (but note the reference here in verse 15 to 'the light of thy countenance'); and 'Shield and Reward' as a pair from Genesis 15.1 (RV, NIV), where the Lord so describes himself to Abram in a vision.

— 380 —

Based on	Psalm 90
Theme	God the Father; the living God
Written	at Ruan Minor, August 1987
Suggested tune	INNSBRUCK based on Heinrich Isaak
Published in	*Songs of Rejoicing* (USA), 1989 to REFUGE by Dorothy H. Sheets
	Psalms for Today, 1990 to INNSBRUCK
	Moravian Book of Worship (USA), 1995 to INNSBRUCK

K. L. Parry in the *Companion to Congregational Praise* (London 1953) tells the story of how

'Dr. Jowett, the famous Master of Baliol, is said to have asked a company of dons to make a list of the best hymns. They each returned one hymn only, "Our God, our help". It seemed to fulfil all the conditions of a perfect hymn.'

It is a daunting task, therefore, to attempt a modern metrical version of Psalm 90, 'the great psalm of human mortality', nearly 300 years after Isaac Watts. This was intended for a new book of metrical psalms then in preparation; and it can be seen that (as with Isaac Watts) it is scarcely possible to include all of the psalm. Watts' intention to see 'David converted into a Christian' can be noticed in the final line of the text.

157 SAFE IN THE SHADOW OF THE LORD   86 86 (CM)

Based on	Psalm 91
Theme	Confidence in God
Written	at Sevenoaks, January 1970
Suggested tune	CREATOR GOD by Norman L. Warren
	STANTON by John Barnard
Translated into	Chinese, Welsh
Published in	*Psalm Praise,* 1973 to (1) music by Christopher Seaman
	(2) CREATOR GOD
	Hymns II (USA), 1976 to CREATOR GOD
	Hymns for Today's Church, 1982 to (1) CREATOR GOD (2) STANTON
	Rejoicing (Australia), 1986 to CREATOR GOD
	Mission Praise 2, 1987 to CREATOR GOD
	Anglican Praise, 1987 to CREATOR GOD
	Supplement to Lutheran Hymnal (Australia), 1987 to CREATOR GOD
	Rejoice! (Australia), 1987 to ST ANNE by William Croft
	Sing Alleluia, 1987 to CREATOR GOD
	Church Family Worship, 1988 to (1) LLOYD by C. Howard
	(2) CREATOR GOD (3) STANTON
	Come Rejoice!, 1989 to CREATOR GOD
	Irish Church Praise (Ireland), 1990 to CREATOR GOD
	Psalms for Today, 1990 to (1) CREATOR GOD (2) STANTON
	The Worshiping Church (USA), 1990 to CREATOR GOD
	Mission Praise Combined, 1990 to CREATOR GOD

Sounds of Grace (Hong Kong), 1991 to CREATOR GOD (with a
   Chinese translation)
Worship Songs Ancient & Modern, 1992 to STANTON
Anthem (USA), 1992 by Paul Inwood
Hymns for the People, 1993 to CREATOR GOD
Fifteen Hymn Anthems, 1994 to an arrangement of CREATOR
   GOD
Glory to God (Ireland), 1994 to CREATOR GOD
Celebration Hymnal for Everyone, 1994 to (1) music by Paul
   Inwood (2) CREATOR GOD
Songs for the People of God (USA), 1994 to ST BENEDICT by Keith
   Landis
Sing we Merrily, 1995 to CREATOR GOD
Worship Together (USA), 1995 to CREATOR GOD
Songs of Fellowship 2, 1998 to CREATOR GOD
Spring Harvest Praise, 1998 to CREATOR GOD (with a translation
   by Hywel M. Griffiths in the Welsh edition)
Common Ground (Scotland), 1998 to CREATOR GOD
People of the Blessing, 1998 (words only)
Anthems Old and New, 1998 to music by Norman L. Warren
Songs of Victory (Scotland), 1998 to CREATOR GOD
Laudate, 1999 to CREATOR GOD
Complete Mission Praise, 1999 to CREATOR GOD
Sing Glory, 1999 to (1) CREATOR GOD (2) STANTON
Together in Song (Australia), 1999 to CREATOR GOD
Keswick Praise, 2000 to CREATOR GOD
Church Hymnal (Ireland), 2000 to CREATOR GOD
Praise!, 2000 to CREATOR GOD
Sing to the Lord, 2000 to CREATOR GOD
Worship Today, 2001 to CREATOR GOD

Recorded on   *Psalm Praise - Sing a New Song*, 1978 to CREATOR GOD
                    Keswick Praise 8, 1993 to CREATOR GOD
                    Keswick Praise 9, 1994 to CREATOR GOD
                    The Hymn Makers: 'Tell out, my soul', 1996 to CREATOR GOD
                    Twenty Favourite Hymns 3, 2000 to CREATOR GOD

Written for *Psalm Praise*, the repeated phrase which forms the third and fourth line of every verse is intended as an affirmation of confidence, the keynote of the text as it is of the psalm. As can be judged from the list of publications above, this text, to Norman Warren's evocative tune, has proved among the most widely-sung of my metrical psalms. I value letters which have been sent to me telling of how it has been used in trouble, sickness and sorrow, read in private as well as sung in the congregation.

158 GOD IS KING! THE LORD IS REIGNING   87 88 87 77

Based on   Psalm 93
Theme   Praise and worship; the living God
Written   at Ruan Minor, August 1982

Suggested tune	CRAIL by Peter Cutts
Published in	*Psalms for Today,* 1990 to CRAIL

In my original note on this text, written in 1983 for *Lift Every Heart,* I had to say 'awaiting a composer' since I knew of no tune in this metre. Peter Cutts supplied one, CRAIL, written in 1985; and text and tune were published together in 1990.

The metre of this text is drawn from No. XXIX in A. E. Housman's *Last Poems,* 'Wake not for the world-heard thunder'. I chose it because of its unusual and attractive quality; and its suitability for such a theme as the psalmist here expounds. The text owes more than its metre to the poem and its author: 'founded' is a word much used by Housman; thunder and lightning appear in both texts; even 'imperishable' is found in 'Parta Quies', No. XLVIII of *More Poems.*

I hesitated a little over rhyming 'ascended' with 'splendid' in verse 1. They sound the same in ordinary speech; but can one equate the final -ed of one with the -id of the other, without false rhyme? Then I recalled Wordsworth's 'Intimations of immortality' with the lines:

> 'And by the vision splendid
> Is on his way attended...'

and took courage.

159 COME, LET US PRAISE THE LORD   66 66 44 44

Based on	Psalm 95, the Venite
Theme	Praise and worship; morning; witness
Written	at Ruan Minor, August 1981
Suggested tune	CHILEAN FOLK-SONG arranged by Michael Paget
	DARWALL'S 148TH by John Darwall
	LOVE UNKNOWN by John Ireland
Published in	*Lift High your Songs!,* 1988 to CHILEAN FOLK-SONG
	New Songs of Praise, 1988 to CHILEAN FOLK-SONG
	Mission Praise Supplement, 1989 to CHILEAN FOLK-SONG
	Songs from the Psalms, 1990 to CHILEAN FOLK-SONG
	The Worshiping Church (USA), 1990 to DARWALL'S 148TH
	Mission Praise Combined, 1990 to CHILEAN FOLK-SONG
	Baptist Praise and Worship, 1991 to CHILEAN VENITE
	(CHILEAN FOLK-SONG)
	BBC Songs of Praise, 1997 to COME, LET US PRAISE (CHILEAN
	FOLK-SONG)
	Complete Mission Praise, 1999 to CHILEAN VENITE
	Church Hymnal (Ireland), 2000 to DARWALL'S 148TH
	Worship & Rejoice (USA), 2001 to DARWALL'S 148TH

In January 1972 Michael Baughen, editor of *Psalm Praise,* wrote to ask me for a metrical Venite (Psalm 95, so called from the opening word of the Latin title in the *Book of Common Prayer,* where it is set for daily use, as indeed it has been for nearly 1,500 years). I wrote one, but in the end withdrew it as unsuitable; and it was only nine years later that I returned to this psalm.

The phrase in my verse 3, 'The Lord our Righteousness', is a borrowing from the Messianic prophecy of Jeremiah (23.6; 33.16); but the concept of God's righteousness, and the word itself, runs through the whole psalter, at least from Psalm 4 to Psalm 119.

160 THE EVERLASTING LORD IS KING · 86 86 (CM)

Based on	Psalm 97
Theme	God the Father; the living God
Written	at Ruan Minor, August 1987
Suggested tune	CAMPMEETING (American traditional)
	KILMARNOCK by Neil Dougall
Published in	*Psalms for Today*, 1990 to NEVILLE COURT by Derek Williams
	Daily Office, Community of the Holy Name,1990 (words only)
	Anthem (USA), 1991 by John Carter

Psalm 97 suffers, perhaps, from comparison with its neighbours, as less likely to inspire the Christian hymn writer. Its theme has been called 'the awesome approach of a conqueror' rather than the rejoicings that gave us 'Joy to the world' from Psalm 98, or even 'Sing a new song to the Lord' from Psalm 96.

Even so, *Psalm Praise* (1973) contained an early unrhymed text by Christopher Idle, and *Praise!* (2000) includes a LM paraphrase by David G. Preston. Those who have attempted to put the whole psalter into verse have had difficulties here: *The Scottish Psalter* offers the convoluted lines:

> 'Ye that are called gods, see that
> ye do him worship all.'

John Keble in his *The Psalter in English Verse* (London n.d.) is not at his best:

> 'Glad Sion heard; 'twas joy and glee
> To Judah's loyal daughters...'

Isaac Watts included in his *Psalms of David* four hymns derived from this psalm. They too may not be Watts at his finest; but they have their share of striking imagery and poetic fire.

161 SING A NEW SONG TO THE LORD · 7 7 11 8

Based on	Psalm 98, Cantate Domino
Theme	Praise and worship; music in praise
Written	at Ruan Minor, September 1971.
Suggested tune	ONSLOW SQUARE (CANTATE DOMINO) by David G. Wilson
Translated into	Swedish
Published in	*Psalm Praise*, 1973 to (1) ONSLOW SQUARE (2) music by A. H. Davies
	Sound of Living Waters, 1974 to ONSLOW SQUARE

Worship II (USA), 1975 to ONSLOW SQUARE
Hymns II (USA), 1976 to ONSLOW SQUARE
Sing to the Lord (USA), 1978 (words only)
Partners in Praise, 1979 to ONSLOW SQUARE
New Harvest (New Zealand), 1979 (words only)
Catholic Book of Worship II (Canada), 1980 to CANTATE DOMINO
Hymns Plus (USA), 1980 to ONSLOW SQUARE
Praise & Worship 2 (Australia), 1981 to CANTATE DOMINO
Their Words, My Thoughts, 1981 to ONSLOW SQUARE
Anthem (USA), 1982 by John F. Wilson
Jesus Praise, 1982 to ONSLOW SQUARE
Hymns for Today's Church, 1982 to ONSLOW SQUARE
Gather to Remember (USA), 1982 to CANTATE DOMINO
Hymns and Psalms, 1983 to (1) ONSLOW SQUARE
     (2) BARNARDO by Alan Gulliver
Mission England Praise, 1983 to ONSLOW SQUARE
Songs for Celebration (USA), 1984 to ONSLOW SQUARE
The Singing Church (USA), 1985 to CANTATE DOMINO
Seventh Day Adventist Hymnal (USA), 1985 to ONSLOW
     SQUARE
Choral Musicianship & Voice Training (USA), 1986 to music by
     John F. Wilson
Hymns Old & New (Anglican Edition), 1986 to ONSLOW SQUARE
Worship III (USA), 1986 to CANTATE DOMINO
Celebration, 1986 (words only)
'We Celebrate' Hymnal (USA), 1986 to CANTATE DOMINO
Sing a New Song 1 (Australia), 1987 to ONSLOW SQUARE
Alive Now! (USA), 1987 to CANTATE DOMINO
Carol Praise, 1987 to ONSLOW SQUARE
A Survey of Christian Hymnody (USA), 1987 to CANTATE DOMINO
Church Family Worship, 1988 to (1) ONSLOW SQUARE
     (2) LITTLEBOURNE by John Barnard
Gather (USA), 1988 to CANTATE DOMINO
Anthem (Sweden), 1988 to ONSLOW SQUARE in a translation
     by Gun-Britt Holgersson
Segertoner (Sweden), 1989 to ONSLOW SQUARE in a translation
     by Gun-Britt Holgersson
Psalms for Today, 1990 to (1) to ONSLOW SQUARE (2) LITTLE-
     BOURNE
The Worshiping Church (USA), 1990 to ONSLOW SQUARE
Mission Praise Combined, 1990 to ONSLOW SQUARE
GIA Hymnal Supplement 1991 (USA), 1991 to CANTATE DOMINO
Worship Songs Ancient & Modern, 1992 to ONSLOW SQUARE
Junior Praise 2, 1992 to ONSLOW SQUARE
Christian Worship: a Lutheran Hymnal (USA), 1993 to CANTATE
     DOMINO
Gather, 2nd edition (USA), 1994 to CANTATE DOMINO
Glory to God (Ireland), 1994 to ONSLOW SQUARE
Songs for the People of God (USA), 1994 to A NEW SONG by Keith
     Landis
Catholic Book of Worship III (Canada), 1994 to ONSLOW SQUARE
Celebration Hymnal for Everyone, 1994 to CANTATE DOMINO

	Moravian Book of Worship (USA), 1995 to CANTATE DOMINO
	Renew! (USA), 1995 to ONSLOW SQUARE
	RitualSong (USA), 1996 to CANTATE DOMINO
	The Covenant Hymnal (USA), 1996 to ONSLOW SQUARE
	As One Voice 2 (Australia), 1996 to ONSLOW SQUARE
	Junior Praise Combined, 1997 to ONSLOW SQUARE
	Word and Song 2000 (USA), 1999 to ONSLOW SQUARE
	Complete Mission Praise, 1999 to ONSLOW SQUARE
	Jesus' People Sing Songbook (USA), 1999 to CANTATE DOMINO
	Worship & Rejoice (USA), 2001 to ONSLOW SQUARE
Recorded on	*Psalm Praise - Sing a New Song*, 1978 to ONSLOW SQUARE
	The Best of Rhapsody in Praise (USA), 1986 to music by John F. Wilson
	He to whom Wonders Belong, 1993 to music by Steve Layfield
	Jesus' People Sing 2 (USA), 1999 to CANTATE DOMINO
	Junior Praise Combined 31, 2000 to ONSLOW SQUARE

Much of the popularity of this hymn, not least among US editors, must be attributed to David Wilson's stirring tune which well expresses the rejoicing of the psalmist. The tune was untitled in *Psalm Praise* (for which both text and tune were written); but in 1979 with its inclusion in *Partners in Praise* it carried the name ONSLOW SQUARE (used retrospectively in the list of hymnals above), no doubt because David Wilson had been curate of St Paul's, Onslow Square, 1969–73. CANTATE DOMINO, used mainly in North America and Australia, is an alternative name for the same tune and is the title given to this psalm when used as the alternative canticle to the Magnificat in the *Book of Common Prayer* Order for Evening Prayer.

Line 3 of verse 3 gave some trouble. The 'shawms' of the Prayer Book version (verse 6 of the psalm) are given as 'cornets' in both AV and RV, but as 'horns' in more recent translations. Derek Kidner points out in his *Leviticus-Deuteronomy* (London 1971) that 'The "trumpets and...horn" of Psalm 98.6 are of more than musical significance: they voice the nation's jubilant prayer.' The 'voices in chorus' are a reference back to the 'joyous song' and 'sing praises' of verses 4 and 5 of the psalm.

162 LET THE EARTH ACCLAIM HIM   66 65 D

Based on	Psalm 100, Jubilate Deo
Theme	Praise and worship; thanksgiving
Written	at Bramerton, August 1991
Suggested tune	see below
Published in	*Songs for the People of God* (USA), 1994 to MONTEBELLO

Psalm 100 is set as one of the canticles (Jubilate Deo) for Morning Prayer in the *Book of Common Prayer* of the Church of England, and listed in *Common Worship* as 'suitable for use as the opening canticle at Morning Prayer' (p. 57).

The metre and rhyming scheme of this brief metrical version are borrowed from a poem by C.S. Lewis, 'Evensong'. David Perry's *Hymns and Tunes Indexed* (Croydon 1980), gives only two tunes for 66 65 D, LEMON'S FARM and DAY OF THE SPIRIT (also known by the rather unfortunate title of WHITSUN JINGLE) and neither appears to fit this text.

Based on	Psalm 103
Theme	Praise and worship; trust in God
Written	at Ruan Minor, August 1986
Suggested tune	WELLS by D.S. Bortniansky
Published in	*Lift High your Songs!*, 1988 to AIR OF AVALON by Michael Paget
	Singing Faith, 1988 to MOW COP by Brian Hoare
Recorded on	*Singing Faith*, 1999 to MOW COP

This text stands in the shadow of a great and familiar hymn, Henry Lyte's version, 'Praise, my soul, the King of heaven'. Verse 3 of my text is a reminder of a verse of Lyte's omitted in most modern hymnals, beginning 'Frail as summer's flower we flourish'.

John Stott in his *Favourite Psalms* (Milton Keynes 1988) subtitles this psalm 'The Benefits of God's Grace' and Psalm 104 'The Works of God in Nature'. He writes:

> 'Psalms 103 and 104 form a perfect pair and illustrate the balance of the Bible. Both begin and end with the words "Praise the Lord, O my soul". Psalm 103 goes on to tell of the goodness of God in salvation, Psalm 104 of the greatness of God in creation (verse 1). Psalm 103 depicts God as the Father with His children, Psalm 104 as the Creator with His creatures. Psalm 103 catalogues His *benefits* (verse 2), Psalm 104 His *works* (verses 13,24,31).'

164 SERVANTS OF THE LIVING LORD 77 77 77

Based on	Psalm 113
Theme	Praise and worship; grace; the living God
Written	at Ruan Minor, August 1983
Suggested tune	PETRA by Richard Redhead
	WELLS by D.S. Bortniansky
Published in	*The Book of Praises*, 1986 (words only)
	Psalms for Today, 1990 to SLOVENIA by Colin Evans
	Grace Praise (New Zealand), 1999 (words only)

This is one of a group of six psalms which were sung by custom before the Passover meal; and as such, probably among the last psalms sung by Jesus immediately before Gethsemane.

Two conscious quotations need to be identified: the repeated 'All who stand before his face' comes from the reference to 'all who stand before you in earth and heaven' in (for example) Eucharistic Prayer A from *Common Worship*, borrowed from Holy Communion in the Church of England *Alternative Service Book, 1980*; and the line 'hears from heaven his dwelling-place' is taken from Solomon's prayer of dedication in, for example, 1 Kings 8. 30, 39, 43, 49.

Verse 2, line 3, originally written as 'Utmost east to utmost west' was changed in the process of revision both because in this metre it is not easy to sing; and also because that has strong associations with Prebendary A. C. Ainger's 'God is working his purpose out'.

The four verses are intended to point to the Lord of heaven, the Lord of time and space, the Lord of creation, and the Lord who is Father and Redeemer of his children.

Based on	Psalm 115
Theme	The living God
Written	at Sevenoaks, April 1970
Suggested tune	HYFRYDOL by Rowland H. Pritchard
	LUX EOI by Arthur S. Sullivan
Published in	*Psalm Praise*, 1973 to (1) music by John Wycliffe-Jones (2) LUX EOI
	Grace Hymns, 1975 to BETHANY by Henry T. Smart
	A Panorama of Christian Hymnody, 1979 (words only)
	Hymnal Supplement (USA), 1984 to HYFRYDOL
	Rejoice in the Lord (USA), 1985 to HILLINGDON by Walter S. Vale
	The Book of Praises, 1986 to ARWELFA by John Hughes
	Psalms for Today, 1990 to LUX EOI
	Sing Glory, 1999 to LUX EOI
	Grace Praise (New Zealand), 1999 (words only)
	Praise!, 2000 to BETHANY
	Methodist Hymns Old & New, 2001 to LUX EOI

Written for *Psalm Praise*, this text is now associated in my mind with Erik Routley's choice of it for his *Panorama of Christian Hymnody* (Collegeville, Minnesota 1979) and for his over-generous reference to it in *The Hymn* of October 1982 as 'a model of how a modern metrical psalm should look'. I had earlier pointed out to him one or two of its manifest weaknesses...but I could only be delighted that it took his fancy.

The text is concerned to make three parallel contrasts: that it is not to us, but to God that glory belongs; not in idols but in the living God that hope of blessing rests; and not the dead 'but we the living' who can sing his praise in the here and now of life on earth.

166 THE WILL OF GOD TO MARK MY WAY   86 86 (CM)

Based on	Verses from Psalm 119.129-144
Theme	God's will and word
Written	at Sevenoaks, September 1970
Suggested tune	BALLERMA by François H. Barthélémon
	GERONTIUS by John B. Dykes
	MANOAH from Greatorex's *Collection*, 1851
Published in	*Psalm Praise*, 1973 to (1) music by Norman L. Warren (2) GERONTIUS
	Keswick Praise, 1975 to CONTEMPLATION by Frederick A.G. Ouseley
	Church Family Worship, 1988 to (1) ST PETER by Alexander R. Reinagle (2) UNIVERSITY by Charles Collignon
	Psalms for Today, 1990 to UNIVERSITY
	Hymns for the People, 1993 to UNLESS THE LORD by Christopher Norton
	New Anthem Book 2: SA Men, 1994 to music by Norman L. Warren
	Praise!, 2000 to HOVE by Andrew Worton-Steward

Written for *Psalm Praise* (where a single metrical version of Psalm 119 would clearly be impossible), the text does little more than echo certain dominant themes from verses 129–144. Though this text is included here as a metrical psalm, another CM text from selected verses of this psalm is placed in Section 3 among the hymns suitable for Bible Sunday: see 124 'Open our eyes, O Lord, we pray'.

167 I LIFT MY EYES   98 97 or 458 457

Based on   Psalm 121
Theme   Confidence and peace
Written   at Sevenoaks, December 1968
Suggested tune   DAVOS (UPLIFTED EYES or LIFT MY EYES) by Michael A.
                       Baughen and Elisabeth Crocker
Translated into   Chinese
Published in   *Psalm Praise,* 1973 to DAVOS
                   Hymns II (USA), 1976 to DAVOS
                   Partners in Praise, 1979 to UPLIFTED EYES
                   Songs of Worship, 1980 to LIFT MY EYES
                   Hymnal Supplement (USA), 1984 to UPLIFTED EYES
                   Anthem (USA), 1985 by John Carter
                   Praise and Thanksgiving, 1985 to UPLIFTED EYES
                   Mission Praise 2, 1987 to DAVOS
                   Supplement to Lutheran Hymnal (Australia), 1987 to LIFT MY EYES
                   The Wedding Book, 1989 to DAVOS
                   The Rainbow Songbook, 1987 to UPLIFTED EYES
                   Sing the Seasons, 1990 to music by Norman L. Warren
                   Psalms for Today, 1990 to DAVOS
                   The Worshiping Church (USA), 1990 to UPLIFTED EYES
                   Mission Praise Combined, 1990 to UPLIFTED EYES
                   The Song Goes On (USA), 1990 to UPLIFTED EYES
                   With Almost Every Voice, 1991 to music by Norman L. Warren
                   Rejoice and Sing, 1991 to DAVOS
                   Baptist Praise and Worship, 1991 to DAVOS
                   Sounds of Grace (Hong Kong), 1991 to DAVOS (with a Chinese
                       translation)
                   Anthem (USA), 1994 by Bret Heim
                   Glory to God (Ireland), 1994 to DAVOS
                   Catholic Book of Worship III (Canada), 1994 to UPLIFTED EYES
                   Songs for the People of God (USA), 1994 to CARRELL by Keith Landis
                   Worship Together (USA), 1995 to UPLIFTED EYES
                   Anthem (USA), 1995 by Carl Johengen
                   The Covenant Hymnal (USA), 1996 to UPLIFTED EYES
                   With Almost Every Voice, 1997 to music by Norman L. Warren
                   BBC Songs of Praise, 1997 to DAVOS
                   Songs of Fellowship 2, 1998 to DAVOS
                   Anthems Old and New, 1998 to music by Norman L. Warren
                   Complete Mission Praise, 1999 to DAVOS
                   Sing Glory, 1999 to DAVOS

Praise the Lord, 2000 to DAVOS
Complete Anglican Hymns Old & New, 2000 to DAVOS
Church Hymnal (Ireland), 2000 to DAVOS
The Poetic Bible, 2001 (words only)
Worship Today, 2001 to DAVOS
Worship & Rejoice (USA), 2001 to DAVOS
Anthem (USA), 2001 by Ronald Arnatt
Anthem, 2001 by Ian Kellam

Recorded on   *Here is Psalm Praise,* 1975 to DAVOS
I Lift my Eyes to the Quiet Hills (USA), 1976 to DAVOS
Vespers from Westonbirt, 1987 to DAVOS
Kings Men (USA), 1992 to music by Brian Dunbar
Sing a New Song, 1992 to DAVOS
Prom Praise on Tour, 1994 to DAVOS
The Hymn Makers: 'Tell out, my soul', 1996 to DAVOS
Catholic Book of Worship III (Canada), 1998 to DAVOS
Twenty Favourite Hymns 2, 1999 to DAVOS
50 Golden Hymns, 2000 to DAVOS
I Will Sing with the Spirit, 2001 to DAVOS

This is one of a pair of 'metrical psalms' written for *Psalm Praise* when recovering from an attack of 'flu (the other is 157 'Safe in the shadow of the Lord'). Some of its popularity must be attributed to the haunting tune which Michael Baughen wrote for it with Elisabeth Crocker when he was Vicar of Holy Trinity, Platt.

The tune was untitled in *Psalm Praise;* but in 1979 with its inclusion in *Partners in Praise* it was called UPLIFTED EYES. Later the composer changed its title to DAVOS, and this is the name used retrospectively in the list of hymnals above where no other title is attached to the tune. The hymn was sung at Michael Baughen's consecration as Bishop of Chester in York Minster in 1982.

The imagery of the hymn in my own mind owes something to my affection for a hill called 'Caesar's Camp' (which indeed it once was) above the town of Folkestone, where we lived before and after the 1939–45 war.

The text is a good example of why I prefer the description 'based on...' for my metrical psalms; it indicates that they make no claim to be 'translations' (I have no Hebrew) or even versions of the inspired originals; but hymns which owe their form, theme and content to the psalm.

Note that while the keeping, guarding and preserving are all objective, 'secure' (verse 2) is subjective. See R.C. Trench, *A Select Glossary* (London 1859) for the distinction between safe and secure: literally, *sine cura,* without anxiety. The point is illuminated further in Henry Bett, *The Hymns of Methodism* (London 1945).

See Index 6.

168 THE FAITHFUL ARE KEPT AS THE MOUNTAINS THAT NEVER SHALL MOVE
14 14 14 15

Based on   Psalm 125
Theme   God our strength
Written   at Ruan Minor, August 1987
Suggested tune   SHEEN by Gustav Holst

This short text, with its long lines, seeks to bring out the varied use the psalm makes of mountain imagery and metaphor. Psalm 125 is one of the 'Songs of Ascents' sung by pilgrims on their way to the temple at Jerusalem, through territory not without danger. As they look at the hills around Jerusalem, they see in them an image of their security, held permanently in the Lord's keeping. But these same hills remind them also of God's unchangeable character, and how he is himself 'round about his people' to protect them. In the last couplet of my text, the singers are invited both to pray that their faith may have the same stability; and that they may know God's encircling love and peace about them in their earthly pilgrimage.

169 BLESS THE LORD AS DAY DEPARTS   78 78

Based on	Psalm 134
Theme	Evening
Written	at Ruan Minor, August 1978
Suggested tune	ASTHALL by John Barnard
	ST ALBINUS (omitting 'Alleluia') by Henry J. Gauntlett
Published in	*The Book of Praise*, 1986 to HESPERUS by David G. Preston
	Hymns for Today's Church (enlarged second edition), 1987 to ASTHALL
	Hymn Sampler Eighty Nine (USA), 1989 to LAWTON WOODS by John Carter
	Psalms for Today, 1990 to ASTHALL
	The Book of Praise (Canada), 1997 to ASTHALL
	Praise!, 2000 to ASTHALL

This is an evening hymn, which would have been placed in Section 2, 'Daily Services', had it not been a metrical psalm

Psalm 134 is the last of the fifteen Songs of Ascents. See 1 Chronicles 9.33 for a reference to the Levitical singers 'day and night' about their work; and 1 Timothy 2.8 for a New Testament reference to 'lifting holy hands'. The reciprocal blessing (from man to God, in thankfulness, and God to man in benediction) is the keynote of the psalm, as it is of verse 3 of this text.

170 THE HEARTFELT PRAISE OF GOD PROCLAIM   86 86 (CM)

Based on	Psalm 138
Theme	Praise and worship; the living God
Written	at Ford, December 1999
Suggested tune	BISHOPTHORPE by Jeremiah Clarke
	DUNDEE (Scottish traditional)
	ST STEPHEN by William Jones

The theme of the psalm is the goodness of God, known in the personal experience of the singer, leading to thankfulness and praise. The one here praised is a God who has chosen to make himself known: his 'Name' stands for his nature and character revealed from eternity in his unchanging word of promise. The central verses of the hymn each contain a deliberate contrast: in verse 2 between the heavens and the earth, represented, for example in the RSV by 'before the gods' and 'toward thy...temple'. Verse 3 compares the kings of earth with the King eternal; he is the theme and they merely the singers; while verse 3 contrasts the humble of heart, looking to God for mercy, with the proud of whom God 'takes note' (REB) or whom he 'marks down' (JB) from afar. Perhaps the Good News Bible captures the sense for us: 'the proud cannot hide from you'. Finally the concluding verse of the text takes up the idea of 'the works of your own hands', linking this with the 'steadfast love' (RSV) of the concluding verse of the psalm.

For another hymn based on this psalm, see 171 below.

171 WITH UNDIVIDED HEART AND CEASELESS SONGS   10 4 10 4 666 4

Based on	Psalm 138
Theme	Trust in God
Written	at Ford, January 1993
Suggested tune	HILLCREST by Greg Leavers
Published in	*New Mission Praise*, 1996 to HILLCREST
	Complete Mission Praise, 1999 to HILLCREST

The psalmist's prayer 'unite my heart to fear thy name' speaks to us all. Which of us has not been conscious of a divided heart? Paul has given classic expression to this in Romans 7: 'Wretched man that I am!' Here in Psalm 138 the thought of wholeheartedness comes not so much as a prayer but as a resolve, expressed in worship which is a response to his 'Name' (Psalm 138, verse 2), known in experience (verse 3), set forth in his word (verses 2, 4), and revealed in his purposes of love (verses 7, 8). It is this sequence of the psalmist's song that I have sought to follow in the text and to emphasise in the particular structure of the verses, with line 2 repeated as lines 4 and 8 in each verse.

See Index 6.

172 COME QUICKLY, LORD, AND HEAR THE CRIES   88 88 88

Based on	Psalm 141
Theme	Prayer; pilgrimage; trust in God; judgment
Written	at Ford, December 1997
Suggested tune	ST CATHERINE by Henri F. Hemy
	ST MATTHIAS by William H. Monk
	SURREY by Henry Carey
Published in	*Supplement 99* (USA), 1999 to COWDEN by David W. Music
	Praise!, 2000 to BENEDICTION by C.J. Dickinson

For the circumstances behind this text, see the Note on 137 'The Lord be near us as we pray'.

Commentators admit that the Hebrew of the middle verses is obscure. Certainly, having consulted a variety of translations, it seems best for a hymn intended to be sung in public worship to take the 'plough' (REB, NIV) as a metaphor for judgment, and to relate the discovered bones to the thought of resurrection to judgment. It is in this light that we pray the prayer and make the affirmations of the final couplet of this verse.

In something of the same way, this text seeks to relate the thought of the psalm in verse 5 (NIV: 'Let a good man strike or rebuke me in kindness...') to Proverbs 27.6: 'Faithful are the wounds of a friend'; and to interpret the 'journey' (Knox, verse 10) as the Christian's pilgrimage through life, from the dark of time to the daybreak of eternity.

173 TO GOD OUR GREAT SALVATION   76 76 D

Based on	Psalm 145
Theme	Praise and worship
Written	at Bramerton, May 1988
Suggested tune	CRÜGER by Johann Crüger
	MORNING LIGHT by George J. Webb
Published in	*Psalms for Today*, 1990 CRÜGER

Derek Kidner, in his *Tyndale Commentary* (London 1975) calls this psalm 'a great outpouring of worship' and says of the last doxology (verse 21):

'So ends David's contribution to the Psalter, on a note of praise which is wholly his own (21a), yet as wide as mankind and as unfading as eternity.'

I have tried to echo this inspiring exposition in my last four lines, by including the personal ('our hearts...'), the worldwide ('his earth...'), and the eternal ('for evermore...').

174 PRAISE THE GOD OF OUR SALVATION   87 87

Based on	Psalm 146
Theme	Praise and worship; thanksgiving; redemption
Written	at Ruan Minor, August 1982
Suggested tune	ANIMAE HOMINUM by Alfred T. Blanchet
	OMNI DIE from Corner's *Gesangbuch*, 1631
	SHIPSTON (English traditional)
Published in	*Psalms for Today*, 1990 to CANTERBURY CATHEDRAL by Alan Ridout
	Grace Praise (New Zealand), 1999 (words only)

This is one of a small number of metrical psalms written in the summer of 1982 at the request of David G. Preston, the compiler of a projected collection. The verse proved very intractable, as may indeed be evident from the result, and the work was done in several attempts and with much discarded material.

175 FILL YOUR HEARTS WITH JOY AND GLADNESS   87 87 87

Based on	Psalm 147
Theme	Praise and thanksgiving; creation; harvest

Written	at Sevenoaks, March 1970
Suggested tune	REGENT SQUARE by Henry T. Smart
	NEANDER (UNSER HERRSCHER) by Joachim Neander
Published in	*Psalm Praise*, 1973 to music by Robin Coulthard

Come and Praise, 1978 to (1) REGENT SQUARE (2) LAUS ET
    HONOR by Gordon Hartless

BBC Radio: A Service for Schools, Teacher's Notes, Autumn 1980
    (words only)

Hymns for Today's Church, 1982 to REGENT SQUARE

More Songs of the Spirit, 1982 to ODE TO JOY by Ludwig van
    Beethoven

Sing Praise, 1982 to ODE TO JOY

Hymns Old & New, 1984 to ODE TO JOY

Hymns Old & New (Anglican Edition), 1986 to ODE TO JOY

Mission Praise 2, 1987 to REGENT SQUARE

Anglican Praise, 1987 to UNSER HERRSCHER

Rejoice! (Australia), 1987 to FILL YOUR HEARTS by Robin
    Coulthard

Church Family Worship, 1988 to REGENT SQUARE

Best of Songs of the Spirit 1 & 2, 1988 to ODE TO JOY

Sing for Joy (USA), 1989 to LAUS ET HONOR

Anthem (USA), 1989 to music by Eugene Englebert

Psalms for Today, 1990 to REGENT SQUARE

Mission Praise Combined, 1990 to REGENT SQUARE

Sing to the Lord (Wales), 1990 (words only)

Baptist Praise and Worship, 1991 to (1) REGENT SQUARE
    (2) LAUS ET HONOR

Junior Praise 2, 1992 to REGENT SQUARE

Hymns for the People, 1993 to REGENT SQUARE

Praise the Lord, 1993 to RHUDDLAN

Worship Together (USA), 1995 to REGENT SQUARE

Hymns Old & New, 1996 edition, to ODE TO JOY

New Hymns and Worship Songs, 1996 to ODE TO JOY

Junior Praise Combined, 1997 to (1) REGENT SQUARE (2) LAUS
    ET HONOR

Songs of Fellowship 2, 1988 to REGENT SQUARE

Laudate, 1999 to REGENT SQUARE

Liturgical Hymns Old & New, 1999 to ODE TO JOY

Complete Mission Praise, 1999 to REGENT SQUARE

Sing Glory, 1999 to REGENT SQUARE

Praise the Lord (revised edition), 2000 to RHUDDLAN

Praying in Song, 2000 to ODE TO JOY

Complete Anglican Hymns Old & New, 2000 to ODE TO JOY

New Hymns and Worship Songs, 2001 to ODE TO JOY

Methodist Hymns Old & New, 2001 to REGENT SQUARE

Recorded on	*Sing a New Song*, 1992 to LAUS ET HONOR

The Hymn Makers: 'Tell out, my soul', 1996 to REGENT SQUARE

Junior Praise Combined 23, 1999 to (1) REGENT SQUARE
    (2) LAUS ET HONOR

This is a psalm linking the wonders of creation with the glories of providence and grace. Verse 4 in the Coverdale version is one to touch the imagination: 'He telleth the number of the stars: and calleth them all by their names.' So in my first attempts to come to grips with this psalm I tried:

> 'Great is the Lord: His wisdom great;
> his might and power proclaim.
> He counts the number of the stars
> and calls them all by name.'

But this will hardly do, since Isaac Watts, I find, has in one his versions:

> 'He form'd the stars, those heavenly flames,
> He counts their numbers, calls their names.'

In the BBC Schools Collection, *Come and Praise,* verse 2 is omitted, which makes a hymn suited for use in schools under the general heading of 'The Created World'. But for congregational use the theme of the psalm (which is in any event compressed in these four verses) requires the second verse with its references to the inner experiences of the heart.

With the tune ODE TO JOY the last two lines of each verse are repeated.

---

176 PRAISE THE LORD OF HEAVEN   65 65 D

Based on	Psalm 148
Theme	Praise and worship
Written	at Sevenoaks, January 1972
Suggested tune	CAMBERWELL by Michael Brierley
	KING'S WESTON by Ralph Vaughan Williams
	PRAISE THE LORD OF HEAVEN by Norman L. Warren
Published in	*Psalm Praise*, 1973 to PRAISE THE LORD OF HEAVEN
	Anthem (USA), 1982 to music by Hal H. Hopson
	Hymns and Psalms, 1983 to PRAISE THE LORD OF HEAVEN
	Songs from the Psalms, 1990 to LORD OF HEAVEN by
	Christopher Norton
	Psalms for Today, 1990 to CAMBERWELL
	Hymns for the People, 1993 to LORD OF HEAVEN
	New Start Hymns and Songs, 1999 to VICAR'S CLOSE by
	Malcolm Archer
	Complete Anglican Hymns Old & New, 2000 to VICAR'S CLOSE
	New Hymns and Worship Songs, 2001 to VICAR'S CLOSE
Recorded on	*Christ Triumphant* (The English Hymn, 1), 1999 to VICAR'S CLOSE

Originally written for *Psalm Praise,* it was only after publication that I became aware of the similarities between this version and that of T. B. Browne, No. 381 in *Hymns Ancient & Modern Revised.* Samuel Johnson complained of Isaac Watts' devotional poetry that 'the paucity of its topicks enforces perpetual repetition'; and it is perhaps not surprising that two versifiers at work on the same psalm should find their results to have much in common. Certainly Browne's first line is identical with my first two lines, and his second line very similar to my third and fourth. I considered, when I discovered this unconscious plagiarism, whether I should withdraw the text. In the event I decided not to do so, since Browne's original was published over 100 years ago in 1862; and because the similarities can be traced directly to the common source in the Coverdale version of the psalm.

177 O GOD WHO BROUGHT THE LIGHT TO BIRTH   88 88 88

Based on	Genesis 1–3
Theme	Creation; the fall
Written	at Ruan Minor, August 1990
Suggested tune	PATER OMNIUM by Henry J.E. Holmes
	RYBURN by Norman Crocker
	ST CATHERINE by Henri F. Hemy
Published in	*100 Hymns of Hope,* 1992 to MALLORY by William J. Reynolds
	The Poetic Bible, 2001 (words only)

This is one of two hymns (the other is 187 'O God of everlasting light') commissioned by Dan McKinley, then organist and choirmaster of the First Christian Church, Columbus, Indiana. His letter to me of January 1990 said 'We have not found an appropriate hymn dealing with the first chapter, or the first three chapters, of Genesis. Thus our Hymn Number One—as the hymnal now stands—will be from Exodus 15, not Genesis. Somehow this seems incomplete...!'

The first three chapters of the Bible are of course particularly rich in setting out origins which go far beyond the bare facts of God's creation of our world. These verses contain references (echoed in this text) to the creation of light, space, galaxies, the solar system, vegetable, animal and then human life. 'Humankind' is shown as having dominion and sharing God's delight in creative powers. The institution of marriage, and of the principle of a cycle of work and rest, are alluded to in verse 3; while verse 4 goes beyond the first hint of the corruption of nature and the loss of innocence (verse 3, line 4) to sin's enslavement and the entail of shame and bondage.

The final verse extrapolates from the Genesis 3.15 reference (line 1) to the fulfilment in Christ of this promise of redemption; and in the final line to its realization in Christian experience.

178 THE GOD OF GRACE IS OURS   66 86 (SM)

Based on	1 Chronicles 29. 10–14
Theme	Praise and worship; thanksgiving; stewardship
Written	at Ruan Minor, August 1985
Suggested tune	CARLISLE by Charles Lockhart
	FESTAL SONG by William H. Walter
	ST THOMAS from Aaron Williams' *New Universal Psalmodist,* 1770
	VENICE by William Amps

Chapter 29 of 1 Chronicles records the great prayer of King David at the inauguration of Solomon's temple, when he 'blessed the Lord in the presence of all the assembly': it is one of the high peaks of Old Testament devotion. The words have for many of us an additional familiarity because of their use liturgically. For such an occasion, short metre might be inappropriate: the moment demands something with altogether more resonance and grandeur. But then this hymn, though based on David's prayer, is not written with such an occasion primarily in mind. The thought of 'blessing the Name of the Lord' for his graciousness and goodness, for 'our creation, preservation, and all the blessings of this life', is one which is never far from the daily worship of all God's people, both individually and in congregations small as well as great. And though the words may come from the Old Testament, the Christian is unable to sing of 'the God of grace' without calling to mind the culmination of our present-day thanksgiving: 'the redemption of the world by our Lord Jesus Christ'.

179 GOD SHALL MY COMFORT BE   65 65 66 65

Based on	Isaiah 12
Theme	Deliverance; thanksgiving; praise and worship
Written	at Ford, August 1999
Suggested tune	MONK'S GATE (English traditional adapted by R. Vaughan Williams)
Published in	*Evangelicals Now,* March 2000 to PORTREE by Julie A. Skelton *Twelve Hymns,* 2001 to LUDLOW by Maurice Bevan

This self-contained song of Isaiah 12 reflects the prophet's own experience of God; and because his God is the Father of our Lord Jesus Christ, it reflects ours also. I have felt free to take the 'in that day' reference as pointing towards the final day; and to include a specifically Christian emphasis (for does not Isaiah 9 speak of 'a Son given to us'?) in the concluding lines.

'Consolation' in the first verse of the text is taken directly from JB and Knox ('comfort' from most other translators); and is a reminder of the real meaning of the word. 'Solace' carries with it the sense of alleviating, easing, bringing cheer; while 'comfort' has as its primary meaning (as in Luke 22.43 in Tyndale, rendered 'strengthening' in later versions) to make strong.

As can be seen in verse 2, I have borrowed the idea of 'the well(s) of life' from Psalm 36.9 (in the Prayer Book version) to stand for 'the wells of salvation' and when Isaiah speaks of the 'glorious things' which God has done, the Christian mind cannot but turn to the gift of Christ (verse 3).

180 O COMFORT EACH BELIEVING HEART   86 86 D (DCM)

Based on	Isaiah 40.1–11
Theme	Redemption; rejoicing
Written	at Ford, August 1993
Suggested tune	ELLACOMBE (German traditional) KINGSFOLD (English traditional)

Isaiah 40, one of the greatest chapters from one of the greatest books of the Old Testament, speaks of what Dr J.A. Motyer in his *The Prophecy of Isaiah* (Leicester 1993) calls 'the principles of divine action' in the deliverance of the people of Israel from their Babylonian exile, and God's purpose to restore them to their own land. Matthew 3.1–3 is our warrant for seeing in this prophecy a reference to Christ and to his coming; and this is echoed in verse 1 of this text where the references to 'sinners/friends' and 'weary load' are pointers to Luke 7.34 and Matthew 11.28. 'Bondage' in line 2 is the Revised English Bible translation of the more traditional 'warfare' (RSV margin: 'time of service').

Line 6 of verse 3 is the first explicit reference to a fully Christian interpretation of the passage.

Those who have no objection to secular folk-tunes in worship may like to try this to the fine eighteenth-century tune 'Drink to me only with thine eyes', or even to 'Auld Lang Syne'!

181 THE HEAVENS ARE SINGING, ARE SINGING AND PRAISING   12 11 12 11 12 11

Based on	Verses from Isaiah 44 & 45
Theme	Praise; redemption; rejoicing
Written	at Coolham, Sussex, October 1981
Suggested tune	ASH GROVE (Welsh traditional)
	CULVER by Alfred V. Fedak
Published in	*Anthem* (USA), 1988 by John Carter
	Lift High your Songs!, 1988 to SONG OF CREATION by Michael Paget
	Songs of Rejoicing (USA), 1989 to CULVER
	The Alfred V. Fedak Hymnary (USA), 1990 to CULVER
	The Poetic Bible, 2001 (words only)

In my earlier collection, *Lift Every Heart*, this text appeared in both a longer and a shorter form. It is the longer which attracted composers, and I have therefore seen no reason to re-publish the shorter version. The longer was the original, and brings out the use of repetition; which appears centrally in line 1, and at the end of line 3, as well as in lines 5 and 6, of each verse. Repetition is also a characteristic of these two chapters of Isaiah, as can be seen, for example, in verses 22, 23 and 24 of chapter 44 (redemption); or in verses 5, 6, 14, 18, 21, 22 of chapter 45 (cf. verse 4, line 4 of my text).

The phrase in verse 2, line 2, 'the stars in their courses' (which is drawn from Judges 5.20 in the AV) is one I had carried for some time in my MS book, waiting for a chance to incorporate it into a hymn text.

In 1988 the Hymn Society of America invited new tunes for this text. John S. Schlavone's tune SKILLMAN, dedicated to the memory of Dr Erik Routley, was sung to these words at the Annual Conference at Bryn Mawr, Pennsylvania, June 1988.

When sung to ASH GROVE the last three lines of each stanza are repeated in a way which harmonizes well with the use of repetition in the text.

See Index 6.

Based on	Isaiah 55
Theme	The feast of life; redemption and deliverance; the Bible
Written	at Ruan Minor and Poldhu Cove, August 1984
Suggested tune	AURELIA by Samuel S. Wesley
	CRÜGER by Johann Crüger
	KING'S LYNN (English traditional)
	ST THEODULPH by Melchior Teschner
Published in	*Bible Sunday Hymns*, 1990 (words only)
	Common Praise (Canada), 1990 to ES FLOG EIN KLEINS
	WALDVÖGELEIN (German traditional)

The Canadian hymnal listed above included this text in their section 'Christian Initiation'; while the references to invitation, promise and 'fruitful word' explain its suitability for Bible Sunday.

The phrase 'feast of life' is borrowed from the title of a book by Canon John Poulton, *The Feast of Life—A Theological Reflection on the Theme: Jesus Christ, the Life of the World* (Geneva 1982), but used here in the sense of the 'gospel feast'. I do not think the phrase can have been coined by him (Shakespeare in *Macbeth* writes of sleep as 'Chief nourisher in life's feast') but I cannot point to any other source.

In John Wesley's *A Collection of Hymns for the Use of the People called Methodists* of 1780, No. 2 is 'Come sinners, to the gospel feast' and No. 4 is based on Isaiah 55.

183 BELOVED IN CHRIST BEFORE OUR LIFE BEGAN 10 10 10 10

Based on	Jeremiah 29.11
Theme	The love of God; the Christian hope
Written	at Ruan Minor, August 1985
Suggested tune	ELLERS by Edward J. Hopkins
	MORECAMBE by Frederick C. Atkinson

This short composition, together with a companion piece 185 'Let every child of earth that sleeping lies', is an attempt to offer a metrical version of a familiar scripture, perhaps as the basis of an anthem rather than a congregational hymn.

This promise, originally to God's people in the face of conquest, deportation and exile, has often spoken to individual Christians in every generation, who know that God does not change. Note the totality of his providence from the phrase 'before our life began' in the first line, to 'life for evermore' in the last.

184 BEYOND ALL MORTAL PRAISE 66 66 44 44

Based on	Daniel 2.20–23
Theme	Praise and worship
Written	at Ruan Minor and Poldhu Cove, August 1981

Suggested tune	DARWALL'S 148TH by John Darwall
	DOLPHIN STREET by Arthur Hutchings
Published in	*The New English Hymnal,* 1986 to (1) DOLPHIN STREET
	(2) MARLBOROUGH GATE by Wayne Marshall
	Complete Anglican Hymns Old & New, 2000 to DOLPHIN STREET
	The Poetic Bible, 2001 (words only)

One of two texts written to this metre in August 1981, the hymn is based on Daniel's prayer of thanksgiving and praise when God revealed to him King Nebuchadnezzar's dream in Daniel 2: note the reference to answered prayer in verse 4. The text assumed its final shape on a grassy cliff above Poldhu Cove through a long and sunny afternoon.

185 LET EVERY CHILD OF EARTH THAT SLEEPING LIES   10 10 10 6

Based on	Daniel 12.2,3
Theme	Judgment; church and ministry
Written	at Ruan Minor, August 1985
Suggested tune	FLEMMING by Friedrich F. Flemming

This is the second in the pair of texts described in the note to 183 'Beloved in Christ before our life began'. Verse 2 employs the same rhymes as verse 1, but in reverse order.

   Daniel 12 is part of an apocalyptic vision comparable to later chapters in Revelation. In these verses a corner of the curtain is lifted, in celebration of 'those who turn many to righteousness'. This text might well form the basis of an anthem or solo at a Thanksgiving Service for a faithful ministry.

186 OUR SAVIOUR CHRIST ONCE KNELT IN PRAYER   88 88 88

Based on	Mark 9.2–10
Theme	The transfiguration of Christ
Written	at Bramerton, March 1978
Suggested tune	ST PETERSBURG by D.S. Bortniansky
	SURREY by Henry Carey
Published in	*Hymns for Today's Church,* 1982 to (1) DAS NEUGEBORNE
	KINDELEIN by Melchior Vulpius (2) SURREY

The transfiguration of Christ is described in all three of the synoptic Gospels; and finds a place within the calendar both of the *Book of Common Prayer* and of the more recent *Common Worship,* 2000 of the Church of England. Few hymns, however, seem to have taken this as their theme.

   I have followed the traditional view that the scene may have been Mount Hermon, within easy reach of Caesarea Philippi (in which case the hills of Galilee would be in the far distance); and have left open the possibility, often accepted, that the transfiguration occurred at night. It seems reasonable, if that were so, that the journey up the mountain would have been made by daylight, with darkness falling during their time of prayer.

In verse 3, the final lines refer to the representative character of Elijah and Moses, understood to typify the Prophets and the Law which together stand for the Old Testament revelation. Line 6 of verse 4 is an allusion, following Mark and Matthew, to our Lord's immediate reference to his coming suffering and death, about which he spoke with these disciples 'as they came down from the mountain' (Matthew 17.9; Mark 9.9).

'Narration' is one of the classifications of hymnody allowed by Robert Bridges in his *A Practical Discourse on some Principles of Hymn-singing* (Oxford 1901), and he calls it 'a very proper and effective form for general praise'. A century later, most worshippers would look, I think, for some link to be suggested between the narration of the historic events, and our life as Christians today. This need I have tried to meet in the final verse, which moves from a rehearsal of past events to a prayer for ourselves arising out of them.

187 O GOD OF EVERLASTING LIGHT 86 86 D (DCM)

Based on	John 3.3–16
Theme	The new birth
Written	at Ruan Minor and Bramerton, August 1991
Suggested tune	CLONMELL (Irish traditional)
	FOREST GREEN (English traditional)
	KINGSFOLD (English traditional)

In January 1990 I was asked by Dan McKinley, on behalf of the hymnal committee of the First Christian Church, Columbus, Indiana, for a versification of the first part of chapter 3 in the Gospel of John. This text, which took over a year to come to its final form, draws on some of the themes of our Lord's talk with Nicodemus, but does not attempt narrative form. So there are references to seeing the kingdom of God, to being born 'a second time' or 'anew' (both are translations of the original), to water and the Spirit and to new life in Christ. Verse 3 of the text draws on John 3.16 (with a reference back to the 'lifting up' of verse 14); while the thought of 'naming him Lord...' serves as a synonym for 'believing in him' (cf. John 1.12).

188 LIVING LORD, OUR PRAISE WE RENDER 87 87

Based on	Romans 6.5–11
Theme	New life in Christ; Eastertide
Written	at Sevenoaks, February 1972
Suggested tune	by Michael A. Baughen (see below)
	ALL FOR JESUS by John Stainer
	STUTTGART from *Harmonia Sacra*, 1715
Translated into	Danish
Published in	*Psalm Praise*, 1973 to music by Michael A. Baughen
	Keswick Praise, 1975 to ST OSWALD by John B. Dykes
	Irish Church Praise (Ireland), 1990 to KILLALOE by Edward F. Darling
	Daily Office, Community of the Holy Name, 1990 (words only)
	Anthem (Denmark), 1994 to music by Michael A. Baughen, in a translation by B. Højlund.

This text was written as a 'New Testament psalm' or canticle for *Psalm Praise*. 'Splendour', in verse 1, line 3, is the New English Bible version of the AV's 'by the glory of the Father'. It is the NEB which by its rendering 'in union with Christ Jesus' paves the way for 'One with Christ' at the start of verse 3 of the hymn. Verse 10 of this passage provides the title and the six-times-repeated refrain for one of Dylan Thomas's best-known lyrical poems 'And death shall have no dominion'.

See Index 6.

189 BORN BY THE HOLY SPIRIT'S BREATH   88 88 (LM)

Based on	Selected verses from Romans 8
Theme	Life in the Spirit; Whitsun; Pentecost
Written	at Sevenoaks, November 1972
Suggested tune	FULDA (GERMANY, WALTON) from William Gardiner's *Sacred Melodies*, 1815
	TALLIS'S CANON by Thomas Tallis
	WHITSUN PSALM by Noël Tredinnick
Published in	*News Extra*, June 1973 (words only)
	Psalm Praise, 1973 to WHITSUN PSALM
	Keswick Praise, to EISENACH by Johann H. Schein
	Living Songs (Africa), 1975 to BRESLAU by Christian Gall
	Songs of Worship, 1980 to (1) WHITSUN PSALM (2) FULDA
	Hymns for Today's Church, 1982 to (1) WHITSUN PSALM (2) FULDA
	Making Melody, 1983 to (1) WHITSUN PSALM (2) FULDA
	Hymns and Psalms, 1983 to CHURCH TRIUMPHANT by James W. Elliott
	Hymns for Praise and Worship (USA), 1984 to MISSIONARY CHANT by Charles H. Zeuner
	Exalt Him (USA), 1984 to GERMANY
	The Singing Church (USA), 1985 to GERMANY
	The New Redemption Hymnal, 1986 to WALTON
	Mission Praise 2, 1987 to WHITSUN PSALM
	Mission Praise Combined, 1990 to WHITSUN PSALM
	Baptist Praise and Worship, 1991 to (1) WHITSUN PSALM (2) ANTWERP by W. Smallwood
	Sing to the Lord (USA), 1993 to GERMANY
	Songs for the People of God (USA), 1994 to ST MARK'S VAN NUYS by Keith Landis
	Complete Mission Praise, 1999 to WHITSUN PSALM
	Sing Glory, 1999 to FULDA
	Grace Praise (New Zealand), 1999 (words only)
	Praise!, 2000 to FULDA
	The Poetic Bible, 2001 (words only)
	Methodist Hymns Old & New, 2001 to CHURCH TRIUMPHANT
	Hymns of Heritage & Hope (USA), 2001 to GERMANY
Recorded on	*Come, Christians, Join to Sing!* (USA), 1992 to GERMANY
	The Hymn Makers: 'Tell Out, my Soul', 1996 to WHITSUN PSALM

This is one of a number of New Testament canticles for the great festivals written for *Psalm Praise*, in this case for Pentecost. For such a theme, Romans 8 is an obvious starting point, even though a single hymn can barely allude to, let alone encompass, a fraction of what the chapter contains.

WALTON and GERMANY in the list above are alternative names for FULDA, normally attributed as I do here, though perhaps owing something to Beethoven. The editors of the *Companion to Hymns & Psalms* (Peterborough 1988) write:

'Numerous suggestions as to what this source of the tune might have been were discussed in the *Bulletin of the Hymn Society*, January 1984, but its identity remains a mystery, and the tune is probably best ascribed to Gardiner himself. It quickly became popular, and both melody and harmony have been published in variant forms.'

I have heard the text sung to EASTER SONG which, with the appropriate Alleluias, makes a joyful carol for Pentecost. At the Festival of Praise of the Jubilee Conference of the Hymn Society of Great Britain and Ireland in 1986 the hymn was sung in Guildford Cathedral to WELLINGTON by Michael Fleming.

See Index 6.

190 NOT FOR TONGUES OF HEAVEN'S ANGELS 87 87 6

Based on	1 Corinthians 13
Theme	Love
Written	at Ruan Minor, August 1984
Suggested tune	BRIDEGROOM by Peter Cutts
Translated into	Japanese
Published in	*New Songs of Praise 1*, 1985 to BRIDEGROOM
	Worship III (USA), 1986 to BRIDEGROOM
	Gather (USA), 1988 to COMFORT by Michael Joncas
	Winter Name of God (USA), 1988 to COMFORT
	Hymn Sampler Eighty Nine (USA), 1989 to BRIDEGROOM
	Songs of Rejoicing (USA), 1989 to REINLYN by Roy Hopp
	Irish Church Praise (Ireland), 1990 to BRIDEGROOM
	The Presbyterian Hymnal (USA), 1990 to BRIDEGROOM
	The Worshiping Church (USA), 1990 to BRIDEGROOM
	The Roy Hopp Hymnary (USA), 1990 to REINLYN
	GIA Hymnal Supplement 1991 (USA), 1991 to BRIDEGROOM
	Anthem (USA), 1991 by Roy Hopp
	United as One (USA), 1993 to music by Dan Schutte
	Drawn by a Dream (USA), 1993 to music by Dan Schutte
	Christian Worship: a Lutheran Hymnal (USA), 1993 to BRIDEGROOM
	New Songs of Rejoicing (USA), 1994 to REINLYN
	Gather, 2nd edition (USA), 1994 to COMFORT
	Songs for the People of God (USA), 1994 to LAKE FOREST by Keith Landis
	Moravian Book of Worship (USA), 1995 to BRIDEGROOM
	RitualSong (USA), 1996 to COMFORT
	The Covenant Hymnal (USA), 1996 to BRIDEGROOM

Voices United (Canada), 1996 to BRIDEGROOM
Glory and Praise (USA), 1997 to music by Dan Schutte
The Hymnal 21 (Japan), 1997 to BRIDEGROOM in an unattributed
    translation
Anthem (USA), 1997 by Richard W. Gieseke
Anthem (USA), 1997 by John A. Behnke
The Book of Praise (Canada), 1997 to BRIDEGROOM
The Growing Years (USA), 1998 to BRIDEGROOM
Laudate, 1999 to HEAVEN'S ANGELS by Stephen Dean
Common Praise (Canada), 1999 to COMFORT
Word and Song 2000 (USA), 1999 to COMFORT
Reformed Worship (USA), June 2000 to BRIDEGROOM
Rejoice in God (USA), 2000 to STRIPLING by K. Lee Scott
The Poetic Bible, 2001 (words only)
Worship & Rejoice (USA), 2001 to BRIDEGROOM

Recorded on	He Has the Power (USA), 1992 to music by Roy Hopp
	Singing our Faith (USA), 1992 to music by Roy Hopp
	United as One (USA), 1993 to music by Dan Schutte
	Drawn by a Dream (USA), 1993 to music by Dan Schutte

In 1984 Bob Batastini of GIA talked with me following a hymn festival during the Hymn Society of America Conference at Elmhurst, Illinois. The collection *Worship III* was in preparation, and he was looking for a new text to Peter Cutts' tune BRIDEGROOM, usually set to Emma Bevan's 'As the bridegroom to his chosen' (a paraphrase of a fourteenth-century original), for which it was originally written. I do not now recall if he or I proposed the theme of 1 Corinthians 13; but the final shape of the text was the result of correspondence with GIA, Hope Publishing, Derek Kidner and Peter Cutts himself. This suggested the plural of the final line (originally 'May love be mine...') and the recasting of the final verse to a form closer to the meaning of 1 Corinthians 13.13.

191 OUT OF DARKNESS LET LIGHT SHINE   77 77

Based on	2 Corinthians 4.6 (NEB translation)
Theme	The gospel; new life in Christ
Written	at Ruan Minor, August 1978
Suggested tune	HARTS by Benjamin Milgrove
	MERCY by Louis M. Gottschalk
	NORTHAMPTON by Charles J. King
Published in	*Hymns for Today's Church*, 1982 to HARTS
	Christingle Songbook, 1997 to HARTS

In 2 Corinthians 4.6 St Paul draws a deliberate parallel, which forms the theme of this text, between God's creative 'Let there be light' of Genesis 1.3 and the light of the gospel (verse 4) shining in the heart of the believer who is 'turned from darkness to light, and from the power of Satan to God' (Acts 26.18). Verse 1 of this text, therefore, is rooted in the creation story of Genesis 1, with the word of the Lord bringing order to an earth 'without form, and void' and without light (Genesis 1.2).

It is this parallel that explains the phrase 'dawn of dawn' in verse 3; meaning the very first sunrise of the very first morning. My notes show some hesitation between a number of alternatives, including as the most likely 'as the new-made dawn on earth'; but 'dawn of dawn', once considered, is to me more expressive of my meaning.

192 FRUITFUL TREES, THE SPIRIT'S SOWING   87 87

Based on	Galatians 5.22,23
Theme	The fruit of the Spirit
Written	at Ruan Minor, August 1981
Suggested tune	ALL FOR JESUS by John Stainer
	CROSS OF JESUS by John Stainer
	STUTTGART from *Harmonia Sacra*, 1715
Published in	*On the Move* (Australia), April 1981 (words only)
	Seventh Day Adventist Hymnal (USA), 1985 to ALL FOR JESUS
	Songs of Rejoicing (USA), 1989 to ORCHARD VIEW by Roy Hopp
	Irish Church Praise (Ireland), 1990 to BEECHGROVE by W. Donald Davison
	The Roy Hopp Hymnary (USA), 1990 to ORCHARD VIEW
	Songs for the People of God (USA), 1994 to LEAVITT by Keith Landis
	Anthem (USA), 1995 by Bret Heim and Roy Hopp
	Hymnal Supplement 1998 (USA), 1998 to DOROTHY by Ralph C. Schultz
	Church Hymnal (Ireland), 2000 to BEECHGROVE
	The Poetic Bible, 2001 (words only)
Recorded on	*Irish Church Praise* (Ireland), 1990 to BEECHGROVE

In the summer of 1981, I copied into my MS book an analysis of the fruits of the Spirit from a variety of English translations of Galatians 5. The AV, the RSV, J. B. Phillips, the New English Bible, the Jerusalem Bible, and R. A. Knox's translation all agree on *love, joy* and *peace*. The moderns all have *patience* and *kindness* for AV's *longsuffering* and *gentleness*, and mostly use *gentleness* where AV has *meekness*. On the other fruits there is a little more divergence of vocabulary. This metrical version of the passage follows the RSV (and therefore most of the moderns) with the one exception that it retains the AV *faith* where RSV (alone) has *faithfulness*, and the other versions give fidelity, trustfulness, forbearance.

193 BE STRONG IN THE LORD   10 10 11 11

Based on	Ephesians 6.10–18
Theme	The armour of God; pilgrimage and conflict
Written	at Ruan Minor, August 1982
Suggested tune	OLD 104TH from Thomas Ravenscroft's *Psalmes*, 1621
	LAUDATE DOMINUM by C. Hubert H. Parry

Published in	Irish Church Praise (Ireland), 1990 to LAUDATE DOMINUM
	Songs for the People of God (USA), 1994 to KINGSBRIDGE from
	Genuine Church Music, 1832
	Hymnal Supplement 1998 (USA), 1998 to LAUDATE DOMINUM

It is easy to overlook the fact that this passage supplies the theme of one of Charles Wesley's greatest hymns, 'Soldiers of Christ arise', since the versions usually printed in the hymnals often give only a selection of the sixteen verses, making of course *general* references to the armour (including the famous use of 'panoply' drawn directly from the Greek text) but not to all the individual items. His complete hymn contains explicit allusions to the girdle, the breastplate, 'the gospel greaves', the shield, the helmet and the Spirit's sword.

'Armour of light' in verse 1 of this text is a reference to Romans 13.12; arguably a different image, but one I take to be related (or relatable) to the Ephesians passage. The reference in the final line is to the cross of Christ as the source of all victory, and his crown as its symbol and reward.

---

194 THE BEST OF GIFTS IS OURS 66 86 (SM)

Based on	Philippians 4.4–9
Theme	The Christian mind; peace and blessing
Written	at Ruan Minor and Gwithian beach, August 1990
Suggested tune	NARENZA adapted by William H. Havergal
	SCHUMANN from Mason and Webb, *Cantica Laudis*, 1850
	VENICE by William Amps
Published in	*Anthem* (USA), 1996 by K. Lee Scott
	Rejoice in God (USA), 2000 to MARJORIE by K. Lee Scott

The text seeks to include the well-known elements of Philippians 4.8 ('Whatsoever things are true... honest... just...') from a number of translations of the passage. The first two stanzas of the text refer to earlier verses of Paul's exhortation, starting at 'Rejoice in the Lord always...' and continuing with his verse 7, often used as a liturgical blessing in the form 'The peace of God, which passes all understanding, keep your hearts and minds...' as in the *Book of Common Prayer*.

'The mind of Christ' in the final stanza is a Pauline expression (1 Corinthians 2.16) though not found in so many words in this passage. The metaphor of 'God's garden' is developed from the idea of the Spirit's fruit in Galatians 5.22.

---

195 PRAISE BE TO CHRIST IN WHOM WE SEE 88 88 D (DLM)

Based on	Colossians 1.15–20
Theme	Praise; the Lord Jesus Christ
Written	at Bramerton, March 1980
Suggested tune	CREATION by Franz Joseph Haydn
	LONDON by John Sheeles
	YE BANKS AND BRAES (Scottish traditional)

Translated into	Welsh
Published in	*Glory to God* (Ireland), 1994 to YE BANKS AND BRAES
	Spring Harvest Praise, 1998 to JERUSALEM by C. Hubert H. Parry
	(with a translation by Daffyd M. Job in the Welsh edition)
	Praise!, 2000 to YE BANKS AND BRAES
	The Poetic Bible, 2001 (words only)

This text, unusual for me in its rhyming structure (abbacdcd), arose directly out of a reading of Colossians as expounded by R. C. Lucas in his book *Fulless and Freedom* (Leicester 1980). He notes there how:

'within three decades of the crucifixion, language like this was in normal circulation among the churches to describe Jesus of Nazareth. What such testimony shows is that there never was a time, from the beginning of the church's life, when the highest honours of the Godhead were not given to his name.'

The same chapter goes on to work out the connections between the supremacy and sufficiency of Christ; between Christ as creator and redeemer; and between Christ before time, on earth, and over all. Traces of these differing emphases can be discerned in my text, which is at the same time directly drawn from a number of modern translations.

196 NO TEMPLE NOW, NO GIFT OF PRICE   886 D

Based on	Hebrews 10.1–25
Theme	Grace; redemption; discipleship
Written	at Ruan Minor, August 1983
Suggested tune	CORNWALL by Samuel S. Wesley
	INNSBRUCK based on Heinrich Isaac
	INNSBRUCK NEW based on Heinrich Isaac
Published in	*Hymnal Supplement 1998* (USA), 1998 to KIRKWOOD by Joseph Herl
	Grace Praise (New Zealand), 1999 (words only)

Hebrews 10 is a chapter that features in the Index of Scripture References of many hymnals; but the texts referred to are often based on a single verse (verse 12 is particularly popular); and perhaps only Isaac Watts' hymn 'Not all the blood of beasts/On Jewish altars slain' explicitly sets out to celebrate the main theme of the chapter with its contrast between the law and the gospel.

I hope it is not fanciful to see the 'way into the holiest' of Hebrews 10.20 (cf. verse 3 of this text) as linked with 'the pilgrim path of faith' hinted at in verses 23–25. They are, in my mind, different stages on the journey but the same road, the road of John 14.6, which is Christ himself.

'Imperishable' (verse 3) is open to the comment that it is more commonly used of what is abstract or impersonal. However the OED gives 'immortal' as a synonym; and in the RSV 1 Corinthians 15.52 reads '...the dead will be raised imperishable...' It serves, I hope, to point the contrast with the Old Testament priesthood, in accordance with the theme of Hebrews 10.

197 FATHER OF LIGHTS, WHO BROUGHT TO BIRTH   88 88 (LM)

Based on	James 1.17,18
Theme	God our light; discipleship; light on the way
Written	at Ruan Minor, August 1976
Suggested tune	BODMIN by Alfred S. Scott-Gatty
	TRURO from Thomas Williams' *Psalmodia Evangelica*, 1789

The title comes from James 1.17, a passage picked up again in verse 3 of this text. Verse 1, speaking of the creation of light, is drawn from Genesis 1.2–4. Other references are to 1 Timothy 6.16 and to John 8.12. Note also the Trinitarian references to Father, Son, and Spirit; and how the light of God's glory, revealed in creation (verse 1) and in redemption ('his mercies', verse 3) inspire the confident prayer for our enlightenment in faith, love and assurance; and in heart, mind and will ('obey', verse 4).

198 O CHRIST THE KING OF GLORY   76 76 D

Based on	1 Peter 1.11 and other verses
Theme	The Lord Jesus Christ; suffering and glory; the worldwide church
Written	at Ford, July 1992
Suggested tune	AURELIA by Samuel S. Wesley
	DIES DOMINICA by John B. Dykes
	THORNBURY by Basil Harwood
Published in	*Compasrose,* Advent 1992 (words only)
	Anglican World, Lent/Easter 1993 (words only)
	New Mission Praise, 1996 to ROEWEN by Roger Mayor
	Supplement 99 (USA), 1999 to CROSS AND GRAVE AND GLORY by William Llewellyn
	Complete Mission Praise, 1999 to ROEWEN

In January 1993 the Primates of the Anglican Communion met in Capetown, South Africa, together with the Anglican Consultative Council; the first time such a joint meeting had been held. The theme was 'A transforming vision: suffering and glory in God's world', based on 1 Peter 1.11.

My friend Canon James Rosenthal of the Secretariat of the Anglican Consultative Council asked me in June 1992 if I would write a hymn for this gathering, bearing in mind that the Anglican Communion needed to attend to its own unity in the face of various divisive forces, theological and secular. This text is the result.

199 HE WALKS AMONG THE GOLDEN LAMPS   86 88 86

Based on	Revelation 1.12–18
Theme	Christ in glory
Written	at Sevenoaks, March 1972

Suggested tune	GOLDEN LAMPS by Norman L. Warren
	REVELATION by Noël Tredinnick
	WITHINGTON by John Barnard
Published in	*Psalm Praise*, 1973 to (1) REVELATION (2) GOLDEN LAMPS
	Grace Hymns, 1975 to GOLDEN LAMPS
	Hymns II (USA), 1976 to REVELATION
	Hymns for Today's Church, 1982 to REVELATION
	Worship III (USA), 1986 to REVELATION (LE BLANC) by Robert Le Blanc
	Trinity Hymnal, revised edition (USA), 1990 to REVELATION
	The Collegeville Hymnal (USA), 1991 to GOLDEN LAMPS (McKENNA) by Edward J. McKenna
	Praise!, 2000 to REVELATION
	The Poetic Bible, 2001 (words only)
Recorded on	*Here is Psalm Praise*, 1975 to REVELATION
	He to Whom Wonders Belong, 1993 to music by Steve Layfield

The text of this hymn follows closely the vision of the aged John on the island of Patmos, described in the first chapter of the book of Revelation. The golden lamps are the churches: the one in the midst of them is described in terms recalling Daniel, chapter 7, as 'like a son of man'. In this text, the robe, the feet, the eyes, the hair, the voice are all drawn directly from John's vision; the description of the robe is an, (I hope, legitimate) extrapolation; the stars and the sword remind us that John's imagery is symbolic rather than pictorial. John is told 'Write what you see'—and the hymn takes up John's description and seeks to make of it an act of worship.

No existing hymn tune known to me fitted the metre of this text—which is not in fact a complicated one. But as can be seen above, editors have been glad of the opportunity to use one or other of the two tunes composed to these words for *Psalm Praise*, the book for which the text was written. Alec Wyton wrote a tune, AUDEN, for this text which appeared in 1979 in the *Book of Worship* of St Luke's Church, St Paul, Minnesota. The two tunes, GOLDEN LAMPS, listed above are unrelated to each other, separated by some twenty years and by the Atlantic ocean. Much the same could be said of the two tunes entitled REVELATION. The name refers to the earlier tune in each instance, unless the composer's name is added in brackets.

---

200 HEAVENLY HOSTS IN CEASELESS WORSHIP   87 87 D

Based on	Revelation 4 & 5
Theme	Praise and worship
Written	at Sevenoaks, September 1972
Suggested tune	ABBOT'S LEIGH by Cyril V. Taylor
	BEECHER (LOVE DIVINE) by John Zundel
	BLAENWERN by William P. Rowlands
Published in	*Psalm Praise*, 1973 to (1) HEAVENLY HOSTS by Noël Tredinnick (2) music by Norman L. Warren
	Grace Hymns, 1975 to MAESYNEUADD by W.R. Thomas
	Worship II (USA), 1975 to HEAVENLY HOSTS

Sixty Hymns from Songs of Zion (USA), 1977 to LINCOLNWOOD
    by Keith Landis
Hymns for Today's Church, 1982 to (1) BLAENWERN (2) ABBOT'S
    LEIGH
Worship III (USA), 1986 to HEAVENLY HOSTS
Anglican Praise, 1987 to LOVE DIVINE (ZUNDEL)
Psalter Hymnal (USA), 1988 to BETHANY by Henry T. Smart
Psalms for Today, 1990 to BLAENWERN
The Baptist Hymnal (USA), 1991 to HARWELL by Lowell Mason
Hymns for the People, 1993 to BLAENWERN
Songs for the People of God (USA), 1994 to TAYLOR by Keith
    Landis
Sing we Merrily, 1995 to BLAENWERN
Worship Together (USA), 1995 to HARWELL
RitualSong (USA), 1996 to HEAVENLY HOSTS
Sing Glory, 1999 to BLAENWERN
Praise!, 2000 to ARWELFA by John Hughes
Sing to the Lord, 2000 to BLAENWERN

The two verses of this hymn appear in my MS book substantially in their present form from the beginning. They occupy a single page, and the corrections are more to individual lines than to the construction or form of the text.

This hymn is based on what John describes in a vision through a door open into heaven (Revelation 4.1). He sees there the throne and 'One seated on the throne', worshipped by the elders and the living creatures round about him; with special reference not only to his glory, honour and power, but to his creation. And then John sees also the Lamb of God who by his blood 'did ransom men for God' (chapter 5, verse 9) worshipped by 'myriads and myriads and thousands and thousands' of the citizens of heaven. Indeed, 'every creature in heaven and earth and under the earth and in the sea' (verse 13) joins in the chorus of praise: and the 'Glory, honour and power' of the first song swells to 'Power and wealth and wisdom and might and honour and glory and blessing... for ever and ever' (verses 12,14).

201 THE GLORY OF OUR GOD AND KING   86 86 (CM)

Based on	Revelation 15.3,4
Theme	God the Father, the living God
Written	at Ford, August 1995
Suggested tune	ASHFORD by Eric H. Thiman
	BISHOPTHORPE by Jeremiah Clarke
	RICHMOND adapted from Thomas Haweis

Written as a New Testament canticle, this is a metrical rendering of 'the song of Moses', the servant of God, and 'the song of the Lamb' from Revelation 15. It is the song of the church triumphant, yet free from false triumphalism since the universal sovereignty it celebrates belongs to God alone. The fact that the passage draws heavily on the Book of Psalms (e.g. 92.5; 139.14; 145.17) makes it particularly suitable for use in public worship.

202 A CITY RADIANT AS A BRIDE   86 86 D (DCM)

Based on	Revelation 21 & 22
Theme	Citizens of heaven; the new Jerusalem
Written	at Ruan Minor, Cornwall, August 1986
Suggested tune	FOREST GREEN (English traditional)
	LADYWELL by William H. Ferguson
Published in	*News of Hymnody,* January 1987 (words only)
	Songs of Rejoicing (USA), 1989 to RADIANT CITY by John Worst
	Day Trips to Heaven, 1991 (words only)
	Songs for the People of God (USA), 1994 to WALKER by Keith Landis
	Common Praise, 2000 to LADYWELL
	Rejoice in God (USA), 2000 to WIEBERG by K. Lee Scott

In the *Alternative Service Book, 1980* of the Church of England, whose authorization expired in 2000, each Sunday was allotted a Sunday Theme for those who wished to follow it. 'Citizens of heaven' was the theme for the last Sunday after Pentecost; and although the suggested themes do not feature in *Common Worship* (the successor to the *Alternative Service Book, 1980*), Revelation 21 is one of the lectionary readings for All Saints' Day.

The phrase 'fields of asphodel' (verse 2, line 4)—which was the starting point of the whole text—is a reference to Isaiah 35.2 in the New English Bible. Asphodel is traditionally the immortal flower of the Elysian Fields. 'Colours none can name' may be taken as an indication that the identification (and so translation) of precious stones from ancient sources has often an element of uncertainty!

203 FATHER WHO FORMED THE FAMILY OF MAN   10 10 10 6

Based on	The Lord's Prayer
Theme	Prayer
Written	at Sevenoaks, July 1968
Suggested tune	by Michael A. Baughen (see below)
Published in	*Youth Praise II,* 1969 to music by Michael A. Baughen
	Thirty Hymns, 1972 (words only)
	New Creation Song Book (Australia), 1983 (words only)
	New Creation Hymn Book (Australia), 1991 (words only)

Originally written for *Youth Praise 2,* this hymn pre-dated the use of a MS book; it is however one of the few such for which the original MS survives. The alternating pattern at the start of each verse ('Father...Lord...') was not an original intention; verse 2, for instance, was originally drafted as 'Father of all the nations of the earth' and 'verse 3 as 'Ruler of all the ordered realms above'. The 'new song' of verse 2 is not yet the new song of Revelation 5.9 but rather of (for example) Psalm 40.3. The two titles in verse 6, line 2 are from the Psalms (18, 40, 70 and 144) and from Genesis 15.1.

Based on	The Collect for aid against all perils
Theme	Evening
Written	at Ruan Minor, August 1977
Suggested tune	CHRISTE SANCTORUM (French traditional)
Published in	*Anglican Hymnbook Supplement*, 1978 (words only)
	Hymns for Today's Church, 1982 to CHRISTE SANCTORUM
	Anglican Praise, 1987 to CLOISTERS by Joseph Barnby
	Church Family Worship, 1988 to CLOISTERS
	Songs for the People of God (USA), 1994 to JUDSON by Keith Landis
	Sing Glory, 1999 to CHRISTE SANCTORUM
Recorded on	*The Hymn Makers: 'Tell Out, My Soul'*, 1996 to CHRISTE SANCTORUM

The Third Collect, 'for aid against all perils', at Evening Prayer in the *Book of Common Prayer*, on which this hymn is based, goes back in its original form for well over a thousand years, and perhaps as far back as the sixth or seventh century. Verse 2 of my text carries echoes of Romans 13.12, the passage which St Augustine found himself reading when he heard in the garden the voice chanting 'Take up and read'; and to Psalm 130.6.

205 LORD GOD ALMIGHTY, FATHER OF ALL MERCIES   11 11 11 5

Based on	The General Thanksgiving
Theme	Thanksgiving
Written	at Ford, August 1983
Suggested tune	CHRISTE SANCTORUM (French traditional)
	FLEMMING by Friedrich F. Flemming
Published in	*New Mission Praise*, 1996 to CHRISTE SANCTORUM
	Glory Be (New Zealand), 2000 to CHRISTE SANCTORUM

Ever since serving in the Diocese of Norwich whose Bishop, Edward Reynolds (1599–1676), gave us the General Thanksgiving, the prayer has been a favourite of mine, both for personal and congregational use. He wrote it just in time for inclusion in the *Book of Common Prayer*, 1662; and it found an honoured place, only slightly recast in its use of language, in the *Alternative Service Book, 1980*, while *Common Worship*, 2000 includes the Prayer Book version intact.

Copying that prayer, this text is built on a framework of 'creation...preservation...all the blessings of this life...the redemption of the world...the means of grace...the hope of glory'; concluding, as Bishop Reynolds does, with the plea that thanksgiving may issue in 'thanksliving'.

The text is clearly meditative; it surveys an incomparable wealth of blessing in only a few lines. It was originally drafted as two stanzas of eight lines each (11 11 11 5 D) following the pattern of Percy Dearmer's 'As the disciples, when thy Son had left them'; and can be sung in that way if a particular tune requires it (for example, the version of DIVA SERVATRIX with first and second endings, as in *Songs of Praise, Ancient & Modern New Standard* or *Common Praise*, 2000).

Based on	A prayer of St Augustine
Theme	Christ in experience
Written	at Ruan Minor, August 1976
Suggested tune	KING'S LYNN (English traditional)
	MOVILLE (Irish traditional)
	NYLAND (Finnish traditional)
Published in	*Songs of Worship*, 1980 to WOLVERCOTE by W.H. Ferguson
	A Supplement to Congregational Praise, 1982 (words only)
	Hymns for Today's Church, 1982 to KING'S LYNN
	The New English Hymnal, 1986 to AU FORT DE MA DÉTRESSE
	from the *Genevan Psalter*, 1542
	Rejoice and Sing, 1991 to NYLAND
	A New Hymnal for Colleges and Schools (USA), 1992 to MOVILLE
	New Songs of Rejoicing (USA), 1994 to CAVANAUGH by Keith
	Landis
	Songs for the People of God (USA), 1994 to CAVANAUGH
	Evangelical Lutheran Hymnary (USA), 1996 to MOVILLE
	The Book of Praise (Canada), 1997 to MEIRIONYDD by W. Lloyd
	Anglican World, Advent 1999 (words only)
	Sing Glory, 1999 to KING'S LYNN
	Complete Anglican Hymns Old & New, 2000 to AU FORT DE MA
	DÉTRESSE
	Common Praise, 2000 to LLANGLOFFAN (Welsh traditional)
	Church Hymnal (Ireland), 2000 to MOVILLE
	Twelve Hymns, 2001 to PARSONAGE FARM by Maurice Bevan

This text was written to the tune MOVILLE and takes its theme from a passage in the *Meditations* of St Augustine, frequently adapted as a traditional and beautiful prayer. It is an example of how much more easily hymns can be addressed to God using 'Thee and Thou' language: 'Light of the minds that know thee' would be an excellent opening line, whereas '...that know you' I find less acceptable.

I have been taken to task for presuming that the reference to the Emmaus road will be self-evident to modern worshippers. But while convoluted imagery from the typology of the Old Testament may be questioned for modern hymns, a familiarity with the Gospels is surely a reasonable expectation. Proper names can be powerful in their associations; but require careful handling. Harold Nicolson in his book *Tennyson* (London 1923) refers to 'this device, so popular with English poets from Milton to Flecker, of enlivening the gray colours of our native speech by the introduction of resonant and flamboyant foreign names'. Similarly B.L.Manning says of Charles Wesley in his *The Hymns of Wesley and Watts* (London 1942):

> 'He knew that the use of a proper name with associations may start or clinch a train of thought more effectively than a flood of colourless words will start or clinch it. To you and to me, with our beggarly knowledge of Holy Scripture, this magic is less potent than it was to Wesley.'

The reference in verse 4 to heaven is based on some words from the Sarum Antiphoner, dating back certainly to the fourteenth century. I used to see them when, as a member of the General Synod of the Church of England, I spent long days in the debating chamber at Church House, London. It is a fine circular hall, and around the base of the dome are inscribed these words:

> 'Holy is the true light and passing wonderful, lending radiance to them that endured in the heat of the conflict; from Christ they inherit a home of unfading splendour, wherein they rejoice with gladness evermore.'

207 O GOD OF OUR SALVATION   76 76 D

Based on	A prayer of St Chrysostom
Theme	Prayer
Written	at Ford, July 2000
Suggested tune	AURELIA by Samuel S. Wesley
	KING'S LYNN (English traditional)

Thomas Cranmer took this lovely prayer, which concludes both Morning and Evening Prayer in the *Book of Common Prayer,* from the liturgy of St John Chrysostom (the name means 'golden-mouthed') attributed, on doubtful evidence, to the fourth-century Bishop of Constantinople. Cranmer placed it, appropriately enough, at the close of the Litany in his Prayer Book of 1549.

This hymn follows the prayer in references to the agreement of those who are met to pray ('with one accord') following Matthew 18.19,20. 'Our common supplications' speaks of agreement and is followed by the Lord's promise to 'two or three gathered together in my name.'

The second stanza picks up the word *petition,* with the acknowledgment that God knows better than we do what is truly for our good ('most expedient for us'). Finally comes the prayer for knowledge of truth and for life everlasting, to which the last four lines of the text refer.

208 GOD OF GODS, WE SOUND HIS PRAISES   87 87 88 87

Based on	The Te Deum
Theme	Praise and worship
Written	at Sevenoaks, April 1970
Suggested tune	AUSTRIA by Franz Joseph Haydn
	GOD OF GODS by Christian Strover
Translated into	Chinese, Estonian
Published in	*Psalm Praise,* 1973 to GOD OF GODS
	Hymns II (USA), 1976 to GOD OF GODS
	Anglican Hymn Book Supplement, 1978 (words only)
	Hymns for Today's Church, 1982 to GOD of GODS
	Hymnal Supplement (USA), 1984 to GOD OF GODS

Songifts, 1986 to GOD OF GODS
Hymns of Life, 1986 to GOD OF GODS
Anglican Praise, 1987 to GOD OF GODS
Church Family Worship, 1988 to GOD OF GODS
Come Rejoice!, 1989 to GOD OF GODS
Psalms for Today, 1990 to GOD OF GODS
Trinity Hymnal, revised edition (USA), 1990 to GOD OF GODS
Baptist Praise and Worship, 1991 to GOD OF GODS
Sounds of Grace (Hong Kong), 1991 to GOD OF GODS (with a
    Chinese translation)
Hymns for the People, 1993 to HICKLING by Roger Mayor
Vaimulikud Laulud (Estonia), 1997 to GOD OF GODS in an
    unattributed translation
Sing Glory, 1999 to GOD OF GODS

Recorded on   Psalm Praise - Sing a New Song, 1978 to GOD OF GODS

It was part of the conception of *Psalm Praise* that it should contain metrical canticles as well as metrical psalms. The Te Deum (from the opening words of the Latin version; translated as 'We praise thee, O God') is a very ancient hymn, thought to come originally from Niceta, Bishop of Remesiana in the fifth century; in the *Book of Common Prayer* it is part of the daily Service for Morning Prayer of the Church of England. This metrical version was fortunate to find a composer who provided it with a strong and attractive tune since it fits no hymn tune already extant. 'God of gods' is not an epithet drawn from the Te Deum; but is used in Scripture (e.g. Daniel 2.47) and the similar phrase 'a great King above all gods' comes in the canticle immediately preceding the Te Deum at Morning Prayer (Psalm 95).

209 WE COME WITH SONGS OF BLESSING   76 76 D

Based on	The Te Deum
Theme	Praise and worship
Written	at Ford, and at Crantock, Cornwall, March and April 1993
Suggested tune	CRÜGER by John Crüger
	OFFERTORIUM from J. Michael Haydn
	ST THEODULPH by Melchior Teschner
Published in	*Rejoice in God* (USA), 2000 to FAITH CHURCH by K. Lee Scott
	Twelve Hymns, 2001 to BOUGHTON ALUPH by Maurice Bevan
	Anthem (USA), 2001 by K. Lee Scott

For many people, adoration is not the easiest part of daily prayer. Sometimes it may be helpful, therefore, to use the matchless words of the Te Deum in one's personal prayers. From this there sprung a second attempt at a metrical version; the first, 208 'God of gods, we sound his praises', was written for *Psalm Praise* over twenty years earlier.

    Bernard Lord Manning, a name revered by all lovers of hymns for his engaging studies of Watts and Wesley (and one 'who cannot be accused of lack of reverence for the Puritan tradition') said of Free Church worship that too often the prayers were 'too long, too woolly, too wordy, too casual': a verdict quoted by Gordon Wakefield in his *Robert Newton Flew* (London 1971). You do not need to be a Free Churchman to know that experience! Perhaps a prayer such as the Te Deum may, from time to time, offer a welcome refreshment.

Based on	The Benedicite
Theme	Praise; creation
Written	at Bramerton and at Oakworth, Yorkshire, April 1986
Suggested tune	MONKLAND by John Antes
	MOZART by W.A. Mozart
	ST GEORGE'S, WINDSOR by George J. Elvey
	UNIVERSITY COLLEGE by Henry J. Gauntlett
Published in	*Hymns for Today's Church* (enlarged second edition), 1987 to
	(1) HUMILITY by John Goss (2) UNIVERSITY COLLEGE
	Church Family Worship, 1988 to MELLING by John Fawcett

The Benedicite, one of the canticles at Morning Prayer in the *Book of Common Prayer*, is based on part of the Apocryphal book, 'The Song of the Three Holy Children'. It is sometimes headed 'A Song of Creation', and three versions of it appear in *Common Worship*, 2000, one considerably shortened. This metrical version, which was commissioned by the editors of *Hymns for Today's Church* for their second edition, can be similarly abbreviated by using only verses 1, 7 and 8.

The Benedicite has been used in Christian worship from the earliest times, and by the fifth century was described as 'sung by Christians throughout the world'.

To a 77 77 D tune, such as ST EDMUND, this text may be sung as four eight-line stanzas. For the shorter version of the text, include verse 6 to give two stanzas.

Based on	The Benedictus, Luke 1.68-79
Theme	Advent; redemption
Written	at Bramerton and Ruan Minor, August 1986
Suggested tune	HOUSTON by Peter Cutts
Published in	*100 Hymns of Hope* (USA), 1992 to HOUSTON

In the *Book of Common Prayer*, the Monastic Offices of Lauds and Matins both contributed elements to Cranmer's service of Morning Prayer; and this 'Gospel Canticle' is carried over from Lauds, through the *Book of Common Prayer* to *Common Worship*, 2000. It comes from the Song of Thanksgiving of Zacharias for the birth of his son John (the Baptist), forerunner of the promised Messiah.

This is my second attempt at a metrical version of the Benedictus. The first, 'Our God has turned to his people' was written for *Psalm Praise*, 1973 but listed in *Lift Every Heart*, 1984 under 'Discontinued texts'; though I allowed its inclusion in *Carol Praise*, 1987 where it can still be found by anyone interested.

No tune to this exact metrical pattern was known to me when this text was written. It is Peter Cutts' tune HOUSTON which allows the text to be sung as a hymn.

Based on	Luke 1.46–55, the Magnificat (NEB translation)
Theme	Praise; the song of Mary
Written	at Blackheath, May 1961
Suggested tune	WOODLANDS by Walter Greatorex
Translated into	Chinese, Japanese, Latvian, Welsh
Published in	*Anglican Hymn Book*, 1965 to TIDINGS by William Llewellyn

Youth Praise 1, 1966 to TELL OUT MY SOUL by Michael A.
    Baughen (see Note, p. 421)
100 Hymns for Today, 1969 to WOODLANDS
Thirteen Psalms, 1970 (words only)
Sing Praise to God, 1971 to WOODLANDS
Family Worship, 1971 (words only)
The Hymn Book (Canada), 1971 to ELING by Geoffrey Ridout
Catholic Book of Worship (Canada), 1972 to WOODLANDS
The Book of Praise (Canada), 1972 to WOODLANDS
Psalm Praise, 1973 to (1) TELL OUT MY SOUL (2) WOODLANDS
Giver of Bread and Justice: Acts of Worship for Christian Aid Week,
    1973 (words only)
Church Hymnary 3, 1973 to MAPPERLEY by Frank Spedding
The Hymnal (Canada), 1973 to WOODLANDS
The Hymnal of the United Church of Christ (USA), 1974 to
    WOODLANDS
Praise for Today, 1974 to MORESTEAD by Sydney Watson
Keswick Praise, 1975 to TELL OUT MY SOUL
New Church Praise (Scotland), 1975 to WINTON by George
    Dyson
Sing a Celebration (Australia), 1975 to TELL OUT MY SOUL
Grace Hymns, 1975 to WOODLANDS
English Praise, 1975 to WOODLANDS
Christian Worship, 1976 to WOODLANDS
Cliff Hymns, 1976 to WOODLANDS
Hymns II (USA), 1976 to WOODLANDS
Westminster Praise (USA), 1976 to CALDERON by Martin Shaw
Sixty Hymns from Songs of Zion (USA), 1977 to BENNETT by
    Keith Landis
The Australian Hymnbook (Australia), 1977 to WOODLANDS
Christian Hymns (Wales), 1977 to WOODLANDS
Partners in Praise, 1979 to WOODLANDS
With One Voice, 1979 to WOODLANDS
Hymns III (USA), 1979 to BIRMINGHAM from Francis
    Cunningham's *A Selection of Psalm Tunes*, 1834
Cantate Domino (USA), 1979 to WOODLANDS
Exploring the Bible (USA), 1979 to WOODLANDS
A Panorama of Christian Hymnody (USA), 1979 (words only)
Pocket Praise, 1980 (words only)
Songs of Worship, 1980 to (1) TELL OUT MY SOUL (2) WOODLANDS
Cry Hosanna, 1980 to WOODLANDS
Catholic Book of Worship II (Canada), 1980 to WOODLANDS

Walsingham Devotions, 1980 (words only)
Lion Book of Favourite Hymns, 1980 (words only)
Fullness of Life: an Order of Service for Christian Aid Week, 1981
    (words only)
Declare His Glory, 1981 to WOODLANDS
Broadcast Praise, 1981 to MORESTEAD
Celebration Hymnal II, 1981 to WOODLANDS
A Supplement to Congregational Praise, 1982 (words only)
Hymns for Today's Church, 1982 to (1) WOODLANDS
    (2) TELL OUT MY SOUL
More Songs of the Spirit, 1982 to WOODLANDS
Parish Sunday Vespers, 1982 to WOODLANDS
Sing Praise, 1982 to WOODLANDS
Covenant Songs (Australia), 1982 to TELL OUT MY SOUL
Hymns Ancient & Modern New Standard, 1983 to WOODLANDS
Hymns for Today, 1983 to WOODLANDS
Hymns and Psalms, 1983 to WOODLANDS
Choral Descants 5, 1983 to WOODLANDS
Mission England Praise, 1983 to (1) TELL OUT MY SOUL
    (2) WOODLANDS
New Creation Song Book (Australia), 1983 (words only)
The Summit Choirbook (USA), 1983 to ERFYNIAD (Welsh traditional)
Hymns Old and New (revised and enlarged), 1984 to WOODLANDS
Worship the King, 1984 to WOODLANDS
Hymnal Supplement (USA), 1984 to WOODLANDS
The Iona Community Worship Book (Scotland), 1984 (words only)
Complete Celebration Hymnal, 1984 to WOODLANDS
Hymns of Praise, 1984 (words only)
Anthem (USA), 1985 by John F. Wilson
Today's Missal (USA), 1985 to WOODLANDS
The Singing Church (USA), 1985 to WOODLANDS
Praise and Thanksgiving, 1985 to (1) WOODLANDS (2) TIDINGS
Rejoice in the Lord (USA), 1985 to WOODLANDS
Alternative Services of the Anglican Church in Canada (Canada),
    1985 (words only)
Hymns of Fellowship, 1985 to WOODLANDS
Seventh Day Adventist Hymnal (USA), 1985 to MORESTEAD
The Hymnal 1982 (USA), 1985 to (1) BIRMINGHAM
    (2) WOODLANDS
Today's Missal (USA), 1986 to WOODLANDS
All Praise to his Name, 1986 to WOODLANDS
Rejoising, 1986 to WOODLANDS
The New English Hymnal, 1986 to WOODLANDS
Hymns Old & New (Anglican Edition), 1986 to WOODLANDS
Junior Praise, 1986 to (1) TELL OUT MY SOUL (2) WOODLANDS
Worship III (USA), 1986 to WOODLANDS
Celebration, 1986 (words only)
The Hymnal for Worship and Celebration (USA), 1986 to
    WOODLANDS
The New Redemption Hymnal, 1986 to WOODLANDS
Spirit of Praise 2, 1987 to WOODLANDS
Your Favourite Songs of Praise, 1987 (words only)

The Broadcast Hymn Book, 1987 to MORESTEAD
Supplement to Lutheran Hymnal (Australia), 1987 to WOODLANDS
Carol Praise, 1987 to WOODLANDS
Rejoice! (Australia), 1987 to WOODLANDS
Hymnal Supplement II (USA), 1987 to WOODLANDS
A Survey of Christian Hymnody (USA), 1987 to WOODLANDS
Church Family Worship, 1988 to (1) WOODLANDS
   (2) YANWORTH by John Barnard
Breaking Bread (USA), 1988 to WOODLANDS
Sing to the Lord, 1988 to WOODLANDS
Psalter Hymnal (USA), 1988 to WOODLANDS
Let's Praise!, 1988 to WOODLANDS
Today's Missal (USA), 1989 to WOODLANDS
The Penguin Book of Hymns, 1989 (words only)
Get Together, 1989 to WOODLANDS
The United Methodist Hymnal (USA), 1989 to WOODLANDS
The Wedding Book, 1989 to (1) YANWORTH (2) WOODLANDS
Spring Harvest Celebration Songbook, 1989 to WOODLANDS
Breaking Bread '90 (USA), 1989 to WOODLANDS
Anthem (USA), 1990 by V. Earle Copes
Sing Joyfully (USA), 1990 to WOODLANDS
Irish Church Praise (Ireland), 1990 to WOODLANDS
Anthem (USA), 1990 by Scott Soper
The Worshiping Church (USA), 1990 to WOODLANDS
Spring Harvest Songbook, 1990 to WOODLANDS
Mission Praise Combined, 1990 to (1) TELL OUT MY SOUL
   (2) WOODLANDS
The Song Goes On (USA), 1990 to WOODLANDS
New Creation Hymn Book (Australia), 1990 (words only)
Trinity Hymnal, revised edition (USA), 1990 to WOODLANDS
Sing & Pray (Ireland), 1990 to WOODLANDS
Sing to the Lord (Wales), 1990 (words only with a translation by
   Dyfnallt Morgan)
The Baptist Hymnal (USA), 1991 to WOODLANDS
Today's Missal (USA), 1991 to WOODLANDS
Songs of Fellowship, 1991 to (1) TELL OUT MY SOUL
   (2) WOODLANDS
Spring Harvest Songbook, 1991 to WOODLANDS
Rejoice and Sing, 1991 to WOODLANDS
Baptist Praise and Worship, 1991 to WOODLANDS
The Popular Carol Book, 1991 to WOODLANDS
GIA Hymnal Supplement (USA), 1991 to WOODLANDS
Thora Hird's Praise Be! Christmas Book, 1991 (words only)
The Complete Celebration Hymnal, 1991 to WOODLANDS
Christmas Praise (USA), 1991 to WOODLANDS
Sounds of Grace (Hong Kong), 1991 to WOODLANDS (with a
   Chinese translation)
The Puffin Book of Hymns, 1992 (words only)
A New Hymnal for Colleges and Schools (USA), 1992 to
   WOODLANDS
Spring Harvest Praise, 1992 to WOODLANDS

Breaking Bread (USA), 1993 to (1) WOODLANDS (2) music by
  Scott Soper
Anthem (USA), 1993 by K. Lee Scott
Hymns for the People, 1993 to TELL OUT MY SOUL
Praise the Lord, 1993 to WOODLANDS
Spring Harvest Praise, 1993 to WOODLANDS
Breaking Bread (USA), 1994 to music by Scott Soper
Spring Harvest Praise, 1994 to WOODLANDS
Glory to God (Ireland), 1994 to WOODLANDS
Catholic Book of Worship III (Canada), 1994 to WOODLANDS
Songs for the People of God (USA), 1994 to BENNETT
Power Praise 3, 1994 to WOODLANDS
More Hazel's Hymns, 1994 (words only)
Journeysongs (USA), 1994 to (1) music by Scott Soper
  (2) WOODLANDS
Celebration Hymnal for Everyone, 1994 to WOODLANDS
Breaking Bread (USA), 1995 to music by Scott Soper
Worship Together (USA), 1995 to WOODLANDS
Renew! (USA), 1995 to WOODLANDS
Spring Harvest Praise, 1995 to WOODLANDS
Hymns Old & New (new edition), 1996 to WOODLANDS
The Covenant Hymnal (USA), 1996 to WOODLANDS
Visa Zeme Kungam Dzied (Latvia), 1996 to WOODLANDS in a
  translation by Marta Jance
The Companion Hymn Book, 1997 (words only)
Design Your Own Wedding Ceremony, 1997 (words only)
Junior Praise Combined, 1997 to (1) TELL OUT MY SOUL
  (2) WOODLANDS
The Hymnal 21 (Japan), 1997 to WOODLANDS in an unattributed
  translation
BBC Songs of Praise, 1997 to WOODLANDS
The Source, 1998 to WOODLANDS
Jesus Through Art, 1998 to WOODLANDS
Youth Challenge Chorus Book (Ireland), 1998 (words only)
Our Growing Years (USA), 1998 to WOODLANDS
Get Together, 1998 (words only)
Celebrate! Songs for Renewal (USA), 1998 to BENNETT
Lambeth Praise (USA), 1998 to WOODLANDS
The Catholic Hymn Book, 1998 to WOODLANDS
Hymnal Supplement 1998 (USA), 1998 to WOODLANDS
Poems of Grace (USA), 1998 (words only)
Songs of Victory (Scotland), 1998 to (1) TELL OUT MY SOUL
  (2) WOODLANDS
Common Praise (Canada), 1998 to WOODLANDS
Laudate, 1999 to WOODLANDS
Liturgical Hymns Old & New, 1999 to WOODLANDS
Anthem (USA), 1999 by David Hurd
Word and Song 2000 (USA), 1999 to WOODLANDS
A Survey of Christian Hymnody (USA), 1999 to WOODLANDS
Complete Mission Praise, 1999 to (1) TELL OUT MY SOUL
  (2) WOODLANDS
Sing and Praise, 1999 to WOODLANDS

Sing Glory, 1999 to WOODLANDS
Grace Praise (New Zealand), 1999 (words only)
Together in Song (Australia), 1999 to WOODLANDS
Praise the Lord, 2000 to WOODLANDS
Praying in Song, 2000 to WOODLANDS
Complete Anglican Hymns Old & New, 2000 to WOODLANDS
Common Praise, 2000 to WOODLANDS
Keswick Songbook, 2000 to WOODLANDS
Church Hymnal (Ireland), 2000 to WOODLANDS
Praise!, 2000 to WOODLANDS
The Bridge, 2001 to WOODLANDS
Caneuon Ffydd (Wales), 2001 to WOODLANDS
Worship Today, 2001 to WOODLANDS
Worship & Rejoice (USA), 2001 to WOODLANDS
Methodist Hymns Old & New, 2001 to WOODLANDS
Favourite Hymns, 2001 (words only)
Hymns of Heritage & Hope (USA), 2001 to WOODLANDS

Recorded on
Hymns from the New Anglican Hymn Book, 1965 to TIDINGS
Here is Psalm Praise, 1975 to TELL OUT MY SOUL
All Souls Celebrates, 1975 to WOODLANDS
Liverpool Cathedral Festival of Praise, 1976 to WOODLANDS
Lydia Servant Songs, 1982 to WOODLANDS
Through Wood and Nails, 1984 to WOODLANDS
Hymns Ancient & Modern 2, 1985 to WOODLANDS
How Can I keep from Singing (USA), 1986 to WOODLANDS
Light and Peace (USA), 1986 to music by David Haas
The Best of Mission Praise 4, 1988 to TELL OUT MY SOUL
Music from Christ College, Brecon, 1992 to WOODLANDS
The Hymn Makers: 'Tell out, my soul', 1996 to WOODLANDS
Twenty Favourite Hymns, 1998 to WOODLANDS
Junior Praise Combined 15, 1999 to TELL OUT MY SOUL
50 Golden Hymns, 2000 to WOODLANDS
Keswick Praise 16, 2001 to WOODLANDS

This metrical version of the Magnificat was not written as a hymn (at that time I believed that hymn writing was closed to me because I lack all musical ability), but simply as an attempt to take the start of the New English Bible translation of Luke 1.46 as the opening line of a lyric, and go on from there. Not long afterwards the editors of the forthcoming Anglican Hymn Book asked if I had written any hymns. I told them I did not write hymns; but, on being pressed, showed them these verses. In 1969 the supplement to Hymns Ancient & Modern Revised, under the title 100 Hymns for Today, included the text set to WOODLANDS. By 1976 Sir John Betjeman could speak of it in a broadcast as 'one of the very few new hymns really to establish themselves in recent years.'

Michael Baughen's original tune for these words in Youth Praise 1 is still often chosen; and appears in hymnals variously as TELL OUT MY SOUL or GO FORTH: in the list above I have used only the former name. As can be seen, different editors have preferred a considerable variety of tunes, with Walter Greatorex's WOODLANDS predominating. The combination is an interesting one, in that both he and I (though we never met, and belong to different generations) were at school in Derbyshire and later associated with Norfolk. Greatorex was music master at Gresham's School, Holt and then Director of Music, from 1900–1936; 'Woodlands' is the name of one of the school boarding houses. He died in 1949.

Based on	Luke 2.29–32, the Nunc Dimittis (NEB translation)
Theme	Fulfilment; consummation; conclusion
Written	at Eastbourne, August 1967
Suggested tune	FAITHFUL VIGIL by David G. Wilson
	GLENFINLAS by Kenneth G. Finlay
	PASTOR PASTORUM by Friedrich Silcher
	QUIETUDE by Harold Green
Published in	*Youth Praise 2*, 1969 to FAITHFUL VIGIL
	Thirteen Psalms, 1970 (words only)
	Family Worship, 1971 (words only)
	Psalm Praise, 1973 to FAITHFUL VIGIL
	English Praise, 1975 to (1) GLENFINLAS (2) PASTOR PASTORUM
	Pilgrim's Manual, 1979 (words only)
	Songs of Worship, 1980 to FAITHFUL VIGIL
	More Hymns for Today, 1980 to PASTOR PASTORUM
	Hymns for Today's Church, 1982 to (1) FAITHFUL VIGIL
	(2) FAWLEY LODGE by Norman L. Warren
	Hymns Ancient & Modern New Standard, 1983 to PASTOR PASTORUM
	Hymns for Today, 1983 to PASTOR PASTORUM
	Rejoice in the Lord (USA), 1985 to PASTOR PASTORUM
	The New English Hymnal, 1986 to GLENFINLAS
	Carols for Today, 1986 to FAITHFUL VIGIL
	Carol Praise, 1987 to FAITHFUL VIGIL
	Church Family Worship, 1988 to FAITHFUL VIGIL
	Mission Praise Supplement, 1989 to FAITHFUL VIGIL
	Irish Church Praise (Ireland), 1990 to PASTOR PASTORUM
	Psalms for Today, 1990 to FAITHFUL VIGIL
	Mission Praise Combined, 1990 to FAITHFUL VIGIL
	Baptist Praise and Worship, 1991 to (1) FAWLEY LODGE
	(2) EUDOXIA by Sabine Baring-Gould
	New Songs of Rejoicing (USA), 1994 to WILLIAM by Leo Nestor
	Anthem (USA), 1995 by Leo Nestor
	Hymns Old & New, 1996 to PASTOR PASTORUM
	Complete Mission Praise, 1999 to FAITHFUL VIGIL
	Complete Anglican Hymns Old & New, 2000 to PASTOR PASTORUM
	Common Praise, 2000 to PASTOR PASTORUM
	Church Hymnal (Ireland), 2000 to PASTOR PASTORUM
Recorded on	*Hymns Ancient & Modern 2*, 1985 to PASTOR PASTORUM

On holiday in August 1967, I set myself to write a metrical version of these verses, sung as the Nunc Dimittis (from the Latin of the opening words) at Evening Prayer in the *Book Common Prayer*, to be a companion to 'Tell out, my soul'. The New English Bible retains the use of 'thee' and 'thy' in references to the Deity; and I therefore wrote my text in that form. In 1981 however, when I was compiling my first collection of texts, it came home to me that there were only two in 'thee and thou' form, and that it would be possible to alter and improve the other (228 'Lord, who left the highest heaven') and to provide a 'you' alternative to this one, with little more than invisible mending. Encouraged by the editors of *Hymns for Today's Church,* which was then in preparation, I provided the alternative text shown, though the original is still available for editors who prefer to follow more closely the usage of the NEB.

See Index 6.

214 ALL GLORY BE TO GOD ON HIGH   86 88 6

Based on	The Gloria in Excelsis
Theme	Praise and worship
Written	at Ruan Minor and at St Julian's, Coolham, August and October 1981
Suggested tune	NICOLAUS by Nicolaus Hermann
	REPTON by C. Hubert H. Parry
Published in	*Music in Worship,* March/April 1986 (words only)
	Hymns for Today's Church (enlarged second edition), 1987 to NICOLAUS
	Lift High your Songs! 1988 to CARILLON DEO GLORIA by Michael Paget
	Singing Faith, 1989 to ENDIKE by Brian Hoare
	Common Praise, 2000 to NICOLAUS
Recorded on	*Singing Faith,* 1999 to ENDIKE

This text represents a second attempt to cast the Gloria in Excelsis (which dates back at least to the fourth-century) into metrical form: my first attempt, 215 'Glory to God in the highest', was two years earlier. This text began with verses of four lines but Common Metre proved altogether too pedestrian for this purpose. Some months later an extensive revision added a fifth line, strengthening the rhyming scheme at the same time and allowing the use of REPTON and the other tunes listed above.

215 GLORY TO GOD IN THE HIGHEST   88 88 88

Based on	The Gloria in Excelsis
Theme	Praise and worship
Written	at Ruan Minor, August 1978
Suggested tune	RUSSWIN by Richard Proulx
Published in	*Two New Hymn Tunes by Richard Proulx* (USA), 1980 to RUSSWIN
	Hymnal Supplement (USA), 1984 to RUSSWIN
	Worship III (USA), 1986 to RUSSWIN
	Hymnal Supplement II (USA), 1987 to RUSSWIN
	Anthem (USA), 1988 by John Carter
	GIA Hymnal Supplement 1991 (USA), 1991 to RUSSWIN

This metrical 'Gloria' was based on that in the Church of England *Alternative Service Book, 1980.* That version derives from the International Consultation on English Texts, which covers all the main denominations in the English-speaking world and most of the principal nations involved. The final two lines of my verse 1 are in fact the opening lines of the ICET text, and they went far to determining structure and metre; though there exists in my MS book an attempt to write the hymn in verses of four rather than six lines.

The hymn preserves the basic structure of the Gloria, described by ICET as 'an opening antiphon based on Luke 2.14, followed by the three stanzas of acclamation, the first addressed to God the Father, the second and third to God the Son'. It amplifies the reference to 'Lamb of God' in the third stanza and substitutes at times an indirect statement, rather than a direct address to God.

216 WE BELIEVE IN GOD THE FATHER

87 87 or 87 87 D

Based on	The Apostles' Creed
Theme	Creed; testimony; trust in God
Written	at Ruan Minor, August 1989
Suggested tune	ABBOT'S LEIGH by Cyril V. Taylor
	LUX EOI by Arthur S. Sullivan
Published in	*Affirmations of Faith*, 1993 (words only): a Report of the Liturgical Commission of the General Synod of the Church of England
	Sing to the Lord (USA), 1993 to RIPLEY arranged by Lowell Mason
	A Service of the Word, 1994 (words only)
	Songs for the People of God (USA), 1994 to OLNEY from *Genuine Church Music*, 1832
	Moravian Book of Worship (USA), 1995 to LUX EOI
	Patterns for Worship, 1995 (words only)
	Supplement '96 (USA), 1996 to OUR CREED by John F. Wilson
	Sing Glory, 1999 to ALLELUIA by Samuel S. Wesley
	Common Praise, 2000 to EBENEZER by Thomas J. Williams
	Common Prayer, 2000 (words only)

In October 1988 the Ven. B.T. Lloyd, Archdeacon of Barnstaple and Chairman of the Urban Priority Area working group of the Church of England Liturgical Commission, wrote to ask for a metrical version of the creed which could be sung to a standard hymn tune. There are, of course, a number of hymns affirming basic Christian doctrines (for example, John Henry Newman's 'Firmly I believe and truly') but few are close enough to a traditional and universal creed for particular liturgical use.

This attempt is based on the version of the Apostles' Creed used in the *Alternative Service Book, 1980,* of the Church of England, following that of the International Consultation on English Texts. It is the only metrical version of a creed approved by the General Synod for use as an Authorized Affirmation of Faith in the public worship of the Church of England and as such is included (page 146) in *Common Worship, 2000.*

217 NAME OF ALL MAJESTY

66 55 666 4

Theme	The Lord Jesus Christ
Written	at Ruan Minor, August 1979

Suggested tune	MAJESTAS by Michael A. Baughen
	NAME OF ALL MAJESTY by Malcolm Archer
Translated into	Chinese, French, Korean
Published in	*Hymns for Today's Church,* 1982 to (1) ALL MAJESTY by Norman L. Warren (2) MAJESTAS

Ten New Hymns in Praise of God, 1982 to CONSERVATION by Michael Dawney

Mission Praise 2, 1987 to MAJESTAS

Anglican Praise, 1987 to MAJESTAS

Rejoice! (Australia), 1987 to MAJESTAS

Church Family Worship, 1988 to MAJESTAS

Let's Praise!, 1988 to MAJESTAS

Come Rejoice!, 1989 to MAJESTAS

The Alfred V. Fedak Hymnary (USA), 1990 to NAME OF ALL MAJESTY by Alfred V. Fedak

Mission Praise Combined, 1990 to MAJESTAS

The Baptist Hymnal (USA), 1991 to MAJESTAS

Songs of Celebration, 1991 to MAJESTAS (with a French translation by Ann Maouyo)

Sing his Praise (USA), 1991 to MAJESTAS

The Carl Schalk Hymnary Supplement, 1991 to MAJESTY by Carl Schalk

Sounds of Grace (Hong Kong), 1991 to MAJESTAS (with a Chinese translation)

Cliff Praise II, 1992 (words only)

100 Hymns of Hope (USA), 1992 to MAJESTAS

A New Hymnal for Colleges and Schools (USA), 1992 to MAJESTY

Hymns for the People, 1993 to MAJESTAS

Together Met, Together Bound (USA), 1993 to PATCHETT by William Rowan

Glory to God (Ireland), 1994 to MAJESTAS

Songs for the People of God (USA), 1994 to COBB by Keith Landis

Worship Together (USA), 1995 to MAJESTAS

Moravian Book of Worship (USA), 1995 to MAJESTAS

Sing We Merrily, 1995 to MAJESTAS

The Celebration Hymnal (USA), 1997 to MAJESTAS

BBC Songs of Praise, 1997 to MAJESTAS

Songs of Fellowship 2, 1998 to MAJESTAS

Celebrate! Songs for Renewal (USA), 1998 to WALLACE by Keith Landis

Korean-English Hymnal (Korea), 1998 to MAJESTAS (with an unattributed translation)

Anthem (USA), 1998 by David W. Music

Spring Harvest Praise 99, 1999 to MAJESTAS

New Start Hymns and Songs, 1999 to NAME OF ALL MAJESTY (Archer)

Songs of Victory (Scotland), 1999 to MAJESTAS

Complete Mission Praise, 1999 to MAJESTAS

Sing Glory, 1999 to MAJESTAS

Complete Anglican Hymns Old & New, 2000 to NAME OF ALL MAJESTY (Archer)

Common Praise, 2000 to MAJESTAS
Keswick Songbook, 2000 to MAJESTAS
Church Hymnal (Ireland), 2000 to MAJESTAS
Praise!, 2000 to MAJESTAS
Sing to the Lord, 2000 to MAJESTAS
Rejoice in God (USA), 2000 to BRIARWOOD by K. Lee Scott
The Bridge, 2001 to NAME OF ALL MAJESTY (Archer)
Worship Today, 2001 to MAJESTAS
New Hymns and Worship Songs, 2001 to NAME OF ALL
    MAJESTY (Archer)
Worship & Rejoice (USA), 2001 to MAJESTAS
Methodist Hymns Old & New, 2001 to (1) MAJESTAS (2) NAME
    OF ALL MAJESTY (Archer)

Recorded on   *Hymns for Today's Church*, 1982 to MAJESTAS
Keswick Praise 3, 1987 to MAJESTAS
Keswick Praise 5, 1990 to MAJESTAS
Keswick Praise 7, 1992 to MAJESTAS
Glory to God 3, 1996 to MAJESTAS
The Hymn Makers: 'Tell out, my soul', 1996 to MAJESTAS
Spread the Word (Australia), 1999 to MAJESTAS

In the early months of 1979 I was enjoying the *Collected Poems* of Walter de la Mare, having only read him previously in anthologies. A page in my MS book at that time shows three extracts from his poems copied out for the sake of their metrical form. It is upon one of these that this text came to be loosely modelled.

When originally published in my privately issued *Collection* it carried the note that it was 'awaiting a composer' since I knew of no existing tune to fit these words. Since then tunes have been supplied, originally by the editorial team of *Hymns for Today's Church*, and by other composers since.

The affirmation of each verse 'Jesus is Lord' is said to be the earliest baptismal creed of the church: cf. Romans 10.9, Philippians 2.11, and 1 Corinthians 12.3, 'No one can say "Jesus is Lord" except by the Holy Spirit.'

218 SAVIOUR CHRIST, IN PRAISE WE NAME HIM   35 33

Theme	The Lord Jesus Christ
Written	at Ruan Minor, August 1978
Suggested tune	SAVIOUR CHRIST by Norman L. Warren
Published in	*Hymns for Today's Church*, 1982 to SAVIOUR CHRIST

The theme of this short hymn is the fullness, perfection and completeness of Christ in his Person and Work; and the key can be found in the word *all*, repeated in every verse. The metre is singularly terse, so much so that a tune had to be written specially, before the text could be included in *Hymns for Today's Church*. The structure, however, is regular from verse to verse, with the exception of the last. Line 1 of each verse takes a title of Christ, line 2 follows on from the title given, line 3 carries the reference to 'all', and line 4 consists of a verb or participle followed by a colon. The whole is therefore governed by the final verse, which adds 'rejoicing' and 'adoring' to the 'praise' of verse 1.

Based on	The seven 'I am' passages of St John's Gospel (6.35; 10.7; 10.11,14; 8.12; 11.25; 14.6; 15.1)
Theme	The Lord Jesus Christ
Written	at Bramerton, August 1991
Suggested tune	ALMSGIVING by John B. Dykes PORTLAND by Cyril V. Taylor THREEFOLD GIFTS by Austin C. Lovelace
Published in	*Songs for the People of God* (USA), 1994 to BRENTWOOD by Keith Landis

To include these seven references in sixteen lines inevitably implies compression.

The hymn seeks to make some reference to Christ's teaching upon each of these 'Parables of the Lord's Person'; though to achieve that, 'Lord of all' must be read as referring to John 14.8–11, where Christ identifies his authority with that of the Father.

Stanza 2 suggests the truth that the Door can be thought of both as open (to allow the sheep to enter and 'to go in and out'); but also as shut to keep them safe.

Theme	The Lord Jesus Christ; the call of God; mission and evangelism
Written	at Ford, August 1992
Suggested tune	LOVE UNKNOWN by John Ireland
Published in	*Songs for the People of God* (USA), 1994 to BUCHANAN by Keith Landis *New Mission Praise*, 1996 to LOVE UNKNOWN *Complete Mission Praise*, 1999 to LOVE UNKNOWN *Glory Be* (New Zealand), 2000 to CROFT'S 136TH by William Croft
Recorded on	*The Hymn Makers: 'Tell out, my soul'*, 1996 to LOVE UNKNOWN

The Lambeth Conference of 1988 proposed to the worldwide Anglican Communion that the closing years of the millennium be named a 'Decade of Evangelism' with a renewed and united emphasis on making Christ known to the people of his world. This Archbishops' Initiative for the Decade of Evangelism, 'Springboard', was launched at a Service in St Paul's Cathedral, London, on 23 September 1992; and it was for this Service that the Archbishop of Canterbury asked me to write a new hymn on the theme of mission.

I have not previously written to the tune LOVE UNKNOWN, considering it to be uniquely dedicated to Samuel Crossman's words from which it takes its name. This is not so; and the tune is used in a number of current hymnals to other words. For example in *Hymns Ancient & Modern, New Standard,* it is set to W. Walsham How's 'Thou art the Christ' and to H. C. A. Gaunt's 'Glory to thee, O God', as well as to 'My song is love unknown'. In *Hymns and Psalms* it is used for F. Pratt Green's marriage hymn 'The grace of life is theirs'. In the *Psalter Hymnal* of the Christian Reformed Church, USA, it carries John Quinn's paraphrase of John 15.1–5, 'I am the holy vine'. With some admitted trepidation (for Crossman's hymn is among my personal favourites) I have therefore written to this metre, with Ireland's tune in mind.

221 CHRIST THE ETERNAL LORD   66 86 D (DSM)

Theme	The Lord Jesus Christ; Christian experience and discipleship; the Bible; mission and evangelism
Written	at Ford, July 1998
Suggested tune	DIADEMATA by George J. Elvey
Published in	*Supplement 99* (USA), 1999 (words only)
	Cantate Domino, 2000 to LAANECOORIE by June Nixon
	Worship & Rejoice (USA), 2001 to DIADEMATA

The text was written at the request of the Scripture Union for whose centenary (as the Children's Special Service Mission) 105 'Lord, for the years' was written rather more than thirty years before. The particular occasion was not an anniversary, but the prospect of two major training events and an international conference from about 100 countries planned for the opening year of the new millennium.

The request was for 'a celebration of our shared commitment to our two aims, namely communicating the good news of Jesus Christ to children, young people and families; and secondly, encouraging people of all ages to meet God daily through Bible reading and prayer.'

The occasion seemed to call for a strong tune; and I had used DIADEMATA once before (for 247 'Lord of all life and power', written for a diocesan celebration) so that it seemed a natural choice. The fourth verse recognizes that the theme of Christ the Light is specially appropriate for a new millennium.

222 FREELY, FOR THE LOVE HE BEARS US   87 85

Theme	The Lord Jesus Christ; faith
Written	at Ruan Minor, August 1989
Suggested tune	DICKEY by Jim Strathdee
	GRIFFIN'S BROOK by John Wilson
	ST LEONARD'S by A. Cyril Barham-Gould
Published in	*Mission Praise Combined*, 1990 to music by Phil Burt
	Songs for the People of God (USA), 1994 to ACCLAMATION by Keith Landis
	Complete Mission Praise, 1999 to music by Phil Burt

The final couplet of each verse is derived directly (with the single addition of the word 'and') from the acclamations which formed part of the Eucharistic Prayer in Rite A Holy Communion of *The Alternative Service Book, 1980* of the Church of England. They have been incorporated unchanged into Holy Communion Order One in *Common Worship*, 2000.

I had been contemplating for some time the inclusion of these acclamations into a hymn text; and, turning over in my mind the tune GRIFFIN'S BROOK, I felt that here was a possible match. That tune is set in *Hymns and Psalms*, 1983, to Kate Barclay Wilkinson's text 'May the mind of Christ my Saviour'.

The repeated acclamation lends itself to variations when sung as a hymn, either antiphonally within a congregation, or with the help of choir or soloist.

Theme	The Lord Jesus Christ
Written	at Ruan Minor, August 1974
Suggested tune	COTTON WEAVER (English traditional)
	GRAFTON (French traditional)
	REGENT SQUARE by Henry T. Smart
Published in	*Songs of Worship*, 1980 to COTTON WEAVER arranged by Robin Sheldon
	Hymns for Today's Church, 1982 to (1) COTTON WEAVER (2) REGENT SQUARE

This hymn owes its origin to a children's TV programme in a series on the BBC entitled 'Bagpuss', about a 'saggy old cloth cat'. I was watching this one day with my young family in the Spring of 1974, when we were living at Postwick, near Norwich. The programme contained a theme tune, charmingly played and sung, which took my fancy as a possible tune for a hymn. I wrote to the creator of the programme, Oliver Postgate, who told me that the tune was an arrangement of a traditional folk song, 'The Lancashire Cotton Weaver' and sent me a tape of the programme. Working from this, the text was written that summer.

224 WHO IS JESUS? FRIEND OF SINNERS 87 87 87

Theme	The Lord Jesus Christ
Written	at Bramerton, May 1975
Suggested tune	GRAFTON (French traditional)
	PICARDY (French traditional)
Published in	*Songs of Worship*, 1980 to GRAFTON
	Anthem (USA), 1991 by Jeffrey Honoré

The theme of this text is the life, death and resurrection to glory of the Lord Jesus Christ. His humanity and divinity are proclaimed in verse 1. Verse 2 includes references to four major themes: the Man of sorrows or Suffering Servant of Isaiah 53; the Prince of life of Peter's sermon in Acts 3; the Lamb of God of John 1 (and pre-eminently also of the Book of Revelation); and (in line 2) the 'emptying of himself' of Philippians 2. In verse 3, 'first-born' is taken from Romans 8.29, seen in the light of the two Colossians references, 1.15 and 1.18.

In verse 3, the epithet in the final line was first written as 'everlasting' (cf. 1 Timothy 6.16). However the line 'Christ, the everlasting Lord' is inseparable from Charles Wesley's use of it in 'Hark! the herald angels sing'; and 'ever-living' is perhaps, on its own merits, a better description in the context of the resurrection (cf. Hebrews 7.25).

See Index 6.

225 O COME TO ME, THE MASTER SAID 86 86 D (DCM)

Theme	The Lord Jesus Christ; Christian experience and discipleship; Holy Communion

Written	at Ruan Minor, August 1987
Suggested tune	KINGSFOLD (English traditional)
	VOX DILECTI by John B. Dykes
Published in	*The Worshiping Church* (USA), 1990 to KINGSFOLD
	Songs for the People of God (USA), 1994 to FOREST GREEN
	(English traditional)
	Supplement '96 (USA), 1996 to THE AULD HOOSE (Scottish
	traditional)
	Worship & Rejoice (USA), 2001 to KINGSFOLD

Hymn writers always need to exercise care when they are paraphrasing Scripture, and never more so than when their words claim to be, in some sense, from the lips of the Lord. It is for this reason that the text includes nothing in inverted commas to indicate direct speech. Nevertheless I hope that all here attributed to 'the Master' can be justified from the Gospels. See in particular the following references:

Matthew 11.28 'Come to me...'
Matthew 6.8 'Your Father knows what you need...'
John 6.35 'I am the bread of life...'
John 15.1,4 'I am the true vine...abide in me...'
Mark 14.24 'This is my blood...which is poured out for many...'
John 14.1 'Believe also in me...'
John 15.15 'I have called you friends...'
John 3.16 '...that whoever believes in him should...have eternal life...'

Note also Luke 19.10; Revelation 21.4; 1 Corinthians 15.26; John 6.40.

226 THE LOVE OF CHRIST WHO DIED FOR ME   86 86 (CM)

Theme	The Lord Jesus Christ; Passiontide; dedication and renewal;
	response to the gospel
Written	at Ruan Minor and Kennack Sands, August 1989
Suggested tune	AZMON by Carl G. Gläser
	DUNDEE (Scottish traditional)
	STRACATHRO by Charles Hutcheson
Published in	*Mission Praise Combined*, 1990 to music by Phil Burt
	The Baptist Hymnal (USA), 1991 to AZMON
	Complete Mission Praise, 1999 to music by Phil Burt

In seeking to write a hymn of response to the gospel some years ago (see 244 'Above the voices of the world around me') I made the mistake of using a metre which severely limited any choice of well-known tune. So for this text I planned to write in CM; though these stanzas could be sung in DCM, were a suitable tune to suggest itself for a particular congregation.

Although I have not indicated that the text is 'based on' any identifiable passage of Scripture, Galatians 2.20 with its reference to 'the Son of God, who loved me and gave himself up for me' is never far away.

Theme	The Lord Jesus Christ
Written	at Ruan Minor, August 1975
Suggested tune	QUAM DILECTA by Henry L. Jenner
	ST CECILIA by Leighton G. Hayne

John Byrom, a Fellow of the Royal Society who taught shorthand to John and Charles Wesley (it is his system which both the brothers used in their journals), wrote a well-known hymn 'My spirit longs for thee' (*Common Praise*, No. 99). He uses there a device, borrowed in this text, of repeating the final line of verse 1 as the opening line of verse 2, and so on throughout. It may well derive from the practice of repeated lines in the French form called 'the villanelle', of which perhaps the best-known modern example is Dylan Thomas's 'Do not go gentle into that good night'. Something of the same can be seen in Richard Wilbur's Christmas hymn 'A stable-lamp is lighted'. Such a pattern requires lines of identical metrical length (in this case 66 66), and rhymes made up of trios rather than pairs.

In this instance, verse 1 of the text introduces the theme of Christ and his praise; verse 2 takes the singer from Christmas to Calvary; verse 3 from cross to grave; verse 4 from death to life; verse 5 from resurrection to immortal praise.

228 LORD, WHO LEFT THE HIGHEST HEAVEN 87 87 77

Theme	The Lord Jesus Christ; home; social concern
Written	at Sevenoaks, February 1962
Suggested tune	ALL SAINTS (German traditional)
	HIGHEST HEAVEN by Michael A. Baughen
Translated into	Chinese
Published in	*Anglican Hymn Book*, 1965 to ALL SAINTS
	Youth Praise 1, 1966 to HIGHEST HEAVEN
	Family Worship, 1971 (words only)
	Thirty Hymns, 1972 (words only)
	Hymns for Today's Church, 1982 to (1) HIGHEST HEAVEN
	(2) OTTOWA by L. Mason
	Hymnal Supplement (USA), 1984 to ALL SAINTS
	Supplement to Lutheran Hymnal (Australia), 1987 to ALL SAINTS
	Carol Praise, 1987 to HIGHEST HEAVEN
	Sounds of Grace (Hong Kong), 1991 to HIGHEST HEAVEN (with a Chinese translation)
	Moravian Book of Worship (USA), 1995 to EDEN CHURCH by Dale Wood
	Common Praise (Canada), 1998 to LATIMER by Keith Landis

This is one of my first texts, written at the request of the editors of the *Anglican Hymn Book*, then in preparation, for something on the theme of 'home'. I was once told that a number of hymns are written by people ill in bed; and this is one of them. At that stage I was so inexperienced that it did not occur to me to see whether each verse would fit a single tune (in fact adjustments had to be made); and I had not quite settled on the use of 'you language' rather than 'thees and thous'. Hence it became one of only two texts using those forms; the other being 213 'Faithful vigil ended' which follows the usage of the New English Bible. I eventually decided to revise both in order to provide versions in 'you form'; and this gave an opportunity to eliminate one or two weaknesses and infelicities. The original version can still be found in the pre-1980 hymnals in the list above.

'Shelter', a national charity concerned with homelessness, included this hymn in their Order of Service for Christmas 1985.

See Index 6.

229 O CHRIST, WHO TAUGHT ON EARTH OF OLD   88 88 88

Theme	The Lord Jesus Christ, his parables; the Bible; harvest
Written	at Bramerton, February 1982
Suggested tune	MELITA by John B. Dykes ST MATTHIAS by William H. Monk
Published in	*Country Way,* Spring/Summer 1999 (words only) *Picture Talk,* 2001 (words only)

'The Parables' was one of the Sunday themes in the *Alternative Service Book, 1980* of the Church of England and although that book has been superseded by *Common Worship,* 2000, a number of our Lord's parables feature in the lectionary (as they do in the gospel readings in the *Book of Common Prayer).* It is to be expected, therefore, that in most churches one or more parables will from time to time be central to the theme of a Service of Worship. It was with that in mind that this text was written. It aims, as far as possible, to allude to certain main groupings of parables rather than to mention them at random; verse 2, for example, could be taken as referring to a wide range of the 'nature' and 'harvest' parables. In verse 3, some of the key words are applicable to more than one of our Lord's parables, and verse 4 takes three of its four allusions from the major parables found only in St Luke: the rich man and Lazarus (Luke 16.19–31), the good Samaritan (Luke 10.25–37) and the prodigal son (Luke 15.11–32).

230 WHEN JESUS LIVED AMONG US HE CAME A CHILD OF EARTH   13 13 13 13 13 13

Theme	The Lord Jesus Christ, his life and teaching; Holy Communion
Written	at Ruan Minor and St Anthony-in-Meneage, August 1980
Suggested tune	THAXTED by Gustav Holst
Published in	*Supplement to Lutheran Hymnal* (Australia), 1987 to THAXTED

This text on the earthly life of Jesus was written to the tune THAXTED at the suggestion of (I think) an editor who felt that there were none too many hymns on this subject, and that the tune could bear more use than it receives with Cecil Spring-Rice's text 'I vow to thee, my country'.

'Likeness' in line 2 is an echo of Philippians 2.7; and the final line of verse 1 refers to St Luke's words in Luke 2.52. I take my use of the verb 'grow' to include a reference to the 'increased in stature' of that verse. Other phrases are designed to bring to mind the biblical narrative; for example, from verse 2, 'friend of sinners' (Luke 7.34); 'the gospel of his kingdom' (Mark 1.14); 'signs and wonders' (John 4.48).

Verse 3 begins with the Lord's own words from Mark 8.31; 'sacrifice for sins' is from Hebrews 10.12; 'our risen life', while not a quotation in that form, is a reference to, e.g. Colossians 2. 12. The final line of verse 3 is based on John 1.12.

231 KINGLY BEYOND ALL EARTHLY KINGS   8 8 8 8 (LM)

Theme	The Lord Jesus Christ; Christ the King
Written	at Ford, December 2000
Suggested tune	LLEDROD (Welsh traditional)
	MARYTON by Henry P. Smith
	SONG 34 by Orlando Gibbons

In the summer of 2000 Dan McKinley, Director of Music at Christ Church, South Hamilton, invited me to consider a visit in 2001 for a hymn festival, and to write a new hymn for the occasion.

Since this was for Christ Church, the theme chosen was 'Christ the King'. Verse 1 speaks of his universal reign. Verse 2 is a reminder of how the title 'King of the Jews' spanned his earthly life, from Matthew 2.2 through Luke 19.30 to the taunts of the soldiers (Mark 15.18) and the title Pilate set above his cross, recorded by all four Evangelists. The following verse moves on to the resurrection and Christ's coming in glory, a theme repeated in the final lines; following a reminder that Christ now reigns, and his kingdom is established, in the hearts of his people.

The phrase 'set at nought' in verse 2, with its echoes of 'Lo, he comes with clouds descending' is used in the AV description of Christ before Herod (Luke 23.11), which Jesus himself had foretold in the same words (Mark 9.12). 'The sum of things' (verse 1) is an echo from A.E.Housman's famous lyric, XXXVII in *Last Poems,* 'Epitaph on an army of mercenaries'; which in turn drew on various Latin sources and on *Paradise Lost,* vi.673.

232 TO CHRIST OUR KING IN SONGS OF PRAISE   86 86 (CM)

Theme	The Lord Jesus Christ; Christ the King; Christ our Light
Written	at Bramerton, October 1976
Suggested tune	AZMON by Carl G. Gläser
	BISHOPTHORPE by Jeremiah Clarke

'Light', 'Life' and 'King' are the key words of this text, found in the opening and final verses in conjunction; and used in turn for the invocation of Christ in each of the other verses. Light out of darkness and life out of death lead on to a dedication to Christ as King, resulting in both worship (verse 5) and mission (verse 4).

Theme	The Lord Jesus Christ; Christ our Light; mission and evangelism
Written	at Bramerton, January 1987
Suggested tune	CWM RHONDDA by John Hughes
	REGENT SQUARE by Henry T. Smart
	RHUDDLAN (Welsh traditional)
Translated into	French, Spanish
Published in	*O Sing with Joy to the Lord,* 1987 to REGENT SQUARE (with a translation into French by Joanna Benson and into Spanish by Felicity Houghton)
	Songs of Celebration, 1991 to REGENT SQUARE (with translations as above)
	Laudate, 1999 to music by James Walsh

In August 1987 the International Fellowship of Evangelical Students held their General Committee in Colombia. For this international gathering I was asked to write a hymn on the theme of the conference, 'Jesus Christ, the Light of the world'. A number of passages from which the hymn is drawn can be readily identified: e.g. Isaiah 9 and 60; Psalm 27; and the Gospel of John. 'Shined' in verse 1, is a deliberate archaism to echo the familiar King James (AV) version of 2 Corinthians 4.6.

Based on	Mark 10.45
Theme	The Lord Jesus Christ; Christ the Servant; discipleship and ministry
Written	at Ford, December 1999
Suggested tune	GRAFTON (French traditional)
	NEANDER (UNSER HERRSCHER) by Joachim Neander
Published in	*Anthem,* 2001 by Maurice Bevan

In 1999 the East Ohio Conference of the United Methodist Church asked for hymns, both text and tune, 'to reflect the conference's mission and vision' and to be used 'as a theme to carry the church into the next millennium'. As their mission, they sought 'to be a servant after the model of Jesus Christ' and as their vision, 'to equip local churches to make and mature disciples of Jesus Christ'.

In the event, this was not the hymn they were looking for; but mission and vision, expressed in service, evangelism and nurture, are themes always relevant to any local church.

Mark 10.45 seemed an obvious starting point, linking in Christ's own words his mission as Saviour ('a ransom for many') and Servant; and this provides the repeated fifth line of the text, with a specific reference to ransom in verse 1. 'Human likeness' is a reference to Philippians 2.7; and God's word as the foundation of the church is taken from Ephesians 2.20 where the Apostles and Prophets (which to us must mean their teaching) are joined with Christ himself, revealed to us in Holy Scripture.

The text thus combines reminders of the Great Commission, to go and make disciples of all nations, with the Great Commandment to care for our neighbour, exemplified in Jesus as Saviour and Servant.

Theme	The Lord Jesus Christ
Written	at Bramerton, February 1975
Suggested tune	OASIS by T. Brian Coleman
Published in	*Partners in Praise*, 1979 to OASIS
	Anthem (USA), 1981 by Hal H. Hopson
	Jesus Praise, 1982 to OASIS
	Word & Music, July-September 1982 to OASIS
	Hymns for Today's Church, 1982 to OASIS
	Hymnal Supplement (USA), 1984 to OASIS
	Anthem (USA), 1985 by John Carter
	Seventh-Day Adventist Hymnal (USA), 1985 to OASIS
	As Water to the Thirsty (USA), 1987 to FREEDOM by David Haas
	Supplement to Lutheran Hymnal (Australia), 1987 to OASIS
	The Worshiping Church (USA), 1990 to OASIS
	Hymns for the People, 1993 to OASIS
	Spring Harvest Praise 94, 1994 to OASIS
	Glory to God (Ireland), 1994 to OASIS
	Songs for the People of God (USA), 1994 to CONVERTED THIEF
	from *The Southern Harmony*, 1835
	Moravian Book of Worship (USA), 1995 to OASIS
	New Mission Praise, 1996 to OASIS
	Sing to the Lord, vol.2, part 3, 1996 to OASIS
	Worship in Song, 1997 to OASIS
	Prom Praise Solos 2, 1997 to OASIS
	The Book of Praise (Canada), 1997 to OASIS
	Songs of Fellowship 2, 1998 to OASIS
	Complete Mission Praise, 1999 to OASIS
	Sing Glory, 1999 to OASIS
	Praise the Lord, 2000 to OASIS
	Common Praise, 2000 to OASIS
	Praise!, 2000 to OASIS
	Worship Today, 2001 to OASIS
	Worship & Rejoice (USA), 2001 to OASIS
Recorded on	*Hymns for Today's Church*, 1982 to OASIS
	As Water to the Thirsty (USA), 1987 to FREEDOM by David Haas
	Crown Him, 1987 to OASIS
	Have you Heard?, 1992 to OASIS
	The Hymn Makers: 'Tell out, my soul', 1996 to OASIS
	'Let the Morning Bring...', 1997 to OASIS
	Prom Solos, 1998 to OASIS
	Twenty Favourite Hymns 3, 2000 to OASIS

My notebook suggests that this text owes more to Simon and Garfunkel's classic phrase of the 1960s, 'Bridge over troubled water', than it does to Emma Bevan's 'As the bridegroom to his chosen'. Erik Routley, in his *Hymns and Human Life* (London, 1952), calls that 'one of the oldest of children's hymns', the translation by Mrs Bevan being based on a 14th-century original by John Tauler. A correspondent suggested to me that my own text must be an unconscious plagiarism of that hymn; but, on the contrary, I felt that there was room for a more modern hymn based on similes. It differs from Emma Bevan's not only in date, but in metre, rhyming structure, and (of course) the imagery chosen. I hope that this imagery is no less biblical in tone, even if sometimes the likeness is to some other facet of Christian experience, rather than an explicit reference to the Lord himself. Perhaps the following references will show what I mean:

Verse 1,	line 1	Psalm 63.1
	2	Psalm 27.4
	3	Psalm 28.7
	4	1 Thessalonians 1.9
	5	Exodus 15.2
	6	Song of Songs, chapter 2
Verse 2,	line 1	1 Kings 19.11,12
	2	Hebrews 13.20
	3	John 20.11–18
	4	Revelation 1.16
	5 and 6	Psalm 104.2
Verse 3,	line 1	Psalm 4.8
	2	Matthew 17.2
	3	Psalm 146.7
	4	Malachi 4.2
	5 and 6	Luke 15.11–24

See Index 6.

236 CHRIST BE THE LORD OF ALL OUR DAYS   86 88 6

Theme	The Lord Jesus Christ; discipleship
Written	at Ruan Minor, August 1975
Suggested tune	GATESCARTH by Caryl Micklem
Published in	*Hymns for Today's Church*, 1982 to GATESCARTH
	Sing We Merrily, 1995 to CLOTH FAIR by John Scott
	Sing to the Lord, 2000 to CLOTH FAIR

This text sprang from the single line 'Christ is the Lord of all our days' which had been running in my head through the weeks preceding our summer holiday in 1975. I had imagined a hymn with that title, and with each succeeding verse following the pattern of 'Christ is the Lord of all our...'. Deeds, hopes and lives were all possible verses. At the same time I had been attracted by the metrical quality of the phrase 'the bright and morning star' (Revelation 22.16 in the AV) as a title of Christ. These came together in this text though originally with the statement 'is' in place of the prayer 'be' in each opening line. Line 4 of verse 1 is an echo of 1 Peter 3.7; and line 5 of verse 3 of the AV rendering of John 14.2.

237 HE COMES TO US AS ONE UNKNOWN   86 88 6

Theme	The Lord Jesus Christ; faith
Written	at Ruan Minor and Poldhu beach, August 1982

Suggested tune	BINNEY'S by Eric H. Thiman
	REPTON by C. Hubert H. Parry
	REST by Frederick C. Maker
Published in	*On the Move* (Australia), July 1983 (words only)
	Word & Music, September/December 1984 to HE COMES TO US
	by Norman L. Warren
	Worship III (USA), 1986 to REPTON
	Carols for Today, 1986 to HE COMES TO US
	GIA Hymnal Supplement 1991 (USA), 1991 to REPTON
	Worship Songs Ancient & Modern, 1992 to REPTON
	A New Hymnal for Colleges and Schools (USA), 1992 to LOBT
	GOTT, IHR CHRISTEN by Nikolaus Hermann
	Hymnal—a Worship Book (USA), 1992 to REPTON
	With One Voice (USA), 1995 to REPTON
	Moravian Book of Worship (USA), 1995 to REPTON
	Anthem (USA), 1996 by Paul Nicholson
	Anthem (USA), 1996 by John Ferguson
	Common Praise (Canada), 1998 to LOBT GOTT, IHR CHRISTEN
	Breaking Bread, Jubilee 2000 (USA), 1999 to REPTON
	Worship & Rejoice (USA), 2001 to REPTON
	Hymns of Heritage & Hope (USA), 2001 to REPTON

The opening line of this hymn is part of a longer sentence from the closing pages of Albert Schweitzer's *The Quest of the Historical Jesus* (London 1919) which says of Christ:

'He comes to us as One unknown, without a name, as of old, by the lakeside, He came to those first men who knew Him not.'

Taking as its theme our perception of God's approach to the soul, and the 'sense of the divine' which is part of human experience, the first two verses were written at a sitting. The third is a reference to Revelation 1.15 and to 1 Kings 19; with the merest allusion to 1 Chronicles 14.15, when a 'sound of going in the tops of the mulberry trees' is a sign or signal from the Lord himself; the NEB translation is a 'rustling sound in the treetops'. By verse 4 the text is explicitly Christian in its reference both to incarnation and to atonement; and by verse 5 there is the personal response of faith to the Lord Jesus Christ of the New Testament (cf. Luke 24.27; 1 Peter 1.8).

238 O CHANGELESS CHRIST, FOR EVER NEW 86 86 (CM)

Theme	The Lord Jesus Christ; Holy Communion
Written	at Ruan Minor and St Julian's, Coolham, August and October 1981
Suggested tune	BALLERMA by François H. Barthélémon
	McKEE (African-American traditional)
	ST BOTOLPH by Gordon Slater
	WILTSHIRE by George Smart
Published in	*Hymns for Today's Church,* 1982 to BALLERMA
	Sing Alleluia, 1987 to ST BOTOLPH
	Baptist Praise and Worship, 1991 to BELMONT from William
	Gardiner's *Sacred Melodies,* 1812
	Celebration Hymnal for Everyone, 1994 to BALLERMA

Voices United (Canada), 1996 to WESTMINSTER by James Turle
Laudate, 1999 to BALLERMA
Sing Glory, 1999 to WILTSHIRE
Together in Song (Australia), 1999 to ST BOTOLPH
Praise!, 2000 to JACKSON by Thomas Jackson
Glory Be (New Zealand), 2000 to SALZBURG (HAYDN)
    by J. Michael Haydn
Spring Harvest Praise, 2001 to WILTSHIRE
Methodist Hymns Old & New, 2001 to WILTSHIRE

In Hebrews 13.8, we read of 'Jesus Christ, the same yesterday, and today, and for ever', and it is to this that the word 'changeless' refers in the opening line of this text. Succeeding verses are drawn from incidents in the Gospels, the Sermon on the Mount and on the Plain, teaching on the beach and from a boat (Matthew 13), the stilling of the storm, the miracles of healing, and the institution of the Lord's Supper.

    This text is the subject of an essay in *Lift Every Heart* which attempts to describe the process of writing such a hymn, from the seed-thought of 'Christ our Contemporary', through six or eight pages of my MS book and the advice of Derek Kidner, to its first publication a year later.

239 OUR LIVING LORD WHOSE NAME WE BEAR   88 88 88

Theme	The Lord Jesus Christ; the call of God; the Bible
Written	at Ford, April and August 1999
Suggested tune	MELITA by John B. Dykes
	SURREY by Henry Carey
Published in	*Cantate Domino,* 2000 to BOORT by June Nixon

This text began life in response to a request from the Scripture Union, looking ahead to a major international conference in 2001. In the event, I did not feel this text was going to serve their purpose, and wrote instead 221 'Christ the eternal Lord'.

    The text uses a number of titles to address the Lord Jesus Christ, beginning with a reminder of the early days of his earthly ministry, and moving on from the opening address as 'Lord' to friend, guide, Saviour, King; becoming fully Trinitarian in the final verse.

    Verse 2, line 5, is an echo of the Collect in the *Book of Common Prayer* for the second Sunday in Advent ('Bible Sunday' as it was commonly called) with its allusion to Romans 15.4 '...that we through patience and comfort of the Scriptures might have hope'. Line 2 of the same verse is taken from Isaiah 55.10,11; and line 3 from Mark 12.37. In the final verse, line 4 borrows from the well-known allusion to Lydia in Acts 16.14.

240 SO THE DAY DAWN FOR ME   64 64

Theme	The Lord Jesus Christ; trust in God; morning
Written	at Ruan Minor and at Poldhu Cove, August 1988
Suggested tune	GLENFINLAS by Kenneth G. Finlay
	RAPHAEL by Kenneth D. Smith
	STANGMORE by W. Donald Davison

As sometimes happens, this is a text that came without my seeking it, when in the middle of writing to a quite different metre and on a different theme. I noted in my MS book, 'I imagine a lilting Irish tune'; and was pleased to discover that there is a choice of tunes to this metre—in fact some five or six, not counting those which are really 10 10.

Because I felt there was something of a Celtic 'feel' to the text, I sent it to Bishop Edward Darling, General Editor of *Irish Church Praise* then just published. He in turn passed it to W. Donald Davison, one of the music editors, who wrote for it the two new tunes to which it appears in *New Songs of Praise 6*.

241 O GOD WHOSE THOUGHTS ARE NOT AS OURS   86 86 D (DCM)

Theme	God the Father, the living God
Written	at Ruan Minor, August 1988
Suggested tune	ST MATTHEW by William Croft
	ST MICHAEL'S from W. Gawler's *Hymns and Psalms*, 1789

The opening line is an echo of Isaiah 55. 8,9; and the hymn goes on to speak of God known in his works (earth, nature, the universe and an eternal world beyond); in his messengers (Sinai, the prophets, God's self-revelation in Scripture); and, beyond all works and words, in his Son. He is a God of power, of righteousness, and of love.

The final phrase of verse 1, 'the edges of his ways' is borrowed from the title of a book by Amy Carmichael of Dohnavur, echoing Job 26.12, '...the outskirts of his ways'. For 'the sum of things', see the Note on 231.

242 CHRIST WHO CALLED DISCIPLES TO HIM   87 87 87

Theme	The call of God; Christian experience and discipleship; church
	membership and confirmation; response to the gospel
Written	at Ruan Minor, August 1989
Suggested tune	REGENT SQUARE by Henry T. Smart
	RHUDDLAN (Welsh traditional)
Published in	*Sing Glory*, 1999 to ASCENDED TRIUMPH by Henry V. Gerike
	Glory Be (New Zealand), 2000 to RHUDDLAN

The four verses follow the sequence of the gospel story, from the calling of the disciples, through the ministry of Jesus to his death 'for our salvation' and his resurrection, and so to the Great Commission and the gift of the Spirit. The word 'defending' in the final verse is an echo of the traditional confirmation prayer of the Church of England: 'Defend, O Lord, your servants with your heavenly grace...'

'No reserve and no delays', verse 4, line 2, is another conscious echo, this time of Marianne Farningham's hymn, first published 1887, 'Just as I am, thine own to be', itself based on Charlotte Elliott's 'Just as I am' of fifty years before.

243 O GOD OF GRACE, TO WHOM BELONGS   88 88 88

Theme	The call of God; the living God; pilgrimage; the Christian hope
Written	at Ford, December 1998
Suggested tune	MELITA by John B. Dykes
	ST CATHERINE by Henri F. Hemy
Published in	*Twelve Hymns*, 2001 to LUSIGNAC by Maurice Bevan

Originally written at the suggestion of 'Spring Harvest', the text takes the twin themes of 'the journeying God' and of 'our future hope in Christ as individuals, as a church and also as a society'.

The four verses progress from 'love eternal', before time or creation, through God's covenant with Israel and Christ's incarnation, towards the 'evermore' of the final stanza and the future hopes which guide and inspire pilgrimage.

244 ABOVE THE VOICES OF THE WORLD AROUND ME   11 10 11 10 D

Theme	Response to the gospel; mission and evangelism
Written	at Ruan Minor, August 1985
Suggested tune	ABOVE THE VOICES OF THE WORLD by Phil Burt
Published in	*Mission Praise 2*, 1987 to ABOVE THE VOICES OF THE WORLD
	Songs of Rejoicing (USA), 1989 to INNER SIGHT by Alfred V. Fedak
	The Alfred V. Fedak Hymnary (USA), 1990 to INNER SIGHT
	Mission Praise Combined, 1990 to ABOVE THE VOICES OF THE WORLD
	Complete Mission Praise, 1999 to ABOVE THE VOICES OF THE WORLD
	Praise!, 2000 to ABOVE THE VOICES OF THE WORLD
	Rejoice in God (USA), 2000 to VESTAVIA HILLS by K. Lee Scott

While there are echoes in this text of many parts of Scripture, Mark 1 is dominant. See the reference in verse 1 of the text to the calling of Christ, in verse 2 to repentance in response to that call, and in verse 3 both to faith and to what Christ shall 'make me', as in Mark 1.17.

The second half of verse 1 draws freely on the words and teaching of Christ in different parts of the Gospels. See, for example:

'I gave my life'   John 10.15
'the cords that bind you'   John 8.33–36
'I rose from death'   Luke 28.46
'to set your spirit free'   John 8.36
'turn from your sins'   Mark 1.15
'and put the past behind you'   Luke 9.59–62
'take up your cross'   Mark 8.34
'come and follow me'   Matthew 16.24

Line 1 of verse 3 echoes the prayer of the father of the epileptic boy, Mark 9.24.

Phil Burt's tune remained untitled until it was included in *Praise!*, 2000; but I refer to it by that later name throughout.

245 JESUS MY BREATH, MY LIFE, MY LORD   88 88 6

Theme	Commitment to Christ; Christ in experience
Written	at Ruan Minor, August 1979
Suggested tune	BREATH OF LIFE by Roy Hopp
	MANOR PARK by Derek Kidner
Published in	*The Hymn* (USA), April 1981 (words only)
	The Summit Choirbook (USA), 1983 to ES IST GEWISSLICH (German traditional)
	Hymn Sampler Eighty Nine (USA), 1989 to MANOR PARK
	Songs of Rejoicing (USA), 1989 to BREATH OF LIFE
	The Roy Hopp Hymnary (USA), 1990 to BREATH OF LIFE
	Anthem (USA), 1997 by K. Lee Scott

An interviewer asked me once if I was aware how often references to God and to heaven as 'high' appeared in my hymns; and whether this indicated a preoccupation with the transcendence of God, rather than with his immanence—his indwelling, his presence among us. Both aspects of God have been celebrated continually by hymn writers; and this text speaks perhaps more intimately than most in this collection of the sense of God's presence in and near us.

'Breath' is used in Scripture (for example in Genesis 2.7, Job 33.4, Ezekiel 38.9, and John 20.22) as the sign of life imparted by God into both body and spirit.

These notes have recorded already the debts I owe to Derek Kidner; among them that on reading this text in MS he wrote a tune for it, entitled MANOR PARK from the address of his home near Cambridge.

246 O SAVIOUR CHRIST, BEYOND ALL PRICE   86 86 D (DCM)

Theme	Commitment to Christ
Written	at Bramerton, April 1978
Suggested tune	FOREST GREEN (English traditional)

This is a text with a strong repetitive structure, as can be seen from the Collect-like opening, with the vocative 'O Christ' (and 'O Saviour Christ...', 'O Sovereign Christ...')

followed by a descriptive reference to the Lord; and then in the second half of each verse the shift from the Lord to the worshipper in the repeated 'I come....', to plead and to bring, to follow and to find.

Line 3 of verse 1 is a conscious echo of the Communion Service in the *Book of Common Prayer* with its '...full, perfect, and sufficient sacrifice...'. In verse 3, line 4 refers to John 15.15; while 'companion' in line 1 is barely used in the the New Testament, however much the thought is present. As applied, however, to the Christian disciple with his Lord, the true meaning of the word is full of symbolism: Archbishop Trench in his *On the Study of Words* (London 1861) reminds us that 'a companion is one with whom we share our bread'. Line 4 of verse 4 refers to Colossians 1.16, where these spiritual beings are shown as owing their existence to the creative power of the eternal Word, with a view to his glory, and serving his purpose.

247 LORD OF ALL LIFE AND POWER   66 86 D (DSM)

Theme	New life in Christ; dedication and renewal
Written	at Ford, May 1997
Suggested tune	COURT BARTON by Malcolm Archer
	DIADEMATA by George J. Elvey
Published in	*New Start Hymns and Songs*, 1999 to (1) COURT BARTON
	(2) DIADEMATA
	Complete Anglican Hymns Old & New, 2000 to COURT BARTON
	Sing to the Lord, 2000 to COURT BARTON
	Glory Be (New Zealand), 2000 to DIADEMATA
	New Hymns and Worship Songs, 2001 to COURT BARTON
	Methodist Hymns Old & New, 2001 to COURT BARTON

Towards the end of 1996 the Diocese of Lincoln began to plan 'a celebratory event' to be held in the Cathedral during the autumn of the following year. It was suggested that I might write a hymn for the occasion, which would mark the completion of a diocesan initiative 'New ways for new times', and look forward to the millennium.

The title chosen for the event was VIVAT!—'let there be life'—and it is this which runs through the progressive stanzas of the hymn: life in creation, and in God's re-creation of his people; life in the natural order (Lincoln is a diocese with strong rural roots, and traditional links with deep-sea fishing, for example, in the port of Grimsby); life in resurrection and the indwelling Spirit of life; and 'life more abundant' in Christian discipleship and commitment. Part of the brief was 'We want to make our commitment to Christ who is alive for the last 2000 years and will be in the third millennium'.

The opening line of the hymn is also the opening phrase of the Collect of Easter Day in *Common Worship*, 2000: based on a prayer which has been in use for well over a thousand years. Verse 4, line 4, is easily recognized as a direct quotation of the opening line of R.F. Littledale's translation of Bianco da Siena's original Italian; and I hope will carry at this point in my hymn some of the great overtones of his.

Based on	1 Peter 1.18, 19; Isaiah 53.3–6; 2 Corinthians 5.17, 18
Theme	New life in Christ
Written	at Ruan Minor, August 1972
Suggested tune	ARGENT by Noël Tredinnick
	LLANGLOFFAN (Welsh traditional)
	MORDEN PARK by Norman L. Warren
	PASSION CHORALE harmonized by J.S. Bach
Translated into	Chinese
Published in	*Rejoice!* (Australia), 1987 to ARGENT
	Church Family Worship, 1988 to (1) PASSION CHORALE
	(2) EWING by Alexander Ewing
	Psalter Hymnal (USA), 1988 to PASTORALE by Adrian Hartog
	Sounds of Grace (Hong Kong), 1991 to MORDEN PARK (with a
	Chinese translation)
	Hymns for the People, 1993 to BLACKDOWN by Andrew Maires
	Hymns for Prayer & Praise, 1996 to (1) LAURENTIUS by Laurence
	Bévenot (2) DU FONDS DE MA PENSÉE, *Strasburg Psalter*, 1539
	Sing Glory, 1999 to EWING
	Together in Song (Australia), 1999 to KING'S LYNN (English
	traditional)
	Praise!, 2000 to BLACKDOWN
Recorded on	*Here is Psalm Praise*, 1975 to ARGENT

Written originally for *Psalm Praise* as 'a Passiontide Psalm', this text draws heavily on the three passages of Scripture indicated. I cannot claim that the rhyme in lines 6 and 8 of verse 1 is original; indeed, it is probably more common in hymnody than I know. It is however used with great effectiveness in one of the closing sequences of John Masefield's poem 'The Everlasting Mercy':

> '...The corn that makes the holy bread
> By which the soul of man is fed,
> The holy bread, the food unpriced,
> Thy everlasting mercy, Christ.'

The lines in question can be found set as a hymn for congregational use in *Songs of Praise* (Oxford 1925).

The repeated phrase 'Lamb of God' occurs first in Scripture in John 1.29, coined, it seems, by John the Baptist as a description of Jesus in the New Covenant prefigured by the Passover. In Isaiah 53.7 the Servant of the Lord is 'led as a lamb to the slaughter'; while in the 2 Corinthians passage there is the fathomless reference to Christ's atoning death, that 'For our sake he made him to be sin who knew no sin, so that in him we might become the righteousness of God' (2 Corinthians 5.21).

See Index 6.

Based on	John 14.6
Theme	Christian experience and discipleship; youth
Written	at Sevenoaks, July 1961
Suggested tune	SLANE (Irish traditional)
	TRISAGION by Henry T. Smart
Published in	*Anglican Hymn Book*, 1965 to SLANE
	Youth Praise 1, 1966 to music by Michael A. Baughen
	Renewal Songbook, 1971 (words only)
	The Hymnal (Canada), 1973 to SLANE
	Keswick Praise, 1975 to SLANE
	Grace Hymns, 1975 to SLANE
	Anthem (USA), 1978 by Henry V. Gerike
	Lutheran Worship (USA), 1982 to SLANE
	Christian Hymns Observed, 1982 (words only)
	Hymns and Psalms, 1983 to TRISAGION
	Hymnal Supplement (USA), 1984 to SLANE
	Praise God Together, 1984 to SLANE
	Sing Alleluia (Australia), 1987 to BONNIE GEORGE CAMPBELL (Scottish traditional)
	The Worshiping Church (USA), 1990 to SLANE
	The Song Goes On (USA), 1990 to SLANE
	A New Hymnal for Colleges and Schools (USA), 1992 to SLANE
	Junior Praise 2, 1992 to SLANE
	Christian Worship: a Lutheran Hymnal (USA), 1993 to SLANE
	Songs for the People of God (USA), 1994 to SHEPHERD'S STAR from *The Southern Harmony*, 1835
	The Covenant Hymnal (USA), 1995 to SLANE
	Junior Praise Combined, 1997 to SLANE
	Together in Song (Australia), 1999 to BONNIE GEORGE CAMPBELL
	Worship & Rejoice (USA), 2001 to SLANE
	Methodist Hymns Old & New, 2001 to TRISAGION
Recorded on	*Come Meet my Jesus* (USA), 1989 to SLANE
	Junior Praise Combined 22, 1999 to SLANE

At the time this was written, John 14.6 was a text much in my mind; and I have always been an admirer of the economy of Bishop Doane's hymn 'Thou art the Way'. This was one of two hymns written at the general invitation of Canon H.C. Taylor, the Chairman of the editorial committee of the *Anglican Hymn Book* (the other being 228 'Lord, who left the highest heaven') but on its inclusion a year later in *Youth Praise* I changed line 3 of verse 1 to read 'Fears for the future I trust to his care'; and this was followed by the editor of *Renewal Songbook* in 1971. This reading is now discontinued, since it loses the immediate thought of 'following' Christ the Way, paralleled by trusting him as the Truth in verse 2. Note the alliterative references to Christ as victor over darkness, doubt and death.

See Index 6.

250 AFFIRM ANEW THE THREEFOLD NAME   86 86 D (DCM)

Theme   Dedication and renewal; faith; unity; mission
Written   at Ford, September 1996
Suggested tune   ELLACOMBE (German traditional)
                     KINGSFOLD (English traditional)
Published in   *Church of England Newspaper,* 6 March 1998 (words only)
                     Anglican World, Easter 1998 to KINGSFOLD
                     Lambeth Praise (USA), 1998 to KINGSFOLD
                     Common Praise, 2000 to TYROL (Tyrolean traditional)

Since 1867 the 'Lambeth Conference' of Anglican bishops has been held about every ten years, steadily increasing in size. It has no legislative powers but considerable authority. The Conference is called, and presided over, by the Archbishop of Canterbury. The 1998 Conference was based in Canterbury, at the University of Kent.

Preparations for such Conferences are laid far ahead; and it was in April 1996 that the Archbishop's Secretary for Anglican Communion Affairs wrote to me, saying that for the daily worship of the 1998 Conference they hoped to have a small selection of hymns, some of them specially written. The major themes had already been identified:

1. Called to full humanity: in the name of the Father, Son and Holy Spirit

2. Called to live and proclaim the Good News

3. Called to be faithful in a plural world

4. Called to be one

It can be seen that the four stanzas of the hymn correspond with these themes, where the call to full humanity includes the experience of sinfulness and of salvation; where the Good News is embodied in God's own 'timeless word'; where Christ alone is Way, Truth and Life amid contemporary relativism; and where the unity of God's church is seen as accompanying other gifts of the Spirit in renewal and revival - a unity which finds its focus as well as its call in the one divine Name of Father, Spirit and Son.

There are a number of fairly well-known DCM tunes to which the text can be sung. ELLACOMBE seems to me to have the necessary force and vigour for the text, and I prefer it to KINGSFOLD for this hymn. Because (at least since the *English Hymnal,* 1906) it is usually associated with 'The Day of Resurrection', an Easter hymn, it is not overworked.

My practice of giving a capital letter to the divine Name follows, e.g., Leviticus 24.11, RSV.

251 BE WITH US, LORD, WHO SEEK YOUR AID   86 86 (CM)

Theme   Dedication and renewal
Written   at Ford, August 1995
Suggested tune   CONTEMPLATION by Frederick A.G. Ouseley
                     MARTYRDOM (Scottish traditional)
                     ST TIMOTHY by Henry W. Baker
Published in   *Glory Be* (New Zealand), 2000 to CRUCIS VICTORIA by M.B.
                     Foster

During 1995 the Bishop of Salisbury asked me for a hymn that would express something of his 'Vision for the Diocese', which was often the theme of particular Services where such a hymn would be appropriate. The three key aspects of this 'Vision' were Christian Action, Christian Confidence and Renewing Worship. We need to be seen to put our faith into action if it is to mean anything to those outside the church. To do this, we need the confidence that comes from knowing what we believe and why. As we understand our faith better and enter into it more deeply, this will be expressed in worship.

A simple text was needed, which could be sung to a tune or tunes already familiar. It will be seen that in the completed version this is achieved by using common metre; and that the three key elements are deployed in a different order. Our worship (verse 2) leads to an increasing confidence (verse 3) in the God we are learning to know better; and this in turn shapes the pattern of our lives as we respond by deed as well as word to the love revealed to us in the Scriptures (verse 4).

252 CHRIST THE WAY OF LIFE POSSESS ME   87 83

Based on	Four images from the Book of Proverbs: 6.23 etc; 10.11; 3.18 etc; 5.6
Theme	Christian experience and discipleship; pilgrimage
Written	at Ruan Minor, September 1988
Suggested tune	CHRIST THE WAY OF LIFE by Phil Burt
	NONINGTON by David H. Grundy
Published in	*Mission Praise Combined*, 1990 to CHRIST THE WAY OF LIFE
	Honour His Name, 1993 to music by Norman L. Warren
	Songs for the People of God (USA), 1994 to STULTZ by Keith Landis
	Supplement '96 (USA), 1996 to NEW FOREST by Carlton R. Young
	Anthem (USA), 1999 by Bob Moore
	Complete Mission Praise, 1999 to CHRIST THE WAY OF LIFE
	Anthems Old & New for SA Men, 1999 to music by Norman L. Warren
	Common Praise, 2000 to CHRIST THE WAY OF LIFE
Recorded on	*This is our Joy and this is our Feast* (USA), 1999 to the music of Bob Moore

Compound images with the word 'life' are not uncommon in Scripture, and are found in the Book of Proverbs, in St John's Gospel, in the Book of Revelation, and in other places also. 'Tree of Life', for example, is an image that begins in Genesis and which, in the words of Henri Blocher's *In the Beginning* (Leicester 1984), 'represents communion with God, the inexhaustible source of life. The communion is made possible by Wisdom...' (see also Revelation 2 and 22). Jesus refers to himself as 'the Way' in John 14.6; and his words about the 'well of water springing up into everlasting life' (John 4.14) stand behind verse 2. The shining path of verse 4 is the path of the just from Proverbs 4.18, which is also the path of life.

'Watered garden' in verse 2 is from Jeremiah 31.12 (cf. Proverbs 11.25 and Isaiah 58.11).

Theme	Love; pilgrimage; heaven
Written	at Ford, October 1994
Suggested tune	HAWKHURST by Henry J. Gauntlett
	PROSPECT (American traditional)
Published in	*Anthem* (USA), 1996 to music by W.A. Mozart arranged by Austin C. Lovelace
	Cantate Domino, 2000 to CRAGDALE by Richard Lloyd
	Rejoice in God (USA), 2000 to FANTO by K. Lee Scott

The reference in the opening verse to 1 Corinthians 13 sets the theme of the text; but this is in no sense a metrical version of the passage; rather, a prayerful meditation on it.

I owe the suggestion of the tune, which was quite new to me, to Dan McKinley, then Director of Music at First Christian Church, Columbus, Indiana who sent it to me, among others, when commissioning a text for his new hymnal. It is not the only tune of that name (a few UK hymnals have a DCM tune, PROSPECT, from the traditional melody 'Drink to me only with thine eyes'); it seems to come originally from a collection *Southern Harmony*, 1835 and is found in e.g. the *Lutheran Book of Worship*, 1978; *Hymnal for the Hours*, 1989; and the *Presbyterian Hymnal*, 1990; all from the US. I do not know of its inclusion in a European hymnal. Though the text can be sung to other tunes it was written for PROSPECT; and it will be seen that the metrically-interesting word 'heaven' occurs in the same place in all three stanzas to meet the demands of the melody. 'Virtues' in verse 1 is a reference to the 'Theological Virtues' of faith, hope and charity, which are grouped together by St Paul in four of his letters (see 1 Corinthians 13.13; Galatians 5.5,6; Colossians 1.4,5; 1 Thessalonians 1.3). The final line echoes Galatians 2.20.

For a text more closely based on 1 Corinthians 13 see 190 'Not for tongues of heaven's angels'.

254 MAY THE LOVE OF CHRIST ENFOLD US 85 85 88 85

Theme	Christian experience and discipleship; morning; pilgrimage
Written	at Ford, December 1992
Suggested tune	CAROLYN by Herbert H.J. Murrill
	KANSFIELD by Erik Routley
Published in	*Anthem* (USA), 1995 by Mary Kay Beall
	Glory Be (New Zealand), 2000 to AR HYD Y NOS (Welsh traditional)

Though this text is a prayer for ourselves and our own daily walk, it began from thoughts of thankfulness and the desire to write a 'litany of thankfulness', a task which still lies ahead of me.

Note that along with the request that we may know Christ's enfolding, upholding, directing, protecting, defending, befriending, goes the call to mission—'his Name confessing' (verse 1); while verse 4 calls us to witness, proclamation and service 'this and every day'.

The final line of each verse suggests that it would be particularly suitable as a morning hymn.

Based on	Ephesians 4.13
Theme	Pilgrimage
Written	at Bramerton, September 1988
Suggested tune	LEONI (from a Synagogue melody)
Published in	*Rejoice in God* (USA), 2000 to MARIETTA by K. Lee Scott

In December 1987 the Bible Institute of Singapore asked me to try my hand at writing for them a College Hymn. Their motto, from Ephesians 4.13, is 'Unity, Knowledge, Perfection'; and the long seventh line of each stanza refers to these in turn. They then come together in the final verse as 'love and truth and grace', since love leads to unity, truth to knowledge, and grace to perfection in the world to come.

256 THOUGH PILGRIM STRANGERS HERE BELOW 88 88 88

Theme	Pilgrimage; social concern and the world's need
Written	at Ford, January 2001
Suggested tune	PATER OMNIUM by Henry J.E. Holmes
	SURREY by Henry Carey

The origin of this text is briefly described in the note on 273 'O God, who gives the fertile seed'. This, however, is the earlier of the two texts, leaving me with the sense that I had more to say: hence the second attempt, which allowed me to offer Christian Aid a choice for their proposed collection. In the event, they chose my second text, 273, and two earlier ones, 272 and 279.

'Pilgrim strangers' of the opening line is drawn from the AV translation of 1 Peter 2.11. In the final line, our Lord's description of himself as 'the Way' includes more than 'the way to heaven'; but in the light of the context in John 14.1–6, and the reference to 'my Father' and 'my Father's house' it seems to me a legitimate expression.

257 WHEN THE WAY IS HARD TO FIND 77 77 77

Theme	Guidance; pilgrimage; the Bible; trust in God
Written	at Ruan Minor, August 1988
Suggested tune	DIX by Conrad Kocher
	HEATHLANDS by Henry T. Smart
	WELLS by D.S. Bortniansky
Published in	*Glory Be* (New Zealand), 2000 to WELLS

The text seeks to affirm the reality of God's guidance, in accordance with his many promises, to those who are willing to obey the light given. Verse 2 speaks of the 'human predicament', in the image of the trackless ocean (to the ancient Jews, a particularly hostile environment), calling forth the prayer of faith. Verse 3 suggests God's guidance through Scripture and the inner witness of the Spirit's voice; while in the final verse 'the light of Christ' is accompanied by faith, confidence, peace and progress.

258 EYE HAS NOT SEEN, NOR EAR HAS HEARD   86 86 (CM)

Theme	The love, wisdom, and purpose of God
Written	at Ruan Minor, August 1985
Suggested tune	CAITHNESS (Scottish traditional)
	ST AGNES by John B. Dykes
	STRACATHRO by Charles Hutcheson

The origin of this text lies in Paul's words in 1 Corinthians 2.9, 10, where he applies to our future hope the words which Isaiah had used centuries before about the vision of God. Verse 5 is based on Romans 8.32, and the final verse carries echoes of 1 Corinthians 3.21, 1 Thessalonians 4.17, and Ephesians 3.18,19.

The passage is sometimes misread, as though Paul is saying that the mysteries of what God has in store for his children are beyond our knowing. In fact, we are being told that though sense cannot discern them, God has revealed them.

The opening line has inspired a number of writers. Isaac Watts has 'Nor eye has seen, nor ear has heard' *(Hymns and Spiritual Songs,* 1707) and John Keble begins verse 4 of his 'A living stream, as crystal clear' *(Hymns Ancient & Modern,* 1916) with the line 'Eye hath not seen, nor ear hath heard'. Apart from the second 'hath' this is an exact rendering of the AV; and the identical line is found in Christina Rossetti's poem 'The heart knoweth its own bitterness'.

259 LORD AND FATHER, FAITH BESTOWING   445 83 or 85 83

Theme	The love of God; the Holy Trinity
Written	at Ford, August 1996
Suggested tune	BULLINGER by Ethelbert W. Bullinger
	CUTTLE MILLS by William Griffith
	VENITE AD ME by Arthur S. Sullivan

The form of this quiet petition and invocation is Trinitarian, asking God as Father, Son and Holy Spirit to draw near, to come with blessing and peace (John 20.19 was in my mind here), with power and with love; and affirming our faith in his presence among those who gather in the Name of Jesus. The Apostle Paul, in Romans 12.3, made it clear that the 'measure of faith' is the gift bestowed on us by God himself; and St John in his first letter (1 John 1.9) gives us the assurance that 'If we confess our sins, he is faithful and just, and will forgive our sins and cleanse us from all unrighteousness': forgiveness and cleansing are the way to peace (stanza 2). It is clear, too, that it was not only Thomas who was 'doubting' among the first disciples (Matthew 28.17); and that the answer to doubt lay in the presence and promise of Jesus.

The metre (85 83) seems to be little-used in contemporary British collections, unless they include Frances Ridley Havergal's 'I am trusting thee (you), Lord Jesus'. But older books carry more texts in this metre with tunes which can be tried against these words. CUTTLE MILLS, dropped from the *English Hymnal,* is retained in *Baptist Praise and Worship,* 1991.

Theme	God the Father, the living God; trust in God
Written	at Ford, February 1992
Suggested tune	AMAZING GRACE (American traditional)
	RICHMOND by Thomas Haweis
	ST PETER by Alexander R. Reinagle

The starting point for this text is Solomon's prayer in 1 Kings 8.22-30. In this context, verse 3 can be seen as the Christian answer to Solomon's question: 'But will God indeed dwell on earth?' In the same way the theme of verse 5 (faith in God, his promises and his care for his children) is one of the concerns of Solomon's great prayer.

Reference can also be found to Lamentations 3.23, 2 Corinthians 5.1, Proverbs 15.8 and Psalm 103.14.

Theme	Trust in God; praise and worship; grace
Written	at Ruan Minor, Holy Week 1976
Suggested tune	DES PLAINES by Carl F. Schalk
	DOMINICA by Herbert S. Oakley
	TRENTHAM by Robert Jackson

Part of the basis for this text is to be found in the thought of the 'God of all grace' of 1 Peter 5.10. My notebook contains the line 'God of grace and King of glory'; with no indication that I was quoting unconsciously from H.E. Fosdick's 'God of grace and God of glory'. I can also recall a few years later being attracted to the line 'who formed and lit the starry height' and wanting to incorporate it into a hymn; with no recollection that I had already done so in verse 2 of this text.

It will be noticed that the first and last verses speak of ourselves turning to God and singing his praise; while the intermediate verses are prayers for divine guidance, inner renewal, and spiritual strength.

Based on	The Prayer of Manasseh
Theme	Prayer and penitence
Written	at Bramerton, January 1987
Suggested tune	MELITA by John B. Dykes
	ST CATHERINE by Henri F. Hemy
Published in	*Praise!*, 2000 to MELITA

This metrical version of part of the Prayer of Manasseh was written at the suggestion of the compilers of the American *United Methodist Hymnal*, 1989. 'The Prayer of Manasseh', one of the books of the Apocrypha, is taken to be the penitential prayer of King Manasseh of Judah whose wickedness, idolatry and corruption is described in 2 Kings 21.1–18. It has been used in Christian worship since at least the early part of the third century, and is perhaps best known for the plea 'Now therefore I bow the knee of mine heart, beseeching thee of grace'.

Almost two years after this text was written, researching for an anthology I read in Philip Doddridge's *Hymns Founded on Various Texts in the Holy Scriptures* (London 1755) the opening lines

> 'Eternal and Immortal King
> Thy peerless Splendors none can bear....'

which I am not conscious of ever having seen before.

263 O LORD, YOURSELF DECLARE   66 86 (SM)

Theme	Prayer; learning to pray
Written	at Ruan Minor, August 1981
Suggested tune	ST GEORGE by Henry J. Gauntlett
	ST MICHAEL adapted by William Crotch

The first of these three short verses contains echoes of Hebrews 10.20 and Luke 11.1. The second, which is the heart of the hymn, draws on the mnemonic ACTS. This stands for a framework of prayer consisting of Adoration, Confession, Thanksgiving and Supplication; in this text the order of the final two is reversed.

For verse 3, with its reference to God's purposes and promises, and to faith in Christ's Name, see for example Ephesians 3.11, Hebrews 10.23, 1 John 2.25, John 14.4 and Acts 3.16.

264 THANKFUL OF HEART FOR DAYS GONE BY   88 88 D (DLM)

Theme	Thankfulness; faith; joy; hope
Written	at Ruan Minor, August 1979
Suggested tune	LAMB OF GOD by Twila Paris

The three verses of this text point to past, present and future with thanksgiving, joy and hope. 'Inward eye' in verse 1, although an expression used also by others (for example, by William Blake), is most familiar from William Wordsworth's poem 'I wandered lonely as a cloud'. 'Tale' (line 4) carries with it the sense not only of story, but of reckoning. The 'sunlit hours' of line 6 have an echo of the sundial, whose boast it is that it only tells the sunny hours. Verse 2, line 5 is a reference to our Lord's words in Matthew 19.6f. 'Hope', of course, in the final line of the text is used in the fully biblical sense of an assurance for the future founded on faith in God, buttressed by recollection of the past and experience of the present, in which the believer will never be disappointed (Romans 5.5).

Based on	Philippians 4
Theme	Peace and blessing; love for God
Written	at Ruan Minor, August 1984
Suggested tune	IBSTONE by Maria Tiddeman
	QUAM DILECTA by Henry L. Jenner
Published in	*Praying with the English Hymn Writers*, 1989 (words only)
	With Almost Every Voice, 1991 to music by Richard Lloyd
	Rejoice in God (USA), 2000 to PEACE by K. Lee Scott

The three verses speak of the peace of God, of peace with God, and of the God of peace. The first and third are found in Philippians 4.7,9, and the middle one in, for example, Romans 5.1.

In verse 1 of the text, peace with God is related to forgiveness, reconciliation, what Dr J.A. Motyer in his *The Prophecy of Isaiah* (Leicester 1993) calls 'the full realization of his favour'. Verse 2 speaks of our experience of God's peace, part of the fruit of the Spirit (Galatians 5.22), 'which will keep constant guard over your hearts and minds as they rest in Christ Jesus' (Philippians 4.7, JBP). 'The God of peace' (verse 3) is a phrase used by the New Testament writers in pronouncing blessing, as in Romans 15.23, 1 Thessalonians 5.23 or Hebrews 13.20.

266 'SET YOUR TROUBLED HEARTS AT REST'   77 77

Based on	John 14.1 (NEB)
Theme	Peace and blessing; confidence and trust
Written	at Ruan Minor, August 1979
Suggested tune	HARROWBY by James Gillespie
	HARTS by Benjamin Milgrove
	LYNCH'S LULLABY by J.P. Lynch
	SONG 13 by Orlando Gibbons
Published in	*Twenty-one Hymns Old and New*, 1985 to SONG 13
	Irish Church Praise (Ireland), 1990 to LYNCH'S LULLABY
	The Roy Hopp Hymnary (USA), 1990 to RENGSTORFF by Roy Hopp
	Aids in Ministry (USA), Summer 1992 to music by Jeffrey Honoré
	Anthem (USA), 1992 by Jeffrey Honoré
	100 Hymns of Hope (USA), 1992 to SAM by John Carter
	Worship Together (USA), 1995 to MERCY by Louis M. Gotteschalk
	Church Hymnal (Ireland), 2000 to LYNCH'S LULLABY
Recorded on	*More Hymns from Irish Church Praise* (Ireland), 1993 to LYNCH'S
	LULLABY

Though begun in the garden at Ruan Minor, much of this text was written on a cliff over-looking Poldhu Cove.

The repetition of a single line in a different place within each verse of a text requires two things: that the line in question is strong enough to stand repetition, and a pattern which allows each line to be metrically identical. The repeated line here is from the New

English Bible translation of John 14.1, the words of the Lord to the disciples following the departure of Judas from the Last Supper, and the foretelling of how short a time Jesus would be with them. It is the NEB version of the familiar AV translation 'Let not your heart be troubled'.

The hymn is addressed to ourselves, fellow-members of a congregation, in exhortation; of which the key is the repeated 'hear again' of verses 1 and 4. Within that context, we urge each other (and our own hearts) to be set at rest, to be at peace, to rejoice, to trust, to find and to embrace that experience.

267 THE GOD WHO SET THE STARS IN SPACE   86 86 D (DCM)

Theme	Creation; conservation; the natural order
Written	at Ford, July 1998
Suggested tune	ELLACOMBE (German traditional)
	KINGSFOLD (English traditional)
Published in	*The Care of Creation*, 2000 (words only)
	Cantate Domino, 2000 to CREATION'S LORD by Alan Rees
	Moral Landscape of Creation (USA), 2001 to ELLACOMBE

In 1994 a group of evangelical Christian leaders in America issued a call for environmental stewardship, 'An Evangelical Declaration on the Care of Creation'. It attempts to address the theology of God's creation in a fallen world, and the responsibility of every Christian to care for God's earth.

A year later Professor R.J. Berry, a former President of the English Ecological Society and Professor of Genetics at University College, London, sought UK signatories for the *Declaration* and in 1997/8 prepared for the publication of a 'Critical and Appreciative Commentary' on it. He wrote asking whether I might contribute a hymn on the subject to this symposium, *The Care of Creation* (see above), perhaps by way of epilogue.

The text contains a number of direct echoes from the wording of the *Declaration* and moves towards a prayer that God will fulfil his purpose in Christ to bring reconciliation and wholeness to the entire created order (Colossians 1.19–20). The final reference is to Hebrews 1.10-12 describing how the earth and the heavens 'shall wax old as doth a garment. And as a vesture shalt thou fold them up and they shall be changed...' And in that day, which Paul calls 'the end' when Christ delivers up the kingdom to God the Father, we read in 1 Corinthians 15.28 that 'God shall be all in all'.

268 THE LORD IN WISDOM MADE THE EARTH   86 86 88

Based on	Proverbs 8.22f; 1 Corinthians 1.24
Theme	The Wisdom of God; creation
Written	at Bramerton, September 1982
Suggested tune	AUCH JETZT MACHT GOTT from Koch's *Choralbuch*, 1816
	CONQUEST by Donald S. Barrows
	O JESU by Johann B. Reimann
	PEMBROKE by Patrick A.S. Hadley
Published in	*Supplement to Lutheran Hymnal* (Australia), 1987 to O JESU

'The Wisdom of God' was one of the Sunday themes of the *Alternative Service Book, 198(*
of the Church of England; and Proverbs 8.22f is set in the current (1997) Lectionary ir
Years A and B for the Second Sunday before Lent. Charles Wesley wrote on 'the divine
Wisdom', and John included two such hymns (14 and 27) in his *A Collection of Hymns for
the Use of the People called Methodists* (London 1780).

In writing my first draft, I followed the Old Testament in personifying Wisdom with a
feminine gender; but I was advised by Derek Kidner, when submitting the draft for criticism, that since the personification of Wisdom in the New Testament is Christ Himself,
the feminine form is found only in the Old Testament and the Apocrypha.

269 WHAT COLOURS GOD HAS MADE   66 86 (SM)

Theme	Creation; the love of God
Written	at Bramerton, February 1990
Suggested tune	SANDYS (English traditional)
	SOUTHWELL from William Damon's *Psalmes, 1579*
Published in	*100 Hymns of Hope* (USA), 1992 to COLORBURST by William J.
	Reynolds
	Anthem (USA), 1992 by Austin Lovelace
	Junior Praise 2, 1993 to music by Michael Paget
	Moravian Book of Worship (USA), 1995 to COLORBURST
	Junior Praise Combined, 1997 to music by Michael Paget

The text, a hymn for children, attempts to weave the theme of colour into that of the
changing seasons. It was written for the recorder group of Thorpe Hamlet First School,
Norwich, at the request of their teacher. They had been learning the tune SOUTHWELL,
but finding the familiar words 'Lord Jesus, think on me, by many a care oppressed...'
inappropriate for six-to-eight-year-olds in school. The Norfolk Agreed Syllabus of
Religious Education included for this age-range ideas of exploring experience through
the natural world and through the Bible; and this text is an attempt to link the two,
together with what the Syllabus calls 'the Christian belief that everyone is special to God'.

270 THE LORD MADE MAN, THE SCRIPTURES TELL   88 88 (LM)

Theme	The fall of man; redemption
Written	at Ruan Minor, August 1977
Suggested tune	BIRLING (English traditional)
	O WALY WALY (English traditional)
	WARRINGTON by Ralph Harrison
Published in	*Songs of Worship,* 1980 to BIRLING
	Hymns for Today's Church, 1982 to (1) THE HOLY SON by Peter
	Hurford (2) BIRLING
	Making Melody, 1983 to BIRLING
	Rejoice! (Australia), 1987 to ALSTONE by Christopher E. Willing
	Lift High your Songs!, 1988 to MEARE HEATH by Michael Paget
	Grace Praise (New Zealand), 1999 (words only)
	Praise!, 2000 to VOM HIMMEL HOCH from Schumann's
	Geistliche Lieder, 1539

In the mid-1970s one or two writers were commenting on the lack of hymns taking the fall of the human race as a major theme. *The Alternative Service Book, 1980* of the Church of England made this subject one of its suggested Sunday themes (for the 8th Sunday before Christmas) and suitable hymns were few in number. Hence this text.

The references to Adam must be understood, not only in terms of the creation story in Genesis, but also of Paul's argument in 1 Corinthians 15. 'Innocence' in verse 3 should be taken with some of the force of its original derivation of 'doing no hurt'.

The text is one in which I do not find it possible to make the changes required if the language were to be fully inclusive since (apart from the problems of verse 2 which, though requiring a change of rhyme, are not insoluble) the opening line would be affected, and the hymn therefore known by alternative titles. Most modern translations use 'Man' here in a generic sense: 'so God created man...' (Genesis 1.27, RSV, NIV) or else in the particular sense, distinguishing him from Eve (see REB, Genesis 2.8; 15f).

271 AS FOR OUR WORLD WE LIFT OUR HEARTS IN PRAISE   10 10 4 10 10 4 10 10

Theme	Social concern and the world's need
Written	at Eastbourne, August 1968
Suggested tune	by Michael A. Baughen (see below)
Published in	*Youth Praise 2*, 1969 to music by Michael A. Baughen
	Thirty Hymns, 1972 (words only)

When *Youth Praise 2* was in preparation, there was a need for new hymns of social concern, but rooted in a personal and biblical spirituality. This text was an attempt at one such, but the experiment in metre means that it is not easy to sing even to the tune written for these words in that book. Perhaps I should have hardened my heart and omitted it from this collection; but the sentiments it expresses, in prayer and thanksgiving, are a necessary part of Christian worship, and I live in hope that some inspired musical setting may add it to the limited repertoire of hymns on this theme.

272 BEHOLD A BROKEN WORLD, WE PRAY   86 86 (CM)

Based on	Micah 4.1–4
Theme	Social concern and the world's need; the peace of the world
Written	at Poldhu Cove and Ruan Minor, August 1984
Suggested tune	MARTYRDOM (Scottish traditional)
	McKEE (African-American traditional)
	ST PETER by Alexander R. Reinagle
Translated into	Japanese
Published in	*The Hymn* (USA), July 1985 (words only)
	Singing for Peace (USA), 1986 to music by Douglas E. Wagner
	Anglican Praise, 1987 to ST MARY from E. Prys's *Llyfr y Psalmau*, 1621
	The United Methodist Hymnal (USA), 1989 to MARSH CHAPEL by Max Miller

Singing for Peace (USA), 1994 to MARTYRDOM
Catholic Book of Worship III (Canada), 1994 to RESIGNATION
(American traditional)
Moravian Book of Worship (USA), 1995 to ST STEPHEN by
William Jones
The Hymnal 21 (Japan), 1997 to MARSH CHAPEL in an
unattributed translation
Praise!, 2000 to BESSELSLEIGH by C.P. Herrington

This text was one of the five chosen entries in the Hymn Society of America hymn search on the theme of 'Peace', 1984/5. Among biblical allusions notice Psalm 46.9 (verse 3, line 3); while in verse 4 'the dreamers of the day' is a phrase from T.E. Lawrence.

273 O GOD, WHO GIVES THE FERTILE SEED   88 88 (LM)

Theme	Social concern and the world's need
Written	at Ford, January 2001
Suggested tune	ANGELUS from Georg Joseph in *Heilige Seelenlust*, 1657
	HERONGATE (English traditional)

In October 2000 Dr Paula Clifford of Christian Aid told me of their plans to co-publish a collection of hymns on social justice, and invited me to contribute. This is one of two texts (the other is 256 'Though pilgrim strangers here below') written in response to that suggestion.

In their careful brief Christian Aid spoke of hymns which should not offer 'unrelieved gloom' nor 'seek to instil a sense of duty', but which should aim 'to inspire and uplift'. Perhaps this is not the obvious sense conveyed by this hymn text, which makes the choice of tune specially important in setting the mood. Verse 2 in particular carries a sober reminder; but the second half of the hymn is a positive turning to seek God's help to do our part towards that 'better world where Christ is Lord'.

274 REMEMBER, LORD, THE WORLD YOU MADE   86 86 (CM)

Theme	Social concern and the world's need
Written	at Ruan Minor, August 1978
Suggested tune	LAND OF REST (American traditional)
	ST BOTOLPH by Gordon A. Slater
Published in	*The Hymn* (USA), April 1981 (words only)
	Hymns for Today's Church, 1982 to LONDON NEW from *Scottish Psalter*, 1635
	Praise!, 2000 to CHARNWOOD by Peter G. White

The opening word of the text, 'Remember', is a prayer used by many characters of Scripture; by Samson (Judges 16.28), by Solomon (2 Chronicles 6.42), by Job (10.9), by the psalmist (e.g. 25.7; 132.1), by Hezekiah (Isaiah 38.3), by Jeremiah (14.21), and by the penitent thief (Luke 23.42). It is a prayer of power. As Derek Kidner reminds us in his *Ezra and Nehemiah* (Leicester 1979), 'God's remembering always implies his intervention, not merely his recollection or recognition.'

As for the word 'seem' in verse 5, it is chosen because a hymn belongs to a whole congregation, none of whom know for a certainty the circumstances of the rest. It is not always those who *appear* the most generous by their response to some need or appeal who necessarily are so. God looks on the heart, we look on the 'outward appearance' (1 Samuel 16.7). There is a further reason; in that like the church at Laodicea (Revelation 3.17) we who seem (to ourselves as well as others) to be rich may in reality be poor indeed.

Verse 2, line 3, contains an echo from the Burial Service in the *Book of Common Prayer*, derived from material at least a thousand years old in Christian worship. Verse 2, line 4 is a reminder of the Lord's special care for orphans, the 'fatherless' of much of Old Testament Scripture (e.g. Psalm 68.5; see also James 1.27).

275 MOST GLORIOUS GOD, FOR BREATH AND BIRTH   86 86 (CM)

Theme	Healing and disability; pilgrimage
Written	at Ford, December 1999
Suggested tune	LONDON NEW from *Scottish Psalter*, 1635
	ST PETER by Alexander R. Reinagle
Published in	*Country Way*, Winter 2000/2001 (words only)

For the tenth anniversary of 'Compass Braille', an acronym for 'Computerised Production of Asian Scripts in Braille', I was asked to write a hymn. This missionary press is housed in a converted Methodist Chapel in Moretonhampstead, Devon, printing Bibles in Braille for the developing world. The hymn was to reflect something of the place that disability—in this case, impaired sight—might have in Christian thinking. I took counsel with my daughter Caroline Gill, herself registered disabled, and tried to offer a text which might be sung by anyone, but which would have a special meaning for those disabled in any way, and which would not embarrass anyone in the singing of it. Verses 1 and 2 offer praise for the inner life of heart and spirit; verse 3 affirms that disability is one of the consequences of a fallen world; yet (it hints) not finally so. Verse 4 reminds us that God does not desert a suffering world, but bears our griefs and carries our sorrows. The final verses speak of God's new creation, and our resurrection bodies; while 'wondering eyes' is a direct allusion to the work of 'Compass Braille'.

276 O LORD, WHOSE SAVING NAME   66 66 44 44

Theme	Hospital and hospice; suffering; healing
Written	at Ford, January 1994
Suggested tune	DARWALL'S 148TH by John Darwall
Published in	*News of Hymnody*, July 1994 (words only)
	New Mission Praise, 1996 to DARWALL'S 148TH
	Supplement 99 (USA), 1999 to DARWALL'S 148TH
	Complete Mission Praise, 1999 to DARWALL'S 148TH

Great Ormond Street Children's Hospital in London is known and honoured the world over. In January 1994 the Chaplain approached me to say that they were planning a Service later in the year for the rededication of the hospital chapel, following extensive reconstruction. He wondered if I might write a hymn for the occasion. He described the hospital as a place where many are far from home; children are in pain, and parents torn between anxiety and hope; death has to be faced, not always as an enemy; and where healing is struggled for, by dedication and devotion, by science, often at the frontiers of knowledge, and by prayer.

He asked for a reflective hymn, suitable for a joyful occasion but touching on the themes of human vulnerability and dependence. He hoped it might not be obtrusively Trinitarian since parents and children of many faiths turn to the Chaplaincy for comfort and support.

Given this difficult but admirably expressed brief, I wondered at first whether I could meet his final request with Christian integrity. Then I remembered that I have in fact written a good many such texts, almost without realizing it (e.g. psalm paraphrases); and I determined to see what could be done to offer a Christ-centred text which was yet appropriate to the needs of such a wide and sensitive constituency. In fact, as can be seen, from the 'saving Name' (the name 'Jesus' means 'Saviour') followed by the allusion to Mark 10, the text moves from Christ the Light of the World, the true and living Way (John 8.12; 14.6), to that cross in which alone our deepest needs can be met; and beyond to the 'endless day' of heaven.

The hymn was first sung at the rededication of St Christopher's Chapel on Sunday 1 May 1994 in a televised Service during which the chapel was rededicated in the Name of Father, Son and Holy Spirit. I would like to think that the hymn may be of use to other hospital chaplains and in Services of Healing, where the two references to 'children' would not seem out of place.

In 1997, at the request of the Precentor of Winchester Cathedral, I made two slight alterations to allow the hymn to be used in a Service celebrating the work of the Hospice movement: see Index 6.

277 WHEN TO OUR WORLD THE SAVIOUR CAME   88 88 (LM)

Theme	Health and healing; medical missions
Written	at Bramerton, December 1977
Suggested tune	by Michael A. Baughen (see below)
	CANONBURY by Robert Schumann
	CHURCH TRIUMPHANT by James W. Elliott
	EISENACH by Johann H. Schein
Translated into	Chinese
Published in	*Medical Missionary Association Centenary Leaflet*, 1978 to music by Michael A. Baughen
	Anglican Hymn Book Supplement, 1978 (words only)
	Songs of Worship, 1980 to CHURCH TRIUMPHANT
	Making Melody, 1983 to CHURCH TRIUMPHANT
	The Lutheran (Australia), 25 May 1987 to SEBASTIENNE by Joanna Booth
	Mission Praise 2, 1987 to CHURCH TRIUMPHANT

Anglican Praise, 1987 to ANGELUS from Georg Joseph in *Heilige Seelenlust,* 1657
Supplement to Lutheran Hymnal (Australia), 1987 to SEBASTIENNE
Mission Praise Combined, 1990 to CHURCH TRIUMPHANT
Sounds of Grace (Hong Kong), 1991 to EISENACH (with a Chinese translation)
Complete Mission Praise, 1999 to CHURCH TRIUMPHANT
Common Praise, 2000 to CHURCH TRIUMPHANT
Praise!, 2000 to ABENDS by Herbert S. Oakeley

In December 1977 I was asked by the Secretary of the Medical Missionary Association if I would write a hymn for their centenary the following year. I was particularly glad to attempt this, since I had lived for four or five years before my marriage in their hostel in Bedford Place, London, a minister among medical students, while working for the Evangelical Alliance whose offices were adjacent. This hymn, to Michael Baughen's specially commissioned tune, was first sung at the Centenary Service of the Association.

The version printed here differs from that in most of the hymnals listed, as being shorter and more inclusive in its language. This is now my preferred version of the text, but the longer form is still available: see Index 6.

278 O GOD, WHOSE ALL-SUSTAINING HAND   88 88 88

Theme	Justice; civic occasions; community
Written	at Swansea and at Ford, March and April 1996
Suggested tune	COLCHESTER by Samuel S. Wesley
	MELITA by John B. Dykes
	SURREY by Henry Carey
Published in	*News of Hymnody,* October 1996 (words only)
	The Shrievalty Magazine, June 1997 (words only)
	Praise!, 2000 to MAGDALEN by John Stainer
	Glory Be (New Zealand), 2000 to ST PETERSBURG by D.N. Bortniansky

In many English counties a part of our civic life, where we are still seen to value our Christian history and inheritance, is the annual 'Justice Service' arranged by the High Sheriff and held in the Cathedral in the presence of one or more of Her Majesty's High Court Judges when on circuit in the county, together with representatives of the legal profession and those responsible for the maintenance of law and order.

In January 1996 I was approached on behalf of Peter Thistlethwayte who was shortly to take up office as High Sheriff of Essex; and asked if I would write a hymn for the Justice Service, using one of his favourite tunes, MELITA.

In commissions of this nature I prefer to be general rather than specific, in a way that will allow those who use the hymn to read into it their own particular concerns and prayers, within a wider framework of thought and petition on the given theme. And since law and justice are part of the foundation of community life, and it is from God himself that all justice ultimately derives, the hymn develops in terms of the just community, and our own hope of mercy through faith in Christ to save.

Theme	Social concern and the world's need; human rights
Written	at Ford, September 1998
Suggested tune	MARTYRDOM (Scottish traditional)
	ST MAGNUS by Jeremiah Clarke
	WILTSHIRE by George T. Smart
Published in	*Sing Glory*, 1999 to ST MAGNUS
	Common Praise, 2000 to WILTSHIRE
	Glory Be (New Zealand), 2000 to BILLING by Richard R. Terry

In August 1998 the Precentor of Salisbury Cathedral, Canon Jeremy Davies, wrote to tell me of a Festival of music and prayer in and around Salisbury Cathedral in December 1998, to celebrate the 50th Anniversary of the Universal Declaration of Human Rights; and to ask me to write a hymn for the occasion.

Because, fifty years on, there was much to celebrate and yet still more remaining to be done, the first line sets the tone as one of both praise and prayer. These receive a stanza each, and join hands again in verse 4. Certain phrases (for example, 'larger freedoms') are taken from the text of the Declaration; and the words 'universal right' in verse 5 echo its title.

The final couplet of verse 3 is a sad reversal of the Messianic prophecy of Isaiah 2.4; echoing the word of judgment of Joel 3.10. The last verse is a reminder to ourselves that our truest welfare must be in terms not only of human rights, but of the gospel and kingdom of our Lord Jesus Christ.

Theme	Writers and broadcasters; the Bible; 'a celebration of the word'
Written	at Ford, March 1998
Suggested tune	CRÜGER by Johann Crüger
	LANCASHIRE by Henry T. Smart
	ST THEODULPH by Melchior Teschner
Published in	*News of Hymnody*, July 1998 (words only)
	Cantate Domino, 2000 to BEATA VIRGO by Andrew Fletcher

In 1988 the Methodist Publishing House, which had been serving the cause of Christian literature since the days of the Wesleys, moved from London to Peterborough. Ten years later they planned to hold a Service of Thanksgiving, marking not only the anniversary, but their long and honourable history. This hymn was written at the request of Brian Thornton, the Chief Executive, to be sung at that Service on 1 June 1998 at Brookside Methodist Church.

But, as with most of my commissions, the text is sufficiently general to be appropriate for other occasions, when the task of Christian communication through the word is to be the theme. The structure of the hymn develops the thoughts of God's gift of words as follows:

Verse 1	The word in creation
Verse 2	The Word incarnate
	The word of Scripture
Verse 3	The word of Christian culture
Verse 4	The word of the gospel

Line 4 of verse 1 echoes Psalm 33.9 (where Coverdale had 'For loke what he sayeth, it is done'). Line 7 of verse 2 is a reminder of the Collect for the second Sunday in Advent ('Bible Sunday') in the *Book of Common Prayer*, transferred in *Common Worship* to the last Sunday after Trinity. Lines 3 and 4 of verse 3 may be recognized as based on a well-known prayer, which can be found in Frank Colqhoun's *Parish Prayers* (London 1967) as in other anthologies. In verse 4, line 3, the phrase 'foolishness of preaching' is the AV translation of 1 Corinthians 1.21.

281 FATHER ON HIGH TO WHOM WE PRAY   88 88 88

Theme	Home and family
Written	at Ruan Minor, August 1977
Suggested tune	ST CATHERINE by Henri F. Hemy
	ST MATTHIAS by William H. Monk
	WYCH CROSS by Erik Routley
Published in	*Songs of Worship*, 1980 to HOLY FAITH by George Martin
	The Hymn (USA), April 1981 (words only)
	Hymns for Today's Church, 1982 to ST MATTHIAS
	The Summit Choirbook (USA), 1983 to MOTHER OF THE
	CHURCH by the Dominican Nuns of Summit, New Jersey
	Baptist Praise and Worship, 1991 to ST MATTHIAS

Two elements combined to create this text. The final line of each verse, familiar as a response to intercessions since the first publication of the 'Alternative Services' of the Church of England, had long been in my mind for such a purpose. Then during 1977 I was asked for a further text on the theme of 'home'. The second and third lines of verse 2 read originally:

> 'and in our nature chose to be
> an alien child of homeless birth...'

It was Erik Routley who suggested that this could give rise to misunderstandings; and that I could not assume that all who might sing the hymn would recognize the circumstances implicit in those lines. Hence the introduction of 'Egypt's land' to show the meaning of the description 'alien'.

The Trinitarian form lends itself, I feel, to such a hymn of intercession and to the movement of thought from the human family and its home to the family of God and the hope of heaven.

Theme	The church; renewal; unity; ministry
Written	at Ruan Minor, August 1976
Suggested tune	LONDONDERRY AIR (Irish traditional)
Translated into	Chinese, French, Spanish
Published in	*Songs of Worship*, 1980 to LONDONDERRY AIR
	Hymns for Today's Church, 1982 to LONDONDERRY AIR
	Making Melody, 1983 to LONDONDERRY AIR
	Mission Praise 2, 1987 to LONDONDERRY AIR
	The Worshiping Church (USA), 1990 to LONDONDERRY AIR
	Mission Praise Combined, 1990 to LONDONDERRY AIR
	Songs of Celebration, 1991 to LONDONDERRY AIR (with a translation into French by Ann Maouyo and into Spanish by Joanna Benson)
	Baptist Praise and Worship, 1991 to LONDONDERRY AIR
	Sounds of Grace (Hong Kong), 1991 to JALAN LEBAN (with a Chinese translation)
	Hymns for the People, 1993 to LONDONDERRY AIR
	Spring Harvest Praise 94, 1994 to LONDONDERRY AIR
	Glory to God (Ireland), 1994 to LONDONDERRY AIR
	Songs of the People of God (USA), 1994 to LONDONDERRY AIR
	Lambeth Praise (USA), 1998 to LONDONDERRY AIR
	Complete Mission Praise, 1999 to LONDONDERRY AIR
	Sing Glory, 1999 to LONDONDERRY AIR
	Keswick Songbook, 2000 to LONDONDERRY AIR
	Church Hymnal (Ireland), 2000 to LONDONDERRY AIR
	Praise!, 2000 to MOORDOWN by Linda Mawson
	Sing to the Lord, 2000 to LONDONDERRY AIR
	The Bridge, 2001 to LONDONDERRY AIR
	Hymns of Heritage & Hope (USA), 2001 to LONDONDERRY AIR
Recorded on	*Keswick Praise 9*, 1994 to LONDONDERRY AIR
	Church Hymnal: Love of God, Life of Faith (Ireland), 2000 to LONDONDERRY AIR

'Christ over all' was the fine watchword of the National Evangelical Anglican Congress held at Keele University in 1967; and though this hymn was not written until nine years later, that was the source of the phrase which both starts and ends the text. The expression 'to turn to Christ' found a new currency in the Church of England with its inclusion as the first of the promises at Baptism and Confirmation in the Alternative Services; even though in Scripture the phrase is usually in the form 'turn to God' (Acts 26.20) or 'turn to the Lord' (Acts 9.35).

Line 4 of the final verse draws on the thought of the 'Prayer for the Church militant' in the *Book of Common Prayer* Service of Holy Communion, that the path to unity is to 'confess thy holy Name' and to 'agree in the truth of thy holy Word'.

Theme	The church; new life in Christ; the call of God
Written	at Ruan Minor, and Poldhu and Gwithian beaches, August 1990
Suggested tune	LUTHER (German traditional)
	JENSEN by William J. Reynolds
Published in	*100 Hymns of Hope* (USA), 1992 to JENSEN

The metre is not as unusual as it might appear at first sight. The CD-Rom *HymnQuest* (London 1997; 2000) lists 30 tunes to this metre, while the rather older *Hymns and Tunes Indexed* by David Perry (Croydon 1980), still an invaluable work of reference, gives 34 tunes. The hymn develops the thought of the church as God's new community, a community of love because it is the community of Jesus Christ.

284 GOOD NEWS OF GOD ABOVE 66 86 D (DSM)

Theme	Mission and evangelism
Written	at Ruan Minor, August 1985
Suggested tune	DIADEMATA by George J. Elvey
	ICH HALTE TREULICH STILL attributed to J.S. Bach
	TERRA BEATA by Franklin L. Sheppard
Published in	*Bible Sunday Hymns*, 1990 (words only)
	The Roy Hopp Hymnary (USA), 1990 to GENESIA by Roy Hopp
	Christian Worship: a Lutheran Hymnal (USA), 1993 to DOUSMAN
	by Kermit G. Moldenhauer
	Praise!, 2000 to BEAVERWOOD by Linda Mawson

Among the many categories into which hymns can be divided, this might be described as 'exhortatory'. It contains urgent encouragements to mission, to tell the news, to spread the seed, to make Christ known, to proclaim his love, sound his praise, and accept his call.

Verbal references to the Scriptures include: Jeremiah 31.3; Luke 8.11; Matthew 11.19; Romans 6.9; Galatians 5.1; Acts 20.21. Line 4 of the final verse looks back to each of the preceding verses with its 'make known, declare, proclaim'.

285 'HOW SHALL THEY HEAR,' WHO HAVE NOT HEARD 88 88 (LM)

Based on	Selected verses from Romans 10, Matthew 28, Isaiah 6
Theme	Mission and evangelism
Written	at Bramerton, December 1979
Suggested tune	BODMIN by Alfred S. Scott-Gatty
	DUKE STREET attributed to John Hatton
	MENDON from *The Methodist Harmonist*, 1821
Translated into	German

Published in   *Consultation Program,* Lausanne Committee for World
                                    Evangelization, Thailand, June 1980 (words only)
                         Programme and Information, Assembly of the National Initiative in
                                    Evangelism, UK, September 1980 (words only)
                         Declare His Glory, 1981 to OMBERSLEY by William H. Gladstone
                         Hymns for Praise and Worship (USA), 1984 to HURSLEY by
                                    William H. Monk from the *Katholisches Gesangbuch,* c.1774.
                         Mission Praise 2, 1987 to OMBERSLEY
                         Bible Sunday Hymns, 1990 (words only)
                         Mission Praise Combined, 1990 to OMBERSLEY
                         Hymnal Supplement 1998 (USA), 1988 to ANGELUS from *Cantica*
                                    Spiritualia, 1847
                         Songs of Victory (Scotland), 1999 to OMBERSLEY
                         Complete Mission Praise, 1999 to OMBERSLEY
                         Sing Glory, 1999 to OMBERSLEY

Late in 1979 Dr John Stott asked me to try my hand at a hymn for the Consultation on World Evangelization arranged by the Lausanne Committee for World Evangelization to be held at Pattaya in Thailand in June 1980.

'How shall they hear' was the theme of the Consultation, so Romans 10 furnished the first of the questions which begin each of the first four verses; but I did not see, when I began, that the other questions from Matthew 28 and Isaiah 6 would fit such a framework. The idea evolved as the text developed.

The text was first printed in the Consultation Program.

INDEXES

1 Index of Hymnals and Other Collections

Details of hymnals and other publications referred to in the Notes, by year of publication. The country of publication is England unless otherwise shown.

1965

Anglican Hymn Book, Church Book Room Press, London

1966

Youth Praise 1, Falcon Books, London

1969

Youth Praise 2, Falcon Books, London

100 Hymns for Today, Hymns Ancient & Modern, London

1970

Thirteen Psalms, Church Pastoral-Aid Society, London

1971

Sing Praise to God, Scolar Press, Menston, Yorkshire

Sing to God, Scripture Union, London

Renewal Songbook, Fountain Trust, London

Family Worship, Falcon Books, London

The Hymn Book, Anglican and United Church of Canada, Toronto, Ontario, Canada

1972

Catholic Book of Worship, Gordon V. Thompson Ltd, Toronto, Ontario, Canada

The Book of Praise, Presbyterian Church in Canada, Don Mills, Ontario, Canada

Thirty Hymns, Church Pastoral-Aid Society, London

1973

Psalm Praise, Falcon Books, London

Church Hymnary (third edition), Oxford University Press, London

The Hymnal, Baptist Federation of Canada, Ontario, Canada

1974

Sound of Living Waters, Hodder & Stoughton, London

The Hymnal of the United Church of Christ, United Church Press, Philadelphia, USA

Praise for Today, Psalms and Hymns Trust, London

Music for Courses 4 (Easter), Royal School of Church Music, Croydon, Surrey

1975

Hear the Bells of Christmas, OMF Publishers, Manila, Luzon, Philippines

Worship II, GIA Publications, Chicago, USA

Living Songs, Africa Christian Press, Achimota, Ghana

Keswick Praise, Trustees of the Keswick Convention, London

New Church Praise, St Andrew's Press, Edinburgh, Scotland

Sing a Celebration, Anglican Church in Western Australia, Perth, Australia

Grace Hymns, Grace Publications Trust, London (music edition 1977)

English Praise, Oxford University Press, London

1976

Westminster Praise, Hinshaw Music Inc., Chapel Hill, North Carolina, USA

Christian Worship, Paternoster Press, Exeter, Devon

Cliff Hymns, Cliff College,Calver, Sheffield

Hymns II, InterVarsity Press, Downers Grove, Illinois, USA

1977

The Australian Hymn Book, Collins, Sydney, Australia

Sixty Hymns from Songs of Zion, Praise Publications, Whittier, California, USA

Christian Hymns, Evangelical Movement of Wales, Bridgend, Mid Glamorgan, Wales

1978

Preist Ihn (in German), STIWA Drück und Verlag, Urbach, Germany

Sing to the Lord, Literature Crusades, Illinois, USA

Carols, Inter-Varsity Press, Downers Grove, Illinois, USA

Come and Praise, British Broadcasting Corporation, London

Anglican Hymn Book Supplement, Vine Books, London

Christmas Carols, Vine Books, London

Merrily to Bethlehem, A & C Black, London

1979

With One Voice (first published as *The Australian Hymn Book,* 1977), Collins, London

Hymns III, The Church Hymnal Corporation, New York, USA

Cantate Domino, GIA Publications, Chicago, USA

Pilgrim's Manual, Walsingham, Norfolk

Partners in Praise, Stainer & Bell, London

New Harvest, St Paul's Outreach Trust, Auckland, New Zealand

A Panorama of Christian Hymnody, The Liturgical Press, Collegeville, Minnesota, USA

1980

Pocket Praise, Stainer & Bell, London

Songs of Worship, Scripture Union, London

Cry Hosanna, Hodder & Stoughton, London

More Hymns for Today, Hymns Ancient & Modern, Colchester, Essex

Walsingham Devotions, Mayhew McCrimmon, Great Wakering, Essex

Lion Book of Favourite Hymns, Lion Publishing, Tring, Hertfordshire

Hymns Plus, Hinshaw Music, Chapel Hill, North Carolina, USA

Catholic Book of Worship II, Gordon V. Thompson Ltd, Toronto, Ontario, Canada

1981

Their Words, My Thoughts, Oxford University Press, Oxford

Declare His Glory, Universities and Colleges Christian Fellowship, Leicester

Broadcast Praise, Oxford University Press, London

Celebration Hymnal II, Mayhew McCrimmon, Great Wakering, Essex

Praise and Worship 2, Resource Christian Music, Victoria, Australia

1982

Lutheran Worship, Concordia, St Louis, USA

Jesus Praise, Scripture Union, London

A Purple Robe (five choral settings in Chinese), China Alliance Press, Hong Kong

A Supplement to Congregational Praise, The Congregational Federation, Nottingham

Hymns for Today's Church, Hodder & Stoughton, London

More Songs of the Spirit, Kevin Mayhew, Leigh-on-Sea, Essex

Gather to Remember, GIA Publications, Chicago, USA

Ten New Hymns in Praise of God, privately published by Michael Dawney, Poole, Dorset

Parish Sunday Vespers, Collins, London

Sing Praise, Kevin Mayhew, Leigh-on-Sea, Essex

Covenant Songs, Covenant Music, Victoria, Australia

Christian Hymns Observed, Prestige Publications, Princeton, New Jersey, USA

1983

Hymns for Today, Hymns Ancient & Modern, Norwich, Norfolk

Mission England Praise, Marshall Morgan and Scott, Basingstoke, Hampshire

Hymns Ancient & Modern New Standard Edition, Hymns Ancient & Modern, Norwich, Norfolk

Son of the Highest, Lillenas Publishing Company, Kansas City, Missouri, USA

Making Melody Hymn Book, Assemblies of God Publishing House, Nottingham

A Song was Heard at Christmas, Hope Publishing Company, Carol Stream, Illinois, USA

Hymns and Psalms, Methodist Publishing House, London

Choral Descants 5, Oregon Catholic Press, Portland, Oregon, USA

Mission Praise, Marshall Morgan and Scott, Basingstoke, Hampshire

New Creation Song Book, New Creation Teaching Ministry, Blackwood, South Australia

The Summit Choirbook, Monastery of Our Lady of the Rosary, Summit, New Jersey, USA

1984

Worship the King, Kingsway Publications, Eastbourne, Sussex

Hymnal Supplement, Agape, Carol Stream, Illinois, USA

Praise God Together, Scripture Union, London

Songs for Celebration, Diocese of Crookston, Minnesota, USA

Exalt Him, Lillenas Publishing Company, Kansas City, Missouri, USA

The Complete Celebration Hymnal, Mayhew McCrimmon, Great Wakering, Essex

Hymns Old & New (revised and enlarged), Kevin Mayhew, Bury St Edmunds, Suffolk

Hymns of Praise: well-loved hymns and their stories, Lion Publishing, Tring, Hertfordshire

Covenant Carols, Covenant Music, Victoria, Australia

Hymns for Praise and Worship, Evangel Press, Nappanee, Indiana, USA

The Iona Community Worship Book, Iona Abbey, Argyll, Scotland

1985

Work in Worship, Hodder & Stoughton, London

Twenty-one Hymns Old and New for use as Simple Anthems, Royal School of Church Music, Croydon, Surrey

The Singing Church, Hope Publishing Company, Carol Stream, Illinois, USA

Praise and Thanksgiving, Gresham Books, Henley-on-Thames, Oxfordshire

Rejoice in the Lord, Eerdmans Publishing Company, Grand Rapids, Michigan, USA

New Songs of Praise 1, Oxford University Press, Oxford

Carols for Christmas, Creative Publishing/Hodder & Stoughton, London

Today's Missal, Music Issue 1985, Oregon Catholic Press, Portland, Oregon, USA

Alternative Services of the Anglican Church of Canada, Anglican Book Centre, Toronto, Ontario, Canada

Hymns of Fellowship, Kingsway Publications, Eastbourne, Sussex

Today's Missal, Music Issue 1986, Oregon Catholic Press, Portland, Oregon, USA

Seventh Day Adventist Hymnal, Review & Herald Publishing Association, Washington DC, USA

Come and Journey, GIA Publications, Chicago, USA

To Be Your Bread, GIA Publications, Chicago, USA

The Hymnal 1982, The Church Hymnal Corporation, New York, USA

1986

The New English Hymnal, Canterbury Press, Norwich, Norfolk

All Praise to his Name, Royal School of Church Music, Croydon, Surrey

Choral Musicianship & Voice Training, Somerset Press, Carol Stream, Illinois, USA

Rejoising, FCYA, Dandenong, Victoria, Australia

Songifts, Hodder & Stoughton, London

Hymns Old & New (Anglican edition), Kevin Mayhew, Bury St Edmunds, Suffolk

Junior Praise, Marshall Pickering, Basingstoke, Hampshire

Singing for Peace, Hope Publishing Company, Carol Stream, Illinois, USA

Worship III, GIA Publications, Chicago, USA

Celebration, Hodder & Stoughton, London

King New-Born: four carols for Christmas, Royal School of Church Music, Croydon, Surrey

The Novello Book of Carols, Novello, London and Sevenoaks, Kent

The Hymnal for Worship and Celebration, Word Music, Waco, Texas, USA

Songs and Hymns of Fellowship, Kingsway Publications, Eastbourne, Sussex

'We Celebrate' Hymnal, J.S. Paluch Company, Schiller Park, Illinois, USA

The Christmas Road; an anthology, Church House Publishing, London

Hymns of Life (with Chinese translations), China Alliance Press, Hong Kong

'Celebrate Christmas with the World Church' pack, Methodist Church Overseas Division, London

Carols for Today, Hodder & Stoughton, London

The New Redemption Hymnal, Word UK, Milton Keynes, Buckinghamshire

Today's Missal, Music Issue 1987, Oregon Catholic Press, Portland, Oregon, USA

Church Family Worship, Hodder & Stoughton, London (words only: music edition 1988)

The Book of Praises, Carey Publications, Liverpool

1987

Spirit of Praise 2, Word Music UK, Milton Keynes, Buckinghamshire

The Lion Easter Book, Lion Publishing, Tring, Hertfordshire

A Pilgrim's Way, Mowbray, London

Your Favourite Songs of Praise, Oxford University Press/BBC Enterprises, Oxford

As Water to the Thirsty, GIA Publications, Chicago, USA

Sing a New Song!, Good News Christian Ministries, Northgate, New South Wales, Australia

The Broadcast Hymn Book, Oxford University Press, Oxford

New Songs of Praise 3, Oxford University Press, Oxford

Alive Now! July/August 1987, Nashville, Tennessee, USA

Mission Praise 2, Marshall Morgan and Scott, Basingstoke, Hampshire

Anglican Praise, Oxford University Press, Oxford

Supplement to Lutheran Hymnal, Lutheran Publishing House, Adelaide, Australia

Carol Praise, Marshall Morgan and Scott, Basingstoke, Hampshire

Together at Christmas, Lutheran Publishing House, Adelaide, Australia

Hymns for Today's Church (enlarged edition), Hodder & Stoughton, London

Rejoice!, Presbyterian Church of Australia, Sydney, Australia

Sing Alleluia, Collins Liturgical Publications, London

The Rainbow Songbook, Word Music UK, Milton Keynes, Buckinghamshire

Hymnal Supplement II, Agape, Carol Stream, Illinois, USA

O Sing with Joy to the Lord, International Fellowship of Evangelical Students, Harrow, Middlesex

A Survey of Christian Hymnody (third edition), Hope Publishing Company, Carol Stream, Illinois, USA

1988

Church Family Worship, Hodder & Stoughton, London

Best of Songs of the Spirit 1 & 2, Kevin Mayhew, Bury St Edmunds, Suffolk

Hymns & Songs for Worship, Cliff College Publishing, Calver, Sheffield

Sing to the Lord, Hodder & Stoughton, London

Winter Name of God, GIA Publications, Chicago, USA

Psalter Hymnal, CRC Publications, Grand Rapids, Michigan, USA

Christmas Carols and their Stories, Lion Publishing, Tring, Hertfordshire

Living Faith Worship Pack 2, Joint Board of Christian Education, Melbourne, Australia

Lift High your Songs, Paget Publications, Ashcott, Somerset

New Songs of Praise 4, Oxford University Press/BBC Publications, Oxford and London

Let's Praise!, Marshall Pickering, Basingstoke, Hampshire

Breaking Bread: Music Issue 1988, Oregon Catholic Press, Portland, Oregon, USA

Gather, GIA Publications, Chicago, USA

Spring Harvest Celebration Songbook 1988, Elm House/BYFC Joint Projects, Heathfield, East Sussex

1989

Today's Missal, Music Issue 1989, Oregon Catholic Press, Portland, Oregon, USA

Light the Candles Round the World, Paget Publications, Ashcott, Somerset

The Penguin Book of Hymns, Viking/Penguin Books, Harmondsworth, Middlesex

Get Together, Longman Group UK, Harlow, Essex

Hymn Sampler Eighty Nine, Agape, Carol Stream, Illinois, USA

The United Methodist Hymnal, United Methodist Publishing House, Nashville, Tennessee, USA

The Presbyterian Hymnal Sampler, Westminster/John Knox Press, Louisville, Kentucky, USA

The Wedding Book, Marshall Morgan & Scott, London

Spring Harvest Celebration Songbook, Spring Harvest, Heathfield, Sussex

Songs of Rejoicing, Selah Publishing Company, New Brunswick, New Jersey, USA

Carolling, Marshall Morgan and Scott, London

Sing for Joy, Review and Publishing Association, Washington DC, USA

Come Rejoice!, Marshall Pickering, Basingstoke, Hampshire/Hope Publishing Company, Carol Stream, Illinois, USA

Breaking Bread '90, Oregon Catholic Press, Portland, Oregon, USA

Segertona (in Swedish), Förlaget Filadelfia, Stockholm, Sweden

Mission Praise Supplement, Marshall Pickering, London

Sing Joyfully, Tabernacle Publishing Company, Carol Stream, Illinois, USA

Hymnal for the Hours, GIA Publications, Chicago, USA

1990

Sing to the Lord/Canwch I'r Arglwydd (in English and Welsh), Church in Wales Publications, Penarth, Glamorgan, Wales

The Keys of Bethlehem, Paget Publications, Ashcott, Somerset

The Promise of his Glory, Church House Publishing, London

Sing the Seasons, Kevin Mayhew, Bury St Edmunds, Suffolk

Irish Church Praise, APCK and Oxford University Press, Oxford

Psalms for Today, Hodder & Stoughton, Sevenoaks, Kent

Songs from the Psalms, Hodder & Stoughton, Sevenoaks, Kent

The Presbyterian Hymnal, Westminster/John Knox Press, Louisville, Kentucky, USA

Mission Praise Combined, Marshall Pickering, London

New Songs of Praise 5, Oxford University Press/BBC Publications, Oxford and London

New Song No 1, Hope Publishing Company, Carol Stream, Illinois, USA

The Alfred V. Fedak Hymnary, Selah Publishing Company, Accord, New York, USA

The Worshiping Church, Hope Publishing Company, Carol Stream, Illinois, USA

Bible Sunday Hymns, Bible Society, Swindon, Wiltshire

Daily Office, Community of the Holy Name, Derby, Derbyshire

Spring Harvest 1990 Songbook, Spring Harvest, Heathfield, Sussex

Sing and Pray, Sunday School Society for Ireland, Dublin, Ireland

The Roy Hopp Hymnary, Selah Publishing Company, Accord, New York, USA

The Song Goes On, Covenant Publications, Chicago, USA

New Creation Hymn Book, New Creation Publications, Blackwood, South Australia

Trinity Hymnal (revised edition), Great Commission Publications, Horsham,
  Pennsylvania, USA

1991

The Collegeville Hymnal, The Collegeville Press, Minnesota, USA

With Almost Every Voice, Kevin Mayhew, Bury St Edmunds, Suffolk

Celebrate the Growing, Scripture Union, Melbourne, Victoria, Australia

Today's Missal, Music Issue 1991, Oregon Catholic Press, Portland, Oregon, USA

A Guide to Prayer for all God's People, Upper Room Books, Nashville, Tennessee, USA

Michael Paget's Gaudeamus!, Paget Publications, Ashcott, Somerset

New Songs of Praise 6, Oxford University Press, Oxford

The Gospels Today, Stanley Thornes, Leckhampton, Cheltenham, Gloucestershire

Carols Old & New, Kevin Mayhew, Bury St Edmunds, Suffolk

The Baptist Hymnal, Convention Press, Nashville, Tennessee, USA

Songs of Fellowship, Kingsway Music, Eastbourne, Sussex

A Song at Christmas, Lion Publishing, Oxford

Twenty New Carols, Kevin Mayhew, Bury St Edmunds, Suffolk

Songs of Celebration, International Fellowship of Evangelical Students, Harrow,
  Middlesex

Spring Harvest Songbook 1991, Spring Harvest, Uckfield, Sussex

Rejoice and Sing, Oxford University Press (for the United Reformed Church), Oxford

Baptist Praise and Worship, Oxford University Press (for the Psalms and Hymns Trust),
  Oxford

The Popular Carol Book, Mowbrays, London

Day Trips to Heaven, Marshall Pickering, London

Thora Hird's Praise! Be Christmas Book, Fount, HarperCollins, London

Morning has Broken, Fount, HarperCollins, London

Sing his Praise, Gospel Publishing House, Springfield, Missouri, USA

Christmas Praise, Westminster/John Knox Press, Louisville, Kentucky, USA

The Complete Celebration Hymnal, McCrimmons, Great Wakering, Essex

GIA Hymnal Supplement 1991, GIA Publications, Chicago, USA

The Carl Schalk Hymnary Supplement, GIA Publications, Chicago, USA

Sounds of Grace (with Chinese translation), Christian Communications Ltd, Hong Kong

Ring of Praise, Anglican Information Office, Sydney, Australia

1992

All Things are Thine, Kevin Mayhew, Bury St Edmunds, Suffolk

The Puffin Book of Hymns, Penguin Books, London

Worship Songs Ancient & Modern, Canterbury Press, Norwich, Norfolk

Cliff Praise II, Cliff College, Calver, Sheffield

100 Hymns of Hope, Hope Publishing Company, Carol Stream, Illinois, USA

A New Hymnal for Colleges and Schools, Yale University Press, New Haven, Connecticut, USA

Hymnal: a worship book, Brethren Press, Elgin, Illinois, USA

Spring Harvest Praise 1992, Spring Harvest, Uckfield, Sussex

Carols Old & New (S.A. & men), Kevin Mayhew, Bury St Edmunds, Suffolk

Carols Old & New (Unison, two and three parts), Kevin Mayhew, Bury St Edmunds, Suffolk

Junior Praise 2, Marshall Pickering, London

New Song No 7, Hope Publishing Company, Carol Stream, Illinois, USA

1993

Breaking Bread 1993, Oregon Catholic Press, Portland, Oregon, USA

Music Issue 1993, Oregon Catholic Press, Portland, Oregon, USA

Affirmations of Faith, GS1038, Church House Publishing, London

The Yes of the Heart, Hope Publishing Company, Carol Stream, Illinois, USA

Honour His Name, Kevin Mayhew, Bury St Edmunds, Suffolk

Sing to the Lord, Lillenas Publishing Company, Kansas City, Missouri, USA

Hymns for the People, Marshall Pickering/Jubilate 2000, London

Praise the Lord, Hoddesdon Christadelphian Services, Bournemouth, Dorset

Hymn Sampler, Anglican Church of Canada Book Centre, Toronto, Ontario, Canada

Give Thanks to God on High: the choral music of Peter Cutts, Hope Publishing Company, Carol Stream, Illinois, USA

Drawn by a Dream: liturgical music by Dan Schutte, OCP Publications, Portland, Oregon, USA

United as One: liturgical music for weddings 2, OCP Publications, Portland, Oregon, USA

Breaking Bread 1994, Oregon Catholic Press, Portland, Oregon, USA

Christian Worship: a Lutheran Hymnal, Northwestern Publishing House, Milwaukee, Wisconsin, USA

Together Met, Together Bound, Selah Publishing Company, Accord, New York, USA

Spring Harvest Praise 1993, Spring Harvest, Uckfield, Sussex

1994

Fifteen Hymn Anthems, Kevin Mayhew, Bury St Edmunds, Suffolk

New Anthem Book 2 (SA men), Kevin Mayhew, Bury St Edmunds, Suffolk

Spring Harvest Praise 94, Spring Harvest, Uckfield, Sussex

Glory to God, Oxford University Press (for the Presbyterian Church in Ireland), Oxford

Power Praise 3, Kingsway Music, Eastbourne, Sussex

New Songs of Rejoicing, Selah Publishing Company, Kingston, New York, USA

Sing for Peace, Herald Publishing House, Independence, Missouri, USA

A Service of the Word and Affirmations of Faith, Church House Publishing, London

More Hazel's Hymns, Foundery Press, Peterborough, Cambridgeshire

The Novena, Redemptorist Publications, Alton, Hampshire

Journeysongs, Oregon Catholic Press, Portland, Oregon, USA

Songs for the People of God, Praise Publications, Whittier, California, USA

Catholic Book of Worship III, Canadian Conference of Catholic Bishops, Ottawa, Ontario, Canada

Gather (enlarged second edition), GIA Publications, Chicago, USA

Celebration Hymnal for Everyone, McCrimmon, Great Wakering, Essex

1995

With One Voice, Augsburg Fortress, Minneapolis, Minnesota, USA

Moravian Book of Worship, Moravian Church in America, Bethlehem, Pennsylvania, USA

Patterns for Worship, Church House Publishing, London

Chalice Hymnal, Chalice Press, St Louis, Missouri, USA

Breaking Bread 1995, Oregon Catholic Press, Portland, Oregon, USA

Worship Together, The Christian Press for the General Conference of the Mennonite Brethren Churches, Fresno, California, USA

Mission Praise Carol Leaflet, HarperCollins Religious, London

Renew! Songs and Hymns for Blended Worship, Hope Publishing Company, Carol Stream, Illinois, USA

Preparing for Worship, Marshall Pickering, London

Spring Harvest Praise 1995, Spring Harvest, Uckfield, Sussex

1996

Evangelical Lutheran Hymnary, Morning Star Publishers, St Louis, Missouri, USA

Supplement '96, Hope Publishing Company, Carol Stream, Illinois, USA

New Mission Praise, HarperCollins Religious, London

Today's Missal, Holy Week/Triduum 1966, Oregon Catholic Press, Portland, Oregon, USA

Today's Missal, Easter/Pentecost 1996, Oregon Catholic Press, Portland, Oregon, USA

Hymns Old & New (1996 edition), Kevin Mayhew, Bury St Edmunds, Suffolk

Songs for the Manger, Kevin Mayhew, Bury St Edmunds, Suffolk

Breaking Bread 1997, Oregon Catholic Press, Portland, Oregon, USA

Hymns for Prayer and Praise, Canterbury Press, Norwich, Norfolk

Sing to the Lord 2, Part 3, Salvationist Publishing and Supplies, London

The Covenant Hymnal, Covenant Publications, Chicago, USA

RitualSong, GIA Publications, Chicago, USA

New Hymns and Worship Songs, Kevin Mayhew, Bury St Edmunds, Suffolk

As One Voice 2, Willow Connection Pty, New South Wales, Australia

Visa Zeme Kungam Dzied (in Latvian), Rïgas metropolijas Romas katoju kārija, Rïga, Latvia

Voices United, United Church Publishing House, Etobicoke, Ontario, Canada

1997

Sing Hallelujah, Kingsway Music, Eastbourne, Sussex

Eleven New Anthems for Unison and Two Parts, Kevin Mayhew, Bury St Edmunds, Suffolk

The Companion Hymn Book, Whytecliffe Trust, Croydon, Surrey

Sing to the Lord (Children's Voice Series) 4, Salvationist Publishing and Supplies, London

Design Your Own Wedding Ceremony, Marshall Pickering, London

Worship in Song, Royal School of Church Music, Dorking, Surrey

Junior Praise Combined, Marshall Pickering, London

The Celebration Hymnal, Word/Integrity, USA

Sing to the Lord (Mixed Voice Series) 4, part 2, Salvationist Publishing and Supplies, London

With Almost Every Voice, Kevin Mayhew, Bury St Edmunds, Suffolk

Glory and Praise, OCP Publications, Portland, Oregon, USA

The Hymnal 21 (in Japanese), The United Church of Christ in Japan, Tokyo, Japan

Wonder, Love and Praise, The Church Publishing Corporation, New York, USA

Vaimulikud Laulud (in Estonian), Eesti Evangeeliumi Kristlaste ja Baptistide Koguduste Liit, Tallinn, Estonia

Today's Missal: Music Issue 1998, Oregon Catholic Press, Portland, Oregon, USA

BBC Songs of Praise, Oxford University Press/BBC Books, Oxford

Christingle Songbook, Children's Society, London

New Carols for Christmas, Kevin Mayhew, Bury St Edmunds, Suffolk

Prom Praise Solos 2, Christian Focus Publications, Tain, Ross-shire, Scotland

The Book of Praise, Presbyterian Church in Canada, Don Mills, Ontario, Canada

1998

Get Together, Longman Group UK Ltd, Harlow, Essex

The Source, Kevin Mayhew, Bury St Edmunds, Suffolk

Hymnal (in Chinese), Taipei Ling-Leung Church, Taiwan

Youth Challenge Chorus Book, Child Evangelism Fellowship of Ireland, Jurgan, Ireland

Songs of Fellowship 2, Kingsway Music, Eastbourne, Sussex

Our Growing Years, GIA Publications, Chicago, USA

Celebrate! Songs for Renewal, Praise Publications, Whittier, California, USA

Lambeth Praise, Morehouse Publishing, Harrisburg, Pennsylvania, USA

Peculiar Honours, Stainer & Bell, London

Spring Harvest Praise 1998 (with Welsh edition *Grym Mawl 2*), Spring Harvest, Uckfield, Sussex

The Catholic Hymn Book, Fowler Wright Books, Leominster, Herefordshire

Jesus Through Art, Religious and Moral Education Press in association with National Gallery Publications, London

Common Ground, Saint Andrew Press, Edinburgh, Scotland

Hymnal Supplement 1998, Concordia Publishing House, St Louis, Missouri, USA

Singing Faith, Methodist Publishing House, Peterborough, Cambridgeshire

Korean-English Hymnal (in Korean and English), Korean Adventist Press, Los Angeles, California, USA

Anthems New & Old, Kevin Mayhew, Stowmarket, Suffolk

Songs of Victory, The Faith Mission, Edinburgh, Scotland

Common Praise (Anglican Church of Canada), Anglican Book Centre, Toronto, Ontario, Canada

Poems of Grace: texts from The Hymnal 1982, Church Publishing, New York, USA

Word and Song 2000, J.S. Paluch Company, Schiller Park, Illinois, USA

1999

Worship 2000!, HarperCollins, London

Spring Harvest Praise 99, Spring Harvest, Uckfield, Sussex

New Start Hymns and Songs, Kevin Mayhew, Stowmarket, Suffolk

Laudate, Decani Music, Mildenhall, Suffolk

Liturgical Hymns Old & New, Kevin Mayhew, Stowmarket, Suffolk

Supplement 99, Hope Publishing Company, Carol Stream, Illinois, USA

The Penguin Book of Carols, Penguin Books, London

Fifty New Anthems for Mixed Voices, Kevin Mayhew, Stowmarket, Suffolk

Catholic Supplement, Kevin Mayhew, Stowmarket, Suffolk

Breaking Bread (an edition of Today's Missal) Jubilee 2000, Oregon Catholic Press, Portland, Oregon, USA

A Survey of Christian Hymnody (revised and enlarged), Hope Publishing Company, Carol Stream, Illinois, USA

Complete Mission Praise, Marshall Pickering, London

Merrily on High, Novello, London

Sing and Praise, Wise Publications, London

Anthems Old & New for SA Men 1, Kevin Mayhew, Stowmarket, Suffolk

Sing Glory, Kevin Mayhew/Jubilate, Stowmarket, Suffolk

Jesus' People Sing Songbook, Concordia Publishing House, St Louis, Missouri, USA

Grace Praise, Grace & Truth Publications, Christchurch, New Zealand

Together in Song (Australian Hymn Book II), HarperCollins, Melbourne, Victoria, Australia

2000

Praise the Lord (revised edition), Hoddesdon Christadelphian Services, Audlem, Cheshire

Praying in Song, Kevin Mayhew, Stowmarket, Suffolk

The Anthems of Malcolm Archer, Kevin Mayhew, Stowmarket, Suffolk

The Care of Creation, IVP, Leicester

Short Anthems for Small Choirs, Kevin Mayhew, Stowmarket, Suffolk

Complete Anglican Hymns Old & New, Kevin Mayhew, Stowmarket, Suffolk

Common Praise (a new edition of *Hymns Ancient and Modern),* Canterbury Press, Norwich, Norfolk

Keswick Songbook, Kevin Mayhew, Stowmarket, Suffolk

Church Hymnal, Oxford University Press (for the Church of Ireland), Oxford

Praise!, Praise Trust, Darlington, Co. Durham

Sing to the Lord, St Paul's Cathedral, London

Cantate Domino, Kevin Mayhew, Stowmarket, Suffolk

Christmas Rhymes and Carols, Lion Publishing, Oxford

Common Worship, Church House Publishing, London

Glory Be, Christchurch Cathedral, Christchurch, New Zealand

Rejoice in God: the K. Lee Scott hymnary, Morning Star Music Publishers, St Louis, Missouri, USA

2001

First Fruits, Canterbury Press (for the Anglican Stewardship Association), Norwich, Norfolk

The Bridge, Kevin Mayhew, Stowmarket, Suffolk

Twelve Hymns (to tunes by Maurice Bevan), Cathedral Music, Chichester, Sussex

The Poetic Bible, SPCK, London

Caneuon Ffydd (in Welsh and English), Pen-y-groes, Caernarfon, Gwynedd, Wales

Spring Harvest Praise 2001, Spring Harvest, Uckfield, Sussex

Worship Today, Spring Harvest, Uckfield, Sussex

New Hymns and Worship Songs (revised and enlarged), Kevin Mayhew, Stowmarket, Suffolk

Worship & Rejoice, Hope Publishing Company, Carol Stream, Illinois, USA

Sing to the Lord no Threadbare Song, Selah Publishing Company, New York, USA

Methodist Hymns Old & New, Kevin Mayhew, Stowmarket, Suffolk

Beneath a Travelling Star, Canterbury Press, Norwich, Norfolk

The Young Choir Songbook, Kevin Mayhew, Stowmarket, Suffolk

Picture Talk, St Edmund's Press, Salisbury, Wiltshire

Favourite Hymns, Continuum International Publishing Group, London

Hymns of Heritage & Hope, Advent Christian General Conference of America Inc., Charlotte, North Carolina, USA

Salmer Underveis (in Norwegian), Norsk, Luthersk Forlag, Oslo, Sweden

Moral Landscape of Creation, 'Christian Reflection', Baylor University, Texas, USA

2 Index of Anthems and Other Sheet Music

Details of anthems and other choral settings referred to in the Notes,
arranged under the opening words of the text and by year of publication.
The country of publication is England unless otherwise shown.

1978

249 *Christ be my leader by night as by day*

    set to SLANE harmonized by Henry V. Gerike for S.A.T.B., Oboe (Flute), and Organ; Concordia Choral Series, Concordia Publishing House, St Louis, Missouri, USA (Ref. 98-2378)

277 *When to our world the Saviour came*

    set to a tune by Michael A. Baughen, arranged by Noël Tredinnick; Medical Missionary Association, London

1980

215 *Glory to God in the highest*

    set by Richard Proulx to his tune RUSSWIN, for unison voices and Organ with S.A.T.B. and descants; in 'Two new hymn tunes by Richard Proulx'; GIA Publications, Inc., Chicago, Illinois, USA (Ref. G-2310)

1981

136 *The stars declare his glory*

    set by Hal H. Hopson for S.A.T.B. with Organ accompaniment; H.W. Gray Publications, Melville, New York, USA (Ref. GCMR 3450)

235 *As water to the thirsty*

    set by Hal H. Hopson for S.A.T.B. a cappella; Agape, Carol Stream, Illinois, USA (Ref. JM 4079)

1982

13 *Chill of the nightfall*

    set by Hal H. Hopson for S.A.B., accompanied; Agape, Carol Stream, Illinois, USA (Ref. HH 3919)

161 *Sing a new song to the Lord*

    set by John F. Wilson, for S.A.T.B. a cappella; for the 75th anniversary of the Chicago Sunday Evening Club; Hope Publishing Co., Carol Stream, Illinois, USA (Ref. A538)

13 *Chill of the nightfall*

    set by Robert Kircher, arranged by Dick Bolks for S.A.T.B.; Beacon Hill Music, Kansas City, Missouri, USA (Ref. AN-3900)

176 *Praise the Lord of heaven*

    set by Hal H. Hopson for S.A.T.B. with accompaniment for Organ and optional Brass Quartet and optional Handbells; H.W. Gray Publications, Melville, New York, USA (Ref. GCMR 3462)

51 *A purple robe, a crown of thorn* (Chinese)

set by David G. Wilson to his tune A PURPLE ROBE as one of five choral settings in Chinese in a collection of the same name, translated and arranged by S.Y. Suen; China Alliance Press, Hong Kong.

13 *Chill of the nightfall*

set by John Horman for mixed voices, S.A.T.B. with Keyboard; Hinshaw Music Inc., Chapel Hill, North Carolina, USA (Ref. HMC-488)

1983

13 *Chill of the nightfall*

set by Richard E. Frey for unison/2 part with Handbells (or Harp or Piano), Organ and optional Strings; distributed by the Lorenz Corporation, Dayton, Ohio, USA for the Choristers Guild, Garland, Texas, USA (Ref. CGA-292)

1984

29 *Hush you, my baby*

set to CRADLE SONG and PASSION CHORALE arranged by Carlton R. Young for unison and mixed voices, Keyboard and Handbells; Agape, Carol Stream, Illinois, USA (Ref. AG 7271)

1985

212 *Tell out, my soul, the greatness of the Lord*

set to WOODLANDS by Walter Greatorex arranged by John F. Wilson for S.A.T.B. Choir, Organ and Brass Quartet (optional); Hope Publishing Co., Carol Stream, Illinois, USA (Ref. F 982)

167 *I lift my eyes*

set by John Carter for S.A.T.B. and Piano; Hope Publishing Co., Carol Stream, Illinois, USA (Ref. JS 294)

73 *Spirit of God within me*

set by Michael Joncas as a concertato to his tune WILLOW RIVER (in honour of the 100th anniversary of St Vincent de Paul Church, Churchville, New York), for S.A.T.B., congregation and Organ; GIA Publications, Inc., Chicago, Illinois, USA (Ref. G-2831)

235 *As water to the thirsty*

set by John Carter for S.A.T.B. and Keyboard; Hope Publishing Co., Carol Stream, Illinois, USA (Ref. JC 297)

85 *This day above all days*

set by Douglas E. Wagner for S.A.T.B. with optional Trumpet (Ref. A-585-B); Hope Publishing Co., Carol Stream, Illinois, USA (Ref. A-585)

38 *The darkness turns to dawn*

set by John F. Wilson based on the tunes ST THOMAS and ST ANDREWS adapted from an arrangement by Phillip Landgrave for S.A.T.B. Choir and congregation with Keyboard and optional Brass Quartet; Hope Publishing Co., Carol Stream, Illinois, USA (Ref. F 981)

1987

35 *See, to us a child is born*

set by Gary Matheny for S.A.T.B. with solo (or treble Choir) and Handbells and/or Keyboard; Agape, Carol Stream, Illinois, USA (Ref. RS 7718)

8   *A song was heard at Christmas*

set by Cindy Johnston for S.A.T.B. and Piano; GIA Publications, Inc., Chicago, Illinois, USA (Ref. G-3060)

36   *Soft the evening shadows fall*

set by John Carter for S.A.T.B. with Keyboard accompaniment; Hope Publishing Co., Carol Stream, Illinois, USA (Ref. A 604)

1988

161   *Sing a new song to the Lord* (Swedish)

set by David G. Wilson to his tune ONSLOW SQUARE in a Swedish translation by Gunn-Britt Holgersson, 'Sjung en ny sang till far Gud', arranged by Lennart Jernestrand; Dagn, Stockholm, Sweden (Ref. 822382)

181   *The heavens are singing, are singing and praising*

set by John Carter for S.A.T.B. Choir, congregation and Keyboard; Beckenhorst Press, Inc., Columbus, Ohio, USA (Ref. BP 1310)

215   *Glory to God in the highest*

set by John Carter for three-part mixed voices with Keyboard accompaniment; Providence Press, Carol Stream, Illinois, USA (Ref. PP 109)

36   *Soft the evening shadows fall*

set by Alec Wyton as 'a carol for Christmas pilgrims' for S.A.T.B., Flute, Handbells, Percussion and Organ; Paraclete Press, Orleans, Massachusetts, USA (Ref. PPM 08806)

90   *We come as guests invited*

set by Judy Hunnicutt for S.A.T.B; Hope Publishing Co., Carol Stream, Illinois, USA (Ref. A-625)

1989

175   *Fill your hearts with joy and gladness*

set by Eugene Englebert for S.A.T.B. and Organ; GIA Publications, Inc., Chicago, Illinois, USA (Ref. G-2867)

117   *God whose love is everywhere*

set by Noël Tredinnick in 'Two new hymns in celebration of Christingle' to his tune · FALLING FIFTHS; The Children's Society, London

1990

212   *Tell out, my soul, the greatness of the Lord*

set by V. Earle Copes to WOODLANDS by Walter Greatorex for S.A.T.B., Organ or Piano; Hope Publishing Co., Carol Stream, Illinois, USA (Ref. CY 3365)

86   *An upper room with evening lamps ashine*

set by David W. Music based on EVENTIDE by William H. Monk for S.A.T.B., optional congregation, and Keyboard; Concordia Publishing House, St Louis, Missouri, USA (Ref. 98-2875); Re-issued by Augsburg Fortress 1990 (Ref. 11-10068)

12   *Child of the stable's secret birth*

set by Valerie Ruddle for S.A.T.B.; Stainer & Bell, London (Ref. W-183)

212   *Tell out, my soul, the greatness of the Lord*

set by Scott Soper for Assembly, two-part Choir, Guitar and Keyboard; OCP Publications, Portland, Oregon, USA (Ref. 9350)

13 *Chill of the nightfall*

set by Gary James for two-part voices and Keyboard; Morning Star Music Publishers, St Louis, Missouri, USA (Ref. MSM-50-1401)

1991

224 *Who is Jesus? Friend of sinners*

set by Jeffrey Honoré for S.A.T.B., Keyboard and optional Flute; Hope Publishing Co., Carol Stream, Illinois, USA (Ref. A 640)

60 *Christ is risen as he said*

antiphon by John Carter for Choir and congregation with Keyboard; Hope Publishing Co., Carol Stream, Illinois, USA (Ref. A 648)

71 *Be present, Spirit of the Lord*

set by Mary Kay Beall for 2-part mixed voices with Keyboard; Providence Press, Carol Stream, Illinois, USA (Ref. PP 128)

46 *Within a crib my Saviour lay*

set by Walt Harrar, arranged by Jack Schrader, under the title 'Glory be to Jesus' for S.A.T.B. and Keyboard; Hope Publishing Co., Carol Stream, Illinois, USA (Ref. GC 924)

103 *Here within this house of prayer*

set by Richard Proulx to the tune CENTRAL CHURCH for S.A.T.B., congregation, Organ, Brass Quartet and Timpani, commissioned by Central Presbyterian Church, Buffalo, New York; GIA Publications, Inc., Chicago, Illinois, USA (Ref. G-3477)

190 *Not for tongues of heaven's angels*

set by Roy Hopp, based on his tune REINLYN, for S.A.T.B., Organ and optional congregation; Selah Publishing Co., Accord, New York, USA (Ref.425-815)

11 *Child of Mary, newly born*

set by Austin C. Lovelace for S.A.T.B. Choir and Keyboard; Randall M. Egan Ltd., The Kenwood Press, Minneapolis, Minnesota, USA

1992

160 *The everlasting Lord is King*

set by John Carter for S.A.T.B. voices, Trumpet and Organ, with the dedication 'Composed in honour of Timothy Dudley-Smith on the occasion of his retirement as Bishop of Thetford'; Hope Publishing Co., Carol Stream, Illinois, USA (Ref. A 659)

89 *The Lord is here*

set by John Carter for S.A.T.B. with Keyboard; Hope Publishing Co., Carol Stream, Illinois, USA (Ref. A 656)

266 *'Set your troubled hearts at rest'*

set by Jeffrey Honoré for S.A.T.B. for Keyboard with optional descant; World Library Publications, Inc., Schiller Park, Illinois, USA (Ref. 8562)

35 *See, to us a child is born*

set by Alan Ridout for S.A.T.B.; Mayhew/Brodt, Charlotte, North Carolina, USA (Ref. KM 505)

157 *Safe in the shadow of the Lord*

set by Paul Inwood for Assembly, S.A.T.B. Choir and Organ; OCP Publications, Portland, Oregon, USA (Ref. 7196)

46 *Within a crib my Saviour lay*

set by Jeffrey Honoré under the title 'All Glory be to Jesus' for S.A.T.B. Choir a cappella, and optional C instrument; World Library Publications, Schiller Park, Illinois, USA (Ref. 8574)

1993

212 *Tell out, my soul, the greatness of the Lord*

set by K. Lee Scott for S.A.T.B., Flute, Handbells and Organ to the 15th century chanson 'L'amour de moi'; Concordia Publishing House, St Louis, Missouri, USA (Ref. 98-3096)

269 *What colours God has made*

set by Austin C. Lovelace for unison voices and Keyboard; Selah Publishing Co., Inc., Accord, New York, USA (Ref. 422-830)

11 *Child of Mary, newly born*

set by Gordon Lawson for S.A.T.B. and Organ in 'Three Carols for Christmas'; Randall M. Egan, Minneapolis, Minnesota, USA (Ref. EC-307)

6 *When the Lord in glory comes*

set by Bob Moore for Choir, congregation, Guitar, Piano, Flute and Oboe; GIA Publications, Inc., Chicago, Illinois, USA (Ref. G-3841)

90 *We come as guests invited*

set by Austin C. Lovelace for S.A.T.B. as an arrangement of the tune WEDLOCK; Augsburg Fortress, USA (Ref. 11-10259)

1994

105 *Lord, for the years your love has kept and guided*

set by Allen Pote for mixed voices and Organ with two optional Trumpets, commissioned for the First Christian Church, Arlington, Texas; The Sacred Music Press, Dayton, Ohio, USA (Ref. 10/1131)

167 *I lift my eyes*

set by Bret Heim for S.A.T.B., Oboe and Organ to his tune PLEASANT HILL; Concordia Publishing House, St Louis, Missouri, USA (Ref. 98-3129)

25 *Here is the centre: star on distant star*

set by Russell Schulz-Widmar under the title 'A Carol for Christmas' for S.A.T.B. voices and Organ; GIA Publications, Inc., Chicago, Illinois, USA (Ref. G-3850)

45 *Where do Christmas songs begin?*

set by Bob Moore for S.A.T.B. voices and Piano; GIA Publications, Inc., Chicago, Illinois, USA (Ref. G-3851)

13 *Chill of the nightfall*

set by Hal H. Hopson for two-part equal voices with Keyboard accompaniment; Agape, Carol Stream, Illinois, USA (Ref. HH3950)

11 *Child of Mary, newly born* (Danish)

set by Donald Davison and T. Larsen to LYNCH'S LULLABY, in a Danish translation by Beate Højlund, 'Lille barn pa krybbestra'; Luthersk Missionsforenings Nodeforlag, Skjern, Denmark (Ref. B-33)

188 *Living Lord, our praise we render* (Danish)

set by Norman Warren and Lars Christensen to a tune by Michael A. Baughen in a Danish translation by Beate Højlund, 'Krist opstanden'; Luthersk Missionsforenings Nodeforlag, Skjern, Denmark (Ref. B-32)

1995

254 *May the love of Christ enfold us*

set by Mary Kay Beall for S.A.T.B. voices, Flute and Keyboard to BEECHER by John Zundel; Hope Publishing Company, Carol Stream, Illinois, USA (Ref. A696)

116 *O Christ the same, through all our story's pages*

set by Michael Conolly for S.A.T.B., congregation, Organ and optional Brass quartet and Timpani; GIA Publications, Inc., Chicago, Illinois, USA (Ref. G-4033)

213 *Faithful vigil ended*

set by Neo Nestor for S.A.T.B. and Organ, to his hymn tune WILLIAM; Selah Publishing Co., Inc., Kingston, New York, USA (Ref. 410-723)

192 *Fruitful trees, the Spirit's sowing*

set by Bret Heim and Roy Hopp for S.A.T.B. and Organ to their tune ORCHARD VIEW; Concordia Publishing House, St Louis, Missouri, USA (Ref. 98-3181)

65 *Now is Christ risen from the dead*

set by Donald Hustad under the title 'An Easter Hodie' for S.A.T.B., Organ and two optional Trumpets based on LASST UNS ERFREUEN; Hope Publishing Co., Carol Stream, Illinois, USA (Ref. A 701)

98 *We turn to Christ anew*

set by Ian Kellam; The Royal School of Church Music, Croydon, Surrey (Ref. A 510)

54 *Dear Lord, who bore our weight of woe*

set by Ian Kellam for S.A.T.B. or Choir in unison, with Piano or Organ accompaniment; The Royal School of Church Music, Croydon, Surrey (Ref. A 511)

167 *I lift my eyes*

set by Carl Johengen for Cantor, assembly, Flute, Oboe and Keyboard; World Library Publications, Schiller Park, Illinois, USA (Ref. 5207)

1996

194 *The best of gifts is ours*

set by K. Lee Scott for S.A.T.B. Choir, Keyboard and congregation; The Beckenhorst Press, Inc., Columbus, Ohio, USA (Ref. BP 1445)

237 *He comes to us as one unknown*

set to REPTON arranged by Paul Nicholson for S.A.T.B., Organ, Cello or Horn; Augsburg Fortress, USA (Ref.11-10736)

28 *How silent waits the listening earth*

set by Richard Proulx for S.A.T.B.; Kevin Mayhew, Bury St Edmunds, Suffolk (Ref. KM213)

34 *Peace be yours and dreamless slumber*

set by Norman Warren for S.A.T.B.; Kevin Mayhew, Bury St Edmunds, Suffolk (Ref. KM214)

237 *He comes to us as one unknown*

set by John Ferguson to REPTON arranged for S.A.T.B. voices; Augsburg Fortress, USA (Ref. 11-10742)

45 *Where do Christmas songs begin?*

set by Malcolm Archer for S.A.T.B. with Keyboard; Hinshaw Music Inc., Chapel Hill, North Carolina, USA (Ref. HMC 1456)

253 *From life's bright dawn to eventide*

set by Austin C. Lovelace for S.A.T.B. a cappella based on music by Mozart, under the title 'The Virtues Three'; Abingdon Press, Nashville, Tennessee, USA (Ref. 502624)

1997

13 *Chill of the nightfall*

set by Richard Jeffrey, arranged by Mark Kellner, for S.A.T.B, Flute, Piano and optional Guitar, under the title 'Carol of the Stable'; Concordia Publishing House, St Louis, Missouri, USA (Ref. 98-3347)

240 *So the day dawn for me*

set by David Haas for Choir, assembly, Guitar, Keyboard and C instrument, from the collection 'Throughout all time'; GIA Publications Inc., Chicago, Illinois, USA (Ref. G-4686)

190 *Not for tongues of heaven's angels*

set by Richard W. Gieseke for S.A.B. or S.A.T.B. and Keyboard under the title 'May love be ours, O Lord'; Concordia Publishing House, St Louis, Missouri, USA (Ref. 98-3349)

245 *Jesus my breath, my life, my Lord*

set by K. Lee Scott for S.A.T.B.; Concordia Publishing House, St Louis, Missouri, USA (Ref. 98-3387)

51 *A purple robe, a crown of thorn*

set by Bret Heim for S.A.T.B. and Keyboard; Concordia Publishing House, St Louis, Missouri, USA (Ref. 98-3399)

190 *Not for tongues of heaven's angels*

set by John A. Behnke to his tune SOFFNER for two-part Choir with Keyboard under the title 'May love be ours, O Lord'; Art Masters Studios, Inc., Minneapolis, Minnesota, USA (Ref.770)

1998

16 *Christ is come! Let earth adore him*

set by Austin Lovelace for unison voices and Keyboard; GIA Publications, Inc., Chicago, Illinois, USA (Ref. G-4697)

29 *Hush you, my baby*

set by Scott M. Hyslop for S.A.T.B., Organ and Oboe; Augsburg Fortress, USA, (Ref.11-10885)

26 *Holy child, how still you lie*

set by Kurt von Kampen for S.A.T.B., Piano and Oboe, with optional Guitar and Flute, to the tune by Michael A. Baughen; Concordia, Publishing House, St Louis, Missouri, USA (Ref.98-3464)

39 *The hush of midnight here below*

set by Valerie Ruddle for S.A.T.B. Choir; Harvey Choral Music, Sevenoaks, Kent

2001

209 *We come with songs of blessing*

set by K. Lee Scott for S.A.T.B. and Organ with optional Brass quartet, Timpani and congregation; Morning Star Music Publishers, St Louis, Missouri, USA (Ref. MSM-50-7045A)

108 *Give thanks to God on high*

set by K. Lee Scott for S.A.T.B. and Organ with optional Brass quartet, Handbells and congregation; Morning Star Music Publishers, St Louis, Missouri, USA (Ref. MSM-50-7046A)

167 *I lift my eyes*

set by Ronald Arnatt for mezzo-soprano Solo, S.A.T.B. Chorus and Organ; ECS Publishing, Boston, Massachusetts, USA (Ref. 5475)

66 *Our risen Lord, our King of kings*

set by Bob Moore for Choir, Cantor, assembly, Guitar and Piano with optional 2 C instruments; GIA Publications, Inc., Chicago, Illinois, USA (Ref. G-5348)

167 *I lift my eyes*

set by Ian Kellam for mixed voices with Organ; Escorial Edition, Norwich, Norfolk

9 *A stone to be the lintel*

set by Steven R. Janco for S.A.B. Choir, Descant, optional assembly, C Instrument, Guitar and Keyboard under the title 'Wood is for the Manger'; World Library Publications, J.S. Paluch Company, Schiller Park, Illinois, USA (Ref. 8707)

234 *Christ, our human likeness sharing*

set by Maurice Bevan as a Hymn Anthem to his tune KESTER; Cathedral Music, Racton, West Sussex (Ref. CM 871)

3 Index of Recordings

*Audio-recordings (LPs, cassettes and CDs) referred to in the Notes,
arranged by year of issue under the title of the recording, followed by
the opening words of the text or texts, and an indication of the tune.
See reference to audio-recordings in the Preface, page ix.
The country of issue is England unless otherwise stated.*

1965

Hymns from the New Anglican Hymn Book: LP LLR 533

> presented by the London Recital Group, conducted by Richard Sinton, organist Robin Sheldon

> > 212 Tell out, my soul, the greatness of the Lord *to* TIDINGS

1969

A Tribute to Youth Praise: Key LP KL 003

> sung by the Crusader Youth Singers, Elim Church, Portsmouth, led by Dave Smith

> > 6 When the Lord in glory comes *to* GLORIOUS COMING

1975

Here is Youth Praise: Reflection LP RL 308

> sung by Charisma, and the congregation of All Souls Church, Langham Place, London

> > 105 Lord, for the years your love has kept and guided *to* LORD OF THE YEARS

> > 51 A purple robe, a crown of thorn *to* A PURPLE ROBE

Here is Psalm Praise: Reflection LP RL 311

> with the choir, orchestra and friends of All Souls Church, Langham Place, London

> > 155 Timeless love! We sing the story *to* TIMELESS LOVE

> > 248 No weight of gold or silver *to* ARGENT

> > 167 I lift my eyes *to* UPLIFTED EYES

> > 212 Tell out, my soul, the greatness of the Lord *to* TELL OUT, MY SOUL

> > 199 He walks among the golden lamps *to* REVELATION

All Souls Celebrates: Word LP WST 9539

> with the choir, orchestra and congregation of All Souls Church, Langham Place, London, conducted by Noël Tredinnick

> > 212 Tell out, my soul, the greatness of the Lord *to* WOODLANDS

Christmas Music: Philips LP 6833 157

> sung by the choir of St Paul's Cathedral, London, directed by Christopher Dearnley, organist Christopher Herrick

> > 12 Child of the stable's secret birth *to* MORWENSTOW

1976

Christmas Praise: Fountain LP LFTN 2501, cassette TC-FTN 2501

> with the Croft children's choir under the direction of Joyce Farrington; and Kerry Eighteen, soloist
>
> > 26 Holy child, how still you lie *to* HOLY CHILD

I Lift my Eyes to the Quiet Hills: InterVarsity Records, USA LP IVR tm

> sung by a choir, with musical ensemble, directed by Hughes Huffman, Director of Music, Christ Church of Oak Brook, Illinois, USA
>
> > 167 I lift my eyes *to* LIFT MY EYES

Liverpool Cathedral Festival of Praise: Abbey LP MVP 774

> with the Cathedral Choir, diocesan church choirs, and the Merseyside Police Band (Brass section), directed by Ronald Woan, organist Noel Rawsthorne
>
> > 212 Tell out, my soul, the greatness of the Lord *to* WOODLANDS

1978

Psalm Praise - Sing a New Song: Word LP WST 9586

> with the choir, orchestra and congregation of All Souls Church, Langham Place, London under the direction of Noël Tredinnick
>
> > 161 Sing a new song to the Lord *to* ONSLOW SQUARE
> >
> > 157 Safe in the shadow of the Lord *to* CREATOR GOD
> >
> > 208 God of gods, we sound his praises *to* GOD OF GODS

1980

Songs of Worship: Word LP WST 9590

> with the All Souls Singers, conducted by Noël Tredinnick, from All Souls Church, Langham Place, London
>
> > 90 We come as guests invited *to* PASSION CHORALE

1982

Lydia Servant Songs: Anchor cassette AR 12

> choir and instrumentalists, with solo voices
>
> > 212 Tell out, my soul, the greatness of the Lord *to* WOODLANDS

Hymns for Today's Church: Word LP WST 9623 (Re-issued in cassette 1998 by Word LANG-C 002)

> with the choir, orchestra and congregation of All Souls Church, Langham Place, London under the direction of Noël Tredinnick
>
> > 235 As water to the thirsty *to* OASIS
> >
> > 51 A purple robe, a crown of thorn *to* A PURPLE ROBE
> >
> > 217 Name of all majesty *to* MAJESTAS

1983

Son of the Highest: Lillenas, USA, LP-9044

> arranged and conducted by Dick Bolks, drama by Paul M. Miller, produced by Paul Stilwell
>
> > 13 Chill of the nightfall *to music by Robert Kircher arranged by Dick Bolks*

1984

Through Wood and Nails: Wild Goose Publications, LP and cassette, 146/RED/S, SRT4KL22I

with a choir of Abbey guests and solo musicians and vocalists from Iona Community members, associates and staff; produced by Ian and Kathy Galloway

212 Tell out, my soul, the greatness of the Lord *to* WOODLANDS

1985

Hymns Ancient & Modern 2: Hymns Ancient & Modern, cassette HAC 851

with singers from the Royal School of Church Music, directed and introduced by Dr Lionel Dakers, from the collections *100 Hymns for Today* and *More Hymns for Today*

212 Tell out, my soul, the greatness of the Lord *to* WOODLANDS

213 Faithful vigil ended *to* PASTOR PASTORUM

Come and Journey: GIA Publications, Inc., USA, LP MS-171

recorded live at the Minneapolis Auditorium, Minneapolis, Minnesota, 4 November, 1984 with Michael Joncas (composer), Marty Haugen, David Haas, and Jeanne Cotter

73 Spirit of God within me *to* WILLOW RIVER

Give Thanks to God on High: Wheaton College Recordings, USA, cassette album 8504-0104

with the Wheaton College Student Body

108 Give thanks to God on high *to* CHRISTO ET REGNO

Covenant Carols: Covenant Music (Australia) distributed by Acorn Press Ltd, Melbourne.

cassette with soloists, instrumentalists and a children's choir from Blackburn Baptist Church, produced by Rick Gordon

26 Holy child, how still you lie *to* HOLY CHILD

31 Not in lordly state and splendour *to* PICARDY

1986

How Can I Keep from Singing: Episcopal Radio TV Foundation, Inc., USA, LP album 721RA/NR16156

with the choir of St Mark's Cathedral, Minneapolis, Minnesota; executive producer Louis C. Schueddig

212 Tell out, my soul, the greatness of the Lord *to* WOODLANDS

To Be Your Bread: GIA Publications, Inc., USA, LP MS-172

with Michael Joncas (cantor) and Jeanne Cotter (handbells); producers David Haas, Marty Haughen

13 Chill of the nightfall *to* PRIOR LAKE

The Best of Rhapsody in Praise: Westmark Custom Records, USA, LP WMC-28563

with the Northwestern College Communique Singers and Orchestra, produced and directed by Richard Edstrom

161 Sing a new song to the Lord *to music by John F. Wilson*

Light and Peace: GIA Publications, Inc., USA, LP MS-175

with the Chorale of the St Paul Seminary School of Divinity, St Paul, Minnesota, directed by Sue Seid-Martin

136 The stars declare his glory *to music by David Haas*

212 Tell out, my soul, the greatness of the Lord *to music by David Haas*

1987

As Water to the Thirsty: GIA Publications, Inc., USA, LP MS-177

 with singers, choir and instrumentalists to music by David Haas, producer

  235 As water to the thirsty *to* FREEDOM

King Forever: Kingsway Publications Ltd, LP SFR 165; cassette SFC 165

 produced by Jackie Williams and Andy Baker

  63 Jesus, Prince and Saviour *to* NORFOLK PARK

Carols for Today: Conifer Ltd, LP CFC 160, CD CDCF 160, cassette MCFC 160

 with the choir of Canterbury Cathedral conducted by Dr Allan Wicks accompanied by Michael Harris, organ; producer Barry Rose

  37 Stars of heaven, clear and bright *to* CUXHAM

  22 Had he not loved us *to* BEACON HILL

The New English Hymnal: Hymns for the Church's Year: Canterbury Press, cassette HAC 872

 with singers from the Royal School of Church Music; organist Andrew Fletcher

  12 Child of the stable's secret birth *to* NEWTOWN ST LUKE

Crown Him: Word (UK) Ltd, LP WSTR 9693, cassette WSTC 9693

 from Prom Praise at Wembley with the All Souls Langham Place Choir and orchestra conducted by Noël Tredinnick

  235 As water to the thirsty *to* OASIS

Festival of Praise: Solent Records, cassette SS(C)080

 from the Methodist Conference, Portsmouth 1987; organist Chris Hyson

  129 Look, Lord, in mercy as we pray *to* LLOYD

Keswick Praise 3: ICC Studios, cassette KC 40/87

 with the All Souls Informal Band, conductor Noël Tredinnick, recorded during the Keswick Convention 1987

  217 Name of all majesty *to* MAJESTAS

Centenary Praise, Kingham Hill School: Abbey Recording Co. Ltd, LP APS 376

 with the choir of Kingham Hill School, Director of Music Terence Mann, organist Robert Stoodley

  105 Lord, for the years your love has kept and guided *to* LORD OF THE YEARS

Vespers from Westonbirt: James Yorke Recordings Ltd, LP WES 001

 recorded in the great hall at Westonbirt School; Director of Music Godfrey Slatter, organist Robin Baggs

  167 I lift my eyes *to* UPLIFTED EYES

1988

Singing Assembly: GIA Publications, Inc., USA, cassette CS-209

 recorded during a concert at St Barbara Church, Brookfield, Illinois with singers, instrumentalists and choir; organist Robert Batastini

  13 Chill of the nightfall *to* PRIOR LAKE

The Best of Mission Praise 4: Reelife Recordings, cassette RRMP 011

with instrumentalists; and staff and students of Capernwray Bible School

212 Tell out, my soul, the greatness of the Lord *to* TELL OUT MY SOUL

Christmas with Haven: Haven of Rest Radio Ministries, Hollywood, USA, cassette 2JC

with quartet and solo voices, keyboard Dwayne Condon

46 Within a crib my Saviour lay *to music by Walt Harrah*

33 O Prince of peace whose promised birth *to music by Walt Harrah*

1989

Joy to the World: carols from Worcester Cathedral: Hyperion Records Ltd, CD CDH88031; cassette KH88031

with the Worcester Cathedral Choir and the Worcester Festival Choral Society, conductor Donald Hunt, organ Adrian Partington

29 Hush you, my baby *to music by William Llewellyn*

Keswick Praise 4: ICC Studios International, cassette ICC 0389

with the Keswick Convention Chorus and the Saltmine Band, recorded during the Keswick Convention 1989

105 Lord, for the years your love has kept and guided *to* LORD OF THE YEARS

Come Meet my Jesus: Concordia Publishing House, USA, cassette 32-8985

with a children's choir and professional song leaders: a teaching cassette including both words with music and accompaniment only

249 Christ be my leader by night as by day *to* SLANE

1990

Keswick Praise 5: ICC Studios International, ICC 2290

with the Saltmine Band, recorded during the Keswick Convention1990

217 Name of all majesty *to* MAJESTAS

Irish Church Praise: Church of Ireland, twin cassette set

with the choir of St Patrick's Cathedral, Dublin, organist John Dexter; the Priory Singers, conductor Harry Grindle; the William Thompson Singers, conductor William Thompson, soloists and instrumentalists

105 Lord, for the years your love has kept and guided *to* MARLBOROUGH PARK

192 Fruitful trees, the Spirit's sowing *to* BEECHGROVE

1991

The Welkin Rings: Kevin Mayhew, cassette

with the choir of Chichester Cathedral, director Alan Thurlow, producer Alan Ridout

35 See, to us a child is born *to* THETFORD

1992

Worship Songs Ancient & Modern: Word (UK) Ltd, cassette and CD, LANGC 006

with the choir and musicians of the Langham Singers, conductor Noël Tredinnick; the St Albans singers, conductor Barry Rose, and the Millmead Church, Guildford Group led by Jonathan Veira

72 Spirit of faith, by faith be mine *to* LITTLE STANMORE

Gaudeamus: Paget Publications, cassette

with 23 participating choirs, soloists and instrumentalists

    26 Holy child, how still you lie *to* HOLY CHILD

Glorify the Lord: Christian Communications, Ltd, Hong Kong, CD and cassette 113O19

    sung in Chinese in a translation by Chua King Ling, from the collection *Sounds of Grace*

        26 Holy child, how still you lie *to* HOLY CHILD

        51 A purple robe, a crown of thorn *to* A PURPLE ROBE

        73 Spirit of God within me *to* LIVING FLAME

He has the Power: Calvin College Alumni Association, USA, cassette HR 014

    with the Calvin College Alumni Choir, conductor Dr Charles K. Smith

        190 Not for tongues of heaven's angels *to music by Roy Hopp*

Sing a New Song: Cambrensis Productions Ltd., Wales, cassette 113

    with the South Wales Baptist Choir, instrumentalists and soloist, director Kelvin Thomas, from the collection *Baptist Praise and Worship*

        175 Fill your hearts with joy and gladness *to* LAUS ET HONOR

        167 I lift my eyes *to* DAVOS

Come, Christians, Join to Sing: Eastern Nazarene College, Quincy, USA, cassette

    with the A Cappella Choir and Madrigal Singers of the Eastern Nazarene College, director Timothy Shetler, organist Lambert Brandes

        189 Born by the Holy Spirit's breath *to* GERMANY

Have your Heard? CH Records, cassette CE 101

    with Cohn Ellis, vocalist

        235 As water to the thirsty *to* OASIS

Keswick Praise 7: ICC Studios, cassette ICC6620

    with the Keswick Convention chorus

        217 Name of all majesty *to* MAJESTAS

Music from Christ College, Brecon: Abbey Recording Co., cassette CPAS 407

        212 Tell out, my soul, the greatness of the Lord *to* WOODLANDS

Singing our Faith: Selah Publishing Co., USA, cassette 520-113

    with Sue Mitchell-Wallace and the Calvin College, Grand Rapids, Cappella; director Merle R. Mustert

        190 Not for tongues of heaven's angels *to music by Roy Hopp*

Kings Men: Back Porch Records, USA, CD BPR4500I

    with the Kings Men group of Biola University, California, executive producer Daniel Radmacher

        167 I lift my eyes *to music by Brian Dunbar*

1993

United as One: OCP Publications, USA, cassette OCP 9750

    with the Trinity Choir of Trinity Episcopal Church, Portland, organist and choirmaster John Strege, organ Lanny Collins, soloists and instrumentalists, from the collection *United as One: Liturgical Music for Weddings, Vol 2*

with soloists, the orchestra of All Souls, Langham Place, conductor Noël Tredinnick, and the Malcolm Sargent Hospitals Choir, from the Symphony Hall, Birmingham

167 I lift my eyes *to* DAVOS

1996

Glory to God 3: Pilgrim Homes, cassette WBCC 3

with the Wessex Baptist Choir

217 Name of all majesty *to* MAJESTAS

The Hymn Makers: 'Tell out, my soul': Kingsway Music, CD KMCD936, cassette KMC936CASS

with the orchestra, choir and congregation of All Souls Church, Langham Place, conductor Noël Tredinnick, soloist Elisabeth Crocker

235 As water to the thirsty *to* OASIS

189 Born by the Holy Spirit's breath *to* WHITSUN PSALM

60 Christ is risen as he said *to* CHRIST IS RISEN AS HE SAID

220 Christ is the one who calls *to* LOVE UNKNOWN

175 Fill your hearts with joy and gladness *to* REGENT SQUARE

26 Holy child, how still you lie *to* HOLY CHILD

167 I lift my eyes *to* DAVOS

204 Lighten our darkness now the day is ended *to* CHRISTE SANCTORUM

105 Lord, for the years your love has kept and guided *to* LORD OF THE YEARS

217 Name of all majesty *to* MAJESTAS

157 Safe in the shadow of the Lord *to* CREATOR GOD

212 Tell out, my soul, the greatness of the Lord *to* WOODLANDS

90 We come as guests invited *to* PASSION CHORALE

6 When the Lord in glory comes *to* GLORIOUS COMING

1997

Let the Morning Bring... : Salvationist Publishing and Supplies, CD SPS112CD, cassette SPS122C

with the International Staff Songsters of the Salvation Army, soloists and instrumentalists, conductor Lee Ballantine, executive producer Lieut-Colonel Michael Williams

235 As water to the thirsty *to* OASIS

Lord of all Hopefulness: Herald AV Publications, CDHAVPCD 205

with the choir of Portsmouth Cathedral, director David Price, organ David Thorne

105 Lord, for the years your love has kept and guided *to* LORD OF THE YEARS

116 O Christ the same, through all our story's pages *to* LONDONDERRY AIR

Throughout All Time: GIA Publications Inc., USA, CD-392

with choir and instrumentalists, director David Haas

240 So the day dawn for me *to music by David Haas*

1998

Twenty Favourite Hymns: Kingsway Music, CD KMCD 2004, cassette KMC 2044

compiled by Bruce Pont from recordings in the Kingsway repertoire

212 Tell out, my soul, the greatness of the Lord *to* WOODLANDS

Prom Solos: Christian Focus Publications, CD 1901212

with Joanne Lunn, soloist; Noël Tredinnick, piano; Helen Sharman, flute; Michael Mace, cello

235 As water to the thirsty *to* OASIS

Breath of Life: Key of Life Productions, USA, cassette 1898

with Vanessa Langer, soloist and keyboard; and Jonathan Langer, bass guitar

13 Chill of the nightfall (under the title 'Song of the Stable') *to music by David Haas*

Catholic Book of Worship III: Publications Service, Canadian Conference of Catholic Bishops, Canada, cassette 9, CCCB

music for the Liturgy of the Hours from *The Catholic Book of Worship III* with choir and instrumentalists, choirmaster Michel Guimont

167 I lift my eyes *to* DAVOS

1999

The Songs of Fellowship Collection 1: Kingsway Music, CD SFCD3I4

compiled from recordings in the Kingsway repertoire from the *Songs of Fellowship* songbook

105 Lord, for the years your love has kept and guided *to* LORD OF THE YEARS

Singing Faith: Methodist Publishing House, cassette MPH 102

with the Northallerton Methodist Church choir, youth choir and worship band, conductor Iris Smith

214 All glory be to God on high *to music by Brian Hoare*

163 Praise the Lord and bless his Name *to music by Brian Hoare*

This is Our Joy and This is Our Feast: GIA Publications, Inc., USA, CD CD-45O

with the Chicago Cathedral Singers, conductor Richard Proulx, and the Metropolis Chamber Players, to the music of Bob Moore

11 Child of Mary, newly born *to music by Bob Moore*

252 Christ the Way of life possess me *to music by Bob Moore*

Spread the Word: Stop the War: Brass for Africa Committee, Australia, CD

with the Brass 4 Africa orchestra and singers, conductor Wendy Toulmin, producer Graham Toulmin, supporting the work of the African evangelist Muhindo Ise-Somo

217 Name of all majesty *to* MAJESTAS

Heavenly Music for Earthly Use: Woman's Weekly, cassette

selections from existing recordings chosen by Roger Royle and distributed as part of a free supplement to *Woman's Weekly,* September 1999

105 Lord, for the years your love has kept and guided *to* LORD OF THE YEARS

Star Child: GIA Publications, Inc., USA, CD CD471

with 'David Haas and friends', choir, children's choir, singers and soloists, instrumentalists, chiefly to the music of David Haas

13 Chill of the nightfall (under the title 'Song of the Stable') *to music by David Haas*

The English Hymn 1: Christ Triumphant: Hyperion, CD CDP12101

with the choir of Wells Cathedral, director Malcolm Archer, organ Rupert Gough, in a selection 'Great Hymn Tunes of the Twentieth Century'

105 Lord, for the years your love has kept and guided *to* LORD OF THE YEARS

176 Praise the Lord of heaven *to* VICAR'S CLOSE

Jesus' People Sing 2: Concordia, USA, CD 97–6815

from the collection of the same name

161 Sing a new song to the Lord *to* CANTATE DOMINO

Twenty Favourite Hymns 2: Kingsway Music, CD KMCD 2216, cassette KMC 2216

compiled by Bruce Pont from recordings in the Kingsway repertoire

167 I lift my eyes *to* DAVOS

Junior Praise Combined 15: HarperCollins, cassette ISBN 0-551-04021-1

from the collection of the same name, Nos 215–229, producer David Anfield

212 Tell out, my soul, the greatness of the Lord *to* GO FORTH

Junior Praise Combined 19: HarperCollins, cassette ISBN 0-551-04025-4

from the collection of the same name, Nos 273-287, producer David Anfield

6 When the Lord in glory comes *to* GLORIOUS COMING

Junior Praise Combined 21: HarperCollins, cassette ISBN 0-551-04037-8

from the collection of the same name, Nos 302–316, producer David Anfield

51 A purple robe, a crown of thorn *to* A PURPLE ROBE

Junior Praise Combined 22: HarperCollins, cassette ISBN 0-551-04036-X

from the collection of the same name, Nos 317–331, producer David Anfield

249 Christ be my leader by night and by day *to* SLANE

Junior Praise Combined 23: HarperCollins, cassette ISBN 0-551-04034-3

from the collection of the same name, Nos 332–346, producer David Anfield

175 Fill your hearts with joy and gladness *to* (1) REGENT SQUARE
(2) LAUS ET HONOR

Junior Praise Combined 24: HarperCollins, cassette ISBN 0-551-04035-1

from the collection of the same name, Nos 347–361, producer David Anfield

117 God whose love is everywhere *to* FALLING FIFTHS

Junior Praise Combined 28: HarperCollins, cassette ISBN 0-551-04031-9

from the collection of the same name, Nos 407–421, producer David Anfield

63 Jesus, Prince and Saviour *to* ST GERTRUDE

2000

Junior Praise Combined 31: HarperCollins, cassette ISBN 0-00-710571-1

from the collection of the same name, Nos 451–464, producer David Anfield

35 See, to us a child is born *to* INNOCENTS

161 Sing a new song to the Lord *to* ONSLOW SQUARE

Church Hymnal: love of God, life of faith: All for Music, Ireland, cassette PDGCD 237A

with seven different choirs and singing groups from Belfast, Limerick and Dublin, producer Stephen Hamill; a two-CD set of 49 hymns from the fifth edition of the Church of Ireland *Church Hymnal*

60 Christ is risen as he said *to* CHRIST IS RISEN AS HE SAID

282 Lord of the church, we pray for our renewing *to* LONDONDERRY AIR

Anno Domini: True Arts, CD TACD 68

with ten choirs, composer, conductor and organist Raymond Smith, the cantata is 'a musical tour of the history of Christianity to celebrate the millennium'

29 Hush you, my baby *to* DIANE

50 Golden Hymns: Kingsway Music, CD KMCD 2243

a three-CD set from recordings in the Kingsway repertoire

167 I lift my eyes *to* DAVOS

212 Tell out, my soul, the greatness of the Lord *to* WOODLANDS

Twenty Favourite Hymns 3: Kingsway Music, CD KCMD 2232, cassette KMC 2232

executive producer, Stephen Doherty; from recordings in the Kingsway repertoire

157 Safe in the shadow of the Lord *to* CREATOR GOD

6 When the Lord in glory comes *to* GLORIOUS COMING

235 As water to the thirsty *to* OASIS

2001

Songs of Praise: BBC Worldwide Ltd, CD 19022472

with the BBC Concert Orchestra, choirs and instrumentalists, conductor Paul Leddington Wright, organist John Scott; recorded at the Royal Albert Hall on the fortieth anniversary of the BBC TV Programme 'Songs of Praise', editor Hugh Faupel.

105 Lord, for the years your love has kept and guided *to* LORD OF THE YEARS

Keswick Praise 16: International Christian Communications, CD ICCD55I3O

from the Keswick Convention, worship leaders John Risbridger and Colin Webster, with instrumentalists; director Adrian Thompson

212 Tell out, my soul, the greatness of the Lord *to* WOODLANDS

I Will Sing with the Spirit: Upstream Recordings, CD KMCOO2CD

with the choir of Knock Methodist Church, Belfast, Northern Ireland, director Stephen Preston, soloist Aimeé Preston, producer Roy Rainey

167 I lift my eyes *to* DAVOS

4 Index of Biblical and other Sources

Some biblical passages on which texts have been based.
Please see the Preface for further details.

See also the *Index of Themes and Subjects,* and section 1 'The Christian Year' for hymns on the Christmas and Easter stories and other festivals.

FROM THE APOCRYPHA

FROM LITURGICAL SOURCES

5 Index of Translations

The following foreign-language translations have been published of the texts in this collection. Copyright, in whole or in part, is held by the administrators of the English original. Enquiries should be addressed to one of the publishers of this collection.

CHINESE

in *A Purple Robe: five choral settings in Chinese,* China Alliance Press, Hong Kong, 1982

    51 A purple robe, a crown of thorn

in *Hymns of Life,* China Alliance Press, Hong Kong, 1986

    208 God of gods, we sound his praises

in *Sounds of Grace,* Christian Communications Ltd, Hong Kong, 1992

    51 A purple robe, a crown of thorn

    208 God of gods, we sound his praises

    22 Had he not loved us

    26 Holy child, how still you lie

    167 I lift my eyes

    63 Jesus, Prince and Saviour

    105 Lord, for the years your love has kept and guided

    82 Lord of the church, we pray for our renewing

    228 Lord, who left the highest heaven

    217 Name of all majesty

    248 No weight of gold or silver

    157 Safe in the shadow of the Lord

    73 Spirit of God within me

    212 Tell out, my soul, the greatness of the Lord

    155 Timeless love! We sing the story

    90 We come as guests invited

    277 When to our world the Saviour came

in *Hymnal 1998,* Taipei Ling-Leung Church, Taiwan, 1998

    212 Tell out, my soul, the greatness of the Lord

DANISH

published individually as sheet music, Luthersk Missionsforenings Nodeforlag, Skjern, Denmark, 1994

ESTONIAN

in *Vaimulikud Laulud,* Eesti Evangeeliumi Kristlaste ja, Baptistide Koguduste Liit, Tallinn, Estonia, 1997

FRENCH

in *Songs of Celebration,* International Fellowship of Evangelical Students, Harrow, 1991

GERMAN

in *Preist Ihn,* STIWA Drück und Verlag, Urbach, Germany 1978

translation by Johannes Jourdan, 1980 for Hanssler-Verlag, Neuhausen-Stuttgart (unpublished)

JAPANESE

in *The Hymnal 21,* The United Church of Christ in Japan, Tokyo 169, 1997

KOREAN

in *Korean-English Hymnal,* Korean Adventist Press, Los Angeles, California, USA, 1998

LATVIAN

in *Visa Zeme Kungam Dzied,* Rïgas metropolijas Romas katoju kürija, Rïga, Latvia, 1996

NORWEGIAN

in *Salmer Underveis,* Norsk Lutheresk Forlag, Oslo, Norway, 2001

    105 Lord, for the years your love has kept and guided

SPANISH

in *Songs of Celebration,* International Fellowship of Evangelical Students, Harrow, 1991

    233 From the night of ages waking

     63 Jesus, Prince and Saviour

    282 Lord of the church, we pray for our renewing

SWEDISH

in *Segertoner,* Förlaget Filadelfia, Stockholm, Sweden, 1989

    161 Sing a new song to the Lord

WELSH

in *Rhaglan 1972,* the programme of the North Wales Baptist Union Festival of Song. Privately published, Garth Uchaf, Bangor, Wales, 1972

     26 Holy child, how still you lie

in *Sing to the Lord/Canwch I'r Arglwydd,* Church in Wales Publications, Penarth, Glamorgan, Wales, 1990

    212 Tell out, my soul, the greatness of the Lord

in *Grym Mawl 2 (Spring Harvest Praise 1998, Welsh edition),* Spring Harvest, Uckfield, East Sussex, 1998

    105 Lord, for the years your love has kept and guided

    195 Praise be to Christ in whom we see

    157 Safe in the shadow of the Lord

6 Index of Discontinued or Altered Texts

The first four texts below (unnumbered) were shown in Appendix 6 of Lift Every Heart, *1984, as 'discontinued'. It seems right to refer to them here for the sake of completeness, though I would not want to encourage their further use. One text from the same 1984 list was republished in 1987 and appears in the second group of hymn texts below, identified by the number given to them in this collection, now altered and revised.*

Father, we bring you love as your children
written on request for a Bible Society leaflet published in connection with the Queen's Silver Jubilee, 1976

O God, our Father and our King
Written on request for the Church of England Board of Education and published in *Our Mum: five themes for Family Services,* 1975 and in the leaflet *A Service for Mothering Sunday,* Church Information Office, 1975

O thank the Lord for he is good
based on Psalm 136 and written for *Psalm Praise,* 1973

Our God has turned to his people
based on Luke 1.68–79 (the Benedictus), and written for *Psalm Praise,* 1973; reprinted in *Carol Praise,* Marshall Pickering, 1987

4　*High peaks and sunlit prairies*
　　v.3, line 2, 'hark' now becomes 'mark'

8　*A song was heard at Christmas*
　　v.2, line 3, 'men' now becomes 'all'

12　*Child of the stable's secret birth*
　　v.4, line 6, misprinted in *Lift Every Heart* with 'to' omitted

26　*Holy child, how still you lie*
　　v.5, line 2, 'sons of men' now becomes 'all the lost'

51　*A purple robe, a crown of thorn*
　　v.3 is omitted in some books

57　*All shall be well*
　　v.4 is omitted in some books

59　*By loving hands the Lord is laid*
　　v.2, lines 3 and 4 have been revised since publication in 1976

63　*Jesus, Prince and Saviour*
　　v.1, lines 4, 5, 6 have been revised since *Lift Every Heart*

73　*Spirit of God within me*
　　v.2, line 7, 'men' now becomes 'all'

105　*Lord, for the years your love has kept and guided*
　　Alternative versions of this text, especially v.4, appear in a number of hymnals. Where possible, the text as it is printed here should be regarded as definitive. In communities where the word 'commonwealth' may be misunderstood, permission may be sought for the following alteration:

v.3, line 3, the words 'for this and every nation' to be substituted for the words 'for commonwealth and nation'. An additional verse, written on request for the Queen's Golden Jubilee, 2002, is now discontinued.

130 *Lord, give us eyes to see*
v.3 has been wholly re-written

133 *In my hour of grief or need*
v.3, line 1, 'man' becomes 'host' with consequential changes in this and the following verse.

146 *Merciful and gracious be*
Excluded from *Lift Every Heart,* but now revised with v.2 wholly re-written and v.3 considerably altered.

149 *Every heart its tribute pays*
v.1, line 5, 'all mankind' now becomes 'humankind'

167 *I lift my eyes*
v.4, line 5, misprinted in *Lift Every Heart* with 'day' for 'days'

171 *With undivided heart and ceaseless songs*
v.1, line 3 has been re-written

181 *The heavens are singing, are singing and praising*
The shorter version (*Lift Every Heart,* p. 147) is discontinued.

188 *Living Lord, our praise we render*
v.3, line 4, 'sons of God' now becomes 'life is ours'

189 *Born by the Holy Spirit's breath*
v.3, line 1, 'Sons, then,' now becomes 'Children'

213 *Faithful vigil ended*
The version printed is definitive; but that printed on p. 72 of *Lift Every Heart* (using 'thy' for 'your') remains a permitted alternative.

224 *Who is Jesus? Friend of sinners*
v.1, line 6, 'sons of men' now becomes 'Son of Man'

228 *Lord, who left the highest heaven*
Some early versions differ from this definitive text.

235 *As water to the thirsty*
v.3, line 6, 'he longs' now becomes 'we long'

248 *No weight of gold or silver*
v.1, line 5, 'no sinner finds his' now becomes 'no sinners find their'

249 *Christ be my leader by night as by day*
An earlier version of v. 1, line 3 is discontinued (see the Note)

276 *O Lord, whose saving Name*
Following a request to use this hymn at a Service for a Children's Hospice, the following alterations are available for such a purpose: v.2, lines 7 and 8 may read,

> for ease again,
> for peace restored.

277 *When to our world the Saviour came*
To reduce the length of the hymn from 7 verses to 5, a new final verse replaces the original verses 5, 6 and 7. The longer version (*Lift Every Heart,* p. 167) remains a permitted alternative.

7 Index of Tunes

as published or suggested in the Notes

When one of these texts is included in a hymnal, the tune used and the name of the composer, together with the title and date of the book, are given in the Notes. The publisher is listed in Index 1.

Where a tune is shown or 'suggested' (whether or not the text has been published to that tune) a brief indication of a few hymnals which include it is usually given in the following Index of Tunes. This is done by means of up to five abbreviations, each referring to a specific hymnal, which are listed immediately below the title of the tune. Otherwise, the phrase 'See Note' refers the user to the Note on the text in question which generally will show at least one book or other source where the tune has been published. Where possible, entries include hymnals both from the UK and from North America, taken from the representative list below, though the choice is inevitably somewhat arbitrary.

The list of hymnals provides the key to the abbreviations. Where both UK and North American hymnals are cited below a particular tune, they are divided by a double colon. Where a hymnal provides more than one tune the figure i, ii , etc., is added to the number. For example, H&P 60 ii means the second tune of hymn 60 in the UK Methodist collection of 1983, *Hymns and Psalms,* namely ALL SAINTS, set to 'Timeless love! We sing the story'.

Selected Hymnals cited as Sources of Tunes

BRITISH PUBLICATIONS

some of which appear also in American editions

AHB	*Anglican Hymn Book,* 1965 (Anglican)
BBC	*BBC Songs of Praise,* 1997 (British Broadcasting Corporation, ecumenical)
BPW	*Baptist Praise and Worship,* 1991 (Baptist Union)
CH3	*The Church Hymnary,* third edition, 1973 (Presbyterian)
CHI	*Church Hymnal,* 2001 (Church of Ireland)
CMP	*Complete Mission Praise,* 1999 (ecumenical)
CPE	*Common Praise,* 2000 (current edition of *Hymns Ancient & Modern,* Anglican)
H&P	*Hymns and Psalms,* 1983 (Methodist)
HTC	*Hymns for Today's Church,* second edition, 1987
NEH	*The New English Hymnal,* 1986 (Anglican)
PP	*Psalm Praise,* 1973 (ecumenical)
R&S	*Rejoice and Sing,* 1991 (United Reformed Church)

NORTH AMERICAN PUBLICATIONS

BP	*The Book of Praise,* 1997 (Presbyterian, Canada)
CH	*Chalice Hymnal,* 1995 (Disciples of Christ, USA)

CPC	*Common Praise,* 1998 (Anglican, Canada)
H82	*The Hymnal 1982* (Episcopal, USA)
LBW	*Lutheran Book of Worship,* 1978 (Lutheran, USA)
MBW	*Moravian Book of Worship,* 1990, 1992 (Moravian, USA)
PH	*The Presbyterian Hymnal,* 1990 (Presbyterian, USA)
PsH	*Psalter Hymnal,* 1987 (Christian Reformed, USA)
TH	*Trinity Hymnal,* 1990 (Orthodox Presbyterian, USA)
TWC	*The Worshiping Church,* 1990 (ecumenical, USA)
UMH	*The United Methodist Hymnal,* 1989 (Methodist, USA)
VU	*Voices United,* 1996 (United Church, Canada)
W	*Worship, third edition,* 1986 (Roman Catholic, USA)
W&R	*Worship and Rejoice,* 2001 (ecumenical, USA)
WT	*Worship Together,* 1995 (Mennonite Brethren, Canada and USA)

THE TUNES

A

A NEW SONG
See Note
161 Sing a new song to the Lord

A PURPLE ROBE
HTC 122 :: CPC 152 W&R 279
  51 A purple robe, a crown of thorn

ABBOT'S LEIGH
CPE 418 R&S 530 :: CPC 273
  W&R 536 UMH 584
  16 Christ is come! Let earth adore him
200 Heavenly hosts in ceaseless worship
143 Tell his praise in song and story
216 We believe in God the Father

ABENDS
See Note
277 When to our world the Saviour came

ABERAFON
See Note
133 In my hour of grief or need

ABERYSTWYTH
CH3 78 i CPE 96 ii NEH 383 ii ::
  CPC 249 PH 20
  11 Child of Mary, newly born
  45 Where do Christmas songs begin?

ABOVE THE VOICES OF THE WORLD
CMP 5
244 Above the voices of the world
    around me

ACCLAMATION
See Note
222 Freely, for the love he bears us

AD ASTRA
See Note
151 Help me, O God, and hear my cry

ADDISON'S
See LONDON

ADVENIT
See Note
  3 Here on the threshold of a new
    beginning

AIR OF AVALON
See Note
163 Praise the Lord and bless his Name

ALBERTA
BBC 300 i CPE 495 i NEH 392
  56 We turn in faith to Christ the Lamb
    of God

ALDINE
See Note
136 The stars declare his glory

ALFORD
CHI 678 CPE 196 :: PsH 619
  TH 323
  8 A song was heard at Christmas
  73 Spirit of God within me

ALL FOR JESUS
AHB 556 CMP 948 :: TWC 570
192 Fruitful trees, the Spirit's sowing
188 Living Lord, our praise we render

ALL MAJESTY
See Note
217 Name of all majesty

ALL SAINTS (or ZEUCH MICH, ZEUCH MICH)
CPE 229   H&P 60 ii   ::   H82 286
  TWC 344   VU 565
 75 God and Father, ever giving
 64 Long before the world is waking
228 Lord, who left the highest heaven
155 Timeless love! We sing the story

ALLELUIA
See Note
143 Tell his praise in song and story
216 We believe in God the Father

ALMSGIVING
CPE 540 ii   H&P 337 i   ::   BP 518
  TH 418   TWC 789
219 Christ is the Bread of life indeed
 84 Lord, for the gift of this new day

ALSTONE
See Note
270 The Lord made man, the Scriptures
      tell

AMAZING GRACE
BBC 282   CPE 375   H&P 215   ::
  MBW 783   UMH 378
260 Draw near to God, whose steadfast
      love

ANGELS' SONG
See SONG 34

ANGELUS (1657)
CH3 52   CPE 12   R&S 644   ::   BP 516
  TH 417
273 O God, who gives the fertile seed
277 When to our world the Saviour came

ANGELUS (1847)
See Note
285 'How shall they hear,' who have not
      heard

ANIMA CHRISTI
CHI 444   CPE 322   NEH 305
128 God is the giver of all things that are

ANIMAE HOMINUM
AHB 480 ii   HTC 443
174 Praise the God of our salvation

ANTWERP
See Note

189 Born by the Holy Spirit's breath

AR HYD Y NOS
See Note
254 May the love of Christ enfold us

ARFON
AHB 370   ::   BP 281   CPC 603   TH 250
 15 Christ from heaven's glory come
 19 Donkey plod and Mary ride

ARGENT
HTC 138 i   PP 50
248 No weight of gold or silver

ARWELFA
See Note
200 Heavenly hosts in ceaseless worship
165 Not to us be glory given

ASCENDED TRIUMPH
See Note
242 Christ who called disciples to him

ASH GROVE
CHI 443   ::   BP 338   MBW 136
  TWC 53
181 The heavens are singing, are singing
      and praising

ASHBURTON
See Note
103 Here within this house of prayer

ASHFORD
AHB 636
201 The glory of our God and King

ASHLANDS
See Note
 25 Here is the centre: star on distant
      star

ASTHALL
BP 94
169 Bless the Lord as day departs

ASTRO
See Note
136 The stars declare his glory

AU FORT DE MA DÉTRESSE
See Note
206 Light of the minds that know him

AUCH JETZT MACHT GOTT
TWC 740   UMH 649
 52 Approach with awe this holiest place
268 The Lord in wisdom made the earth
131 To heathen dreams of human pride

AULD HOOSE
See THE AULD HOOSE

AURELIA
CPE 585   NEH 167   ::   MBW 309
  TWC 689   VU 331
152   A King on high is reigning
182   From all the wind's wide quarters
 88   God gives a new beginning
198   O Christ the King of glory
207   O God of our salvation
113   Saint Luke, beloved physician
 90   We come as guests invited

AUS DER TIEFE
See HEINLEIN

AUSTRIA (or AUSTRIAN HYMN)
CPE 556   H&P 222   ::   CPC 388
  H82 522   W&R 17
208   God of gods, we sound his praises

AVE VERUM CORPUS
See Note
143   Tell his praise in song and story

AZMON
CPC 230   MBW 99   TWC 130   W&R 96
226   The love of Christ who died for me
232   To Christ our King in songs of praise

B

BALDWIN
See Note
108   Give thanks to God on high

BALLERMA
CPE 221 ii   R&S 688   ::   BP 364
 53   Behold, as love made manifest
 27   How faint the stable-lantern's light
238   O changeless Christ, for ever new
166   The will of God to mark my way

BANGOR
CH3 452   CHI 396 ii   CPE 256 ii   ::
  CPC 189   H82 164
 51   A purple robe, a crown of thorn
 54   Dear Lord, who bore our weight of
        woe
 89   The Lord is here
 55   Upon a tree the sin of man

BANNER OF HOPE
See Note
 81   Rejoice in God! Let trumpets sound

BARN RISE
See Note

 63   Jesus, Prince and Saviour

BARNARDO
See Note
161   Sing a new song to the Lord

BATTLE HYMN
BBC 156   CHI 113   CMP 681   ::
  UMH 717   W&R 730
 80   Let us sing the God of glory who has
        set the stars in place

BEACON HILL
See Note
 22   Had he not loved us

BEALL
See Note
 36   Soft the evening shadows fall

BEATI SUNT
See Note
141   Happy are those, beyond all measure
        blessed

BEATITUDO
CPE 561   H&P 792 ii   ::   CPC 280
  H82 683
119   All flowers of garden, field and hill
124   Open our eyes, O Lord, we pray

BEATO VIRGO
See Note
280   Before the world's foundation

BEAVERWOOD
See Note
284   Good news of God above

BEECHER (or LOVE DIVINE, ZUNDEL)
BP 587   H82 470   W&R 358
120   Faith and truth and life bestowing
200   Heavenly hosts in ceaseless worship

BEECHGROVE
See Note
192   Fruitful trees, the Spirit's sowing

BELMONT
CH3 549 ii   CPE 282   R&S 441   ::
  TH 143   VU 614
 53   Behold, as love made manifest
 54   Dear Lord, who bore our weight of
        woe
101   Lord of our lives, our birth and breath
238   O changeless Christ, for ever new
147   When troubles come and hopes depart

BENEDICTION
See Note
172 Come quickly, Lord, and hear the cries

BENNETT
See Note
212 Tell out, my soul, the greatness of the Lord

BESSELSLEIGH
See Note
272 Behold a broken world, we pray

BETHANY
See Note
200 Heavenly hosts in ceaseless worship
165 Not to us be glory given

BILLING
See Note
279 We bring you, Lord, our prayer and praise

BINNEY'S
R&S 213   TWC 339
71 Be present, Spirit of the Lord
237 He comes to us as one unknown

BINSCOMBE
See PSALM 67

BIRLING
CHI 295   CPE 264   HTC 143 ii
270 The Lord made man, the Scriptures tell

BIRMINGHAM
See Note
212 Tell out, my soul, the greatness of the Lord

BISHOPTHORPE
CPE 475   NEH 378   ::   CPC 58   TH 41
VU 811
124 Open our eyes, O Lord, we pray
201 The glory of our God and King
170 The heartfelt praise of God proclaim
232 To Christ our King in songs of praise

BLACKDOWN
See Note
248 No weight of gold or silver

BLAENWERN
CPE 301   H&P 267 i   ::   CPC 447
CH 690   W&R 671
200 Heavenly hosts in ceaseless worship

BLAIRGOWRIE
H&P 187

23 He comes, the Way that all may tread

BLUFF PARK
See Note
108 Give thanks to God on high

BODAFON FIELDS
See Note
155 Timeless love! We sing the story

BODMIN
AHB 486   CMP 433 ii   ::   TH 555
197 Father of lights, who brought to birth
285 'How shall they hear,' who have not heard

BONNIE GEORGE CAMPBELL
See Note
249 Christ be my leader by night as by day

BOORT
See Note
239 Our living Lord whose Name we bear

BOUGHTON ALUPH
See Note
209 We come with songs of blessing

BRAMERTON
See Note
149 Every heart its tribute pays

BREATH OF LIFE
See Note
245 Jesus my breath, my life, my Lord

BRENTWOOD
See Note
219 Christ is the Bread of life indeed

BRESLAU
See Note
189 Born by the Holy Spirit's breath

BRIARWOOD
See Note
217 Name of all majesty

BRIDEGROOM
R&S 517   ::   TWC 597   UMH 544
VU 604
190 Not for tongues of heaven's angels

BROOKSHILL
See Note
137 The Lord be near us as we pray

BROTHER JAMES' AIR
HTC 591   ::   TH 86   TWC 615
VU 748

DAVID
See Note
  5 When he comes

DAVOS (or UPLIFTED EYES or LIFT MY EYES)
BBC 229 R&S 64 :: TWC 81 W&R 488
  WT 588
167 I lift my eyes

DEBEN
See Note
  73 Spirit of God within me

DEDICATION CAROL
See Note
  91 This cherished child of God's creation

DEERFIELD
See Note
136 The stars declare his glory

DES PLAINES
LBW 162
261 God of eternal grace

DIADEMATA
CH3 298 CPE 166 R&S 262 :: BP 274
  CH 234
221 Christ the eternal Lord
284 Good news of God above
247 Lord of all life and power
  97 We turn to Christ alone

DICKEY
BP 436 VU 415
222 Freely, for the love he bears us

DIES DOMINICA
CPE 331
198 O Christ the King of glory

DINBYCH
See Note
  97 We turn to Christ alone

DIX
H&P 121 R&S 184 :: MBW 119
  TWC 562 VU 81
103 Here within this house of prayer
146 Merciful and gracious be
257 When the way is hard to find

DOLPHIN STREET
NEH 340 i
184 Beyond all mortal praise

DOMINICA
CHI 382 CPE 240 NEH 342 i ::
  MBW p.21
261 God of eternal grace
130 Lord, give us eyes to see

DONCASTER
CHI 302 ii CPE 458 H&P 306 ii
100 Lord, hear us as we pray

DONEYDADE
See Note
240 So the day dawn for me

DOROTHY
See Note
192 Fruitful trees, the Spirit's sowing

DOUSMAN
See Note
284 Good news of God above

DU FONDS DE MA PENSÉE
See Note
248 No weight of gold or silver

DUKE STREET
CPE 429 NEH 322 :: CPC 363
  UMH 101 W&R 341
132 How great our God's majestic Name
285 'How shall they hear,' who have not
      heard

DUNDEE
AHB 433 CPE 38 NEH 396 :: CPC 282
  H82 126a
125 Teach us to love the Scriptures, Lord
170 The heartfelt praise of God proclaim
226 The love of Christ who died for me
  89 The Lord is here

DUNSTAN
TH 622
  23 He comes, the Way that all may tread

E

EASTER HYMN
CPE 147 NEH 110 :: CPC 203
  H82 207 TWC 234
  30 In our darkness light has shone

EASTER SKIES
See Note
  57 All shall be well

EASTER SONG (or LASST UNS
ERFREUEN)
CHI 274   CPE 149   ::   CPC 231
  UMH 62   W&R 23
   24 Hear how the bells of Christmas play
   65 Now is Christ risen from the dead

EBENEZER (or TON Y BOTEL)
CPE 363   R&S 360   ::   H82 381
  MBW 507   VU 198
143 Tell his praise in song and story
216 We believe in God the Father

EDEN CHURCH
See Note
228 Lord, who left the highest heaven

EGHAM
See Note
   95 This child from God above

EISENACH (LONG METRE)
AHB 597   CPE 118   ::   BP 80   CPC 79
  W 715
189 Born by the Holy Spirit's breath
132 How great our God's majestic Name
277 When to our world the Saviour came

EISENACH (88 88 88)
AHB 527
   58 And sleeps my Lord in silence yet

ELING
See Note
212 Tell out, my soul, the greatness of
         the Lord

ELLACOMBE
CPE 157   H&P 208   ::   CPC 205   PH 89
  TWC 52
250 Affirm anew the threefold Name
   79 In endless exultation
129 Look, Lord, in mercy as we pray
180 O comfort each believing heart
267 The God who set the stars in space
126 To God who gave the Scriptures

ELLERS
CPE 20   H&P 643   ::   CPC 31
  UMH 663   W&R 385
   86 An upper room with evening lamps
         ashine
183 Beloved in Christ before our life began
   47 Christ our Redeemer knew
         temptation's hour
   22 Had he not loved us

ELLESDIE
MBW p.111   PsH 171   TH 443
208 God of gods, we sound his praises

ENDIKE
See Note
214 All glory be to God on high

ENGLAND'S LANE
CHI 52 ii   CPE 253 i   NEH 285 i   ::
  CPC 429   H82 88
   15 Christ from heaven's glory come
   19 Donkey plod and Mary ride
103 Here within this house of prayer

ERFYNIAD
See Note
212 Tell out, my soul, the greatness of
         the Lord

ES FLOG EIN KLEINS WALDVÖGELEIN
See Note
182 From all the wind's wide quarters

ES IST GEWISSLICH
See Note
245 Jesus my breath, my life, my Lord

EST IST KEIN TAG (or MEYER)
CH3 145 i   CPE 269   NEH 422   ::
  BP 432
   84 Lord, for the gift of this new day

ESCAMBIA
See Note
   73 Spirit of God within me

EUDOXIA
See Note
213 Faithful vigil ended

EVENTIDE
CPE 10   H&P 665   R&S 336   ::
  H82 662   W&R 274
   86 An upper room with evening lamps
         ashine
128 God is the giver of all things that are

EVERLASTING LOVE
CMP 452   HTC 482   ::   TH 703
   61 Come and see where Jesus lay

EWHURST
AHB 624   HTC 432
   46 Within a crib my Saviour lay

EWING
CHI 670   CPE 482   ::   CPC 278
  H82 624   TWC 754

79 In endless exultation
248 No weight of gold or silver
126 To God who gave the Scriptures

EYTHORNE
See Note
136 The stars declare his glory

F

FAIRMILE
See Note
 26 Holy child, how still you lie

FAITH CHURCH
See Note
209 We come with songs of blessing

FAITHFUL VIGIL
CMP 125   HTC 55   PP 30
213 Faithful vigil ended

FALERA
See Note
141 Happy are those, beyond all measure
     blessed

FALLING FIFTHS
See Note
117 God whose love is everywhere

FANTO
See Note
253 From life's bright dawn to eventide

FARLEY CASTLE
CH3 649 i   CPE 151   H&P 391   ::
  CPC 305   LBW 211
 86 An upper room with evening lamps
     ashine
112 Praise be to God for servants of the
     word

FAWLEY LODGE
See Note
213 Faithful vigil ended

FESTAL SONG
CPC 496   H82 551   VU 79
130 Lord, give us eyes to see
178 The God of grace is ours

FINLANDIA
CMP 98   CPE 384   ::   CPC 540
  MBW 757   W&R 372
 17 Come now with awe, earth's ancient
     vigil keeping
114 If on our hearts the light of Christ
     has shone

FLEMMING (or INTEGER VITAE)
MBW 383   TH 107   VU 492
185 Let every child of earth that sleeping
     lies
205 Lord God Almighty, Father of all
     mercies

FOREST GREEN
CHI 174 i   CPE 63 i   ::   PH 292
  VU 518   W&R 540
202 A city radiant as a bride
102 Give thanks to God, and honour those
 32 O child of Mary, hark to her
225 O come to me, the Master said
187 O God of everlasting light
246 O Saviour Christ, beyond all price

FOYE
H&P 124 ii
 12 Child of the stable's secret birth

FRAGRANCE (or QUELLE EST CETTE
ODEUR)
AHB 101   CMP 700   CPE 72   ::   BP 134
  TH 230
121 God in his wisdom, for our learning
 67 Who is there on this Easter morning

FRAMLINGHAM
HTC 424
137 The Lord be near us as we pray

FRANCONIA
CH3 74   CMP 934   CPE 391   ::
  CPC 439   MBW 318
154 For God my spirit longs
100 Lord, hear us as we pray

FRANKLIN
See Note
108 Give thanks to God on high
 74 When God the Spirit came

FREEDOM
See Note
235 As water to the thirsty

FULDA (or GERMANY or WALTON)
CPE 111   NEH 486   ::   CPC 592
  MBW 221   W&R 591
189 Born by the Holy Spirit's breath

G

GATESCARTH
HTC 256   R&S 497   ::   PH 351   VU 513
236 Christ be the Lord of all our days
134 Lord, when the storms of life arise

HARWELL
See Note
200 Heavenly hosts in ceaseless worship

HAWKHURST
CPE 176   NEH 347
253 From life's bright dawn to eventide

HE COMES TO US
See Note
237 He comes to us as one unknown

HEATHLANDS
BBC 227   BPW 48   CHI 695   ::   BP 177
146 Merciful and gracious be
257 When the way is hard to find

HEAVENLY HOSTS
See Note
200 Heavenly hosts in ceaseless worship

HEAVEN'S ANGELS
See Note
190 Not for tongues of heaven's angels

HEINLEIN (or AUS DER TIEFE)
CH3 210   CHI 207   CPE 95   ::
  CPC 175   MBW 760
133 In my hour of grief or need

HERMANN
See NICOLAUS

HERONGATE
BBC 82 i   CPE 109   R&S 425   ::   BP 92
  CPC 584
273 O God, who gives the fertile seed

HESPERUS
See Note
169 Bless the Lord as day departs

HICKLING
See Note
208 God of gods, we sound his praises

HIGHEST HEAVEN
HTC 97
228 Lord, who left the highest heaven

HILASTERION
See Note
141 Happy are those, beyond all measure
        blessed

HILLCREST
CMP 963
171 With undivided heart and ceaseless
        songs

HILLINGDON
See Note
165 Not to us be glory given

HOLDERNESS
See Note
107 With all who in this hallowed place

HOLY APOSTLES
See Note
  8 A song was heard at Christmas

HOLY CHILD
CMP 236   HTC 60 ii
 26 Holy child, how still you lie

HOLY FAITH
AHB 535
281 Father on high to whom we pray
145 Lord, may our hearts within us burn

HOLY PRESENCE
See Note
 89 The Lord is here

HOLY VINE
See Note
 83 Lord, as the day begins

HOPE PARK
See Note
120 Faith and truth and life bestowing

HOUSTON
See Note
211 Our God and Father bless

HOVE
See Note
166 The will of God to mark my way

HUMILITY
See Note
210 Bless the Lord, creation sings

HUNTINGDON
See Note
 47 Christ our Redeemer knew
        temptation's hour

HUNTLEY
See Note
104 In the Name of Christ rejoicing

HURSLEY
See Note
285 'How shall they hear,' who have not
        heard

HUSHABY
See Note
  29 Hush you, my baby

HUSTAD
See Note
  39 The hush of midnight here below

HYFRYDOL
CPE 628 NEH 271 :: CH 450
  TWC 492 VU 486
  16 Christ is come! Let earth adore him
  104 In the Name of Christ rejoicing
  165 Not to us be glory given
  143 Tell his praise in song and story

I

IBSTONE
CMP 950 H&P 730 :: BP 494 CH 409
  265 For peace with God above

ICH HALTE TREULICH STILL
CHI 563 CPE 518 :: PH 418 VU 295
  284 Good news of God above
  97 We turn to Christ alone
  153 What blessings God bestows

IMPACT (or MONKSGATE)
PP 34 i
  150 Mercy, blessing, favour, grace

INNER SIGHT
See Note
  244 Above the voices of the world
        around me

INNOCENTS
H&P 738 i HTC 566 :: UMH 675
  60 Christ is risen as he said
  35 See, to us a child is born

INNSBRUCK (or O WELT, ICH MUSS
DICH LASSEN)
CPE 23 NEH 75 :: CPC 19 H82 309
  UMH 631
  196 No temple now, no gift of price
  123 O God who shaped the starry skies
  156 Our God eternal, reigning
  44 To this our world of time and space

INNSBRUCK NEW
AHB 510
  196 No temple now, no gift of price
  123 O God who shaped the starry skies
  44 To this our world of time and space

INTEGER VITAE
See FLEMMING

IRBY
CMP 539 CPE 66 :: PH 49 VU 62
  W&R 183
  75 God and Father, ever giving
  64 Long before the world is waking
  155 Timeless love! We sing the story

IVYTHORN HILL
See Note
  149 Every heart its tribute pays

J

JACKSON (or BYZANTIUM)
AHB 276 CHI 116 CPE 288 H&P 698
  :: BP 183
  238 O changeless Christ, for ever new
  279 We bring you, Lord, our prayer and
        praise

JALAN LEBAN
See Note
  282 Lord of the church, we pray for our
        renewing

JENSEN
See Note
  283 The church of God on earth, we
        come

JERUSALEM
See Note
  195 Praise be to Christ in whom we see

JESU, MEINE FREUDE
CMP 840 CPE 484 H&P 259 ::
  H82 701 VU 667
  69 Heaven's throne ascending

JESUS ALIVE
See Note
  57 All shall be well

JORDAN
See Note
  40 The King of glory comes to earth

JUDSON
See Note
  204 Lighten our darkness now the day is
        ended

JULIUS
H&P 140
  76 God is not far, whose threefold
        mercies shine
  22 Had he not loved us

K

KANSFIELD
TWC 428
254 May the love of Christ enfold us

KILLALOE
See Note
188 Living Lord, our praise we render

KILMARNOCK
BPW 87 i   CH3 603   CPE 477   ::   BP 194
54 Dear Lord, who bore our weight of woe
160 The everlasting Lord is King

KING'S LYNN
AHB 470   CHI 451   CPE 314   ::
CPC 283   H82 231
182 From all the wind's wide quarters
206 Light of the minds that know him
248 No weight of gold or silver
207 O God of our salvation
90 We come as guests invited

KING'S WESTON
CPE 380 ii   H&P 199   NEH 50   ::
PH 148   VU 97
176 Praise the Lord of heaven

KINGSBRIDGE
See Note
193 Be strong in the Lord

KINGSFOLD
CPE 469   R&S 201   ::   CPC 508   W 490
W&R 434
250 Affirm anew the threefold Name
18 Come, watch with us this Christmas night
28 How silent waits the listening earth
49 No tramp of soldiers' marching feet
32 O child of Mary, hark to her
225 O come to me, the Master said
180 O comfort each believing heart
187 O God of everlasting light
78 The everlasting Father reigns
267 The God who set the stars in space
40 The King of glory comes to earth

KIRKWOOD
See Note
196 No temple now, no gift of price

KONOMICHI
See Note
89 The Lord is here

L

LAANECOORIE
See Note
221 Christ the eternal Lord

LADYWELL
BPW 276 ii   CPE 364
202 A city radiant as a bride
28 How silent waits the listening earth
129 Look, Lord, in mercy as we pray
49 No tramp of soldiers' marching feet
78 The everlasting Father reigns
40 The King of glory comes to earth

LAKE FOREST
See Note
190 Not for tongues of heaven's angels

LAMB OF GOD
WT 364
264 Thankful of heart for days gone by

LANCASHIRE
BP 742   TWC 747   UMH 303
280 Before the world's foundation

LANCASHIRE COTTON WEAVER
See COTTON WEAVER

LAND OF REST
H&P 621 i   ::   CPC 60   H82 304
TWC 200   W&R 252
274 Remember, Lord, the world you made

LANGRAN
See ST AGNES

LANTERN'S LIGHT
27 How faint the stable-lantern's light

LASST UNS ERFREUEN
See EASTER SONG

LATIMER
See Note
228 Lord, who left the highest heaven

LAUDATE DOMINUM (PARRY)
CPE 543 i   R&S 293   ::   CPC 330
H82 432   TWC 704
193 Be strong in the Lord
43 Through centuries long the prophets of old

LAUDS
CPE 198   R&S 329   ::   CH 257   VU 582
W&R 133
2 From the Father's throne on high
35 See, to us a child is born

LAURENTIUS
See Note
248 No weight of gold or silver

LAUS ET HONOR
See Note
175 Fill your hearts with joy and gladness

LAWES' PSALM 47
See Note
83 Lord, as the day begins

LAWNDALE
See Note
72 Spirit of faith, by faith be mine

LAWTON WOODS
See Note
169 Bless the Lord as day departs

LE MAIRE
See Note
152 A King on high is reigning

LEAVITT
See Note
192 Fruitful trees, the Spirit's sowing

LEOMINSTER
CMP 455   H&P 714   ::   MBW 604
  PsH 260   TH 169
139 In judgment, Lord, arise
97 We turn to Christ alone
153 What blessings God bestows

LEONI
CPE 586   NEH 148   ::   H82 372
  PsH 621   TWC 336
148 God is my great desire
255 The pilgrim church of God
98 We turn to Christ anew

LES COMMANDEMENS DE DIEU
CH3 586   CPE 298   H&P 603   ::
  CPC 16   PH 550
91 This cherished child of God's
    creation

LIFT MY EYES
See DAVOS

LIMERICK
See Note
74 When God the Spirit came

LINCOLNWOOD
See Note
200 Heavenly hosts in ceaseless worship

LITTLE CORNARD
CPE 4   NEH 7   ::   VU 277   W 365
83 Lord, as the day begins

LITTLE STANMORE
See Note
72 Spirit of faith, by faith be mine

LITTLEBOURNE
See Note
161 Sing a new song to the Lord

LIVING FLAME
BPW 296   HTC 243
73 Spirit of God within me

LLANFAIR
CPE 167   NEH 130 i   ::   CPC 206
  H82 214   TWC 40
30 In our darkness light has shone

LLANGLOFFAN
BPW 581   CPE 501   ::   CPC 593
  TH 371   W&R 626
206 Light of the minds that know him
248 No weight of gold or silver

LLANGOLLEN
See LLEDROD

LLANSANNAN
See Note
120 Faith and truth and life bestowing

LLEDROD (or LLANGOLLEN)
CHI 351 ii   R&S 602   ::   CPE 41
  H82 299
231 Kingly beyond all earthly kings

LLOYD
See Note
129 Look, Lord, in mercy as we pray
157 Safe in the shadow of the Lord

LOBE DEN HERREN
BBC 19   CPE 558   NEH 440   ::
  CPC 384   PH 482
109 Thanks be to God for his saints of
    each past generation

LOBT GOTT, IHR CHRISTEN
See NICOLAUS

LONDON (or ADDISON'S)
CHI 35   CPE 265   NEH 267
195 Praise be to Christ in whom we see

LONDON NEW
BBC 6 i   CH3 6   NEH 365   ::
  CPC 546

275 Most glorious God, for breath and birth

274 Remember, Lord, the world you made

LONDONDERRY AIR
CHI 103   NEH 258   R&S 265   ::
  VU 586   W&R 433

282 Lord of the church, we pray for our renewing

116 O Christ the same, through all our story's pages

LORD OF HEAVEN
See Note

176 Praise the Lord of heaven

LORD OF LOVE
HTC 70   ::   TH 212

46 Within a crib my Saviour lay

LORD OF THE YEARS
CPE 81   CMP 428   HTC 328   ::
  W&R 70   WT 462

105 Lord, for the years your love has kept and guided

LOVE DIVINE (ZUNDEL)
See BEECHER

LOVE UNKNOWN
CPE 112   NEH 86   ::   CPC 184   PH 76
  VU 143

220 Christ is the one who calls

159 Come, let us praise the Lord

LUDLOW
See Note

179 God shall my comfort be

LUDY
See Note

108 Give thanks to God on high

LUMEN CHRISTI
See Note

240 So the day dawn for me

LUSIGNAC
See Note

243 O God of grace, to whom belongs

LUTHER (or LUTHER'S HYMN)
CPE 370   NEH 170 i   R&S 484   ::
  BP 106   TH 321

283 The church of God on earth, we come

LUX
See Note

30 In our darkness light has shone

LUX EOI
CHI 251   CPE 137   NEH 103   ::
  H82 191   MBW 71

16 Christ is come! Let earth adore him

165 Not to us be glory given

216 We believe in God the Father

LUX PRIMA
CH 266   MBW 475   PsH 481

19 Donkey plod and Mary ride

LYNCH'S LULLABY
CHI 626 i

11 Child of Mary, newly born

266 'Set your troubled hearts at rest'

M

MAESYNEAUADD
See Note

200 Heavenly hosts in ceaseless worship

MAGDALEN
See Note

278 O God, whose all-sustaining hand

MAGISTER
See Note

70 Risen Lord in splendour seated

MAIDSTONE
AHB 563   BPW 485 ii

149 Every heart its tribute pays

37 Stars of heaven, clear and bright

45 Where do Christmas songs begin?

MAJESTAS
BBC 129   CPE 525   HTC 218 ii   ::
  MBW 407   W&R 101

217 Name of all majesty

MAJESTY
See Note

217 Name of all majesty

MALLORY
See Note

177 O God who brought the light to birth

MALONE
See Note

74 When God the Spirit came

MANOAH
MBW 39   TH 56

166 The will of God to mark my way

MANOR PARK
See Note
245 Jesus my breath, my life, my Lord

MAPPERLEY
See Note
212 Tell out, my soul, the greatness of
the Lord

MARCH OF THE CHRISTMAS PILGRIMS
See THE MARCH OF THE CHRISTMAS
PILGRIMS

MARCH OF TRIUMPH
See Note
51 A purple robe, a crown of thorn

MARIANDYRYS
See Note
95 This child from God above

MARIETTA
See Note
255 The pilgrim church of God

MARJORIE
See Note
194 The best of gifts is ours

MARLBOROUGH GATE
See Note
184 Beyond all mortal praise

MARLBOROUGH PARK
See Note
105 Lord, for the years your love has
kept and guided

MARSH CHAPEL
See Note
272 Behold a broken world, we pray

MARTYRDOM
CPE 379 :: BP 235 TWC 208
UMH 294
51 A purple robe, a crown of thorn
251 Be with us, Lord, who seek your aid
272 Behold a broken world, we pray
279 We bring you, Lord, our prayer and
praise

MARYTON
BPW 17 H&P 11 i :: CH 602
CPC 70 W&R 589
231 Kingly beyond all earthly kings

McKEE
H&P 758 i :: BP 480 H82 529
W&R 600

272 Behold a broken world, we pray
238 O changeless Christ, for ever new

MEAD HOUSE
AHB 383 H&P 36 :: TH 742
120 Faith and truth and life bestowing

MEARE HEATH
See Note
270 The Lord made man, the Scriptures
tell

MEDITATION
See Note
135 Within the love of God I hide

MEIRIONYDD
See Note
206 Light of the minds that know him

MELITA
CPE 413 R&S 58 :: H82 579 VU 322
W&R 74
262 Almighty Lord Most High draw near
151 Help me, O God, and hear my cry
93 Lord Jesus, born a tiny child
48 O Christ, who faced in deserts bare
229 O Christ, who taught on earth of old
243 O God of grace, to whom belongs
278 O God, whose all-sustaining hand
239 Our living Lord whose Name we
bear

MELLING
AHB 550 CPE 335 NEH 344
210 Bless the Lord, creation sings

MENDON
CPC 332 H82 419 TWC 714
285 'How shall they hear,' who have not
heard

MERCIFUL AND GRACIOUS
See Note
146 Merciful and gracious be

MERCY
TH 387 TWC 302 WT 587
191 Out of darkness let light shine
266 'Set your troubled hearts at rest'

MEYER
See ES IST KEIN TAG

MILLENNIUM
H&P 226
41 The light of glory breaks

RIPLEY
See Note
216 We believe in God the Father

ROEWEN
See Note
198 O Christ the King of glory

ROUNDHAY
See Note
22 Had he not loved us

RUACH
H&P 294
73 Spirit of God within me

RUSSWIN
W 542
215 Glory to God in the highest

RUSTINGTON
CH3 353   CPE 605   ::   BP 663   H82 278
TWC 39
120 Faith and truth and life bestowing

RUXLEY
See Note
26 Holy child, how still you lie

RYBURN
CPE 133 i   H&P 349   HTC 480   ::
BP 263   LBW 336
177 O God who brought the light to birth

S

SAFFRON WALDEN
BBC 274 i   CPE 308 i   HTC 440
20 Exult, O morning stars aflame
72 Spirit of faith, by faith be mine

SAIGON
HTC 68   PP 46
38 The darkness turns to dawn

SALTASH
See PLEADING SAVIOR

SALVATOR MUNDI
HTC 263
3 Here on the threshold of a new
beginning

SALZBURG (HAYDN)
See Note
238 O changeless Christ, for ever new

SALZBURG (HINTZ)
CHI 254   CPE 138   ::   BP 176   CPC 162
H82 135

14 Choirs of angels, tell abroad
37 Stars of heaven, clear and bright

SAMUEL
CH3 123   HTC 268   ::   MBW 609
TH 399
83 Lord, as the day begins

SANDON
CHI 653 ii   CPE 495 ii   ::   TH 552
VU 842   W&R 409
56 We turn in faith to Christ the Lamb
of God

SANDYS
CHI 601   CPE 460   R&S 538   ::   BP 89
38 The darkness turns to dawn
95 This child from God above
269 What colours God has made

SARA
See Note
118 Our Father God in heaven

SAVIOUR CHRIST
HTC 216
218 Saviour Christ, in praise we name him

SCHOLA
See Note
73 Spirit of God within me

SCHUMANN
MBW 657   PH 428   W&R 688
194 The best of gifts is ours

SEBASTIENNE
See Note
277 When to our world the Saviour came

SECRET BIRTH
See Note
12 Child of the stable's secret birth

SELFLESS LOVE
BPW 435 i   CMP 214   HTC 405
102 Give thanks to God, and honour those

SERENITY
See Note
51 A purple robe, a crown of thorn

SHANTY CREEK
See Note
22 Had he not loved us

SHEEN
CPE 299   NEH 286   ::   CPC 339
168 The faithful are kept as the mountains
that never shall move

SHEPHERD'S STAR
See Note
249 Christ be my leader by night as by day

SHIPSTON
AHB 348   H&P 344   NEH 360   ::
  BP 512   CPC 261
174 Praise the God of our salvation

SIBFORD FERRIS
See Note
 89 The Lord is here

SIGNIFER
See Note
 61 Come and see where Jesus lay

SLANE
CHI 643   CPE 386   ::   CPC 505
  MBW 719   TWC 107
249 Christ be my leader by night as by day

SLOVENIA
See Note
164 Servants of the living Lord

SONG 1
BBC 196   NEH 302   ::   CPC 57   H82 315
  VU 571
127 Eternal God, before whose face we
       stand
141 Happy are those, beyond all measure
       blessed
 25 Here is the centre: star on distant star
114 If on our hearts the light of Christ
       has shone
 50 In the same night in which he was
       betrayed

SONG 13
AHB 165   CPE 259   H&P 183   ::
  BP 394   PH 321
266 'Set your troubled hearts at rest'

SONG 22
AHB 374   CPE 186   NEH 409   ::
  H82 703
 87 As in that upper room you left your
       seat
112 Praise be to God for servants of the
       word

SONG 34 (or ANGELS' SONG)
BBC 390   CH3 45   H&P 381   ::
  CPC 266   H82 21
231 Kingly beyond all earthly kings

SONG 46
CPE 106   HTC 149   ::   CPC 49
  H82 328   TWC 236
 57 All shall be well

SONG OF CREATION
See Note
181 The heavens are singing, are singing
       and praising

SONG OF THE HOLY SPIRIT
See Note
 42 The shining stars unnumbered

SOUND OF WIND
See Note
 74 When God the Spirit came

SOUTHWELL (DAMAN)
BBC 276   CPE 564   H&P 533   ::
  PH 301   VU 607
269 What colours God has made

SPIRITUS FIDEI
See Note
 72 Spirit of faith, by faith be mine

SPIRITUS VITAE
BBC 159R&S 302   ::   BP 384   TH 341
  W&R 328
 91 This cherished child of God's creation

ST AGNES (DYKES)
CPE 485   CMP 386   ::   CPC 85
  PsH 480   W&R 420
258 Eye has not seen, nor ear has heard

ST AGNES (LANGRAN)
CHI 418 ii   H&P 608 i   ::   BP 543
  MBW 421   TWC 783
 47 Christ our Redeemer knew
       temptation's hour
128 God is the giver of all things that are
112 Praise be to God for servants of the
       word

ST ALBINUS
CHI 272   CPE 148   NEH 112   ::
  CPC 239   H82 194
169 Bless the Lord as day departs

ST ANNE
See Note
157 Safe in the shadow of the Lord
 89 The Lord is here

ST BENEDICT (LANDIS)
See Note

157 Safe in the shadow of the Lord

ST BENEDICT (STAINER)
See Note
150 Mercy, blessing, favour, grace

ST BOTOLPH
CPE 338   H&P 610 i   NEH 385   ::
  CPC 617   H82 209
 27 How faint the stable-lantern's light
274 Remember, Lord, the world you
  made

ST CATHERINE (HEMY)
BBC 331 ii   H&P 747   ::   H82 558
  TWC 692   VU 580
262 Almighty Lord Most High draw near
172 Come quickly, Lord, and hear the
  cries
281 Father on high to whom we pray
145 Lord, may our hearts within us burn
 48 O Christ, who faced in deserts bare
243 O God of grace, to whom belongs
177 O God who brought the light to birth

ST CECILIA
CH3 322   CPE 607   HTC 334   ::   BP 269
  H82 613
227 Let hearts and voices blend

**ST CHARLES, QUEENSBOROUGH
TERRACE**
See Note
240 So the day dawn for me

ST CHRYSOSTOM
CPE 603 ii   ::   TH 410
151 Help me, O God, and hear my cry
 96 When Jesus taught by Galilee

ST EDMUND (STEGGALL)
CHI 197   CPE 90 i   HTC 98 i
 14 Choirs of angels, tell abroad
 61 Come and see where Jesus lay
 45 Where do Christmas songs begin?

ST GEORGE
BPW 201   R&S 429   ::   BP 326   H82 267
263 O Lord, yourself declare

ST GEORGE'S, WINDSOR
CPE 270   NEH 259   ::   CPC 262   TH 420
  W&R 243
210 Bless the Lord, creation sings
 14 Choirs of angels, tell abroad
 61 Come and see where Jesus lay
149 Every heart its tribute pays

 37 Stars of heaven, clear and bright
 45 Where do Christmas songs begin?

ST GERTRUDE
CPE 549   NEH 435   ::   CPC 499
  H82 562   W&R 509
 63 Jesus, Prince and Saviour

ST GODRIC
CMP 392   H&P 374   ::   TH 356
 41 The light of glory breaks

ST HUGH
CPE 98   H&P 679 i   NEH 406
125 Teach us to love the Scriptures, Lord

ST JOHN'S
See Note
  6 When the Lord in glory comes

ST JUDE
See Note
136 The stars declare his glory

ST LEONARDS (GOULD)
CHI 636   H&P 739 ii   ::   PsH 291
  W&R 464   WT 207
222 Freely, for the love he bears us

ST MAGNUS
CPE 172   NEH 134   ::   BP 368
  CPC 491   H82 447
  1 Awake, as in the skies above
 53 Behold, as love made manifest
279 We bring you, Lord, our prayer and
  praise
147 When troubles come and hopes
  depart

ST MARK'S VAN NUYS
See Note
189 Born by the Holy Spirit's breath

ST MARY
See Note
272 Behold a broken world, we pray

ST MATTHEW
BPW 18   CPE 347   R&S 472   ::   H82 567
 32 O child of Mary, hark to her
241 O God whose thoughts are not as ours
107 With all who in this hallowed place

ST MATTHIAS (MONK)
AHB 60   BPW 499   H&P 396
172 Come quickly, Lord, and hear the cries
281 Father on high to whom we pray

93   Lord Jesus, born a tiny child
229   O Christ, who taught on earth of old

ST MAUGHAN
See Note
87   As in that upper room you left your
seat

ST MICHAEL (or OLD 134TH)
CHI 477 i   CPE 33   ::   BP 277
MBW 546   W&R 381
100   Lord, hear us as we pray
263   O Lord, yourself declare
95   This child from God above

ST MICHAEL'S
CPC 293   PsH 363   TWC 409
241   O God whose thoughts are not as ours
107   With all who in this hallowed place

ST OSWALD
See Note
188   Living Lord, our praise we render

ST PETER
CHI 92   CPE 338   ::   BP 517   PH 439
W&R 603
272   Behold a broken world, we pray
260   Draw near to God, whose steadfast
love
275   Most glorious God, for breath and
birth
166   The will of God to mark my way
96   When Jesus taught by Galilee
147   When troubles come and hopes depart

ST PETERSBURG
NEH 154 ii   ::   CPC 442   H82 574
TWC 779
278   O God, whose all-sustaining hand
186   Our Saviour Christ once knelt in
prayer
111   What debt of sin that none can pay
96   When Jesus taught by Galilee

ST STEPHEN
CPE 37   NEH 317   ::   CPC 343
H82 73   PH 250
1   Awake, as in the skies above
272   Behold a broken world, we pray
170   The heartfelt praise of God proclaim

ST THEODULPH
CHI 217   R&S 208   ::   BP 115
MBW 391   W&R 265

7   A new song God has given
280   Before the world's foundation
182   From all the wind's wide quarters
118   Our Father God in heaven
209   We come with songs of blessing

ST THOMAS (WILLIAMS)
CPE 36   NEH 14   ::   CPC 350
MBW 513   W&R 11
154   For God my spirit longs
178   The God of grace is ours

ST TIMOTHY
AHB 41   CPE 5   HTC 296
251   Be with us, Lord, who seek your aid

STANGMORE
See Note
240   So the day dawn for me

STANTON
HTC 445 ii
157   Safe in the shadow of the Lord

STELLA
CPE 341   H&P 47   NEH 384   ::
PsH 90   TH 510
99   At Cana's wedding, long ago
145   Lord, may our hearts within us burn

STOCKPORT
See YORKSHIRE

STREETS OF BETHLEHEM
See THE STREETS OF BETHLEHEM

STRACATHRO
BBC 311 ii   CPE 195   R&S 101
258   Eye has not seen, nor ear has heard
89   The Lord is here
226   The love of Christ who died for me
55   Upon a tree the sin of man

STRENGTH AND STAY
BBC 14 i   CPE 18   H&P 366   ::   TWC 573
94   Now to the Lord we bring the child
he gave us

STRIPLING
See Note
190   Not for tongues of heaven's angels

STULTZ
See Note
252   Christ the Way of life possess me

STUTTGART
CHI 123   CPE 85   ::   CPC 158   H82 66
W&R 677
192   Fruitful trees, the Spirit's sowing

THEODORA
See Note
133 In my hour of grief or need

THETFORD
See Note
 35 See, to us a child is born

THIS ENDRIS NYGHT
CH3 197   CPE 595   NEH 23   ::
   BP 286   H82 116
 27 How faint the stable-lantern's light

THORNBURY
BBC 179   CPE 606   NEH 485   ::
   CPC 444   H82 444
198 O Christ the King of glory

THORNTON
See Note
  5 When he comes

THREEFOLD GIFTS
MBW 598
219 Christ is the Bread of life indeed

TIDINGS
See Note
212 Tell out, my soul, the greatness of
    the Lord

TIMELESS LOVE
H&P 60 i   HTC 47 ii   CMP 707
155 Timeless love! We sing the story

TON-Y-BOTEL
See EBENEZER

TOULON
See OLD 124TH

TRAITOR'S KISS
See Note
 50 In the same night in which he was a
    betrayed

TRENTHAM
BBC 160 i   BPW 282 ii   ::   CPC 649
   TWC 295   UMH 420
261 God of eternal grace

TRISAGION
CPE 247 i   H&P 709   NEH 193 ii   ::
   BP 820
249 Christ be my leader by night as by
    day

TRURO
CMP 379   H&P 190   ::   CH 129
   VU 158   W&R 176

197 Father of lights, who brought to
    birth

TRUSTING GOD
See Note
137 The Lord be near us as we pray

TYROL (or TYROLESE)   76 76 D
AHB 351   CH3 464   CHI 36   ::
   MBW 658
  9 A stone to be the lintel

TYROL (or TYROLESE) DCM
CPE 200   ::   CPC 260   TWC 88
250 Affirm anew the threefold Name
 40 The King of glory comes to earth

U

UNDE ET MEMORES
CPE 559   NEH 273   ::   CPC 66   H82 337
127 Eternal God, before whose face we
    stand
114 If on our hearts the light of Christ
    has shone
 50 In the same night in which he was
    betrayed

UNIVERSITY
CH3 435   CPE 325 ii   NEH 77   ::
   CPC 22
119 All flowers of garden, field and hill

UNIVERSITY COLLEGE
AHB 584   CH3 539   NEH 434
210 Bless the Lord, creation sings

UNIVERSITY HILLS
See Note
 97 We turn to Christ alone

UNLESS THE LORD
See Note
166 The will of God to mark my way

UNSER HERRSCHER
See NEANDER

UPLIFTED EYES
See DAVOS

UPTON VALE
See Note
 29 Hush you, my baby

URCHFONT
See Note
150 Mercy, blessing, favour, grace

WHITSUN PSALM
BPW 281 i   CMP 61   HTC 225
189 Born by the Holy Spirit's breath

WIE LIEBLICH IST DER MALEN
See Note
 90 We come as guests invited

WIEBERG
See Note
202 A city radiant as a bride

WILDRIDGE
See Note
240 So the day dawn for me

WILLIAM
See Note
213 Faithful vigil ended

WILLOW RIVER
See Note
 73 Spirit of God within me

WILTSHIRE
BBC 22   CPE 604   NEH 467   ::   BP 18
238 O changeless Christ, for ever new
279 We bring you, Lord, our prayer and
      praise

WINCHESTER OLD
CPE 76   NEH 42   ::   H82 94   TWC 172
VU 75
 27 How faint the stable-lantern's light

WINDERMERE
CPE 174   H&P 589   NEH 497
 95 This child from God above

WINTON
See Note
212 Tell out, my soul, the greatness of
      the Lord

WITHINGTON
BP 8
199 He walks among the golden lamps

WOLVERCOTE
BBC 339 i   CPE 538   ::   CPC 438
H82 289
206 Light of the minds that know him
118 Our Father God in heaven

WOODLANDS
BBC 39   CPE 362   NEH 186   ::
CPC 362   UMH 200
115 Give praise to God for his Apostle
      Paul
 76 God is not far, whose threefold
      mercies shine
212 Tell out, my soul, the greatness of
      the Lord

WOODWAY
See Note
  9 A stone to be the lintel

WOOLLEY
See Note
108 Give thanks to God on high

WYCH CROSS
AHB 60 ii   R&S 362
 99 At Cana's wedding, long ago
281 Father on high to whom we pray

WYE VALLEY
CMP 421   HTC 463   ::   MBW 582
TH 699   W&R 435
 63 Jesus, Prince and Saviour

Y

YANWORTH
See Note
212 Tell out, my soul, the greatness of
      the Lord

YE BANKS AND BRAES (or CANDLER)
CHI 514   HTC 220   ::   CPC 304
W&R 628
195 Praise be to Christ in whom we see

YORKSHIRE (or STOCKPORT)
CH3 190   CMP 80   R&S 158   ::
BP 135   H82 106
 25 Here is the centre: star on distant
      star

Z

ZEUCH MICH, ZEUCH MICH
See ALL SAINTS

8 Metrical Index

35 33
218 Saviour Christ, in praise we name
  him

3 3 11 8 8 11 and refrain
 5 When he comes

445 83 (see also 85 83)
259 Lord and Father, faith bestowing

446 D (see also 86 86 CM)
 89 The Lord is here

4486 8886
 81 Rejoice in God! Let trumpets sound

458 457 (see also 98 97)
167 I lift my eyes

46 46 (see also 10 10)
 57 All shall be well

55 46 55 55
 22 Had he not loved us

55 54 D
 13 Chill of the nightfall

55 65 D
 29 Hush you, my baby

64 64
240 So the day dawn for me

65 65
213 Faithful vigil ended
 92 Father, now behold us

65 65 D
176 Praise the Lord of heaven

65 65 D and refrain
 63 Jesus, Prince and Saviour

65 65 66 65
179 God shall my comfort be
 21 Gold for a manger bed

664 6664
 10 Carols to Christ be sung

66 55 666 4
217 Name of all majesty

665 665 786
 69 Heaven's throne ascending

66 65 D
162 Let the earth acclaim him

66 66
265 For peace with God above
227 Let hearts and voices blend

66 66 44 44 (see also 66 66 88)
184 Beyond all mortal praise
220 Christ is the one who calls
159 Come, let us praise the Lord
276 O Lord, whose saving Name
140 We sing the Lord our light

66 66 88 (see also 66 66 44 44)
 83 Lord, as the day begins
 41 The light of glory breaks

66 84 D
148 God is my great desire
255 The pilgrim church of God
 98 We turn to Christ anew

66 86 (Short metre: SM)
154 For God my spirit longs
261 God of eternal grace
130 Lord, give us eyes to see
100 Lord, hear us as we pray
263 O Lord, yourself declare
194 The best of gifts is ours
 38 The darkness turns to dawn
178 The God of grace is ours
 95 This child from God above
269 What colours God has made

66 86 66
108 Give thanks to God on high
 85 This day above all days
 74 When God the Spirit came

66 86 D (Double short metre: DSM)
221 Christ the eternal Lord
284 Good news of God above
139 In judgment, Lord, arise
247 Lord of all life and power
 97 We turn to Christ alone
153 What blessings God bestows

66 88 86
211 Our God and Father bless

9 Index of Themes and Subjects

10 Index of First Lines

Each text carries the same number as the page on which it appears.